Organisational Behaviour

(Text and Cases Including Internet Exercises and Skill Tests)

[For B Tech. VIII Semester students of West Bengal University of Technology]

Organisational Behaviour

(Text and Cases Including Internet Exercises and Skill Tests)

[For B Tech. VIII Semester students of West Bengal University of Technology]

Prof. (Dr.) S Shajahan

MBA, PhD

Founder Member & Ex-Dean
Indian Institute of Management (IIM), Shillong

and

CEO, Benjamin Wright Infrastructure Ltd.
New Delhi and Jharkhand

NEW AGE
WBUT

An Imprint of

NEW AGE INTERNATIONAL (P) LIMITED, PUBLISHERS

New Delhi • Bangalore • Chennai • Cochin • Guwahati
Hyderabad • Kolkata • Lucknow • Mumbai
Visit us at www.newagepublishers.com

Published by New Age International (P) Ltd., Publishers
First Edition: 2015

BRANCHES

- **Bangalore** 37/10, 8th Cross (Near Hanuman Temple), Azad Nagar, Chamarajpet, Bangalore-560 018
Tel.: (080) 26756823, Telefax: 26756820, **E-mail: bangalore@newagepublishers.com**
- **Chennai** 26, Damodaran Street, T. Nagar, Chennai-600 017
Tel.: (044) 24353401, Telefax: 24351463, **E-mail: chennai@newagepublishers.com**
- **Cochin** CC-39/1016, Carrier Station Road, Ernakulam South, Cochin-682 016
Tel.: (0484) 2377004, Telefax: 4051303, **E-mail: cochin@newagepublishers.com**
- **Guwahati** Hemsen Complex, Mohd. Shah Road, Paltan Bazar, Near Starline Hotel, Guwahati-781 008
Tel.: (0361) 2513881, Telefax: 2543669, **E-mail: guwahati@newagepublishers.com**
- **Hyderabad** 105, 1st Floor, Madhiray Kaveri Tower, 3-2-19, Azam Jahi Road, Near Kumar Theater Nimboliadda, Kachiguda, Hyderabad-500 027, Tel.: (040) 24652456, Telefax: 24652457
E-mail: hyderabad@newagepublishers.com
- **Kolkata** RDB Chambers (Formerly Lotus Cinema) 106A, 1st Floor, S.N. Banerjee Road, Kolkata-700 014
Tel.: (033) 22273773, Telefax: 22275247, **E-mail: kolkata@newagepublishers.com**
- **Lucknow** 16-A, Jopling Road, Lucknow-226 001
Tel.: (0522) 2209578, 4045297, Telefax: 2204098, **E-mail:lucknow@newagepublishers.com**
- **Mumbai** 142C, Victor House, Ground Floor, N.M. Joshi Marg, Lower Parel, Mumbai-400 013
Tel.: (022) 24927869, Telefax: 24915415, **E-mail: mumbai@newagepublishers.com**
- **New Delhi** 22, Golden House, Daryaganj, New Delhi-110 002
Tel.: (011) 23262368, 23262370, Telefax: 43551305, **E-mail: sales@newagepublishers.com**

ISBN: 978-81-224-3779-9

₹ 200.00

C-14-03-7484

Printed in India at Nisha Enterprises, Delhi.
Typeset at In-house, Delhi.

PUBLISHING GLOBALLY
NEW AGE INTERNATIONAL (P) LIMITED, PUBLISHERS
7/30 A, Daryaganj, New Delhi-110002
Visit us at **www.newagepublishers.com**

Dedicated This Edition

to

ASIN, ADHIL & RASEENA

"...Organization does not really accomplish anything. Plans do not accomplish anything either. Theories of Management don't much matter. Endeavours succeed or fail because of the people involved. Only by attracting the best people you will accomplish great deeds. It's people who count..."

Colin Powell
Former US Secretary of State

PREFACE

Organizational behaviour is the study of human behaviour in organizational settings, the interface between human behaviour and the organization, and the organization itself. The author believes that the people starts learning when they join any organization then all other individual process will centered on their personality. Again, any relationship that will be formed later also based on the job characteristics. Hence interpersonal and group activities are centered on the job. Finally the organization starts functioning only when there is a free flow of communication throughout the organization. This will leads to developing criteria for measuring individual and organization process.

A Dominant theme affecting organization is change. Change has become a constant. After liberalization process, the domestic firms have been passing through a period of transition, from a seller's market to buyer's market and from rationing shortages to marketing of surpluses. Now effective use of Information Technology has been identified as an important strategy for enhancing the competitiveness of any organization in this millennium. Today, the global economy is increasingly influenced by Internet Technology. Effects of an emerging global economy. Internet, Employee Relationship Management (ERM) and free flow of information and people across the national boundaries and culture. In a bid to strengthen the Indian economy and organization, "Organization Behaviour" is included as one of the fundamental subjects for various Management and Technology courses offered in Indian Universities who are the major sources of employee recruitment and training centers. This book presents an overview of updated, multifaceted, and latest global information systems. This book covers syllabi requirements of B.Tech (Engineering) of West Bengal, MBA, MCA, BBA, BCA, MIT, MIB and other postgraduate, degree, and diploma level engineering and management course of Indian universities.

Further, this book has adopted the latest concepts, practices and cases of organization behaviour by utilizing the author's 24 years of domestic and international experience and learning cum teaching in various universities/curricula in USA, China, India and KSA. The author strongly believes in the potential of internet and information technology in revolutionizing the ongoing organization restructuring and practices in India and EMEs.

This book comprises 11 chapters with 10 self improvement tests, 5 cases, 6 internet exercises and the latest OB concepts and practices like virtual team, empowerment, development management potential performance programming, indigenization of western management of varying lengths and levels of difficulty. This book will focus primarily on four levels of change in people such as (*a*) knowledge changes, (*b*) attitudinal changes, (*c*) behavioural changes and (*d*) group or organizational performance changes and conflict management. This is enforced through the application of internet technology, case study method, and student exercise; test yourself—an individual management skill-developing inventory, discussion questions, and review questions. Finally, author examined several contextual perspectives that provide a general framework for a more comprehensive examination of e-organization behaviour and faceless world in the era of Facebook and Google.

This book is about those people. It is also about the organization itself and the managers who operate it. The studies of organizations and of the people who work in them together constitute the field of organizational behaviour. In the first chapter, we begin with a comprehensive definition of organizational behaviour and discuss a framework for its study. Then we trace the field's historical roots and its emergence as an independent field. Next, we discuss contemporary organizational behaviour and present future of OB in AD 2020. In short, emphasis is placed on discussing contemporary organizational settings and challenges, identifying change agent and management frameworks and tools as they relate to OB principles and applications, providing a framework for managing diversity and the international and ethical dimensions of workplace behaviour and using diagnostic models to examine OB issues in this introductory chapter.

In Chapter 2 Personality, this focuses on the individual as the "unit" of analysis. The importance of personality and the personal system is emphasized as ways to understand and read individual differences and work effectiveness are examined. Personality characteristics that hinder and facilitate relationships are discussed. Similarly this chapter also describes attitude formation and types changes in attitude formation and job satisfaction at the end. Again in Chapter 3 Perception which perception and attribution theory with particular reference to workforce diversity and cross-national workforces. How individuals see, avoid stereotyping, and evaluate problems and opportunities is a first step in understanding organizational problems. Further, in Chapter 4, Motivation which deals with classical theory and contemporary issues and guidelines for diagnosing and motivating members of workforce 2000. How to motivate professionals during organizational changes is also discussed.

In Chapter 6, Group Dynamics narrates various type and formation of groups, group decision-making process and techniques in detail. Again in Chapter 7, Leadership which explains the distinctive competencies of organizational leaders and how leaders can be viewed as partners with followers. Organizational behaviour at the team and individual levels are greatly affected by the leadership's choice of vision and mobilization around strategy. The role of leadership skills in setting a vision and formulating a strategy for obtaining it is emphasized. Classical studies and approaches to leadership are summarized. Similarly in Chapter 8, Organizational Politics describes models and skills for effectively using and managing power and politics in organizations in socially responsible ways. A changed model that incorporates power is also presented. Further in Chapter 9 Conflict and Communication, presents different sources of conflict and various approaches for resolving conflict, effective negotiation and bargaining skills in organizations with reference to international and culturally diverse workforces.

In Chapter 10, Culture and Organizational effectiveness define culture and describe symptoms of cultures in trouble and attributes of those that are successful. Methods for diagnosing and changing culture are presented. International perspectives that influence organizational culture are given. A holistic model was developed for assessing the organization design and its effect on OB. Emerging concepts in Organization Development in the new millennium, discusses the current topic of research and gives an inside view of development management, self management, potential performance programming, OB in Indian perspective and research studies on India management. Finally in Chapter 11, Case study and Internet exercise which describes various case study from the global and Indian scenario for providing a comprehensive coverage of the corporate world and issues in OB to the students.

At the end, all chapters are provided with Test Yourself, which will help the reader to assess himself or herself and also provide an opportunity to chat with the author for further consultation. *Review question focuses on the examination type question and discussion question and student exercise assist the student to extend the learning to the real world situation*. In fact this is the first attempt ever made by an Indian author in this subject to do so as early as in 2003.

Prof. (Dr) S. SHAJAHAN
www.linkedin.com/in/drsshajahan2009

ACKNOWLEDGEMENT

Author wishes to acknowledge the support and guidance rendered by Mr. Joseph Manuel, Founder Director Society for Self Management Service, Trivandrum, in completing this work successfully. Further author also acknowledges with sincere gratitude, the cooperation and encouragement given to him by his colleagues, friends and Professors from various Universities during 1989–2013 such as his OB teacher Mr. Alex P Luckose (SMS CUSAT Kochi), his PhD guide Prof. N. Rangathan (School of Management Studies (SMS) CUSAT, Kochi).

Again, author thankfully acknowledges the teaching input, subject knowledge and international advisory support from his own Professors from a dozen global universities such as Professors from University of Pennsylvania Wharton School (Prof. Barbara Kahn, Prof. Peter Fade & Prof. David Bell), Legendary Personality in Management Prof. Michael Porter (HBS), Prof. Scotty Page (University of Michigen), Prof. Gilbert Probst (University of Geneva), Prof. James V Green (University of Maryland), Prof. Tobias Kretschmer PhD (Institute for Strategy, Technology & Organization, Munich School of Management LUDWIG-MAXMILIANS, Universitat Munchen), Prof. Walter Sinnott & Prof. Armstrong(Duke University), Prof. Mark Zupan (University of Rochester), Prof. Peter Navarro (University of California-Irvine), Prof. Michael J. Orlando (University of Colorado), Prof. Conway (Princeton University), Prof. Rolf Storm Olsen (IE Business School, Madrid) and Prof. R. Edward Freeman (University of Virginia, Darden School of Business) in various academic programmes during 2005–2013. The above global personalities groomed him as the youngest Dean in the 50 year old Indian Institute of Management (IIM) fraternity in 2008 and also helped him in reviving this title after 10 years of first edition.

This book would not have been completed without the support and cooperation of his wife Raseena, daughter Asin and son Adhil who have compromised a lot for their family time during his writing while staying alongwith them in an alien country which is far away from his home country and people in 2014. Finally author wishes to thank New Age International (P) Ltd., Publishers, New Delhi in preparing this volume.

A request to my dearest readers who procured the book legally; keep sending your comments/ views to on this book shaangrila@gmail.com for further improvement and suggestions or maintain continuous engagement in the discussion forum through drs.shajahan/facebook.com. I will promise you that investment made in this book is going to mould your career or profession better than the degree which you procure from your college.

Wishing all of you a happy reading and successful career in OB

Prof. (Dr) S.SHAJAHAN

Drs.shajahan/facebook.com

CONTENTS

1

CHAPTER

OVERVIEW OF ORGANISATION BEHAVIOUR IN AD 2020

LEARNING OBJECTIVES

This chapter aims at introducing both fundamental and emerging concepts as a prerequisite for explaining the present organisation behaviour theories and practices to the readers:

- *Definition, importance and fundamental concepts of organisation behaviour*
- *Need for studying organisational behaviour*
- *Major characteristics and nature and scope of organisation behaviour*
- *Fundamental theories and approaches of organisation behaviour*
- *Historical backgrounds of organisation behaviour*
- *Emerging trends of organisation behaviour in AD 2020*
- *Paradigm shift in organisation behaviour and modern approach to organisational behaviour*
- *Interactionalism and virtual organisation in AD 2020*
- *Converging global organisation behaviour through social media interaction*
- *Challenges and opportunities for organisation behaviour in AD 2020*
- *Future of organisational behaviour: Beyond AD 2020*
- *Limitations of organisation behaviour*

1.1 DEFINITION, NEED AND IMPORTANCE OF ORGANISATION BEHAVIOUR

The knowledge and information explosion, ICT revolution and deeper penetration of social media like facebook and twitter, global competition, total quality management and work force diversity are some of the realities that the managers are facing today. There are many solutions being offered to deal with these complex challenges. Yet the simple but most profound solution may be found in the words of Sam Walton, the richest person in the world and the founder of Wal-Mart. Sam was once asked the key to successful organisations and management; Sam quickly replied, "People are the key".

According to Gary Johns, "organisations are social inventions for accomplishing goals through group efforts". This definition covers wide variety of groups such as businesses, schools, hospitals, fraternal groups, religious bodies, government agencies and so on. There are three significant aspects in the above definition, which require further analysis. They are as follows:

- ***Social Inventions:*** The word 'social' as a derivative of society basically means gathering of people. It is the people that primarily make up an organisation.
- ***Accomplishing Goals:*** All organisations have reasons for their existence. These reasons are the goals towards which all organisational efforts are directed. While the primary goal of any commercial organisation is to make money for its owners, this goal is inter-related with many other goals. Accordingly, any organisational goal must integrate in itself the personal goals of all individuals associated with the organisation.
- ***Group Effort:*** People, both as members of the society at large and as a part of an organisation interact with each other and are inter-dependent. Individuals in themselves have physical and intellectual limitations and these limitations can only be overcome by group efforts.

In general, organisation as two or more individuals who are interacting with each other within a deliberately structured set up and working in an interdependent way to achieve some common objectives. Organisations play a major role in our lives. We possibly cannot think of a single moment in our lives when we are not depending on organisations in some form or the other. Right from the public transport that you use, to come to your institute, the institutes itself, the class you are attending at this moment, are all examples of organisations.

(a) Definition of Organisational Behaviour

Organisational Behaviour is concerned with people's thoughts, feelings, emotions and actions in setting up a work. Understanding an individual behaviour is in itself a challenge, but understanding group behaviour in an organisational environment is a monumental managerial task.

Organisational Behaviour (OB) is a field of study that investigates the impact that individuals, groups and structures have on behaviour within an organisation for the purpose of applying such knowledge towards improving an organisation's effectiveness. It is an interdisciplinary field that includes sociology, psychology, communication, and management; and it complements the academic studies of organisational theory (which is focused on organisational and intra-organisational topics) and human resource studies (which is more applied and business-oriented). As you are aware, an organisation is a system of two or more persons, engaged in cooperative action, trying to reach some purpose. Organisations are bounded systems of structured social interaction featuring authority relations, communication systems, and the use of incentives. Example of organisations includes businesses, hospitals, colleges, retail stores, and prisons.

As Nadler and Tushman put it, "Understanding one individual's behaviour is challenging in and of itself; understanding a group that is made up of different individuals and comprehending the many relationships among those individuals is even more complex". Ultimately, the organisation's work gets done through people, individually or collectively, on their, own or in collaboration with technology. Therefore, the management of organisational behaviour is central to the management task—a task that involves the capacity to 'understand' the behaviour patterns of individuals, groups and organisations, to 'predict' what behavioural responses will be elicited by various managerial actions and finally to use this understanding and these predictions to achieve 'control'.

It is the behaviour of the people working in an organisation to achieve common goals or objectives. Organisation comprises of people with different attitudes, cultures, beliefs, norms and values. The term Organisational behaviour is a little misleading because it actually refers to the behaviour of people in organisations—organisations themselves do not behave. It may also be referred to as organisational studies or organisational science. Organisational Behaviour tries to understand the behaviour, attitudes, and performance of people in organisations organisational theory focuses on the design and structure of organisations. Organisational Behaviour is an applied behavioural science that is built upon contributions from a number of behavioural disciplines. Now, as perhaps never before, there is a growing awareness that the success of our organisations is directly dependent on the effective use of human resources based on the applied behavioural sciences. To meet these challenges we need special tools and the skills to use these tools. This is what this book is all about. It not only presents fundamental behavioural science concepts and theories but also suggests proven simple-to-use tools based on the behavioural sciences.

Organisational behaviour can then be defined as: "The study of human behaviour in organisational settings, the interface between human behaviour and the organisational context, and the organisation itself". The above definition has three parts—the individual behaviour, the organisation and the interface between the two. Each individual brings to an organisation a unique set of beliefs, values, attitudes and other personal characteristics and these characteristics of all individuals must interact with each other in order to create organisational settings. The organisational behaviour is specifically concerned with work-related behaviour, which takes place in organisations.

Organisational Behaviour is concerned with the characteristics and behaviours of employees in isolation; the characteristics and processes that are part of the organisation itself; and the characteristics and behaviours directly resulting from people with their individual needs and motivations working within the structure of the organisation. One cannot understand an individual's behaviour completely without learning something about that individual's organisation. Similarly, he cannot understand how the organisation operates without studying the people who-make it up. Thus, the organisation influences and is influenced by individuals.

In addition to understanding; the on-going behavioural processes involved, in their own jobs, managers must understand the basic human element of their work. Organisational behaviour offers three major ways of understanding this context; people as organisations, people as resources and people as people. Above all, organisations are people; and without people there would be no organisations. Thus, if managers are to understand the organisations in which they work, they must first understand the people who make up the organisations.

As resources, people are one of the organisation's most valuable assets. People create the organisation, guide and direct its course, and vitalize and revitalize it. People make the decisions, solve the problems, and answer the questions. As managers increasingly recognize the value of potential contributions by their employees, it will become more and more important for managers and employees to grasp the complexities of organisational behaviour.

Finally, there are people as people, an argument derived from the simple notion of humanistic management. People spend a large part of their lives in; organisational settings, mostly as employees. They have a right to expect something in return beyond wages and benefits. They have a right to expect satisfaction and to learn new skills. An understanding of organisational behaviour can help the manager better appreciate the variety of individual needs and expectations.

Organisational behaviour encompasses the study of organisations from multiple viewpoints, methods, and levels of analysis. For instance, some authors divide these multiple viewpoints into three perspectives: modern, symbolic, and postmodern. Another traditional distinction, present especially in American academia, is between the study of 'micro' organisational behaviour—which refers to individual and group dynamics in an organisational setting and 'macro' strategic management and organisational theory which studies whole organisations and industries, how they adapt, and the strategies, structures and contingencies that guide them. To this distinction, some scholars have added an interest in 'meso' scale structures—power, culture, and the networks of individuals and i.e., ronit units in organisations and "field" level analysis which study how whole populations of organisations interact.

The organisational behaviour has a goal to help the managers make a transition to the new paradigm. Some of the new paradigm characteristics include coverage of second-generation information technology and total quality management such as empowerment, reengineering and benchmarking, and learning organisation for managing diversity of work. The new paradigm sets the stage for the study, understanding, and application of the time-tested micro-variables, dynamics and macro-variables. One must know why management needs a new perspective to meet the environmental challenges and to shift to a new paradigm.

We have all known courageous men and women who have provided the vision and energy to make things happen in very difficult situations. But even after decades of research, we are still unable to identify with certainty the specific causal factors that determine managerial success at a specific time and place. This is because real-life situations are never static. They are in a constant state of change, with many factors or variables interacting at the same time. Because of this, the behavioural sciences, unlike the physical sciences, deal in probabilities. In developing these ideas and skills, we wanted to build upon the considerable legacy of the behavioural sciences by using a common language so managers could easily master the key ideas and skills. Many of our most critical problems are not in the world of things but in the world of people. Our greatest failure as human beings has been the inability to secure cooperation and understanding with others. Shortly after World War II, Elton Mayo recognized this problem when he reflected, "the consequences for society of the unbalance between the development of technical and of social skills have been disastrous".

Again, whenever people interact in organisations, many factors come into play. Modern organisational studies attempt to understand and model these factors. Like all modernist social sciences, organisational studies seek to control, predict, and explain. There is some controversy over the ethics of controlling workers' behaviour, as well as the manner in which workers are treated (see Taylor's Scientific Management approach compared to the human relations movement of the 1940s). As such, Organisational Behaviour (and its cousin, Industrial Psychology) have at times been accused of being the scientific tool of the powerful. Those accusations notwithstanding, organisation behaviour can play a major role in organisational development, enhancing organisational performance, as well as individual and group performance/satisfaction/commitment. One of the main goals of organisational theorists is, according to Simms (1994), to revitalize organisational theory and develop a better conceptualization of organisational life. An organisational theorist should carefully consider levels assumptions being made in theory, and is concerned to help managers and administrators.

So let us understand organisational behaviour and what it exactly means. "Organisational Behaviour" can be defined as the study of what people think, feel, and do, in and around organisations. The study of organisational behaviour facilitates the process of explaining, understanding, predicting, maintaining, and changing employee behaviour in an organisational setting. The value of organisational behaviour is that: it isolates important aspects of the manager's job and offers specific perspective on the human side of management: people as organisations, people as resources and people as people.

In other words, organisation behaviour involves the understanding, prediction and control of human behaviour and factors affecting their performance and interaction among the organisational members. And because organisational behaviour is concerned specifically with employment-related situations, you should not be surprised to find that it emphasizes behaviour as related to concerns such as jobs, work, absenteeism, employment turnover, productivity, human performance and management.

(b) Need for Studying Organisational Behaviour

The rules of work are different from the rules of play. The uniqueness of rules and the environment of organisations forces managers to study organisational behaviour in order to learn about normal and abnormal ranges of behaviour. More specifically, organisational behaviour serves three purposes:

- What causes behaviour?
- Why particular antecedents cause behaviour?
- Which antecedents of behaviour can be controlled directly and which are beyond control?

A more specific and formal course in organisational behaviour helps an individual to develop more refined and workable sets of assumption that is directly relevant to his work interactions. Organisational behaviour helps in predicting human behaviour in the organisational setting by drawing a clear distinction between individual behaviour and group behaviour.

Organisational Behaviour does not provide solutions to all complex and different behaviour puzzles of organisations. It is only the intelligent judgment of the manager in dealing with a specific issue that can try to solve the problem. Organisational behaviour only assists in making judgments that are derived from tenable assumptions; judgement that takes into account the important variables underlying the situation; judgement that are assigned due recognition to the complexity of individual or group behaviour; judgement that explicitly takes into account the managers own goals, motives, hang-ups, blind spots and weaknesses.

(c) Importance of Organisational Behaviour

Organisational Behaviour offers several ideas to management as to how human factor should be properly emphasized to achieve organisational objectives. Barnard has observed that an organisation is a conscious interaction of two or more people. This suggests that since an organisation is the interaction of persons, they should be given adequate importance in managing the organisation. Organisational behaviour provides opportunity to management to analyze human behaviour and prescribe means for shaping it to a particular direction.

Further, organisational behaviour provides understanding the human behaviour in all directions in which the human beings interact. Thus, organisational behaviour can be understood at the individual level, interpersonal level, group level and inter-group level. Organisational behaviour helps to analyze 'why' and 'how' an individual behaves in a particular way. Human behaviour is a complex phenomenon and is affected by a large number of factors including the psychological, social and cultural implications. Organisational behaviour integrates these factors to provide simplicity in understanding the human behaviour primarily at three levels such as:

***Interpersonal Level*:** Human behaviour can be understood at the level of interpersonal interaction. Organisational behaviour provides means for understanding the interpersonal relationships in an organisation. Analysis of reciprocal relationships, role analysis and transactional analysis are some of the common methods, which provide such understanding.

***Group Level*:** Though people interpret anything at their individual level, they are often modified by group pressures, which then become a force in shaping human behaviour, thus, individuals should be studied in groups also. Research in group dynamics has contributed vitally to organisational behaviour and shows how a group behaves in its norms, cohesion, goals, procedures, communication pattern and leadership. These research results are advancing managerial knowledge of understanding group behaviour, which is very important for organisational morale and productivity.

***Inter-group Level*:** The organisation is made up of many groups that develop complex relationships to build their process and substance. Understanding the effect of group relationships is important for managers in today's organisation. Inter-group relationship may be in the form of co-operation or competition.

The Co-operative Relationships help the organisation in achieving its objectives. Organisational behaviour provides means to understand and achieve co-operative group relationships through interaction, rotation of members among groups, avoidance of win-lose situation and focusing on total group objectives.

***Controlling and Directing Behaviour*:** After understanding the mechanism of human behaviour, managers are required to control and direct the behaviour so that it conforms to the standards required for achieving the organisational objectives. Thus, managers are required to control and direct the behaviour at all levels of individual interaction. Therefore, organisational behaviour helps managers in controlling and directing in different areas such as use of power and sanction, leadership, communication and building organisational climate favourable for better interaction.

***Use of Power and Sanction*:** The behaviours can be controlled and directed by the use of power and sanction, which are formally defined by the organisation. Power is referred to as the capacity of an individual to take certain action and may be utilised in many ways. Organisational behaviour explains how various means of power and sanction can, be utilised so that both organisational and individual objectives are achieved simultaneously.

***Leadership*:** Organisational behaviour brings new insights and understanding to the practice and theory of leadership. It identifies various leadership styles available to a manager and analyses which style is more appropriate in a given situation. Thus, managers can adopt styles keeping in view the various dimensions of organisations, individuals and situations.

***Communication*:** Communication helps people to come in contact with each other. To achieve organisational objectives, the communication must be effective. The communication process and its work in inter-personal dynamics have been evaluated by organisational behaviour.

***Organisational Climate*:** Organisational climate refers to the total organisational situations affecting human behaviour. Organisational climate takes a system perspective that affect human behaviour. Besides improving the satisfactory working conditions and adequate compensation, organisational climate includes creation of an atmosphere of effective supervision; the opportunity for the realization of personal goals, congenial relations with others at the work place and a sense of accomplishment.

***Organisational Adaptation*:** Organisations, as dynamic entities are characterized by pervasive changes. Organisations have to adapt themselves to the environmental changes by making suitable, internal arrangements such as convincing employees who normally have the tendency of resisting any changes.

(d) Aggregative View of Contemporary Organisational Behaviour Literature

Organisational Behaviour can be treated as a distinct field of study. It is yet to become a science. Now efforts are being made to synthesize principles, concepts and processes in this field of study. Much of what you read in this book may have an impact on your knowledge and attitudes, but this book becomes relevant only if you are willing to "try on" some new behaviours. This means that a behavioural scientist integrates concepts and theories and the results of empirical studies from the areas of cultural anthropology, economics, political science, psychology, sociology, and social psychology. Organisational behaviour is an applied behavioural science that is built on contributions from a number of behavioural disciplines such as psychology, sociology, social psychology, anthropology and economics. As we shall learn, psychology's contributions have been mainly at the individual or micro level of analysis; the other four disciplines have contributed to our understanding of macro concepts such as group processes and organisation.

1. Psychology: Psychology is the study of human behaviour which tries to identify the characteristics of individuals and provides an understanding why an individual behaves in a particular way. This thus provides us with useful insight into areas such as human motivation, perceptual processes or personality characteristics.

2. Sociology: Sociology is the study of social behaviour, relationships among social groups and societies, and the maintenance of social order. The main focus of attention is on the social system. This helps us to appreciate the functioning of individuals within the organisation which is essentially a socio-technical entity.

3. Social psychology: Social psychology is the study of human behaviour in the context of social situations. This essentially addresses the problem of understanding the typical behavioural patterns to be expected from an individual when he takes part in a group.

4. Anthropology: Anthropology is the science of mankind and the study of human behaviour as a whole. The main focus of attention is on the cultural system, beliefs, customs, ideas and values within a group or society and the comparison of behaviour among different cultures. In the context of today's organisational scenario. It is very important to appreciate the differences that exist among people coming from different cultural backgrounds as people are often found to work with others from the other side of the globe.

5. Economics: Any organisation to survive and sustain must be aware of the economic viability of their effort. This applies even to the non-profit and voluntary organisations as well.

6. Political science: Although frequently overlooked, the contributions of political scientists are significant to understand arrangement in organisations. It studies individuals and groups within specific conditions concerning the power dynamics. Important topics under here include structuring of conflict, allocation of power and how people manipulate power for individual self-interest etc.

7. Interdisciplinary approach: It is a fact that behavioural scientists borrowed from other areas of knowledge such as engineering, physics, quantitative analysis, and statistics. For example, force field analysis, developed by Kurt Lewin, which we will be talking about later in this book, is directly related to concepts in physics. So, perhaps the best way to look at the field is to say that a behavioural scientist attempts to integrate all of those areas or disciplines that can be useful to us as practitioners in better understanding, predicting, and having an impact on the behaviour of individuals and groups. Thus Organisational behaviour essentially follows an interdisciplinary approach. It draws heavily from other disciplines like psychology, sociology and anthropology. Besides, it also takes relevant things from economics, political science, law and history.

It shows the linkages among human behaviour in organisational settings, the individual-organisation interface, the organisation, and the environment surroundings the organisation. Each individual brings to an organisation a unique set of personal background and characteristics, and experiences from other organisations. In considering the people who work in organisations, therefore, a manager must look at the unique perspective each individual brings to the work setting. Further, organisational behaviour integrates the relevant contents of these disciplines to make them applicable for organisational analysis. e.g., it addresses issues, which may be relevant to the case, such as the following:

- What facilitates accurate perception and attribution?
- What influences individual, group and organisational learning and the development of individual attitudes towards work?
- How do individual differences in personality, personal development, and career development affect individual's behaviours and attitudes?
- What motivates people to work, and how? Does the organisational reward system influence worker's behaviour and attitudes?
- How do managers build effective teams?
- What contributes to effective decision-making?
- What are the constituents of effective communication?
- What are the characteristics of effective communication?
- How can power be secured and used productively?
- What factors contribute to effective negotiations?
- How can conflict (between groups or between a manager and subordinates) be resolved or managed?
- How can jobs and organisations be effectively designed?
- How can managers help workers deal effectively with change?

1.2 HISTORICAL BACKGROUND OF ORGANISATION BEHAVIOUR

The history of organisation behaviour as a discipline in India is comparatively of recent origin. But Kautilya had dealt with some of the important aspects of organisation behaviour in his 'Arthasastra' 400 BC. Government in those days adopted the techniques of H.R.M. and motivation techniques as suggested by Kautilya. Organisation behaviour, in its modern sense, had developed only since independence. Though the importance of labour and welfare officers was recognized and organisation behaviour issues gained momentum only after the enactment of the Factories Act of 1948. The earliest labour legislation in India dealt with certain aspects of Indian labourers (Regulation of Recruitment, Forwarding and Employment) sent to various British Colonies in 1830. Over a period of five decades since independence, now the corporate have identified intellectual capitals and intangible assets in a slightly elevated position in comparison with their physical assets and inventories. The organisation behaviour techniques act as foundations for the HR department to function. Now the corporate are looking for proactive people and policies to build up their organisation for the new millennium.

In general, Scientist theories and related organisation behaviour concepts are like the way that photographers use zoom lenses or lenses of different focal lengths to picturise the organisational scenario/culture prevalent at that time. The consequences of organisational behaviour can be examined using functional analysis, an analytical tool borrowed from anthropology. When anthropologists study a society, they divide their organisational behavioural observations into two major groups. First, they decide whether the consequences of organisational behaviour are manifest or latent. Then they determine whether the consequences are functional or dysfunctional for the society. Functional consequences are results of organisational behaviour that are good for the organisation and help its adjustment and adaptation. Such results contribute to the organisation's progress toward its goals. Dysfunctional consequences are results of organisational behaviour that have a negative effect on the organisation. These results restrict the organisation adjustment and adaptation, impeding it from reaching its goals.

For scientist, universal principles provide simplicity and thus lead to models that can be applied in all situations. For managers universal principles provide ready guides to action in all situations. Some of the early writing predating the field of organisation behaviour is of this universal type. For example, Max Weber prescribed the use of a highly structured bureaucracy for all organisations. His prescriptions were succeeded in the 1950s and 1960s by an equally prescriptive set of guides that argued the opposite. Rennis Likert and McGregor, for example, advocated it from fearless formality. Unfortunately, as most practicing managers soon learn the real world is not so simple and refuses to lend itself to universal theories and principles. Abraham Maslow, another pioneer in the human relations movement, developed the well-known hierarchy of human needs. Organisational behaviour began to emerge as a mature field of study in the late 1950s and early 1960s. Contemporary organisational behaviour has an interdisciplinary focus, drawing from fields such as psychology, sociology, and other related areas. Organisational behaviour attempts to describe relationships between two or more behavioural variables. Table 1.1 describes the major scientific studies/principles contributed to the development of organisation behaviour as a major subject in modern organisational management literature.

Table 1.1: Showing historical phase of organisation behaviour

Agrarian	**Industrial**	**Post-industrial**		**Information**		**ICT era**
Scientific and classical management	Bureaucracy human relations	Group dynamics	Decision-making approaches; leadership	Socio-technical systems theory	Contin-gency theory	Global management, internet and mobile technologies quality, speed, customer empowerment and CRM diversity and ethics
1910–1920	1921–1940	1941–1950	1951–1960	1961–1980	1981–1990	1991–2020

(a) Scientific Management: Frederick W.Taylor (1911)

Scientific management approach was developed by F.W. Taylor at the beginning of the 20th century. This theory supported the use of certain steps in scientifically studying each element of a job, selecting and training the best workers for the job and making sure that the workers follow the prescribed method of doing the job.

The principal object of management should be to secure the maximum prosperity for the employer, coupled with the maximum prosperity for each employee. Those words are from the opening paragraph of Frederick W. Taylor's book, The Principles of Scientific Management. Taylor felt he had developed a new approach to management that produced positive results for both employer and employee. Management wanted to maximize profits, and workers wanted the highest possible wages. Disputes between management and labor centered on what each viewed as mutually exclusive goals. Taylor felt his system of Scientific Management could maximize both goals. Both sides had to undergo a "mental revolution". Each side had to rid itself of antagonistic views of the other. Taylor felt they should view profits as the result of cooperation between management and workers. In short, management needed the workers and workers needed management to get what they each wanted. Taylor based his Scientific Management on the following four principles:

- Carefully study the jobs to develop standard work practices. Standardize the tools used by workers.
- Scientifically select each worker.
- Management and workers must cooperate to ensure that work is done according to standard procedures.
- Management plans and makes task assignments; workers carry out tasks assigned by managers.

These four principles describe a division of work between management and workers. Managers planned and designed the work. They made task assignments, set performance goals, and made time schedules. Managers also selected and trained the workers to do the tasks according to standard procedures and gave the workers quick feedback about how they were doing. They rewarded increased individual productivity with economic incentives.

In short, this approach has provided a scientific rationale for job specialization and mass production. His assumption was that employees are motivated largely by money. To increase the output, Taylor advised managers to pay monetary incentives to efficient workers. Yet, his theory was criticized by many employers and workers. Workers objected to the pressure of work as being harder and faster. Critics worried that the methods took the humanity out of labor, reducing workers to machines responding to management incentives. Therefore, Taylor's view is now considered inadequate and narrow due to the points given by the critics.

(b) Theory of Administration: Henry Fayol (1919)

Fayol took a broad view of administration. He felt his theory of administration applied to all types of organisations, public or private. Fayol's live functions of management were planning, organizing, command, co-ordination, and control. Fayol's five management functions have endured the test of time. A review of research that focused on managerial activities showed that an impressive number of activities fell into Fayol's five functions. Managers not only did those classical functions, but they should do them. The time spent on these areas and the skills required to do them were associated with higher performance of the organisation. Fayol believed that manager "all must observe the same general principles". These principles were central to his theory of administration. They are a set of tools, a manager needs to perform the functions of management. He did not believe managers should apply his principles rigidly and absolutely in all circumstances. They must tailor the application of the principles to the specific circumstances they face, using a clear sense of proportion. Several relationships exist among the principles. Delegation of authority gets the desired degree of centralization or decentralization. Delegation also leads to a division of labor in the organisation. Unity of command and unity of direction are guides for the design of the organisation.

(c) Bureaucracy: Max Weber (1922)

Max Weber was a prominent German political scientist, economist, and sociologist. He made a major contribution to several fields of study with his analysis of bureaucracy as a form of organisation and management. He believed bureaucracy was an efficient and successful form of administration. Weber believed the following features account for the efficiency of bureaucracies:

- Clearly defined and specialized functions
- Use of legal authority
- Hierarchical form
- Written rules and procedures
- Technically trained bureaucrats
- Appointment to positions based on technical expertise
- Promotions based on technical competence
- Clearly defined career path.

Weber felt bureaucracies were rational and predictable systems. The rationality followed from the objectivity and impersonality of decisions. Decisions were based on fact and made according to existing written rules and procedures so they would be consistent. The unusual features of any specific case were not to be considered. Predictability followed from the fixed formal relationships among clearly defined hierarchically organized functions.

In short, Weber argued that bureaucracy was the application of rational-legal authority to the organisation of work: Through the application of rationality, bureaucracy was the most technically efficient form of organisation. Charles Perrow has extended this work, showing the continuing application of bureaucratic concepts to the study of organisations. Perrow argues that all organisations can be understood in terms of bureaucracy and that organisational failures are more often a result of insufficient application of bureaucratic principles. Weber's principles of bureaucratic organisation can be summarized as: A formal organisational hierarchy, management by rules, organisation by functional speciality and selecting people based on their skills and technical qualifications. An "up-focused" (to organisation's board or shareholders) or "in-focused" (to the organisation itself) mission and purposefully impersonal to apply the same rules and structures to all people.

(d) Mary Parker Fillet's Observations on Organisations and Management (1925)

Mary Parker Fillet worked mainly as a social worker among the poor in the Roxbury section of Boston. Although her work career did not involve management, she made several basic and enduring observations about organisations and management, during the mid-1920s to the early 1930s. The following three of her observations on organisations and management are power, conflict, and leadership. Fillet conceived of power as capacity. Although her point was not completely clear, she apparently meant the capacity to get things done. Power cannot be delegated, but authority can. She clearly distinguished between power and authority, treating each separately in her analysis. Integration of desires was Fillet's creative suggestion about how to manage conflict. This approach finds a solution that fully meets the goals of each party in dispute. Both parties get what they want. Neither party gives up anything. Invigoration of desire unshackles us from existing alternatives and let us creatively discover alternatives that are not mutually exclusive. With integration, conflict is put to work to help discover new, creative solutions to problems and issues in organisations. Follett's view of the personal qualities of a leader gives a vivid picture of the characteristics of a good leader. "Tenacity, steadfastness of purpose, tactfulness, steadiness in stormy periods".

(e) The Functions of the Executive: Chester I. Barnard (1938)

Chester Barnard was an engineer who became the President of the New Jersey Bell Telephone Company and later the first executive head of the United Services Organisation. His book, The Functions of the Executive, is rich in basic contributions to our thinking about organisations and management. Barnard believed organisations formed because individuals had a purpose or purposes, but also had limitations. The limitations could be knowledge, financial resources, or physical resources. The person with the purpose needed the cooperation of one or more other people to achieve that purpose. Purpose plus limitation leads to a system of cooperative action. Barnard distinguished between two types of motivation in organisations motivation to participate and motivation to perform. Motivation to participate is the motivation of an individual to join and stay with the organisation and perform at a minimally acceptable level.

Barnard felt managers must first attend to the motivation to participate. After they have solved the problem of membership, they can attend to the second type of motivation, the motivation to perform. This type of motivation focuses on performance level higher than the minimum expectation. Managers use both monetary and non-monetary incentives to get higher performance levels.

(f) Theory X and Theory Y: Douglas McGregor (1960)

Douglas McGregor, and MIT psychologist, proposed two sets of assumptions about human motivation that a manager can hold. McGregor called the assumptions Theory X and Theory Y. They are as follows:

The Theory X assumptions are as follows: A manager's behaviour towards his workers and his management style will differ based on the assumptions guiding his behaviour.

- The average person dislikes working and will avoid it if possible.
- Because people dislike working, they must be directed, tightly controlled, and pressured to get them to work toward organisational goals.
- The average person wants security, avoids responsibility, and has little ambition.
- McGregor believed that many managers held Theory X assumption about workers. Such managers give their workers little latitude, closely supervise them, and punish poor performance. They use few rewards and typically give only negative feedback.

The Theory Y assumptions are as follows:

- The average person does not dislike work; it is as natural as play.
- If a person is committed to a set, he will work toward them without an external control.
- Goal commitment follows from the satisfaction of a person's desire to achieve.
- The average person can learn to accept responsibility. Lack of ambition is not a basic human characteristic.
- Creativity, ingenuity, and imagination are human characteristics that are widely dispersed in the population.
- Modern organisations only partially use and tap the potentialities of its workers.

Managers who hold Theory Y assumptions have a positive view of people; believe they have much hidden potential, and that people will work toward organisational goals. These managers will give workers more job responsibility and reply on self-motivation more than coercion. These two sets of different assumptions reigned in the academic literature for many years. They were widely understood by practicing managers. Although called a theory, they are not theories as described earlier. They are assumptions or beliefs about human motivation that can strongly affect management behaviour.

(g) Chris Argyris Model of Immaturity-Maturity Continuum

In attempting to analyze this situation, Chris Argyris, has compared bureaucratic pyramidal values (the organisational counterpart to Theory X assumptions about people) that still dominate most organisations with a more humanistic/democratic value system (the organisational counterpart to Theory Y assumptions about people), as illustrated in Table 1.2 .

Table 1.2: Two different value systems as seen by Chris Argyris

Bureaucratic/Pyramidal value system	Humanistic/Democratic value system
1. Important human relationships—the crucial ones are those related to achieving the organisation's objectives, i.e., getting the job done.	1. The important human relationships are not only those related to achieving the organisation's objectives but those related to maintaining the organisation's internal system and adapting to the environment as well.
2. Effectiveness in human relationships increases as behaviour becomes more rational, logical, and clearly communicated; but effectiveness decreases as behaviour becomes more emotional.	2. Human relationships increase in effectiveness as all the relevant behaviour (rational and interpersonal) becomes conscious, discussible, and controllable.
3. Human relationships are most effectively motivated by carefully defined direction, authority, and control, as well as appropriate rewards and penalties that emphasize rational behaviour and achievement of the objective.	3. In addition to direction, controls, and rewards and penalties, human relationships are most effectively influenced through authentic relationships, internal commitment, psychological success, and the process of confirmation.

According to Argyris, following bureaucratic or pyramidal values leads to poor, shallow, and mistrustful relationships. Because these relationships do not permit the natural and free expression of feelings, they are phony or no authentic and result in decreased interpersonal competence. "Without interpersonal competence or a 'psychologically safe' environment, the organisation is a breeding ground for mistrust, intergroup conflict, rigidity, and so on, which in turn lead to a decrease in organisational success in problem solving.'

In short, Chester Barnard recognized that individuals behave differently when acting in their organisational role than when acting separately from the organisation. Organisational behaviour studies these differences to describe and model the behaviour of individuals and groups in organisations. Organisational Behaviour draws most heavily on psychology and social psychology.

According to Argyris, seven changes should take place in the personality of individuals if they are to develop into mature people over the years. First, individuals move from a passive state as infants to a state of increasing activity as adults. Second, individuals develop from a state of dependency upon others as infants to a state of relative independence as adults. Third, individuals behave in only a few ways as infants, but as adults they are capable of behaving in many ways. Fourth, individuals have erratic, casual, and shallow interests as infants but develop deeper and stronger interests as adults. Fifth, the time perspective of children is very short, involving only the present, but as they mature, their time perspective increases to include the past and the future. Sixth, individuals as infants are subordinate to everyone, but they move to equal or superior positions with others as adults. Seventh, as children, individuals lack an awareness of a 'self.' Argyris suggests that these changes reside on a continuum and that the "healthy". Please find below in Table 1.3 about Immaturities - Maturity continuum.

Table 1.3: Immaturities - Maturity continuum

Immaturity	Maturity
Passive	Active
Dependence	Independence
Behave in a few ways	Capable of behaving in many ways
Erratic shallow interests	Deeper and stronger interests
Short time perspective	Long time perspective (past and future)
Subordinate position	Equal or super ordinate position
Lack of awareness of self	Awareness and control over self

Argyris contends that, in many cases, when people join the force, they are kept from maturing by the management practices utilized in their organisations. In these organisations, they are given minimal control over their environment and are encouraged to be passive, dependent, and subordinate; therefore, they behave immaturely. The worker in many organisations is expected to act in immature ways rather than as a mature adult.

Argyris feels that these concepts of formal organisation lead to assumptions about human nature that are incompatible with the proper development of maturity in human personality. He sees a definite incongruity between the needs of a mature personality and the formal organisations as they now exist.

(h) The Hawthorne Studies (1939)

Even, as Taylor and Weber brought attention with their rational, logical approaches to more efficient productivity, their views were criticized on the ground that both approaches ignored worker's humanity.

The real beginning of applied research in the area of organisational behaviour started with Hawthorne Experiments. In 1924, a group of professors began an enquiry into the human aspects of work and working conditions at the Hawthorne plant of Western Electric Company, Chicago.

The plant produced various parts for telephone switching systems. This research was a landmark work done in the social sciences in the United States. The Hawthorne Studies were preceded and stimulated by the illumination experiments done in the Hawthorne Plant in the early 1920s. These studies were designed to determine whether various lighting levels affected human productivity. The experimental design used a control group where lighting was not varied. An experimental group experienced changes in light levels. The results of the experiments baffled the investigators. They increased the lighting and productivity went up. Then it was decreased, and productivity went up. The lighting was severely reduced, and productivity went up. The lighting for the control group was not changed, but the groups' productivity also increased. Eventually, the researchers concluded that simply being part of the experiment, which focused new and greater attention on the workers, increased productivity. Previously, interaction between supervisors and coworkers was limited. It had focused mainly on the work, not on the workers themselves.

Following the illumination experiments, several researchers from Harvard University began studying some groups of workers in the plant. Their goal was to understand the factors that contributed to differences in human productivity. The researchers concluded that a more empathic or people-oriented form of management led to more productivity than a directive, authoritarian, and money-oriented form of management. People wanted more than monetary incentives for working. Some researchers doing secondary analyses of data published in the original reports have come to varying conclusions. One researcher found support for a driving form of management and use of monetary incentives. He felt the researchers moved from presenting descriptive results to promoting a new form of management. By doing so, the original Hawthorne researchers went well beyond the results of their research.

The findings of these studies were given a new name 'human relations' the studies brought out a number of findings relevant to understanding human behaviour at work. The Human element in the workplace was considerably more important. The workers are influenced by social factors and the behaviour of the individual worker is determined by the group. The importance of the Hawthorne went well beyond the results of their research organisations should not be diminished by disputes about research design and research results. Hawthorne studies have been criticized for their research methods and conclusions drawn. But their impact on the emerging field of organisational behaviour was dramatic. They helped usher in a more humanity centered approach to work. Although strong conclusions cannot be drawn directly from the research studies were impetuses to further developing our understanding about behaviour in organisations.

(i) The Twentieth Century's Management Guru: Peter F. Drucker (1995)

Austrian born Peter F. Drucker ranks among the most widely read and widely quoted management scholars of the twentieth century. Drucker is a professor of management a Claremont College in California, a post he has held since 1971. He has written almost 30 books and continued his writing activity into the late 1990s. His 1954 book, The Practice of Management, launched him as a significant management writer. Among his most lasting observations was his proposed philosophy of management by objectives and self-control. General Electric was the first company to adopt Management By Objectives (MBO) and put it into practice with Drucker's help as a consultant. Drucker has an insatiable appetite for statistics. He examines them for a pattern often finds pattern that others miss. Here are his predictions for events unfolding until about 2010.

- A rise in alliance, partnership, and joint ventures on a global scale. Technology will help link these parts of an emerging "Network Society".
- A compelling need for decentralized organisations in an increasing uncertain environment.
- A related increase in the use of teams in organisations.
- An increase in the number of knowledge workers (for example, computer technologists and medical workers) and continual decline in the number of blue-collar and agricultural workers in all developed free-marked countries. The knowledge workers will need continuous learning, a characteristic with implications for educational systems.
- The twenty-first century will see the evolution of knowledge societies in developed countries. These societies will have three sectors: Business, government, and nonprofit. The last is new and helps people's social development. Nonprofit volunteer activities will characterize English-speaking countries but appear fewer elsewhere.
- An unquestionable forming of a world economy in which world markets will be come more important than domestic markets.

1.3 APPROACHES TO ORGANISATIONAL BEHAVIOUR

There are mainly four approaches to organisational behaviour. They are as follows:

(a) Human Resources Approach

The human resources approach is concerned with the growth and development of people towards higher levels of competency, creativity and fulfillment, because people are the central resource in any organisation. This approach help employees become better in terms of work and responsibility and then it tries to create a climate in which they can contribute to the best of their improved abilities. This approach is also known as "supportive approach" because the manager's primary role changes from control of employees to providing an active support for their growth and performance.

The human relations theory lays emphasis on the motivation of the individual and heavily oriented towards psychology and sociology. It should be noted that the exponents of this theory have not produced a complete body of management theory. Their main contribution has been to provide new insights rather than new techniques of management. Industrial sociologists, social psychologists and cultural anthropologists have developed the human relations school. The credit of highlighting the importance of uniformal social groups, good human relation, and the needs for managerial motivation, participation, better communication, good leadership and committee management goes to this school of thought.

McGregor's theory 'Y' is heavily human relation oriented. The theory made it explicit that group relationships are the key to behaviour. It throws light on how and why individuals and group behaviour influences workers motivation, supervision, communication pattern and productivity. Human relations theories also helped to provide a better explanation of why people in organisations behave as they do by stressing and exploring the role of group. Although there were varied and complex reasons for the emerging importance of behavioural approach to management, it is generally recognized that the Hawthorne studies mark the historical roots for the field of organisational behaviour.

In the words of Keith Davis, "Human relations are the integration of people into work situation that motivates them to work together productively, cooperatively and with economic, psychological and social satisfaction". According to McFarland, "Human relation is the study and practice of utilizing human resources through knowledge and understanding of the activities, attitudes, sentiments and inter-relationship of people at work". Raymond Miles defines this subject, as "Human relations approach was simply to, treat people as human beings in the productive process". The above definitions reveal the following important characteristics of human relations such as: The human relations approach focuses on people. When people stimulate more and better work, there will be sound in a given situation in order to achieve a balance of objectives that will yield greater human relations in the organisation. It is a process of study of effective motivation of individuals' satisfaction and to the company as well. It is an integration of people into work situation that motivates them to work through the satisfaction of economic, social, psychological needs. The ultimate goal of creating sound human relations is to help male workers more productive and cooperative.

(b) Contingency Approach

Contingency approach is based on the modern theory of organisation. It is an attempt to provide something more useful to the practicing managers in the present day complex organisations. It seeks to understand the inter-relationship within and among organisational subsystems, as well as between the organized systems. Contingent approach strongly believes that there is no prescribed organisational design, which is appropriate to all situations. In the opinion of Fred Luthens, it is concerned with the relationship between relevant environment variables and appropriate management concepts and techniques that lead to effective goal attainment.

A contingency approach to organisational behaviour implies that different situations require different behavioural practices for effectiveness instead of following a traditional approach for all situations. Each situation must be analyzed carefully to determine the significant variables that exist in order to establish the more effective practices.

According to Kast and Rosenzweig, a contingency approach attempts to understand the inter-relationship within and among organisational units as well as between the organisation and its environment. It emphasizes the complex nature of organisations and attempts to interpret and understand how they operate under varying conditions and in specific situations. The approach strives to aid managers by suggesting organisational design strategies, which have the highest probability of succeeding in a specific situation. The success criteria revolve around the accomplishment of organisational goal. The strength of this approach is that it encourages analysis of each situation prior to action. Thus, it helps to use all the current knowledge about people in the organisation in the most appropriate manner.

(c) Productivity Approach

Productivity is a ratio that compares units of output with units of input. It is often measured in terms of economic inputs and outputs. Productivity is considered to be improved, if more outputs can be produced from the same amount of inputs. But besides economic inputs and outputs, human and social inputs and outputs also are important.

(d) Systems Approach

A system is an inter-related part of an organisation or a society that interacts with everyone related to that organisation or society and functions as a whole. Within the organisation 'people' employ 'technology' in performing the 'task' that they are responsible for, while the 'structure' of the organisation serves as a basis for co-ordinating all their different activities. The systems view emphasizes the interdependence of each of these elements within the organisation, if the organisation as a whole is to function effectively. The other key aspect of the systems view of organisation is its emphasis on the interaction between the organisation and its broader environment, which consists of social, economic, cultural and political environment within which they operate.

The systems framework is also fundamental to organisational theory as organisations are complex dynamic goal-oriented processes. One of the early thinkers in the field was Alexander Bogdanov, who developed his Tectology, a theory widely considered a precursor of Bertalanffy's General Systems Theory, aiming to model and design human organisations. Kurt Lewin was particularly influential in developing the systems perspective within organisational theory and coined the term "systems of ideology", from his frustration with behavioural psychologies that became an obstacle to sustainable work in psychology (see Ash 1992: 198–207). The complexity theory perspective on organisations is another systems view of organisations. German sociologist Niklas Luhmann (1927–1998) developed a sociological system theory and describes organisations—alongside interactions and society as one of three main entities.

Modern organisation theory has its origin from the general systems theory, which is associated with the name of Kenneth Boulding. He worked on various systems from simple to complex. He classified various systems as below:

1. *The static structure*: It also refers to the level of framework. The anatomy of the universe is good example to this system.
2. *The simple dynamic system*: It incorporates necessary predetermined motions.
3. *The cybernetic system*: It is like a thermostat where there is automatic feedback control mechanism.
4. *The open system*: It is a self-maintaining structure.
5. *The genetic social system*: It is generally typified by the plant and preoccupies the empirical work of the botanist.
6. *Animal system*: It is characterised by the increased mobility, technological behaviours, self-unawareness, and goal-oriented approach.
7. *Social system*: Here social organisations are formed and individuals assume organisational goals.
8. *Transcendental system*: Here social organisations are formed and individuals assume organisational goals.

The systems theory visualizes organisation as a system consisting of interacting parts. Specifically, the open-systems concept, which stresses the input-output analysis, has a marked impact on modern theory. System analysis has its own peculiar points under which organisation is considered as a system of mutually dependent variables. Social scientists, management thinkers, operation researchers, psychologists and others, all unanimously agree that organisations are systems. Charles Perrow concludes, one thing all the varied school of organisation analysis now seemed to be agreed; organisations are system-indeed, they are systems.

Organisations are dependent upon their surrounding environment in two main ways: First, the organisation requires 'inputs' from the environment in the form of raw material, people, money, ideas and so on. The organisation itself can be thought of as performing certain 'transformation' processes, on its inputs in order to create outputs in the form of products or services. Secondly, the organisation depends on environment such as, public to accept its output. The systems view of organisation thus emphasizes on the key interdependencies that organisations must manage. Within themselves the organisations must trade off the interdependencies among people, tasks, technology and structure in order to perform their transformation processes effectively and efficiently. Organisations must also recognize their interdependence with the broader environments within which they exist.

The systems approach to organisations relies heavily upon achieving negative entropy through openness and feedback. A systemic view on organisations is transdisciplinary and integrative. In other words, it transcends the perspectives of individual disciplines, integrating them on the basis of a common 'code', or more exactly, on the basis of the formal apparatus provided by systems theory. The systems approach gives primacy to the inter-relationships, not to the elements of the system. It is from these dynamic inter-relationships that new properties of the system emerge. In recent years, systems thinking has been developed to provide techniques for studying systems in holistic ways to supplement traditional reductionistic methods. In this more recent tradition, systems theory in organisational studies is considered by some as a humanistic extension of the natural sciences.

The general system theory of Boulding has been criticized by Von Bertalanffy on the ground that it is descriptive rather than a strictly logical and prescriptive. Von Bertalanffy is credited with coining the "general systems theory". However, the recent social scientist Scott contends that modern organisation theory and the general systems theory are close together.

(e) Moving Towards Holistic Approach in AD 2020

The blending of nature of people and organisation results in a holistic organisational behaviour essence of which are listed less than 1 to 5.

1. An Applied Science: The basic objective of organisational behaviour is to make application of various researches to solve the organisational problems, particularly related to the human behavioural aspect.

2. Normative and Value Centered: Organisational behaviour is a normative science. A normative science prescribes how the various findings of researches can be applied to get organisational results, which are acceptable to the society. Thus, what is acceptable by the society or individuals engaged in an organisation is a matter of values of the society and people concerned.

3. Humanistic and Optimistic: Organisational behaviour focuses the attention on people from humanistic point of view. It is based on the belief that needs and motivation of people are of high concern. Further, there is optimism about the innate potential of man to be independent, creative, predictive and capable of contributing positively to the objectives of the organisation.

4. Oriented towards Organisational Objectives: Organisational behaviour is oriented towards organisational objectives. In fact, organisational behaviour tries to integrate both individual and organisational objectives so that both are achieved simultaneously.

5. A Total System Approach: An individual's behaviour can be analyzed keeping in view his psychological framework, interpersonal-orientation, group influence and social and cultural factors;

thus, individual's nature is quite complex and organisational behaviour by applying systems approach tries to find solutions for this complexity.

1.4 FUNDAMENTAL CONCEPTS IN ORGANISATION BEHAVIOUR

Organisational behaviour starts with the following fundamental concepts revolving around the nature of people which can be summarized as: (*a*)The nature of people includes individual differences, a whole person, motivated behaviour and value of the person and (*b*) the nature of organisation which includes social system and mutual interest of the organisation and stake holders at large. These can be further be illustrated as under:

(a) Individual Differences

Individuals are different in their physical and mental traits. They are different not only in the physical appearance such as sex, age, height, weight, complexion and so on but also different in their psychological trait such as intelligence, attitude, motivation and perception. This belief that each person is different from all others is typically called the "Law of Individual Differences". Individual differences mean that the management has to treat them differently to get the best out of them.

(b) A Whole Person

Though the organisation may feel that they are employing only the individual's skill or intelligence, in fact, they employ the "whole person". This means that individual does not have only the skill and intelligence but he has a personal life, needs and desires as well. In other words, his personal life cannot be separated from his work life since people function as total human beings. When management practices organisational behaviour, it is not only trying to develop a better employee but it also wants to develop a 'better person' in terms of all round growth and development. The benefit will extend beyond the firm into the larger society in which each employee lives.

(c) Motivated Behaviour

It is the urge of the individual to satisfy a particular need that motivates him to do an act. The motivation could be positive or negative. Motivation is essential for the proper functioning of organisations. The organisation can show to its employees how certain actions will increase their need fulfillment.

(d) Value of the Person

It is more an ethical philosophy. It stresses that people are to be treated with respect and dignity. Every job, however simple, entitles the people who do it to proper respect and recognition of their unique aspirations and abilities. Since organisational behaviour involves people, ethical philosophy is involved in one way or the other.

(e) Social System

A system is a group of independent and interrelated elements comprising a unified whole. In context with an organisation, the individuals of a society are considered as a system organized by a characteristic pattern of relationships having a distinctive culture and values. It is also called social organisation or social structure. It can be further divided into following categories:

(*i*) ***Feudal system***: This is a social system, which is developed in Europe in the 8th Century. A political and economic system based on the holding of land and relation of lord to vassal and characterized by homage, legal and military service of tenants, and forfeiture.

(*ii*) ***Patriarchate***: This is social system, in which a male is considered to be the family head and title or surname is traced through his chain. In other words, power lies in his hands.

(*iii*) ***Matriarchate***: This is social system, in which a female is considered to be the family head and title or surname is traced through her chain. In other words, power lies in her hands.

(*iv*) ***Meritocracy***: This is a social system, in which power vests in the hands of the person with superior intellects.

(*v*) ***Class Structure***: This is a social system of different classes with in a society.

(*vi*) ***Segregation***: This is a social system, which provides separate facilities for minority groups of a society.

(*vii*) ***Mutual Interest***: Organisational relationships are most likely to be strong if different groups can negotiate strategies. This can be defined as the interests that are common to both the parties and are related to the accomplishment of their respective goals. This space for sharing ideas builds trust. Individuals who have shared mutual interests are likely to make their organisation the strongest, because even though the views are different they have a shared concern for similar objectives. It is important for the individuals to think about their issues openly, and to incorporate the perspectives of their colleagues. This helps to build sustainable and harmonious activities that can operate in the mutual direct interests of the organisation.

(f) Holistic Organisational Behaviour

When the above concepts of organisational behaviour are considered together, they provide a holistic concept of the subject. Holistic organisational behaviour interprets people-organisation relationships in terms of the whole person, whole group, whole organisation and whole social system.

1.5 NATURE, SCOPE AND CHARACTERISTICS OF ORGANISATION BEHAVIOUR

The field of organisational behaviour attempts to understand human behaviour in organisational settings, the organisation itself, and the individual organisation interface. As illustrated here, these areas are highly interrelated. Thus, although it is possible to focus on only one of these areas at a time, a complete understanding of organisational behaviour requires knowledge of all three areas. Thus, the field of organisational behaviour is both exciting and complex. Myriad variables and concepts accompany the interactions just described, and together these factors greatly complicate the manager's ability to understand, appreciate, and manage others in the organisation. They also provide unique and important opportunities to enhance personal and organisational effectiveness. To most effectively use the knowledge provided by this field, however, managers must thoroughly understand its various concepts, assumptions, and premises as shown in Fig. 1.1.

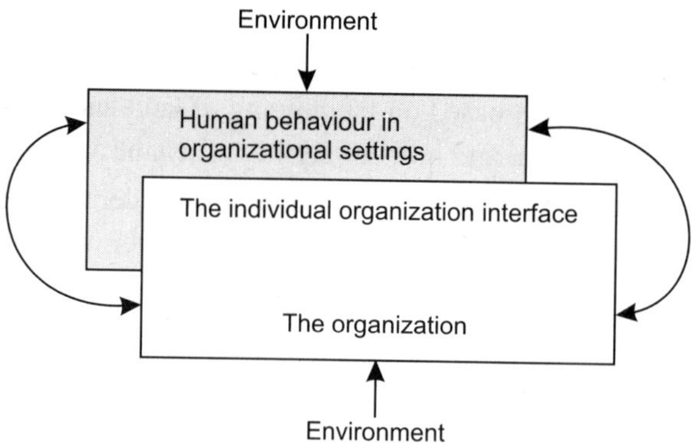

Fig. 1.1: Nature of organisation behaviour

(a) OB is a Field of Study and not a Discipline or Even Emerging as a Discipline

A discipline is an accepted science with a theoretical foundation that serves as the basics for research and analysis.

(b) OB is Interdisciplinary Orientations

It integrates behavioural sciences (psychology, sociology and anthropology) and social sciences (economics, political science and history).

(c) OB has Three Levels of Performance Analyses

Organisation behaviour has three levels of performance analysis—(1) The individual, (2) The group, and (3) The formal organisation. All organisations, regardless of their industry affiliation, size and shape, are made up of individuals and groups. Organisations have unique characteristics in much the same sense, as do individuals and groups. There is a need to study the small group and such characteristics as group, structure, process, development and cohesion. A characteristic that provides some important insight about organisation is its size, formalization policies, levels in hierarchy, degree of centralization, and locus of decision-making. These three levels of analysis are not mutually exclusive. In fact, the field of organisation behaviour embraces therein as being complementary.

(d) OB is a Contingency Orientation Approach

This approach is directed towards developing managerial actions that are most appropriate for a specific situation and the people involved. By considering and weighing situation and the relevant variables in a situation, the manager can proceed to develop the most appropriate action plan needed to accomplish important goals. Managers must be able to recognize, diagnose, and adapt to the given situation to use the contingency approach successfully. To develop most appropriate plan to solve a particular motivation, organisational design, performance appraisal or training problem, the manager must analyse carefully each important variable and link the variables together. Such analysis makes the contingency approach much more than an enticing suggestion for managerial action.

(e) OB as a Source of Knowledge and a Repository of Information

The field of organisation behaviour is being recognized as a source of knowledge and repository of information by theorists, researchers and practitioners. Predicting behaviour and performance is certainly much more elusive. Individuals groups and organisations are separately studied and then interrelated parts before a manager can even hope to make some reasonably good prediction and conducting a thorough review of the variables and the theoretical and research literature, a manager must be satisfied that under the present circumstances a certain action is most appropriate. If not, the manager must decide on an alternative action.

(f) OB is Science, Art or Both

The study of human behaviour in organisations is concerned the science and the skill and the knowledge applying towards the organisation behaviour is an art.

1.6 PARADIGM SHIFT IN OB

The term paradigm comes from the Greek word 'paradigma', which means "model, pattern or example". First introduced over thirty years ago, by the philosophy and science historian Thomas Khun, the term 'paradigm' is now used as, a broad model, a framework, a way of thinking, and a scheme for understanding reality. The impact of information technology, total quality and diversity mentioned earlier has led to a paradigm shift. The organisational behaviour has a goal to help the managers make a transition to the new paradigm. Some of the new paradigm characteristics include coverage of second-generation information technology and total quality management such as empowerment, reengineering and benchmarking, and learning organisation for managing diversity of work. The new paradigm sets the stage for the study, understanding, and application of the time-tested micro-variables, dynamics and macro-variables. One must know why management needs a new perspective to meet the environmental challenges and to shift to a new paradigm.

The modern approach to organisational behaviour is the search for the truth of why people behave the way they do. The organisational behaviour is a delicate and complex process. If one aims to manage an organisation, it is necessary to understand its operation. Organisation is the combination of science and people. While science and technology is predictable, the human behaviour in organisation is rather unpredictable. This is because it arises from deep needs and value systems of people.

(a) Modern Approach to Organisational Behaviour

The modern approach to organisational behaviour is the search for the truth of why people behave the way they do. The organisational behaviour is a delicate and complex process. If one aims to manage an organisation, it is necessary to understand its operation. Organisation is the combination of science and people. While science and technology is predictable, the human behaviour in organisation is rather unpredictable. This is because it arises from deep needs and value systems of people. The roles, in the context of organisational behaviour, are as follows:

1. Interpersonal Roles: In every organisation managers spend a considerable amount of time in interacting with other people both within their own organisations as well as outside. These people include peers, subordinates, superiors, suppliers, customers, government officials and community leaders. All these interactions require an understanding of interpersonal behaviour. Studies show that interacting with people takes up nearly 80% of a manager's time. These interactions involve the following three major interpersonal roles:

(i) ***Figure/lead Role*: ** Managers act as symbolic figureheads performing social or legal obligations. These duties include greeting visitors, signing legal documents, taking important customers to lunch, attending a subordinate's wedding and speaking at functions in schools and churches. All these, primarily, are duties of a ceremonial nature but are important for the smooth functioning of an organisation.

(ii) ***Leadership Role*: ** The influence of the manager is most clearly seen in the leadership role as a leader of a unit or an organisation. Since he is responsible for the activities of his subordinates therefore he must lead and coordinate their activities in meeting task-related goals and motivate them to perform better. He must be an ideal leader so that his subordinates follow his directions and guidelines with respect and dedication.

(iii) ***Liaison Role*: ** The managers must maintain a network of outside contacts. In addition, they need to have a constant contact with their own subordinates, peers and superiors in order to assess the external environment of competition, social changes or changes in governmental rules and regulations. In this role, the managers build up their own external information system. This can be achieved by attending meetings and professional conferences, personal phone calls, trade journals and informal personal contacts with outside agencies.

2. Information Roles: A manager, by virtue of his interpersonal contacts, emerges as a source of information about a variety of issues concerning an organisation. In this capacity of information processing, a manager executes the following three roles.

(i) ***Monitor Role*: ** The managers are constantly monitoring and scanning their internal and external environment, collecting and studying information regarding their organisation. This can be done by reading reports and periodicals, interrogating their liaison contacts and through gossip, hearsay and speculation.

(ii) ***Information Disseminator Role*: ** The managers must transmit the information regarding changes in policies or other matters to their subordinates, their peers and to other members of an organisation. This can be done through memos, phone calls, individual meetings and group meetings.

(iii) ***Spokesman Role*: ** A manager has to be a spokesman for his unit and represent his unit in either sending relevant information to people outside his unit or making some demands on behalf of his unit.

3. Decision Roles: A manager must make decisions and solve organisational problems on the basis of the environmental information received. In that respect, a manager plays four important roles.

(i) ***Entrepreneur Role*: ** Managers, as entrepreneurs are constantly involved in improving their units and facing the dynamic technological challenges. They are constantly on the lookout for new ideas for product improvement or product addition. They initiate feasibility studies, arrange capital for new products and ask for suggestions from the employees to improve organisation. This can be achieved through suggestion boxes, holding strategy meetings with project managers and R&D personnel.

(ii) ***Conflict Handling Role*: ** The managers are constantly involved as judge in solving conflicts among the employees and between employees and management. Mangers must anticipate such

problems and take preventive action and take corrective action once the problem arises. These problems may involve labor disputes, customer complaints, employee grievances, machine breakdowns, cash flow shortages and interpersonal conflicts.

(iii) ***Resource Allocation Role***: The managers establish priorities among various projects or programs and make budgetary allocations to different activities of an organisation based on these priorities.

(iv) ***Negotiator Role***: The managers in their negotiator role represent their organisation in negotiating deals and agreements within and outside of an organisation. They negotiate contracts with the unions. Sales managers may negotiate prices with prime customers. Purchasing managers may negotiate prices with vendors.

All the above ten roles under three sub heads are important in a manager's job and are interrelated, even though some roles may be more influential than others depending upon the managerial position. For example, sales manager gives more importance to interpersonal roles, while the production manager may give more importance to decisional roles.

(b) Organisational Behaviour in AD 2020

Information technology is a major force driving change. We are experiencing the rapid integration of information across all industries everywhere, yet it is still people who invent, direct, guide, and manage change in their own careers and in the boundary less organisation. This text relates organisational behaviour topics to managing dynamic body of knowledge that can be used to understand and manage a wide technological change as a driver of performance and integration. "Business at the speed of thought" is a major factor of competitive advantage. Another set of success factors that lead to competitive advantage are developing and sustaining world-class products and services with Internet speed and meeting and exceeding customer demand. Organisations are adapting by reengineering, reinventing, restructuring, and rethinking their strategies, structures, and expertise around web-based, Internet and Mobile integrated business processes. Not all organisations are changing at the same pace or on the same scale. However, Internet and Mobile driven networks and android applications/tablets in AD 2014 have produced a type of "Digital Darwinism".

The information-based and socially networked organisation has knowledge workers who are specialists and who resist command-and-control procedures based on the military model. Everyone takes responsibility in these workplaces. Structures become flatter, clear, simple, common objectives that lead to action are required. Changing managerial unified vision in the organisation; devising a management structure for task forces; and ensuring the supply, preparation, and testing of top management people. Finally, because of the internationalization of business and continuous merger, acquisition, and divestiture activities, yet another aspect of managerial work is being revised.

Take the example of Google, the search engine of the world today. The name "Google" originated from a misspelling of 'googol' which refers to the number represented by a 1 followed by one-hundred zeros. On October 9, 2006, Google bought the popular online video site YouTube for $1.65 billion and maintained YouTube as a separate brand, rather than merging it with Google Video. As of September 2013, Google operates 70 offices in more than 40 countries. Originally the search engine used the Stanford website with the domain *google.stanford.edu*. The domain *google.com* was registered on September 15, 1997. They formally incorporated their company, *Google*, on September 4, 1998 at a friend's garage in California. The first patent filed under the name "Google Inc." was filed on August 31,

1999. This patent, filed by Siu-Leong Iu, Malcom Davis, Hui Luo, Yun-Ting Lin, Guillaume Mercier, and Kobad Bugwadia, is titled "Watermarking system and methodology for digital multimedia content" and is the earliest patent filing under the assignee name "Google Inc".

Both Brin and Page had been against using advertising pop-ups in a search engine, or an "advertising funded search engines" model, and they wrote a research paper in 1998 on the topic while still students. They changed their minds early on and allowed simple text ads. By the end of 2013, Google had an index of about 600 million pages. It is a fact that Google influences our way of thinking and giving concrete shapes for our idea and information search as well. Infact the employees continue to serve the organisation based on their portal rankings and rating on employee friendliness or most admirable employer in the world. So the technology made the life of every one through e-job search, e-content and even e-shopping. So many organisations in that category now rule the world; for example, Google and facebook became the hot spots and most lovely places to work in the world across all generations' countries and culture in 2014.

In coordination with several of the major corporations, including Microsoft, Nokia, LG, Samsung, and Ericsson, Google provided financial support in the launch of the mobi top level domain created specifically for the mobile Internet, stating that it is supporting the new domain extension to help set the standards that will define the future of mobile content and improve the experience of Google users In early 2006, Google launched *Google.mobi*, a mobile search portal offering several Google mobile products, including stripped-down versions of its applications and services for mobile users. On September 17, 2007, Google launched "Adsense for Mobile", a service to its publishing partners providing the ability to monetize their mobile websites through the targeted placement of mobile text ads. Also in September, Google acquired the mobile social networking site, Zingku.mobi to provide people worldwide with direct access to Google applications, and ultimately the information they want and need, right from their mobile devices. The fate of the world's top mobile phone manufacturer Nokia was sealed in 2013 just because the company failed to migrate to android platform rapidly or even at par with Samsung and Apple.

Further, Rosabeth Moss Kanter calls the new managerial work and practices "post-entrepreneurial" because "they involve the application of entrepreneurial creativity and flexibility to established businesses". Post-entrepreneurial practices include managers involving themselves in networks outside individual empires and thinking cross-functionally and strategically to contribute to other faces of the business. The era of the boundaryless or seamless corporation has arrived. Emphasis is placed on developing co-operative relationships among internal, external, and virtual teams who are part of an expanding economic (or what may become a "Webonomic", *i.e.*, Internet integrated) enterprise. High-performance teams are organized with empowered individuals who work creatively to add value to their company as well as to their units. Knowledge of organisational behaviour and a repertoire of people skills are essential in building and sustaining face-to-face and virtual relationships.

1. Interactionalism: People and Situations: Interactionalism is a relatively new approach to understanding behaviour in organisational settings. First presented in terms of interactional psychology, this view assumes that individual behaviour results from a continuous and multidirectional interaction between characteristics of the person and characteristics of the situation. More specifically, interactionalism attempts to explain how people select, interpret, and change various situations. When people enter an organisation, their own behaviours and actions shape that organisation in various ways. Similarly, the organisation itself shapes the behaviours and actions of each individual who becomes a part of it. This interactionist perspective can be useful in explaining organisational behaviour.

2. Smartphone Integration through facebook and Social Media: The interactionalism cannot be completed unless we touch the facebook, the world's best social media site and platform. Facebook is a social networking service and website started in February 2004. It is owned by Facebook, Inc. As of March 2013, Facebook has 1.10 billion active users. Users may make a personal profile, add other users as friends, and send messages. Facebook users must register before using the site. Users may join user groups. These groups can be for a workplace, school or college, or other interest. The name of the service comes from the name for the book given to students at the start of the school year by some universities in the United States. These books help students get to know each other better. Facebook allows any users who say they are at least 13 years old to become users of the website.

Facebook was started by Mark Zuckerberg with his college roommates and fellow computer science students Eduardo Saverin, Dustin Moskovitz and Chris Hughes. The website's membership was only for Harvard students at first. Later it included other colleges in the Boston area, the Ivy League, and Stanford University. It eventually opened for students at other universities. After that, it opened to high school students, and, finally, to anyone aged 13 and over. Based on Consumers Reports.org in May 2011, there are 7.5 million children under 13 with accounts. This breaks the website's rules.

In January 2009 Compete.com study ranked Facebook as the most used social networking service by worldwide monthly active users. *Entertainment Weekly* put the site on its end-of-the-decade "best-of" list. It said, How on earth did we stalk our exes, remember our co-workers' birthdays, bug our friends, and play a rousing game of Scrabulous before Facebook. According to *Social Media Today*, in April 2013 about 71.6% of the U.S. population had a Facebook account.

As of February 2011, Facebook had become the largest online photo host, being cited by Facebook application and online photo aggregator pixable as expecting to have 100 billion photos by summer 2011. As of March 2013, over 1,110 million users accessed Facebook through their mobile phones, accounting for 33% of all Facebook traffic.

Many new smartphones offer access to the Facebook , the third largest population in the world (if it is considered as a country) services either through their web browsers or applications. The Facebook iPhone-compatible website was launched in August 2007 and as of July 2008 over 1.5 million people used it regularly, at the point when a free application for the iOS named "Facebook for iPhone" was launched. Version 2.0 of this app was released in September 2008 and featured improved services such as being able to respond to friend requests and notifications. Version 3.0 was released in August 2009 and added features such as events, and uploading video with an iPhone 3GS.

Microsoft developed an application for Facebook on their Windows Phone 7 platform, available in the Windows Phone Marketplace. Users can pin elements such as Messages, Events, the News Feed, and Photos directly onto one's home screen. It also includes tile notifications for events, friend requests, tags, and so on. Windows Mobile platform, including features such as messaging, uploading pictures and video straight from the device, managing profile information, contact integration allowing users to call anyone in their friends list that has their number in their profile information. It is also possible to add a chat feature to Windows Mobile via third-party software such as FIM, available in the Windows Mobile Marketplace. Nokia also offers a Facebook app on its Ovi Store for Nokia S60 devices such as the N97 and contains most of the functionality of the full website.

Google's Android 2.0 OS automatically includes an official Facebook app. The first device to use this is the Motorola Droid. The app has options to sync Facebook friends with contacts, which adds profile pictures and status updates to the contacts list. Research In Motion also offers a Facebook application for the BlackBerry. It includes a range of functions, including an ability to integrate Facebook events into the BlackBerry calendar, and using Facebook profile pictures for Caller ID.

"Status updates" (also called as a 'status') allows users to post messages for their friends to read. In turn, friends can respond with their own comments, as well as clicking the "Like" button. A user's most recent updates appear at the top of their Timeline/Wall and are also noted in the "Recently Updated" section of a user's friend list. Originally, the purpose of the feature was to allow users to inform their friends of their current 'status', including feelings, whereabouts, or actions, where Facebook prompted the status update with "Username is"... and users filled in the rest. This feature first became available in September 2006, though on December 13, 2007, the requirement to start a status update with is was removed.

The updates were followed by the "What are you doing right now?" status update question; in March 2009, the question was changed to "What's on your mind?". In 2009, Facebook added the feature to tag certain friends (or groups, etc.) within one's status update by adding an @ character before their name, turning the friend's name into a link to their profile and including the message on the friend's wall. Tagging has since been updated to recognize friends' names by typing them into a status while a list of friends whose names match the inputted letters appears. A large percentage of the updates that are posted are humorous and as a result, many apps, websites and books have sprung up to help users to update their own. Companies like Samsung and Apple have their own application stores apart form Google store to support this customer and employee behaviour globally for large and mini corporate in 2014 which link their facebook and twitter pages and applications as well.

In short, organisational behaviour is concerned with the characteristics and behaviours of employees in isolation; the characteristics and processes that are part of the organisation itself; and the characteristics and behaviours directly resulting from people with their individual needs and motivations working within the structure of the organisation. One cannot understand an individual's behaviour completely without learning something about that individual's organisation. Similarly, he cannot understand how the organisation operates without; studying the people who-make it up. Thus, the organisation influences and is influenced by individuals. Many organisations, social media reporting and postings in the similar web communities and their cross interactions of their employees were also monitored strictly to safeguard the interest of organisation at large.

(c) Organisational Ecology: A New Perspective for Management in 2020

Management is generally considered to have three major dimensions—technical, conceptual and human. The technical dimension consists of the manager's expertise in particular functional areas. They know the requirements of the jobs and have the functional knowledge to get the job done. But the practicing managers ignore the conceptual and human dimensions of their jobs.

Most managers think that their employees are lazy, and are interested only in money, and that if you could make them happy in terms of money, they would be productive. If such assumptions are accepted, the human problems that the management is facing are relatively easy to solve. But human behaviour at work is much more complicated and diverse. The new perspective assumes that employees are extremely complex and that there is a need for theoretical understanding given by empirical research before applications can be made for managing people effectively.

Organisational ecology (also organisational demography and the population ecology of organisations) is a theoretical and empirical approach in the social sciences that is especially used in organisational studies. Organisational ecology utilizes insights from biology, economics, and sociology, and employs statistical analysis to try to understand the conditions under which organisations emerge, grow, and die.

Introduced in 1977 by Michael T. Hannan and the late John H. Freeman in their American Journal of Sociology piece "The population ecology of organisations" and later refined in their 1989 book Organisational Ecology, organisational ecology examines the environment in which organisations compete and a process like natural selection occurs. This theory looks at the death of organisations (firm mortality), the birth of new organisations (organisational founding), as well as organisational growth and change. Organisational ecology contains a number of more specific 'theory fragments', including Inertia and change, Niche width, Resource partitioning , Density dependence and Age dependence.

Organisational ecology also predicts that the rates of founding and mortality are dependent on the number of organisations (density) in the market. The two central mechanisms here are legitimation (the recognition or taken-for-grantedness of that group of organisations) and competition. Legitimation generally increases (at a decreasing rate) with the number of organisations, but so does competition (at an increasing rate). The result is that legitimation processes will prevail at low numbers of organisations, while competition at high numbers.

The founding rate will therefore first increase with the number of organisations (due to an increase in legitimation) but will decrease at high numbers of organisations (due to competition). The reverse holds for mortality rates. Thus, the relationship of density to founding rates has an inverted U shape and the relationship of density to mortality rates follows a U-shaped pattern. Organisational ecology can be usefully compared with evolutionary theories in economics (e.g., Nelson & Winter, 1982). Main similarities between these strands of literature are: (1) the emphasis on organisational routines and the limits to organisational adaptability, (2) the population or system level of analysis and (3) the importance of environmental selection. Organisational ecology's perspective is more Darwinistic provide a more Lamarckian perspective. Another important difference concerns the question what is selected by the environment: "organisational forms", as in organisational ecology, or "routines" as in the evolutionary economics literature? Authors like Joel Baum and Arjen van Witteloostuijn have argued for the potential of cross-fertilization between these two research strands.

1.7 CHALLENGES AND OPPORTUNITIES FOR OB

Positive Organisational Behaviour (POB) is defined by Fred Luthens in 2002 as "the study and application of positively oriented human resource strengths and psychological capacities that can be measured, developed, and effectively managed for performance improvement in today's workplace. For a positive psychological capacity to qualify for inclusion in POB, it must be positive and must have extensive theory and research foundations and valid measures. In addition, it must be state like, which would make it open to development and manageable for performance improvement. Finally, positive states that meet the POB definitional criteria are primarily researched, measured, developed, and managed at the individual, micro level. This is an opportunity as well as challenge for the organisation behaviour practitioners and researchers as well. The state-like criterion distinguishes POB from other positive approaches that focus on positive traits, whereas its emphasis on micro, individual-level constructs separates it from positive perspectives that address positive organisations and their related macro-level variables and measures. Meeting the inclusion criteria for POB are the state-like psychological resource capacities of self-efficacy, hope, optimism, and resiliency and, when combined, the underlying higher-order, core construct of positive psychological capital or PsyCap.

In general, organisation behaviour is the study of the way people interact within groups. Normally this study is applied in an attempt to create more efficient business organisations. The central idea of the study of organisational behaviour is that a scientific approach can be applied to the management of workers. Organisational behaviour theories are used for human resource purposes to maximize the output from individual group members.

Organisational behaviour is a growing field in AD 2020. Organisational studies departments generally form part of business schools, although many universities also have industrial psychology and industrial economics programs. The field is highly influential in the business world with practitioners such as Peter Drucker and Peter Senge, who turned the academic research into business practices. Organisational behaviour is becoming more important in the global economy as people with diverse backgrounds and cultural values must work together effectively and efficiently. It is also under increasing criticism as a field for its ethnocentric and pro-capitalist assumptions. During the last 20 years, organisational behaviour study and practice has developed and expanded through creating integrations with other domains such as Anthropology became an interesting prism to understanding firms as communities, by introducing concepts like Organisational culture, 'organisational rituals' and 'symbolic acts' enabling new ways to understand organisations as communities.

Opportunities in organisation behaviour also arised out of better understanding of sustainable organisation/business and crucial role of leadership at various levels of an organisation in the process of change management and market turbulence. Business ethics and their importance as pillars of any organisation vision and one of the most important driving forces in an organisation especially after 2008 global meltdown and financial crisis. Within the last decades Aesthetics also emerged as a separate filed in organisation behaviour that focuses on the aesthetic sphere of our existence in organisations, drawing on interdisciplinary theories and methods from the humanities and disciplines such as theatre studies, literature, music, visual studies and many more.

There are a variety of different models and philosophies of organisational behaviour. Areas of research include improving job performance, increasing job satisfaction, promoting innovation and encouraging leadership. In order to achieve the desired results, managers may adopt different tactics, including reorganizing groups, modifying compensation structures and changing the way performance is evaluated. In short, organisational behaviour is the field of study that investigates how organisational structures affect behaviour within organisations across the culture, leadership and more importantly over a span of time.

1.8 LIMITATIONS OF OB

Following are the limitations of organisation behaviour taking in a theoretical sense; however for a practitioner the same appears to be offering greater challenge and job satisfaction.

(a) OB will not Abolish Conflict and Frustration; it can Only Reduce Them

It is a way to improve, not an absolute answer to problems. Furthermore, it is but part of the whole of an organisation. We can discuss organisational behaviour as a separate subject, but to apply it we must tie it back to the whole of reality.

(b) Improved Organisational Behaviour will not Solve Unemployment

It will not make up for our deficiencies. It cannot substitute for poor planning inept organizing, or shoddy controls. It is only one of many stems operating within a larger social system.

(c) Existence of Behavioural Bias

Behavioural bias, which gives them a narrow viewpoint that emphasizes "meaningful" employee experiences while overlooking the broader system of the organisation in relation to all its publics. Behavioural bias can be so misapplied that it harms employees as well as the organisation. Some people, in spite of their good intentions so overwhelm others with care that they are reduced to dependent and unproductive indignity. They become content, not fulfilled. They find excuses for failure rather than taking responsibility for progress. They lack of self-discipline and self-respect.

(d) Overemphasis on an Organisational Behaviour Practice

This may produce negative results, as indicated by the law of diminishing returns. It is a limiting factor in organisational behaviour the same way that it is in economics. In economics the law of diminishing returns refers to a declining amount of extra outputs when more of a desirable input is added to an economic situation. The law of diminishing return in organisational behaviour works in a similar way. It states that at some point increases of a desirable practice produce declining returns, eventually zero returns, and then negative returns as more increases are added.

(e) Use of Autonomy

Employ autonomy is a higher-order need that is frequently emphasized. One reason probably is that excess prevents coordination toward central goals. Different units of the organisation cannot work together, so the labour of employees is wasted. At another end of the continuum, the lack of autonomy also is ineffective. When autonomy declines below an appropriate level, the organisation fails to develop and use the talents of employees. The result is that effectiveness declines with both excessive use and miserly use of autonomy.

(f) Manipulation of People without Regard for Human Welfare

A significant concern about organisational behaviour is that its knowledge and techniques can be used to manipulate people as well as to help them develop their potential. People who lack respect for the basic dignity of the human being could learn organisational behaviour ideas and use them for selfish ends. They could use what they know about motivation or communication to manipulate people without regard for human welfare. People who lack ethical values could use people without regard for human welfare. People who lack ethical values could use people in unethical ways. The possibility of manipulation means that people in power in organisations need to be people of high ethical and moral integrity who will not misuse their power. Without ethical leadership, the new knowledge that is learned about people becomes a dangerous instrument for possible misuse.

In short, organisational behaviour cannot abolish conflict and frustration but can only reduce them. It is a way to improve but not an absolute answer to problems. It is only one of the many systems operating within a large social system. People who lack system understanding may develop a 'behavioural basis', which gives them a narrow view point, *i.e.*, a tunnel vision that emphasizes on satisfying employee experiences while overlooking the broader system of an organisation in relation to all its public. The law of diminishing returns also operates in the case of organisational behaviour. It states, that at some point increase of a desirable practice produce declining returns and sometimes, negative returns. The concept implies that for any situation there is an optimum amount of a desirable practice. When that point is exceeded, there is a decline in returns. For example, too much security may lead to less employee initiative and growth. This relationship shows that organisational effectiveness is achieved not by maximizing one human variable but by working all system variables together in a balanced way. A significant concern about organisational behaviour is that its knowledge and techniques could be used to manipulate people without regard for human welfare. People who lack ethical values could use people in unethical ways.

1.9 FUTURE OF ORGANISATIONAL BEHAVIOUR: BEYOND AD 2020

The growing interest in organisational behaviour stems from both a philosophical desire by many people to create more humanistic work places and a practical need to design more productive work environments. As a result of these forces, organisational behaviour is now a part of the curriculum of almost all courses including engineering and medical. A separate branch has been now opened for studying the employee behaviour of IT and software industries and the organisation researches are focusing on how to retain talent in the organisation as they realized that employees are their real assets.

The field of organisational behaviour has grown in depth and breadth. The keys to its past and future success revolve around the related processes of theory development, research and managerial practice. Although organisational behaviour has certain limitations, it has a tremendous potential to contribute to the advancement of civilization. It has provided and will provide much improvement in the human environment. By building a better climate for people, organisational behaviour will release their creative potential to solve major social problems. In this way organisational behaviour will contribute to social improvements. Improved organisational behaviour is not easy to apply but opportunities are there. It should produce a higher quality of life in which there is improved harmony within each individual, among people and among the organisations of future. The best examples in this regard are companies like Microsoft, Apple, Google and Facebook are maintaining their supremacies in the world through the acquisition and retention of the world's best talents from 195 countries every year for their business operations and R&D activities.

SUMMARY

- Organisational behaviour is the study of human behaviour in organisational settings, the interface between human behaviour and the organisation, and the organisation itself. The study of organisational behaviour is important because organisations have a powerful influence over our lives.
- Serious interest in the study of management first developed around the beginning of this century. Two of the earliest approaches were scientific management (best represented by the work of Taylor) and classical organisation theory (exemplified by the work of Weber).
- Organisational behaviour began to emerge as a scientific discipline as a result of the Hawthorne studies. McGregor and Maslow led the human relations movement that grew from those studies.

- Management is a relatively new field of study, having emerged only within the last 100 years. Key contributors to scientific management included Frederick W. Taylor, Frank and Lillian Gilbreth, Henry Gantt, and Harrig ton Emerson. Taylor identified a phenomenon he called "soldiering"—the practice of working considerably slower than one can. Classical organisation theory focused on how organisations can be structured most effectively to meet their goals.
- Key contributors to classical organisation theory included Henri Fayol, Lyndall Urwick, and Max Weber. The bureaucracy model, as described by Weber, was an early universal approach to organisation structure. In ideal form, a bureaucracy is logical, rational, and efficient. Robert Owen, Hugo Munsterberg, and Mary Parker Follett were among the first to recognize the importance of individual behaviour to organisations.
- While scientific management was focusing on the interaction between workers and the task, more researchers were studying how to structure the organisation more effectively. Instead of trying to make each worker more efficient, classical organisation theory sought the most effective overall organisational structure for workers and managers. The theory's most prominent advocate, Max Weber, proposed a bureaucratic form of structure, which he thought would work for all organisations. Weber's idea of bureaucracy was, logical, rational and efficient. He made the naive assumption that one structure would work best for all organisations. Henry Ford, Henry Fayol and Frederick W. Taylor, the early management pioneers, recognized the behavioural side of management. However, they did not emphasize the human dimensions.
- The Hawthorne studies, conducted between 1927 and 1932, led to some of the first discoveries of the importance of human behaviour in organisations. Following the Hawthorne studies, the human relations movement emerged. Human relationists believed that employee satisfaction is a key determinant of performance.
- A prominent human relations writer, Douglas McGregor, developed the concepts of Theory X and Theory Y. Theory X takes a negative and pessimistic view of workers, Theory Y a more positive perspective. McGregor advocated the adoption of Theory Y.
- Contemporary organisational behaviour attempts to describe, rather than prescribe, behavioural forces in organisations. Ties to psychology, sociology, anthropology, political science, economics, engineering, and medicine make organisational behaviour an interdisciplinary field.
- The basic concepts of the field are divided into three categories: Individual processes, interpersonal processes, and organisational process and characteristics. Those categories from the framework for the organisation of this book.
- Important contextual perspectives on the field of organisational behaviour are the systems and contingency perspectives, interactionalism, and contemporary applied perspectives.
- By its very nature, management requires an understanding of human behaviour, to help managers better comprehend those at different levels in the organisation, those at the same level, those in other organisations, and themselves.
- The manager's job can be characterized in terms of four functions, three sets of roles, and four skills. The basic managerial functions are planning, organizing, leading, and controlling. The roles consist of three interpersonal roles, three informational roles, and four decision-making roles. The four basic skills necessary for effective management are technical, interpersonal, conceptual, and diagnostic skills.

- Several organisational challenges confront managers. One major organisational challenge is downsizing and cutbacks. Another is increasing workforce diversity. The new workforce also poses significant organisational challenges for managers, as does organisation change. Information technology and new ways of organizing are two other important organisational challenges.
- There are also several important environmental challenges to consider. Determining the most effective competitive strategy and matching people to that strategy is one important challenge. Today, global competition is one of the most critical environmental challenges. Ethics and social responsibility are significant as well. The manager must also emphasize product and service quality and manage technology successfully.
- Managing for effectiveness involves balancing a variety of individual-level, group and team-level, and organisation-level outcome variables. Organisation behaviour is all about attitudes of individuals and groups toward one another and toward the organisation as a whole, and its effect on the organisation's functioning and performance.
- The term contingency orientation in organisation behaviour reflects the need to consider the situation and individuals involved before drawing conclusions about behaviour. The organisation behaviour field has no universally applicable set of prescriptions for managers. The organisation behaviour researcher must always be concerned with understanding real events in actual organisations and with communicating results in a meaningful fashion to practicing managers.
- Finally, we can summarize Organisational Behaviour is the study of human behaviour in organisation. It is an interdisciplinary approach and studies individuals, groups, organisations and the environment. It borrows heavily from theories, models and concepts from the behavioural sciences. Knowledge about human behaviour would be useful in improving organisational effectiveness. Organisational behaviour offers both challenges and opportunities for managers. It recognizes differences and help managers to see the value of workforce diversity and practices that may need to be changed when managing in different countries. It can help improve quality and employee productivity by showing managers how to empower their people as well as how to design and implement change programs. Lastly, organisation behaviour can offer managers guidance in creating an ethically healthy global work climate.

REVIEW QUESTIONS

1. What do you mean by organisation behaviour? How important it is for an organisation in the 21st century?
2. Comment on the Human Relation approach of organisation behaviour.
3. Explain system theory of organisation behaviour in the current context.
4. Theory X and Theory Y helped managers to practice organisation behaviour as a discipline. Do you agree or not? Explain.
5. How do you visualise the application of fundamental concepts of organisation behaviour in an e-commerce organisation?

DISCUSSION QUESTIONS

1. In what ways is organisational behaviour comparable to functional areas such as finance, marketing, and production? In what ways, organisation behaviour is different from these areas?
2. Identify some managerial jobs that are highly affected by human behaviour and others that are less so. Which one would you prefer? Why?
3. Get a recent issue of a popular business magazine and newspapers like Business Week, Business Standard, Economic Times or Fortune and scan its major articles. Do, any of them reflect concepts which you learned from organisational behaviour? Describe.
4. The author believes that we cannot understand organisations without understanding the behaviour of the people within them. Do you agree or disagree with this assertion? Why?
5. Interview a local manager or business owner to find out his or her views on the importance of individual behaviour to the success of the organisation. Report your findings to the class.
6. What advice would you give managers to help them prepare better to cope with changes in workforce demographics?
7. How information technology changed your role as a student? Have the changes been positive or negative?

STUDENT EXERCISE

Visit your nearest business organisation say India Cements/Asian Paints/Ford Motors and comment on the organisation practices followed by them for nurturing both its internal and external customers. Compare with the theories, which you have read in the chapter and comment on its impact on its survival.

SKILL TEST

Are you a Human Relation Oriented Manager?

Gauge your ability as a human relation oriented manager by responding to the following statements, and mark the options closest to your experience. Be as honest as you can; if your answer is **never**, mark option 1; if it is **always**, mark option 4; and so on. Add your scores together, and refer to the Analysis to see how you scored. Use your answers to identify the areas that need improving.

OPTIONS

1. Never
2. Occasionally
3. Frequently
4. Always

1. I apply Theory Y management principles rather than Theory X.

1	2	3	4

2. I avoid office politics and discourage others from politicking.

1	2	3	4

3. I involve people in issues at the earliest possible opportunity.

1	2	3	4

4. I thank people for good work face to face or by handwritten note.

1	2	3	4

5. If I feel it is necessary, I bend the rules and avoid working by the book.

1	2	3	4

6. I look out for and move people who are not using their full potential.

1	2	3	4

7. I seek opportunities for radical change and take them where possible.

1	2	3	4

8. I reward, recognize, and promote on merit alone.

1	2	3	4

9. I give reasons for my actions and for any disagreements with people.

1	2	3	4

10. I seek consensus and encourage others to do the same.

1	2	3	4

11. I react to failure not by blame but by analysis and correction.

1	2	3	4

12. I try to persuade and influence staff rather than force them to do what I want.

1	2	3	4

13. I try to ensure that work is enjoyable for my staff.

1	2	3	4

14. I interview people who leave to find out their reasons for going.

1	2	3	4

15. I use my knowledge of non-verbal communication to influence discussions.

1	2	3	4

16. I am honest with my staff and keep them as informed as possible.

1	2	3	4

17. If I enquire into staff attitudes, I make a point of acting on what I find.

1	2	3	4

18. I seek a balance between firm control and giving people independence.

1	2	3	4

19. I make conscious efforts to improve on my motivational skills.

1	2	3	4

20. I change benchmarks to keep targets at stimulating heights.

1	2	3	4

21. I revise the system in order to remove obstacles to performance.

1	2	3	4

22. I look at more than just financial results when assessing staff performance.

1	2	3	4

23. I encourage people to be open about how much they and others are paid.

1	2	3	4

24. In appraisal interviews, I request and receive appraisals of myself.

1	2	3	4

25. I get full, clear feedback from people whose behaviour I have had to criticize.

1	2	3	4

26. I organise work so that one person can own and complete an entire task.

1	2	3	4

27. I look at assignments and moves as ways to develop people.

1	2	3	4

28. I encourage people to act on their own initiatives.

1	2	3	4

29. I delegate work that does not have to be done by me.

1	2	3	4

30. If difficult 'people decisions' are needed, I take them without hesitation.

1	2	3	4

31. I act to avert or settle disputes and personality clashes.

1	2	3	4

32. I make changes only after full consultation with those affected.

1	2	3	4

KEY TO THE TEST SCORE

Now you have completed the self-assessment, add up your total score and check your performance by reading the corresponding evaluation.

ANALYSIS AND INTERPRETATION

32–64 : You are demotivating rather than motivating people. Find actions that work and practice them often to achieve results.

65–95 : Your motivational skills are fairly sound, but your weak points need to be addressed.

96–128 : You are a great motivator. Be careful not to become complacent or to let your high standards slip.

If you wish to know more insight on your test score, then you are welcome to contact author via e-mail. shaangrila@gmail.com or social media drs.shajahan.7@facebook.com

2

CHAPTER

PERSONALITY AND ATTITUDES

LEARNING OBJECTIVES

This chapter aims at introducing fundamental concepts for explaining the personality and attitudes and its influence in organisational behaviour to the readers:

- *Definition, importance and fundamental concepts of personality, attitudes and job satisfaction in the organisational context*
- *Meaning and importance of personality*
- *Personality determinants and traits*
- *Development of personality*
- *Types of attitudes*
- *Job satisfaction*

INTRODUCTION

The word personality originated from the Latin word "persona" which means the mask worn by the player. When categorically used it means the false appearance. Later on it became the player himself with distinct qualities. As far as psychologists are concerned personality is neither the false appearance over the distinct qualities. According to them people are the product of biological structures and their environments. It emerges from the interaction between the biological organism and a social physical world. It is expressed form of behaviour. It refers to the whole individual.

Personality consists of certain surface traits and depth factors. Traits such as friendliness, vigour sociability etc. are only the surface traits which are measured using Rating Scales, questionnaires etc. while the depth factors contribute the inner personality of an individual. They include fears, anxieties, aspirations etc. A person may be conscious or unconscious about his inner wants. This inner personality is revealed through psychoanalysis especially dream analysis and force association. Certain tests also are used in measuring it. This gives us a fair understanding regarding the complexity and the multiplicity of personality traits. It consists of a constellation of traits such as intelligence, interests, aptitude, value etc. In short we can only say that personality is a configuration of many traits, which influence his total behaviour.

2.1 DEFINITION OF PERSONALITY

In the popular sense most people as an intangible quality that makes people or an individual attractive or non-attractive to others understand personality, we often hear people using the term to mean many things. To psychologist personality is a much wider term. In every individual we see characteristics, which in a given situation result in a typical reaction. This pattern of reaction to a particular situation makes the personality of an individual unique.Personality is a complex, multi-dimensional construct and there is no simple definition of what personality is. Maddi defines personality as, "A stable set of characteristics and tendencies that determine those commonalities and differences in the psychological behaviour and that may not be easily understood as the sole result of the social and biological pressures of the moment".

From the above definition we can infer that all individuals have some universally common characteristics. Yet they differ in some other specific attributes. This makes it difficult for the managers to assume that they can apply same reward types or motivation techniques to modify different individual behaviours. The definition, however, does not mean that people never change. In simple terms, it asserts that individuals do not change all at once. Their thoughts, feelings, values and actions remain relatively stable over time. Changes in individual's personality can, however, occur gradually over a period of time. The managers should, therefore, attempt to understand certain dimensions of personality. This can enable them to predict the behaviour of their employees on a daily basis.

In the words of Kolasa, "Personality is a broad, amorphous designation relating to fundamental approaches of persons to others and themselves. To most psychologists and students of behaviour, this term refers to the study of the characteristics traits of an individual, relationships between these traits, and the way in which a person adjust to other people and situations".

According to Gluck, "Personality is a pattern of stable states and characteristics of a person that influences his or her behaviour toward goal achievement. Each person has unique ways of protecting these states".

Szilagyi and Wallace assume "Personality is the combination of psychological characteristics or variable one uses to type or classify someone". If a manager describes a job applicant as "client-oriented", for example, he is employing a one-dimensional definition of personality. If, on the other hand, he describes an applicant for the position as a high-need achiever with very little mathematical skill who also possesses high levels of interpersonal skills, he has used a three-dimensional definition.

Further, many personality theorists stress the need of identifying person-situation as interaction. This is equivalent to recognizing the social learning aspects related to personality. Such a social learning analysis is one of the most comprehensive and meaningful ways included in the overall study of organisational behaviour. From this perspective, personality means the way people affect others. It also involves people's understanding themselves, as well as their pattern of inner and outer measurable traits, and the person and situation interaction. People affect others depending primarily upon their external appearance such as height, weight, facial features, colour and other physical aspects and traits.

2.2 DETERMINANTS TO PERSONALITY

Several factors influence the shaping of our personality. Chief among these are heredity, culture, family background, our experiences through life, and the people we interact with.

(a) Heredity

There are some genetic factors, which play a part in determining certain aspects of what we tend to become. Whether we are tall or short, experience good health or ill health, are quickly irritable or patient, are all characteristics which can, in many cases, be traced to heredity.

(b) Culture

The cultural values we are surrounded by significantly tend to shape our personal values and predisposition. Thus people born in different cultures have different personalities, which significantly influence their behaviours. People in the West, for instance, generally tend to be more assertive than people in oriental cultures.

(c) Family Background

The socio-economic status of the family, the number of children in the family and birth order, and the background and education of the parents and extended members of the family such as uncles and aunts, influence the shaping of personality to a considerable extent. Experiences in Life whether one trusts or mistrusts others, is miserly or generous has a high or low self esteem, and the like, is at least partially related to the past experiences the individual has had.

A person we interact with "a person is known by the company he or she keeps" is a common adage. The implication is that people influence each other and tends to associate with members who are more like them in their attitudes and values. From childhood, the people we interact with influence us. First our parents and siblings, then our teachers and class mates, later our friends and colleagues, and so on. The influence of these various individuals and groups shapes our personality.

In sum, our personality is a function of both heredity and other external factors that shape it. It is important to know what specific personality predisposition influence work behaviour.

Jung's Psychological Functions: Carl Jung (1923) identified four psychological functions used in gathering and evaluating information. They are sensation, intuition, thinking, and feeling. The first two functions are important for gathering information and the last two for evaluating or judging the situation. Individuals are strong in either sensation or intuition while gathering information and they are strong in either thinking or feeling while evaluation or processing the information.

(*i*) ***Sensation and Intuition***: Individuals gather data either through processing the facts and details in the environment in a very methodical fashion—sensation types or through global visualizations of what the scene depicts intuition types. The sensation type individual depends on a lot of information to assess the situation, is pragmatic and down to earth, and concentrates on the present time. The intuitive type, on the other hand, relies on hunches and nonverbal cues, simultaneously considers several alternatives and quickly discards the non-viable ones, is very imaginative, and is more futuristically oriented. Both sensing and intuitive type have their advantages and disadvantages.

(*ii*) ***Thinking and Feeling*:** People evaluate and make judgements either in impersonal and objective fashions—the thinking types or in a more personal and subjective fashion—the feeling types. The thinking type person makes systematic inquiry, is unemotional, and highly analytical and rational in making judgements. The feeling type in contrast, places much reliance on human feelings and emotions, is very empathic, sentimental, and tries to "read between the lines" while evaluating situations. The thinking type individuals feel comfortable when logic and good analysis are the bases of decision-making and such individuals are generally unemotional and not very sensitive to the feelings of others. Feeling types enjoy pleasing others, dislike telling people unpleasant things, and heavily emphasise the human aspects of dealing with organisational matters (Hellriegel, Slocum and Woodsman, 1986). Both the thinking and feeling types have their strengths and weaknesses.

(*iii*) ***Sensation Thinkers*:** Managers with these predispositions create effective structures for organisations, which insure stability. They are seldom wrong with their facts and they are dependable leaders. Some of their weaknesses include extreme impatience with delays and imperfections and their ineffectiveness when quick changes are necessary since they are unable to act quickly.

(*iv*) ***Intuitive Thinkers*:** Managers with these predispositions are the proactive change masters. They see relationships among the various goals and activities and they build new systems giving much thought to the effects of their ideas on operating effectiveness. Their main weakness is that they may be insensitive to the feelings of others and are likely to face difficulty in handing interpersonal relations.

(*v*) ***Sensation Feelers*:** Manager with these orientations is pragmatic and can deal with the problems they confront in a very systematic fashion. They have the cooperation of the people working for them, and they know how to effectively use available resources rather than "fight the system". Their main weakness is that they are unable to conceptualize a new scheme of things and hence the status quo may prevail in the system.

(*vi*) ***Intuitive Feelers*:** Managers who are intuitive feelers very effective in group settings where new ideas are to be formulated to move the organisation towards success. The intuitive feeler managers are also good mentors, developing their subordinates personally and professionally. Their possible weakness includes their basing certain decisions on personal likes or dislikes rather than on objective criteria, and spending too much time seeking approval from others.

(d) Personality Traits

Personality traits are very important in organisational behaviour. In particular, five personality traits especially related to job performance have recently emerged from research. Characteristics of these traits can be summarized as follows:

1. **Extroversion:** Sociable, talkative and assertive.
2. **Agreeableness:** Good-natured, cooperative and trusting.
3. **Conscientiousness:** Responsible, dependable, persistent and achievement-oriented.
4. **Emotional Stability:** Viewed from a negative standpoint such as tense, insecure and nervous.
5. **Openness to Experience:** Imaginative, artistically sensitive and intellectual.

Identifying the above "big five" traits related to performance reveals that personality plays an important role in organisational behaviour. Besides physical appearance and personality traits, the aspects of personality concerned with the self-concept such as self-esteem and self-efficacy and the person-situation interaction also play important roles.

2.3 DEVELOPMENT OF PERSONALITY

The personality development of an individual starts at birth and continues throughout his life. Three major types of factors play important roles in personality development, which are as follows:

- ***Determinants***: The most widely studied determinants of personality are biological, social and cultural. People grow up in the presence of certain hereditary characteristics (body shape and height), the social context (family and friends) and the cultural context (religion and values). These three parts interact with each other to shape personality. As people grow into adulthood, their personalities become very clearly defined and generally stable.
- ***Stages***: According to Sigmund Freud human personality progresses through four stages: Dependent, compulsive, oedipal and mature. This concept of stages of growth provides a valuable perspective to organisational behaviour. Experienced managers become aware of the stages that their employees often go through. This helps them 19 deals with these stages effectively and promotes maximum growth for the individual and for the organisation.
- ***Traits***: Traits to personality are also based on psychology. According to some trait theories, all people share common traits, like social, (political, religious and aesthetic preferences but each individual's nature differentiates that person from all others.

(a) Personality Factors in Organisations

Some of the important personality factors that determine what kind of behaviours are exhibited at work place include the following:

1. ***Need Pattern***: Steers and Braunstein in 1976 developed a scale for the four needs of personality that became apparent in the work environment. They are as follows:

- **The need for achievement:** Those with a high achievement need engage themselves proactively in work behaviours in order to feel proud of their achievements and successes.
- **The need for affiliation:** Those in greater need for affiliation like to work cooperatively with others.
- **The need for autonomy:** Those in need for autonomy function in the best way when not closely supervised.
- **The need for dominance:** Those high in need for dominance are very effective while operating in environments where they can actively enforce their legitimate authority.

2. ***Locus of Control***: Locus of control is the degree to which an individual believes that his or her behaviour has direct impact on the consequences of that behaviour. Some people, for example, believe that if they work hard they will certainly succeed. They strongly believe that each individual is in control of his or her life. They are said to have an internal locus of control. By contrast, some people think that what happens to them is a result of fate, chance, luck or the behaviour of other people, rather than the lack of skills or poor performance on their part. Because these individuals think that forces beyond their control dictate the happenings around them, they are said to have an external locus of control.

As a personality attribute, locus of control has clear implications for organisations. For example, certain individuals have an internal locus of control, which means they have a relatively strong desire to participate in the management of their organisations and have a freedom to do their jobs. Thus, they may prefer a decentralized organisation where they have a right of decision-making and work with a leader who provides them freedom and autonomy. They may like a reward system that recognizes individual performance and contributions.

Conversely, people with an external locus of control, are likely to prefer a more centralized organisation where they need not take any decisions. They may incline to structured jobs where standard procedures are defined for them. They may prefer a leader who makes most of the decisions and a reward system that considers seniority rather than merit.

3. *Introversion and Extroversion*: Introversion is the tendency of individuals, which directs them to be inward and process feelings, thoughts and ideas within themselves. Extroversion, on the contrary, refers to the tendency in individuals to look outside themselves, searching for external stimuli with which they can interact. While there is some element of introversion as well as extroversion in all of us, people tend to be dominant as either extroverts or introverts.

Extroverts are sociable, lively and gregarious and seek outward stimuli or external exchanges. Such individuals are likely to be most successful while working in the sales department, publicity office, personal relations unit, and so on, where they can interact face to face with others. Introverts, on the other hand, are quiet, reflective, introspective, and intellectual people, preferring to interact with a small intimate circle of friends. Introverts are more likely to be successful when they can work on highly abstract ideas such as R&D work, in a relatively quiet atmosphere. Since managers have to constantly interact with individuals both in and out of the organisation and influence people to achieve the organisation's goals, it is believed that extroverts are likely to be more successful as managers.

4. *Tolerance for Ambiguity*: This personality characteristic indicates the level of uncertainty that people can tolerate to work efficiently without experiencing undue stress. Managers have to work well under conditions of extreme uncertainty and insufficient information, especially when things are rapidly changing in the organisation's external environment.

Managers who have a high tolerance for ambiguity can cope up well under these conditions. Managers, who have a low tolerance for ambiguity may be effective in structured work settings but find it almost impossible to operate effectively when things are rapidly changing and much information about the future events is not available. Thus, tolerance for ambiguity is a personality dimension necessary for managerial success.

5. *Self-esteem and Self-concept*: Self-esteem denotes the extent to which individuals consistently regard themselves as capable, successful, important and worthy individuals. Self-esteem is an important personality factor that determines how managers perceive themselves and their role in the organisation. Self-esteem is important to self-concept, *i.e.*, the way individuals, define themselves as to who they are and derive their sense of identity.

High self-esteem provides a high sense of self-concept, which, in turn, reinforces high self-esteem. Thus, the two are mutually reinforcing. Individuals with a high self-esteem will try to take on more challenging assignments and be successful. Thus, they will be enhancing their self-concept i.e., they would tend to define themselves as highly valued individuals in the organisational system. The higher the self-concept and self-esteem, the greater will be their contributions to the goals of the organisation, especially when the system rewards them for their contributions.

6. *Authoritarianism and Dogmatism*: Authoritarianism is the extent to which an individual believes that power and status differences are important within hierarchical social systems like organisations. For example, an employee who is highly authoritarian may accept directives or orders from his superior without much questioning. A person who is not highly authoritarian might agree to carry out appropriate and reasonable directives from his boss. But he may also raise questions, express disagreement and even refuse to carry out requests if they arc for some reason objectionable.

Dogmatism is the rigidity of a person's beliefs and his or her openness to other viewpoints. The popular terms 'close-minded' and 'open-minded' describe people who are more and less dogmatic in their beliefs respectively. For example, a manager may be unwilling to listen to a new idea related to doing something more efficiently. He is said to be a person who is close-minded or highly dogmatic. A manager who is very receptive to hearing about and trying out new ideas in the same circumstances might be seen as more open-minded or less dogmatic. Dogmatism can be either beneficial or detrimental to organisations, but given the degree of change in the nature of organisations and their environments, individuals who are, not dogmatic are most likely to be useful and productive organisational members.

7. *Risk Propensity*: Risk propensity is the decree to which an individual is willing to take chances and make risky decisions. A manager with a high-risk propensity might be expected to experiment with new ideas and to lead the organisation in new directions. In contrast, a manager with low risk propensity might lead to a stagnant and overly conservative organisation.

8. *Machiavellianism*: Machiavellianism is manipulating or influencing other people as a primary way of achieving one's goal. An individual tends to be Machiavellian, if he tends to be logical in assessing the system around, willing to twist and turn facts to influence others, and try to gain control of people, events and situations by manipulating the system to his advantage.

9. *Type A and B Personalities*: Type A persons feel a chronic sense of time urgency, are highly achievement-oriented, exhibit a competitive drive, and are impatient when their work is slowed down for any reason. Type B persons are easy-going individuals who do not feel the time urgency, and who do not experience the competitive drive. Type A individuals are significantly more prone to heart attacks than Type B individuals. While Type A persons help the organisation to move ahead in a relatively short period of time they may also suffer health problems, which might be detrimental to both themselves and the organisation in the long run.

10. *Work-ethic Orientation*: Some individuals are highly work-oriented while others try to do the minimum Work that is necessary to get by without being fired on-the-job. The extremely work oriented person gets greatly involved in the job. Extreme work ethic values could lead to traits of "workaholics" where work is considered as the only primary motive for living with very little outside interests.

For a workaholic turning to work can sometimes become a viable alternative to facing non-work related problems. A high level of work ethic orientation of members is good for the organisation to achieve its goals. Too much "workaholic", however, might lead to premature physical and mental exhaustion and health problems, which is dysfunctional for both organisation and the workaholic members.

The above ten different personality predispositions are important for individual, managerial and organisational effectiveness.

(b) Desired Personality Characteristics for Effective Managers

Obviously, there are some personality "predispositions, which are favourable" to managerial effectiveness and to the success of managers. Apart from possessing the necessary skills and abilities, managers need to develop a high tolerance for ambiguity. There are many changes taking place in the internal and the external environment of an organisation. Naturally, several unpredictable factors are involved in any complex situation, which are beyond the managers' control. Therefore, they should be able to, handle situations as they come, without experiencing undue stress. Thus, a high tolerance for ambiguity is a desired managerial trait. Managers with a good mix of achievements, affiliations and power will be successful in most situations. This is because they will have the drive to achieve the goals and the interpersonal orientation to get the job done through others. In sales and other people-oriented roles, extrovert managers will fit better in their jobs. Similarly, managers with internal locus of control will be more efficient as intellectual and skilled performers. Managers with good work ethic values will get more involved in their jobs and make things happen. They are likely to be more successful in their jobs. Managers with Type A personalities may suit very well for some jobs, which have inbuilt performance pressures and deadlines, but they need to know how to relax through exercises and self-monitor their stress levels.

Personality is a relatively stable factor, but our predispositions can be changed through conscious choice. For instance, our tolerance for ambiguity and ability to handle stress can be considerably enhanced; the attributions we make for success such as internal versus external-locus of control can be changed. Also, our latent needs can be activated and our skills in decision-making can be increased through training programs and by deliberately making the necessary changes. Recognizing the essential ingredients for managerial success is the first step towards making the changes.

(c) The Self-concept: Self-esteem and Self-efficacy

People's attempt to understand themselves is called the self-concept in personality theory. The human self is made of many interacting parts and may be thought of as the personality viewed from within. This self is particularly relevant to the concepts of self-esteem and self-efficacy in the field of organisational behaviour.

People's self-esteem has to do with their self-perceived competence and self-image. Considerable research has been done on the role played by self-esteem outcomes in the organisational behaviour. Most recently done studies indicate that self-esteem plays an important moderating role in the areas of emotional and behavioural responses and stress of organisational members. It was recently noted that, "both research and everyday experience confirm that employees with high self-esteem feel unique, competent, secure, empowered and connected, to the people around them".

Self-efficacy is concerned with self-perceptions of how well a person can cope with situations as they arise. Those with high self-efficacy feel capable and confident of performing well in a situation. In the field of organisational behaviour, self-efficacy is conceptually close to self-esteem. Miner points out the differences by noting that self-esteem tends to be a generalized trait (it will be present in any situation), while self-efficacy tends to be situation specific. Self-efficacy; has been shown to have an empirical relationship with organisational performance and other dynamics of organisational behaviour.

2.4 PERSONALITY THEORIES

One of the most important things about individual behaviour is its consistency. That is certain characteristics pursuit over a period of time in the behaviour of a given person and is revoked by situation resembling each other and certain characteristics tend to be associated with one another.

(a) Historical Theories

1. *Fraud's Psycho Analytics Theory*: According to Freud, the human mind is composed of three elements (*i*) the preconscious, (*ii*) the conscious, and (*iii*) the unconscious. According to him the conscious element is concerned with thoughts, feelings, desires etc. and unconscious component is basically related with ideas and wishes that cannot be learned through introspection. This theory has had an enormous impact on psychological and philosophical conceptions of people.

2. *Carl Jung*: A colleague of Freud believed in a collective unconscious in the personality deeper and now unknown for the person than the personal unconscious of. It includes the cumulative experiences of all part generation even those of primitive ancestors. For work or introversions and extraversion are the two opposing attitudes existing in people.

3. *Alfred Adler*: Yet another colleague of Freud. According to him development and personal growth are the result of attempt made by the individual to improve himself and thus overcome or compensate for feelings of inferiority and inadequacy. Adler and young placed fewer attempts as on the sexual nature of man than did Freud. Self is plays more important role there. e.g., Cultural and other environmental factors are more important other Neo-Freudian includes Uniform, Haney Otter and Rank Sullivan. All other historical school such as (structuralism, functionalism behaviourism and gestaltism) also made contribution.

4. *Self theories*: It contains the self-concept. Carl Regim is most closely associated with this approach. According to him it is an organized constant composed of 'I' or 'Me' and the perception of the relationship of the one to other and to other aspects of life. The self is that the individual believes what he is and strives to be consorting of perception, learning and motivation which together from a unique whole. The 'Me' represents social self. The Me is the way a person appear to others and the way he think he appears to others. In that other half of the self. A person's self concept gives him the sense of meaningfulness and according to Gellerman the average individual is not particularly well acquainted with himself but remains quite faithful to his not so accurate of himself and thereby sequences same consistency. The person's self concept will have a direct effect on his behaviour.

(*i*) ***Sullivan (1982-1994)*** observed that personality could not be observed and in fact, did not lent apart from inter personal behaviour. Sullivan's self-system is a psychological structure, which defends the self against anxiety and production continuity and stability.

(*ii*) ***Kurt Lewin (1890–1941)*** described the interaction behaviour the self and the social environment. He introduced the Felga theory according to which behaviour of the organisation is the product of the interaction to form operating in a given field at a given time. It can be described idea graphically and topologically *i.e.*, things schematic diagram representing the various fields where faces on the individual.

Many self-theories call themselves as phenomenologist since they viewed the individual and his environment as 'phenomena'. Rogers, suygg and Couls and Marla have been called existential psychologists because they emphasis 'being' rather their copying and adjusting.

5. *Learning Theory*: It looks upon personality as a more or less integrated collection of habits. But the way in which these habits are acquired operate and disappear is specified by them in terms of such concepts as derive, reinforcement, conditioning extinction generalisation, discrimination etc. Experts of Miller (1948) and Miller and Bugelsk (1948) proved that many of the trends or attributes are learned. Most of what we call personality is nothing but learned behaviour.

6. *Social Learning Theory*: In learning theories on personality development the emphasis is on the effects of reinforcement, reward and punishment on behaviour. In social learning the emphasis is on identification and imitation (Bandure and Walter). Children come to identify with the parents or other adults and they imitate their models. The process of imitation is facilitate by the Childs' anxiety the results of being punished for wrongdoing. This anxiety stimulates the learning of socially acceptable patterns of behaviour. The behaviour that is imitated may include many things such as action of social value gestures habits, attitude etc.

7. *Type Theory*: The physique body type theories try to determine relationship between features of the face or body and personality. Sheldom body type is the most widely know body type theory. The physiological theory concentrates on body chemistry substances are correlated with temperament. The kind attempt for type personality is in terms of psychological factor. For example, Jung's introvert, extrovert types.

8. *Trait Theory*: This is a search for identification of traits. A trait is something, which is competently and repeatedly is manifested in a variety of situation and is an enduring attribute of individual.

(*i*) ***All Port Trait Theory*:** According to him there is the distinction between common trait and personal disposition. Common traits are used to compare people (say social, economic etc.) Then other unique traits called personal disposition. They can be cardinal, central or secondary.

(*ii*) ***Cattell Trait Theory*:** Ray used Cattell came across 17/words that can be used to describe personality traits. He made a distinction between what be called the surface traits and source traits. He has 35 surface traits by fending flusters of traits that correlated say sociable-seclusive, wise-foolish. Using factor analysis Cattell determined 12 source traits such as affect thymia vs. sizothymia, eye strength vs. emotionality and neuroticism, dominance vs. submissiveness, surgency vs. de-surgency.

9. *Biological Theories of Personality Development* have developed from two different sets of research. Ethnological theory describes the ways in which the members of a given species, say, human beings, develop common characteristics as a result of evolution. Behaviour Genetics describe how an individual's unique gene structure affects personality development. The accumulated research evidence points to strong genetic effects on human personality.

(*i*) **The Big-Five Personality Dimensions:** After almost a century of research, personality psychologists largely agree that five dimensions can describe human personality as shown in Fig. 2.1.

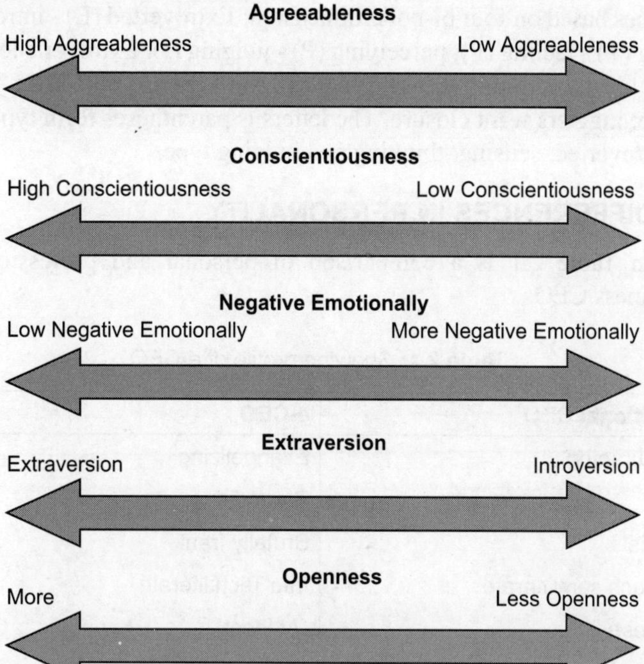

Fig. 2.1: The big five personality frame work

The following are typical traits associated with the high and low characteristics of each Big-Five Personality dimension. *Reflect on your personality as you read the descriptions and traits. Do any of these dimensions describe your personality?*

1. ***Extroversion*** **High:** Talkative, active, sociable, assertive, gregarious.
   Low: Reserved, quiet, introverted.
2. ***Emotional Stability*** **High:** Calm, relaxed, and secure.
   Low: Worried, depressed, anxious, insecure, angry, embarrassed.
3. ***Agreeableness*** **High:** Cooperative, tolerant, good-natured, trusting, courteous, and caring.
4. ***Conscientiousness*** **High:** Dependable, thorough, organized, responsible, playful, achievement-oriented, hardworking.
   Low: Sloppy, careless, and inefficient.
5. ***Openness to Experience*** **High:** Curious, intelligent, broad-minded, creative, imaginative cultured
   Low: Simple, unimaginative, and conventional.

Some dimensions have practical implications for organisations and management. For example, some research found extroversion is positively related to positive affect or attitudes. Other research found conscientious is negatively related to absenteeism and tardiness.

***(ii) Myers-Briggs Type Indicator (MBTI)*:** The Myers-Briggs Type Indicator (MBTI) is a popular personality assessment device based on Jung's personality theory. This device assigns people to one of sixteen personality types based on four bi-polar dimension: Extroverted (E) - introverted (I); sensing (S) - intuitive (I); thinking (T) - feeling (F); perceiving (P) - judging (J). Extroverts look outward; introverts turn inward. Sensors use data; intuitive use hunches. Thinkers are objective; feelers are subjective. Perceivers are flexible; jugglers want closure. The letters is parentheses form type indicators. An ESTJ, for example, is an extroverted, sensing, thinking and judging type.

2.5 INDIVIDUAL DIFFERENCES IN PERSONALITY

The profile shown in Table 2.1 is a comparison of personal and professional characteristics of entrepreneurial e-business CEOs.

Table 2.1: Showing profile of e-CEO

Traditional CEO	e-CEO
Encouraging	Evangelizing
Alert	Paranoid
Cordial	Brutally frank
InfoTech semiliterate	Info Tech literate
(At best)	(At least)
Clearly focused	Intensely focused
Fast moving	Faster moving
Hates ambiguity	Likes ambiguity
Suffers from technology	Suffers from bandwidth
Confrontation anxiety	Separation anxiety

Not everyone working in an e-business environment demonstrates this caricature of e-CEOs or e-professionals. This e-profile does indicate that managing a faster growth environment may require different personal and skill orientations. Understanding personality characteristics can help leaders and professionals deal with individual adaptation and resistance to change. Organisational change, including technologically driven change, can be accomplished only through people. Learning to 'read people' is valuable skill in understanding and leading organisational change.

It should be noted that there is not an ideal personality type or profile for an organisation, a job, or an assignment. Because of the diversity of the workforce, the complexity of work environments, and innovative, changing ways of doing business, the search for ideal personality types is senseless. There are, however, good matches between individuals, organisations, and assignments that can be optimized by using qualitative and quantitative evaluations.

2.6 MEASURING PERSONALITY

The managers benefit from personality theories, which can use for feedback to improve, adjust, train, and make decisions about employee behaviour. Personality assessments are most commonly made through self-report questionnaires, projective tests, and behavioural measures. Projective tests ask individuals to describe what they see in a drawing or photo or to relate a story to the images. It is supposed that unique personality differences will surface and can then be interpreted by a skilled analyst. Following are the important tests carried out in the organisation by HR department at the time of induction/selection and recruitment process

(*a*) Holistic Assessment: The 'Whole' person is taken into consideration. This is a gestation approach to understand the total person through stress interview, spying, observation, etc. Developed by the German Military Psychologists. This was later adopted by the British army and later by the officers of the strategic services (DSS).

(*b*) Projective Tests: When an individual is put in an unstructured situation he projects himself, his wants, aspirations, ambitions, attitude etc. This gives a deeper clue to his inner personality. The important tests are:

1. Thematic Apperception Tests (TAT)
2. Rorschach Ink Blot Test
3. Sentence Completion Test (SCT)
4. Rosanzweig's Picture Frustration Test etc.

(*c*) Measuring Personality Traits:

1. Minnesota Multiphase Inventory (MMPI)
2. Taylor Scale of Manifest Anxiety
3. All Port Vernon Lindsey Study of Values.

Projective tests, however, have low reliability because the results are subjective. In fact, personality tests do not predict job performance. In fact, most such tests are poor predictors of job performance. Secondly, there is an ongoing controversy regarding the "differential validity" of personality tests (*i.e.*, the question of whether or not such tests measure races differently). There are presently too few studies to answer this very relevant question. Personality tests are not used by all, or even most, companies for screening and hiring. For example, Microsoft uses demanding interviews. Personality test results are only one tool to help managers interpret employees 'fit' with an organisation's culture and required skills.

Again, personality tests and results should be administered and interpreted by reputable and licensed psychologists. Personality tests should be used along with others methods of assessing abilities, such as job-related skills tests. Managers who use personality tests should be sensitive and alert to any discriminatory interpretations resulting from such tests. Behavioural measures involve direct observation of a person's behaviour in a controlled environment. Expert analysts then record, for example, the frequency of particular actions on an index of personality characteristics. The necessarily small sample of behaviour can render this measure low in reliability. The self-report method is most commonly used for assessing personality individuals respond to questions in a simple format.

Who has a Normal Personality?

Well, normality is a very relative term. But from a social point of view the normal person is the one who is adjusted to his environment to such as extent that he finds his life enjoyable.

In summary, personality is a very diverse and complex cognitive process. It incorporates almost everything. As defined above, personality means the whole person. It is concerned with external appearance and traits, self and situational interactions. Probably the best statement on personality was made many years ago by Kluckhohn and Murray, "to some extent, a person's personality is like all other people's, like some other people's, and like no other people's".

Organisational behaviour theorists such as Argyris (1957), Likert (1961, 1967), and McGregor (1960), argued that people in organisations need opportunities to use their individual creativity and must have their growth needs met in order to function effectively. However, not all organisational members want to develop and grow on the job or desire to self-actualise at work. Hence, current thinking on the subject is to take a "complex man" approach and recognise that different individuals have different needs and personality predisposition and if there is a "fit' or match between these and the environment that they operate in, functional behaviours will emerge.

By understanding the concept of personality and its primary components as they influence behaviour at work, managers can try to create or structure environments in which people can most effectively function. In addition, such an understanding will help managers to enhance their own functional behaviours and thus increase their own and organisational members' productivity. Moreover an understanding of personality will help managers to predict human behaviour at work (absenteeism, turnover, work involvement, etc.).

Hence we are going to discuss the other related organisation behaviour factors with personality such as Attitudes and job satisfaction in the remaining portion of this chapter in brief.

2.7 ATTITUDES

In simple words, an "attitude" is an individual's point of view or an individual's way of looking at something. To be more explicit, an "attitude" may be explained as the mental state of an individual, which prepares him to react or make him behave in a particular pre-determined way.

An attitude is a learned predisposition to respond in a consistently favourable or unfavourable manner with respect to a give object. The object of an attitude can be anything in a person's environment, including physical objects, issues, ideas, events, and people. The evaluative or affective part of the definition is central to the concept of attitude. It is the affective part that conceptually distinguishes and attitude from other psychological concepts such as need, motive, and trait.

An attitude can be defined as a positive or negative evaluation of people, objects, event, activities, ideas, or just about anything in your environment, but there is debate about precise definitions. Eagly and Chaiken, for example, define an attitude "a psychological tendency that is expressed by evaluating a particular entity with some degree of favour or disfavour." Though it is sometimes common to define an attitude as affect toward an object, affect (*i.e.*, discrete emotions or overall arousal) is generally understood to be distinct from attitude as a measure of favourability.

An attitude is defined as, "a learned pre-disposition to respond in a consistently favourable or unfavorable manner with respect to a given object". Jung's definition of attitude is a "readiness of the psyche to act or react in a certain way". Attitude is the combination of beliefs and feelings that people have about specific ideas, situations or other people. Attitude is important because it is the mechanism through which most people express their feelings.

(a) Characteristics of Attitude

Various definitions of attitude allows for one's evaluation of an attitude object to vary from extremely negative to extremely positive, but also admits that people can also be conflicted or ambivalent toward an object meaning that they might at different times express both positive and negative attitude toward the same object. This has led to some discussion of whether individual can hold multiple attitudes toward the same object.

Whether attitudes are explicit (*i.e.*, deliberately formed) versus implicit (*i.e.*, subconscious) has been a topic of considerable research. Research on implicit attitudes, which are generally unacknowledged or outside of awareness, uses sophisticated methods involving people's response times to stimuli to show that implicit attitudes exist (perhaps in tandem with explicit attitudes of the same object). Implicit and explicit attitudes seem to affect people's behaviour, though in different ways. They tend not to be strongly associated with each other, although in some cases they are. The relationship between them is poorly understood.

***Rao and Narayana identified the following characteristics of attitudes*:**

1. ***Valence*:** It refers to the magnitude of degree of favorableness or unfavourableness toward the event. While measuring attitudes we are basically concerned with the valence. If a person is extremely favourable or unfavourable toward an attitude object, then his attitude will have a high valence.
2. ***Multiplexity*:** It refers to the number or elements constituting attitude. For example, an employee may loyal to the organisation, but another may loyal hardworking, respectful, and dependent also.
3. ***Relation to Needs*:** Attitudes can also vary in relation to the needs they serve. Attitude of an individual toward the pictures may serve only entertainment needs. On the other hand, attitudes of an individual toward task may serve strong needs for security, achievement, recognition, and satisfaction.
4. ***Centrality*:** This refers to the importance of the attitude object to the individual. Centrality indicates the importance of the object. The attitude which has high centrality for an individual will less accessible to change.

(b) Type and Categories of Attitudes

In the broader sense of the word there are only three attitudes, a positive attitude, a negative attitude, and a neutral attitude. Positive attitude is the one which concerns on the positive outcome of the task or problem in hand and negative attitude is the one which concerns on the negative outcome of the task or problem in hand.But in general sense, an attitude is what it is expressed through.

Given below is a list of attitudes that are expressed by people, and are more than personality traits which you may have heard of, know of, or might be even carrying them.

Acceptance, Confidence, Seriousness, Optimism, Pessimism, Interest, Independent Jealous, Courteous, Cooperative, Considerate, Gratitude, Cheerful, Inferiority, Condescending, Happiness, Frankness, Respectful, Authority, Sincerity, Persistent, Honest, Sincere, Sympathetic, Responsible, Realistic, Faithful, Flexible, Decisive, Trusting, Thoughtful, Determined, Loving, Satisfaction, Hostile, Generous, Modest, Reliable, Tolerant, Kind, Humble, Cautious, Suspicious, Sarcasm, Helping, Hardworking, Inclusiveness, and Tenacity.

These were some of the attitudes that you may confuse with personality traits as there is a very thin line between the two. Personality traits are more rigid and permanent whereas attitudes may change with different situations and experiences in life. Personality traits are what humans are endowed with whereas attitudes are learned and acquired. In simple words, attitudes are judgments or conclusions that we draw about certain phenomena in life including our own self.

***(i) Examples of Attitudes*:** Essentially, what you think, what you do, and what you feel is what forms your attitude. For example, if a girl (Sreeja) says, "I like dancing", it represents positive thinking towards dancing. This attitude is formed because she believes that she likes dancing, or feels happy while dancing.

Consider another example, Mohan (another person) says, "I hate working on this project" represents a negative attitude of that person towards the project. He either thinks so, or he believes that this work is boring. In both the cases there could be numerous reasons for developing those attitudes.

In the first case, the girl may think that dancing is good for health or it is 'cool' to dance, or she must be having fun while dancing, in short the reasons could be numerous for her to like dancing or believe that she likes dancing. In the similar manner, in the second case, a man may hate working on a project due to numerous reasons that make him feel so or make him believe and think so.

Attitudes are formed over the years by various means. Sometimes, they are based on our experiences and knowledge and sometimes we acquire them from other people. Sometimes they are based on what is true or what we think is true. Humans manifest their attitudes through their behaviour and actions.

For example, in the first case, the girl may take up dancing classes and in the second case; a man may leave the project. Basically, there are three components of attitude namely, emotional, cognitive, and behavioural that relate to feelings, information or thought process, and the course of action, respectively. All these things result in different people having different attitudes that may or may not change.

It is possible for human beings to change or unlearn their attitudes as attitudes are learned. One needs to change the way he or she thinks, behaves, and feels in order to change the attitude. However, it is very challenging to change our emotions and feelings but they constitute a major part of our attitude and hence changing attitude is a difficult task.

Though vague, feelings are powerful and difficult to control and hence, to change your attitude you must start with other two components, thinking and behaviour, as they are easy to control. By changing these components, it is possible to change different types of attitudes carried by different people. The author would like to quote a famous statement by Winston Churchill which speaks volumes about positive attitude in a single line that you can ponder upon, "Attitude is a little thing that makes a big difference".

***(ii) Categories of Attitudes*:** The most common work attitudes studied by researchers are organisational commitment, satisfaction, and job involvement. These attitudes are important aspects of work experience and play a role in employee turnover. A person with strong attitudes about an object, issue, idea, or another person will usually behave in accord with that attitude. You have undoubtedly seen such strong attitudes in action.

Generally types of attitudes are classified based on the way attitudes serve particular functions for individuals. That is, researchers have tried to understand why individuals hold particular attitudes or why they hold attitudes in general by considering how attitudes affect the individuals who hold them.

Daniel Katz, for example, writes that attitudes can serve "instrumental, adjustive or utilitarian", "ego-defensive", "value-expressive", or "knowledge" functions. The functional view of attitudes suggests that in order for attitudes to change (e.g., via persuasion), appeals must be made to the function(s) that a particular attitude serves for the individual.

According to Katz, attitude serves the following important functions:

1. ***Adjustment Function***: This function is based on the hedonistic principle, which means people strive to maximize the rewards and minimize the penalties in their external environment.
2. ***The Ego-defensive Function***: People normally spend a great deal of their energies in the process of learning to live with themselves. Attitudes serve the function of defending self-image.
3. ***The Value-expressive Function***: This function, according to Katz, not only gives clarity to the self-image but also bring that self-image closer to the heart's desire.
4. ***The Knowledge Function***: This function is based on the need for understanding and making sense of the world. For example, certain attitudes that are suitable to a situation are retained and an employee discards those, which are unsuitable or outdated.

Utilitarian: People adopt attitudes that are rewarding and that help them avoid punishment. In other words any attitude that is adopted in a person's own self-interest is considered to serve a utilitarian function. Consider you have a condo, people with condos pay property taxes, and as a result you don't want to pay more taxes. If those factors lead to your attitude that "Increases in property taxes are bad" you attitude is serving a utilitarian function. Utilitarian provides us with general approach or avoidance tendencies.

Knowledge: People need to maintain an organized, meaningful, and stable view of the world. That being said important values and general principles can provide a framework for our knowledge. Knowledge help people organize and interpret new information.

Ego-Defensive: This function involves psychoanalytic principles where people use defense mechanisms to protect themselves from psychological harm. Mechanisms include:

Denial, Repression, Projection and Rationalization.

The ego-defensive notion correlates nicely with Downward Comparison Theory which holds the view that derogating a less fortunate other increases our own subjective well-being. We are more likely to use the ego-defensive function when we suffer a frustration or misfortune.

These attitudes also can help people protect their self-esteem. As an example, the "ego-defensive" function might be used to influence the racially prejudicial attitudes of an individual who sees themselves as open-minded and tolerant. By appealing to that individual's image of themselves as tolerant and open-minded, it may be possible to change their prejudicial attitudes to be more consistent with their self-concept. Similarly, a persuasive message that threatens self-image is much more likely to be rejected.

Value-Expressive: It serves to express one's central values and self-concept. Central values tend to establish our identity and gain us social approval thereby showing us who we are, and what we stand for. An example would concern attitudes toward a controversial political issue.

Value-expressive is used to express central values or beliefs. Attitudes achieve this goal by making things fit together and make sense.

Examples:

I believe that I am a good person.

I believe that good things happen to good people.

Something bad happens to my friend Shainu.

So I believe Shainu must not be a good person.

(c) Components of Attitude

Attitude has three components, which are as follows: Affective component, Cognitive component and Intentional component.

A person's attitude comprises of three components; namely, affective, cognitive and overt. The "affective" or "feeling" component refers to the emotions associated with an attitude object. It basically consists of the "feeling" a person has toward an attitude object. The "cognitive" component represents the beliefs of a person about an attitude object. Cognitive component is very important and consist of the individual's perceptions, beliefs, and ideas about an object. The "overt" component is concerned with the way one intends to behave toward a particular attitude object. Both the affective and cognitive components (feeling and beliefs) influence the way a person intends to behave towards an attitude object. An attitude has three separate but related parts.

The affective component of an attitude reflects 'feelings and emotions' that an individual has towards a situation. The cognitive component of an attitude is derived from 'knowledge' that an individual has about a situation. Finally, the intentional component of an attitude reflects how an individual 'expects to behave' towards or in the situation. For example, the different components of an attitude held towards a firm, which supplies inferior products and that too irregularly could be described as follows:

- "*I don't like that company*": Affective component.
- "*They are the worst supply firm I have ever dealt with*": Cognitive component.
- "*I will never do business with them again*": Intentional component.

People try to maintain consistency among the three components of their attitudes. However, conflicting circumstances often arise. The conflict that individuals may experience among their own attitudes is called 'cognitive dissonance'.

How the person wants to behave and what the person says about his behaviour toward the object. It is not always the same as the behaviour observed following the expression of the attitude.

(d) Attitude Formation and Change

A person's beliefs about an object and the amount and type of information the person has about the object both contribute to the formation of an about the object. If a person has positive beliefs about an object, the person forms a positive attitude about it. If the person believes the object had negative attributes, the emerging attitude will be negative.

Individual attitude are formed over time as a result of repeated personal experiences with ideas, situations or people. One of the very important ways to understand individual behaviour in an organisation is that of studying attitude, which is situationally specific and learned. An attitude may change as a result of new information. A manager may have a negative attitude about a new employee because of his lack of job-related experience. After working with a new person, a manager may come to realise that he is actually very talented and subsequently may develop a more positive attitude toward him.

Attitudes can be changed through persuasion and an important domain of research on attitude change focuses on responses to communication. Experimental research into the factors that can affect the persuasiveness of a message.

Kolasa classified attitude changes into two groups; congruent and incongruent change. Congruent change means a movement in the same direction; for example, a less serious and idle worker may be converted into a more efficient and serious worker by resorting to attitude change. Incongruent attitude, on the other hand, is a change resorted to other end of the continuum. For example, turning dislike into like, favourable into unfavourable, etc.

When a manager attempts to change an individual worker's attitudes, he should keep in mind the following factors.

1. ***The characteristics of the communicator*:** These include the status and prestige, whether the manager is attractive and liked.
2. ***The method of communication*:** This is another important factor in attitude change. The communication should be easy and convincing so that it creates change without any discomfort.
3. ***The characteristics of the target*:** The most important factor influencing the attitude change is the degree of commitment of the employee (target) to the initial attitude. Moreover, an openly stated attitude is more difficult to change because the person concerned has already shown commitment.
4. ***The situational factors*:** The situational factors play a greater role in influencing the change in attitude of an individual. How one picks up the message is apart, the most important part is the situation or the prevailing context.

There are four major aspects in Attitude change:

(i) ***Target Characteristics*:** These are characteristics that refer to the person who receives and processes a message. One such trait is intelligence - it seems that more intelligent people are less easily persuaded by one-sided messages. Another variable that has been studied in this category is self-esteem. Although it is sometimes thought that those higher in self-esteem are less easily persuaded, there is some evidence that the relationship between self-esteem and persuasibility is actually curvilinear, with people of moderate self-esteem being more easily persuaded than both those of high and low self-esteem levels (Rhodes & Woods, 1992). The mind frame and mood of the target also plays a role in this process.

(ii) ***Source Characteristics*:** The major source characteristics are expertise, trustworthiness and interpersonal attraction or attractiveness. The credibility of a perceived message has been found to be a key variable here; if one reads a report about health and believes it came from a professional medical journal, one may be more easily persuaded than if one believes it is from a popular newspaper. Some psychologists have debated whether this is a long-lasting effect and Hovland and Weiss (1951) found the effect of telling people that a message came from a credible source disappeared after several weeks (the so-called "sleeper effect"). Whether there is a sleeper effect is controversial. Perceived wisdom is that if people are informed of the source of a message before hearing it, there is less likelihood of a sleeper effect than if they are told a message and then told its source.

(iii) ***Message Characteristics*:** The nature of the message plays a role in persuasion. Sometimes presenting both sides of a story is useful to help change attitudes. When people are not motivated to process the message, simply the number of arguments presented in a persuasive message will influence attitude change, such that a greater number of arguments will produce greater attitude change.

(iv) ***Cognitive Routes:*** A message can appeal to an individual's cognitive evaluation to help change an attitude. In the central route to persuasion the individual is presented with the data and

motivated to evaluate the data and arrive at an attitude changing conclusion. In the peripheral route to attitude change, the individual is encouraged to not look at the content but at the source. This is commonly seen in modern advertisements that feature celebrities. In some cases, physician, doctors or experts are used. In other cases film stars are used for their attractiveness.

Attitudes are dynamic change over time. The sources of attitude change are within the person and in the person's social environment. Attitude change happens because, (1) something persuades the person to shift his attitudes; (2) the norms of a social group important to the person affect his attitudes; or (3) the person becomes uncomfortable with some aspects of his beliefs about certain things.

Common sources of attitude change are the persuasive communications designed to affect our beliefs such as those found in radio, television, newspaper, and magazine advertising. Persuasive communication tries to change the cognitive part of an attitude and assumes the affective part will change in either a positive or negative direction. The second major approach to attitude change views people as embedded in a social context and affected by the norms or standards held by the social groups a person experience. People who hold attitudes different from those of a group important to them will feel social pressures to conform to the norms of the group. Such pressures come from the tendency of social groups to reject people who do not conform to their norms.

(e) Attitude Behaviour Relationship

The effects of attitudes on behaviours represent a significant research enterprise within psychology. Two theoretical approaches have dominated this research: The theory of reasoned action and, its theoretical descendant, the theory of planned behaviour, both of which are associated with Icek Ajzen.

Both of these theories describe the link between attitude and behaviour as a deliberative process, with an individual actively choosing to engage in an attitude-related behaviour. An alternative model, called MODE for "Motivation and Opportunity as Determinants" was proposed by Russell H. Fazio, which focuses on motivations and opportunities for deliberative attitude-related behaviour to occur.

MODE is a Dual process theory that expects deliberative attitude-behaviour linkages like those modeled by the theory of planned behaviour—only occur when individuals have motivation to reflect upon their own attitudes.

The Theory of Reasoned Action (TRA), is a model for the prediction of behavioural intention, spanning predictions of attitude and predictions of behaviour. The subsequent separation of behavioural intention from behaviour allows for explanation of limiting factors on attitudinal influence (Ajzen, 1980).

The Theory of Reasoned Action was developed by Martin Fishbein and Icek Ajzen (1975, 1980), derived from previous research that started out as the theory of attitude, which led to the study of attitude and behaviour. The theory was "born largely out of frustration with traditional attitude–behaviour research, much of which found weak correlations between attitude measures and performance of volitional behaviours".

The theory of planned behaviour was proposed by Icek Ajzen in 1985 through his article "From intentions to actions: A theory of planned behaviour". The theory was developed from the theory of reasoned action, which was proposed by Martin Fishbein together with Icek Ajzen in 1975. The theory of reasoned action was in turn grounded in various theories of attitude such as learning theories, expectancy-value theories, consistency theories and attribution theory.

According to the theory of reasoned action, if people evaluate the suggested behaviour as positive (attitude), and if they think their significant others want them to perform the behaviour (subjective norm), this results in a higher intention (motivation) and they are more likely to do so. A high correlation of attitudes and subjective norms to behavioural intention, and subsequently to behaviour, has been confirmed in many studies.

A counter-argument against the high relationship between behavioural intention and actual behaviour has also been proposed, as the results of some studies show that, because of circumstantial limitations, behavioural intention does not always lead to actual behaviour. Namely, since behavioural intention cannot be the exclusive determinant of behaviour where an individual's control over the behaviour is incomplete, Ajzen introduced the theory of planned behaviour by adding a new component, "perceived behavioural control". By this, he extended the theory of reasoned action to cover non-volitional behaviours for predicting behavioural intention and actual behaviour.

(f) Emotion and Attitude Change

Emotion is a common component in persuasion, social influence, and attitude change. Much of attitude research emphasized the importance of affective or emotion components. Emotion works hand-in-hand with the cognitive process, or the way we think, about an issue or situation. Emotional appeals are commonly found in advertising, health campaigns and political messages. Recent examples include no-smoking health campaigns and political campaign advertising emphasizing the fear of terrorism. Attitudes and attitude objects are functions of cognitive, affective and co native components. Attitudes are part of the brain's associative networks, the spider-like structures residing in long term memory that consist of affective and cognitive nodes.

By activating an affective or emotion node, attitude change may be possible, though affective and cognitive components tend to be intertwined. In primarily affective networks, it is more difficult to produce cognitive counterarguments in the resistance to persuasion and attitude change. Affective forecasting, otherwise known as intuition or the prediction of emotion, also impacts attitude change. Research suggests that predicting emotions is an important component of decision making, in addition to the cognitive processes. How we feel about an outcome may override purely cognitive rationales?

In terms of research methodology, the challenge for researchers is measuring emotion and subsequent impacts on attitude. Since we cannot see into the brain, various models and measurement tools have been constructed to obtain emotion and attitude information. Measures may include the use of physiological cues like facial expressions, vocal changes, and other body rate measures. For instance, fear is associated with raised eyebrows, increased heart rate and increase body tension. Other methods include concept or network mapping, and using primes or word cues in the era.

Attitude accessibility refers to the activation of an attitude from memory in other words, how readily available is an attitude about an object, issue, or situation. Issue involvement is the relevance and salience of an issue or situation to an individual. Issue involvement has been correlated with both attitude access and attitude strength. Past studies conclude accessible attitudes are more resistant to change.

(g) Work-Related Attitudes

People in an organisation form attitude about many things such as about their salary, promotion possibilities, superiors, fringe benefits, food in the canteen, uniform etc. Especially some important attitudes are job satisfaction or dissatisfaction, organisational commitment and job involvement.

1. ***Five Attitudes that are Important in Workplaces*****:** It may seem as if skills and experience are the most important characteristics of an employee, but attitude plays just as big of a role. After all, what good are great professional skills without the attitude to see it all through? There are five key attitudes that small businesses should seek out in employees to ensure a harmonious professional environment and a productive staff.

- ***Respectfulness:*** Respect is a very important attitude in the workplace and doesn't solely extend to the way in which employees interact with management. Employees should also have a respectful attitude when interacting with clients and customers as well as co-workers. Employees with this type of attitude are willing to treat other people politely and professionally, even if they disagree with the other person's point of view.
- ***Pridefulness:*** It might seem as if being prideful is a good attitude to have in the workplace, but most employees who have a prideful attitude about their work tend to work harder to excel. A prideful attitude doesn't mean that an employee won't accept help or work in teams; it simply means that the outcomes of tasks the employee does and how they contribute to the company matter a great deal to him.
- ***Commitment:*** A committed attitude is a valued one in the workplace. Small businesses need employees who are not only committed to the goals and initiatives that affect the bottom line, but who also are committed to their particular positions. Employees project a committed attitude by showing a willingness to do whatever it takes to fulfill the duties of their positions and via the development of new ideas to make the company even better.
- ***Innovation:*** Employees with an innovative attitude don't shy away from trying something new or finding a different way to do things. Small businesses need employees who can think outside of the box and innovate new ways to accomplish existing tasks and approach goals. Employees with this type of attitude know their ideas might not work out to be the best way to do something, but that the biggest failure is not at least giving new ideas a shot.
- ***Helpfulness:*** It is important to have a helpful attitude at work, whether that means assisting clients and customers with their needs or helping co-workers accomplish overall company goals. The more helpful an attitude employees have, the more people want to be around them at work and the more willing they are to partner with those employees on key projects and initiatives.

2. ***Organisational Commitment and Involvement*****:** Two other important work-related attitudes are organisational commitment and involvement. Organisational commitment is the individual's feeling of identification with and attachment to an organisation. Involvement refers to a person's willingness to be a team member and work beyond the usual standards of the job. An employee with little involvement is motivated by extrinsic motivational factor and an employee with strong involvement is motivated by intrinsic motivational factors. There are a number of factors that lead to commitment and involvement. Both may increase with an employee's age and years with the organisation, with his sense of job security and participation in decision-making. If the organisation treats its employees fairly and provides reasonable rewards and job security, employees are more likely to be satisfied and committed. Involving employees in decision-making can also help to increase commitment. In particular, designing jobs, which are interesting and stimulating, can enhance job involvement.

3. *Attitude*: *It's Importance in Organisational Behaviour*: Attitudes of both workers and management react to each other and determine mutual relationships. Attitude is an understanding or learning of why employees feel and act the way; they do and help supervisors in winning cooperation from them. So, it is very essential for the efficient working of an organisation. From a personal perspective, attitudes provide knowledge base or prepare, our mental state, for our interaction with others, and with the world around us. This directly affects organisational behaviour, and in turn organisational working.

Shell Oil Co. hired a top survey research firm to study 1,123 Americans in summer 1998 on their attitudes about work. The results showed that people generally fit into one of six categories (*source*: http://www.workforce.com/articles/six-types-of-employee-attitudes).

- ***Fulfillment Seekers*:** A large majority of Fulfillment Seekers believe a good job is one that "allows me to use my talents and make a difference", rather than one that provides a good income and benefits. Most say they have a career as opposed to a job, and a substantial majority say they are team players rather than leaders. Fulfillment Seekers are mostly white, married and satisfied with their jobs. You'll find these teachers, nurses and public defenders in a variety of "rooms": classrooms, emergency rooms and courtrooms.
- ***High Achievers*:** To pass muster as a High Achiever, plan on laying out a career path; a large majority of achievers say they have followed a career plan since a young age. Their planning apparently pays off—The High Achievers group is the highest income group, with nearly a quarter earning more than $75,000, and the group with the highest educational achievement. Most are leaders who take initiative, and a majority hold managerial positions and are male. Look for these lawyers, surgeons and architects in operating rooms and law offices.
- ***Clock Punchers*:** Clock Punchers are the least satisfied of any group surveyed, with nearly all of them saying they have a job rather than a career. An overwhelming majority say they ended up in their jobs largely by chance, and nearly three-quarters say they would make different career choices if they could do it all over again. Clock Punchers are predominately female, have the lowest household income (35 percent below $30,000) and are the least educated—half have a high school diploma or less, and fewer than 1 in 5 has earned a four-year college degree. These cashiers, waitresses and hospital orderlies aren't happy campers. The High Achievers group is the highest income group, with nearly a quarter earning more than $75,000, and the group with the highest educational achievement.
- ***Risk Takers*:** Risk Takers have something in common with bank robbers: They both go where the money is. Members of this group are far more willing than others to take risks for the opportunity for great financial success. They are also the only group that likes to move from employer to employer in search of the best job. This group is young (45 percent are under the age of 35) and largely male. Risk Takers are fairly well-educated and have good incomes (more than 4 in 10 have household incomes above $50,000). Show them the dough: These are software entrepreneurs and car salespeople.
- ***Ladder Climbers*:** Ladder Climbers aren't going anywhere—except up. These are "company people" who prefer the stability of staying with one employer for a long time. A substantial majority prefer a stable income over the chance of great financial success and consider themselves to be leaders rather than team players. Company loyalty matters—4 in 9 say they would change cities to stay with their current employer. They are the opposite of Fullfillment Seekers.

Now we discuss on Job satisfaction in the last segment which is a manifestation of attitude and personality of the individual.

2.8 JOB SATISFACTION

The term 'job satisfaction' refers to an employee's general happiness with his or her job. Locke defines job satisfaction as a 'pleasurable or positive emotional state resulting from the appraisal of one's job experiences". For our purposes job satisfaction will be defined as the amount of overall positive affect or feelings that individuals have towards their job.

Job satisfaction is the result of various attitudes the employee holds towards his job, towards related factors and towards life in general. The importance of job Satisfaction is that if the people are satisfied with their work, then there is an improvement in both the quality and quantity of production. If they are not satisfied, then both the quantity and quality of his output will be low, there will be high absenteeism and employee turnover and increased unionism.

Job satisfaction is an attitude reflects the extent to which an individual is gratified or fulfilled by his or her work. Extensive research conducted on job satisfaction has indicated that personal factors such as an individual's needs and aspirations determine this attitude, along with group and organisational factors such as relationships with co-workers and supervisors, working conditions, work policies and compensation. A satisfied employee also tends to be absent less often, makes positive contributions, and stays with the organisation. In contrast, a dissatisfied employee may be absent more often may experience stress that disrupts co-workers, and may keep continually look for another job. Organisational factors that influence employee satisfaction include pay, promotion, policies and procedures of the organisations and working conditions. Group factors such as relationship with co-workers and supervisors also influence job satisfaction. Similarly, satisfaction depends on individual factors like individual's needs and aspirations. If employees are satisfied with their job, it may lead to low employee turnover and less absenteeism and vice-versa.

Caldur and Schurr in 1981 suggested that there are three different approaches to evaluating job satisfaction. The first approach is that work attitudes such as job satisfaction are dispositional in nature, i.e., they are stable, positive or negative disposition learned through experiences. The second approach is the 'social information processing model', which suggests that job satisfaction and other work place attitudes are developed or constructed out of experiences and information provided by others at the work place. The third approach is the "information processing model", which is based on the accumulation of cognitive information about the work place and one's job. In a sense, this is the most obvious approach, as it argues that a person's job satisfaction is influenced directly by the characteristics of their job.

(a) Factors Relating to Job Satisfaction

Some of the most important factors relating to job satisfaction are briefly stated below:

1. *Personal Factors*: These factors include the individual employee's personality, age, sex, educational level, intelligence etc. Most of the evidence on the relation between age and satisfaction seems to indicate that there is generally a positive relationship between the two variables up to the pre-retirement years and then there is a sharp decrease in satisfaction.

There is no clear research evidence between educational level and job satisfaction. As regards the relationship between the intelligence level and job satisfaction, it usually depends upon the level and range of intelligence and the challenge of the job. There is as yet no consistent evidence as to whether women are more satisfied with their jobs than men.

2. *Job Factors*: These factors include the type of work to be performed, skill required for work performance, occupational status involved in the job etc. The type of work is very important, as a number of research studies have shown that varied work generally brings about more satisfaction than routine work. Where skill exists to a considerable degree it tends to become the main source of satisfaction to the employee. As regards the relation of occupational status to job satisfaction, research evidences indicate that employees are relatively more dissatisfied in those jobs, which have less social status or prestige.

3. *Organisational Factors*: These factors include security, wages and salaries, fringe benefits, opportunities for advancement, working conditions etc. Social and economic security to employees increases job satisfaction, the wages and salaries and fringe benefits are definitely the main factors that affect job satisfaction of employees. As regards the relation of opportunity for advancement to job satisfaction, it has been found that this factor is most important to skilled personnel and least important to unskilled personnel. Desirable working conditions are also important to job satisfaction. Besides, an effective downward flow of communications in an organisation is also important to job satisfaction as employees are keen to know more about the company and its plans, policies etc. Basically, job satisfaction is determined by the discrepancy between what individuals expect to get out of their jobs and what the job actually offers. A person will be satisfied if there is no discrepancy between desired and actual conditions.

(b) Importance of Job Satisfaction

Obviously, job satisfaction significantly contributes to employee productivity and morale. An organisation can be substantially benefited if it develops general attitudes of its employees that can effectively contribute to job satisfaction. If employees are satisfied, turnover and absenteeism will be less and productivity will be more, Further, satisfaction of individual expectations results in group integration and cohesiveness.

(c) Measuring Job Satisfaction

There have been many measures of job satisfaction in the work place from the Job Description index to Job Satisfaction Scales to the more recent job satisfaction scale of the Occupational Stress Indicator (OSI). They all tend to involve scales, which explore pay, work activities, working conditions, career prospects, and relationship with superiors and relationship with colleagues. An example of a measure of job satisfaction from the OSI, which contains all of the elements that usually make up a job satisfaction measure, is given in the Table 2.2.

Table 2.2: An example of a measure of job satisfaction

How you feel about your job?

Very high satisfaction 6
High satisfaction 5
Some satisfaction 4
Some dissatisfaction 3
High dissatisfaction 2
Very high dissatisfaction 1

1.	Communication and the way information flow around your organisation.	6	5	4	3	2	1
2.	The relationships you have with other people at work.	6	5	4	3	2	1
3.	The feeling you have about the way you and your efforts are valued.	6	5	4	3	2	1
4.	The actual job itself.	6	5	4	3	2	1
5.	The degree to which you feel "motivated" by your job.	6	5	4	3	2	1
6.	Current career opportunities.	6	5	4	3	2	1
7.	The level of job security in your present job.	6	5	4	3	2	1
8.	The extent to which you may identify with the public image or goals of your organisation.	6	5	4	3	2	1
9.	The style of supervision that your superiors use.	6	5	4	3	2	1
10.	The way changes an innovations are implemented.	6	5	4	3	2	1
11.	The kind of work or tasks that you are required to perform.	6	5	4	3	2	1
12.	The degree to which you feel that you can personally develop or grow in your job.	6	5	4	3	2	1
13.	The way in which conflicts are resolved in your company.	6	5	4	3	2	1
14.	The scope your job provides to help you achieve your aspirations and ambitions.	6	5	4	3	2	1
15.	The amount of participation which you are given in important decision making.	6	5	4	3	2	1
16.	The degree to which your job taps the range of skills which you feel you possess.	6	5	4	3	2	1
17.	The amount of flexibility and freedom you feel you have in your job.	6	5	4	3	2	1
18.	The psychological "feel" or climate that dominates your organisation.	6	5	4	3	2	1
19.	Your level of salary relative to your experience.	6	5	4	3	2	1
20.	The design or shape of your organisation's structure.	6	5	4	3	2	1
21.	The amount of work you are given to do whether too much or too little.	6	5	4	3	2	1
22.	The degree to which you feel extended in your job.	6	5	4	3	2	1

(d) Measures to Increase Job Satisfaction

Although management cannot change the personal factors in job satisfaction, it should appreciate the role-of such factors and must take care to place the employees where the personal factors of the individual help him in achieving job satisfaction. Similarly, the management can use the factors inherent in the job to plan and administer jobs more advantageously for its personnel. For example, the policy of job rotation, job enrichment, and job enlargement may help increase job satisfaction. Management should also take necessary steps to raise the occupational status of the workers.

The management should carefully develop appropriate policies and practices for promotions and transfers, working conditions, wages, grievance handling, fringe benefits, satisfactory hours of work and adequate rest pausing. Management should also able to recognize and appreciate the good work done by the employees and give respect for their creative suggestion. Proper delegation of authority, freedom to do work will also help increase job satisfaction. Above all, while keeping in view the factors related to job satisfaction, the management must recognize the importance of the stability of employee attitudes that may lead to high morale and production.

It is evident from the above description that there are many factors that influence job satisfaction and the managements must be able to work out a broad strategies that may help increase job satisfaction and must also able to identify the specific factors that causes the individual differences and must evolve appropriate strategies that could raise the job satisfaction of those particular segment.

SUMMARY

We begin this chapter by presenting the framework of the personal system, and then go on to explain major personality theories. Methods for measuring personality are summarized, and personality characteristics that managers and employees can observe and address in organisational settings are discussed. The ethical dimensions of personality are then presented. The characteristics of personal mastery and effectives habits are examined; these are benchmark processes that individuals can use to enhance motivation. Finally, we present general guidelines for understanding and managing individual differences in the workplace.

The workplace and the workforce are rapidly changing as are group and individual values regarding the nature of work, organisations and careers. Personality is a combination of stable physical and mental characteristics that makeup an individual's identity. To understand behaviour, we must understand the interaction between personality and environment Major personality theories and commonly used personality assessment methods have pointed out the fact that focusing a job satisfaction and organisational commitment of any employee will help the organisations to deliver the goods. A person's locus of control is the extent to which he believes his circumstances are a function of either his own actions or of external factors beyond his control. Other important personality traits include self efficacy, authoritarianism, machiavellianisan, self-esteem and risk propensity.

Locus of control is a personality characteristic manifested in individual who attribute causes of their behaviour to either external (environmental) or internal (themselves) sources. "Externals" have an "external locus of control" orientation and tend to focus their attention to "other-oriented" causes and effects of activities. "Internals" have an "internal locus of control" and look within themselves for the causes and effects of activities. Internalisers tend to believe that they control their decisions and livers; externalisers believe that outside forces and events control their decisions and lives.

In contract to the locus of control characteristic, which addresses why a person is behaving in a certain manner, the well-known type A/B classification describes how a person behaves in his life and work. Type A individuals are characterized as compulsive and obsessive, impatient and irritable, high achievers, perfectionists, very competitive, quick movers, and very time conscious. ***Type B*** individuals, on the other hand, are more methodical in getting tasks accomplished, more relaxed and laid back, and more patients with others. Type A personalities, when carried to extremes, can lead to over controlling and conflict-oriented behaviour. A higher incidence of cardiovascular disease has also been linked to type A personalities.

REVIEW QUESTIONS

1. What do you mean by personality? How is it important for a manager?
2. Explain personality theories.
3. Discuss the modern personality theories and its impact in the organisation performance.
4. How personality is measured?
5. State determinants of personality.
6. Explain attitude formation and change. How it is connected to job satisfaction and organisational growth?
7. Describe Job satisfaction. How is it measured for a Service sector company like Telecom?

DISCUSSION QUESTION

Visit a e-CEO of a Telecom company and find out from him the important traits for a successful personality. Also make use of the theories explained in the chapter. State which theory is more applicable. Also form your view on importance of heredity and environment in moulding a successful personality.

STUDENT EXERCISE

"The process by which people attempt to control or manipulate the reactions of others to images of themselves or their ideas" defines *Impression Management*. Impression Management encompasses a wide range including how one speaks, looks, and behaves. Favorable impression management includes the concept of "dress for success", maintaining a positive attitude, and the avoidance of offending others. As a global manager, one must be fully aware of the cultural differences that impact the process of impression management. What may be considered appropriate in one culture (e.g., slapping an employee on the back in the US can be seen as a positive gesture for good work? The same behaviour would be reprehensible in Japan). What specific elements of personality and attitude would a global manager possess when doing business in the UK? What specific personality traits and attitudes appropriate for business meetings? Are there differences in formal and informal meetings?

SKILL TEST

Are you a Type A or Type B Personality?

This test will help you develop insights into your own tendencies toward Type A or Type B behaviour patterns. Answer the questions honestly and accurately about either your job or your college, whichever requires the most time each week. Then calculate your score according to the instructions that follow the questions. Choose from the following responses to answer the questions below:

A. Almost always true
B. Usually true
C. Seldom true
D. Never true
E. Neutral

1. I do not like to wait for other people to complete their work before I can proceed with mine.
2. I hate to wait in most line.
3. People tell me that I tend to get irritated too easily.
4. Whenever possible I try to make activities competitive.
5. I have a tendency to rush into work that needs to be done before knowing the procedure I will use to complete the job.
6. Even when I go on vacation, I usually take some work along.
7. When I make a mistake, it is usually because I have rushed into the job before completely planning it through.
8. I feel guilty about taking time off from work.
9. People tell me I have a bad temper when it comes to competitive situations.
10. I tend to lose my temper when I am under a lot of pressure at work.
11. Whenever possible, I will attempt to complete two or more tasks at once.
12. I tend to race against the clock.
13. I have no patience with lateness.
14. I catch myself rushing when there is no need.

ANALYSIS AND INTERPRETATION

An intense sense of time urgency is a tendency to race against the clock, even when there is little reason to. The person feels a need to hurry for hurry's sake alone, and this tendency has appropriately been called "hurry sickness".

Time urgency is measured by items 1, 2, 8, 12, 13 and 14. Every A or B answer to these six questions scores one point.

Inappropriate aggression and hostility reveals itself in a person who is excessively competitive and who cannot do anything for fun. This inappropriately aggressive behaviour easily evolves in frequent displays of hostility, usually at the slightest provocation or frustration.

Items 3, 4, 9 and 10 measure competitiveness and hostility. Every A or B answers scores one point.

Polyphasic behaviour refers to the tendency to undertake two or more tasks simultaneously at inappropriate times. It usually results in wasted time due to an inability to complete the tasks.

Items 6 and 11 measure this behaviour. Every A or B answers scores one point.

Goal directedness without proper planning refers to the tendency of an individual to rush into work without really knowing how to accomplish the desired result. This usually results in incomplete work or work with many errors, which in turn leads to wasted time, energy, and money.

Items 5 and 7 measure lack of planning. Every A or B response scores one point.

If your score is 5 or more, you may possess some basic components of the Type A personality. If you wish to know more insight on your test score, then you are welcome to contact author via e-mail *shaangrila@gmail.com* or social media *drs.shajahan.7@facebook.com.*

3
CHAPTER

PERCEPTION AND ITS INFLUENCE IN DECISION MAKING PROCESS

LEARNING OBJECTIVES

This chapter aims at introducing fundamental concepts for explaining the perception process and its influence in organisational decision making process to the readers:

- *Definition, importance and fundamental concepts of perception*
- *Major characteristics and importance of perception*
- *Perception process and distortions*
- *Factors influencing perception*
- *Perceptual selectivity*
- *Link between perception and decision making*

INTRODUCTION

Perception (from the Latin *perceptio, percipio*) is the organisation, identification, and interpretation of sensory information in order to represent and understand the environment. All perception involves signals in the nervous system, which in turn result from physical or chemical stimulation of the sense organs. For example, vision involves light striking the retina of the eye, smell is mediated by odormolecules, and hearing involves pressure waves. Perception is not the passive receipt of these signals, but is shaped by learning, memory, expectation, and attention. Perception involves these "top-down" effects as well as the "bottom-up" process of processing sensory input. The "bottom-up" processing transforms low-level information to higher-level information (e.g., extracts shapes for object recognition). The "top-down" processing refers to a person's concept and expectations (knowledge), and selective mechanisms (attention) that influence perception. Perception depends on complex functions of the nervous system, but subjectively seems mostly effortless because this processing happens outside conscious awareness.

For a layman perception may be in terms of his inner experiences. For instance the awareness that he has while listening to pop music of the small of coffee percolating and so on. But for is in the form of a private event. Psychological researching this field is confined to events that can be observed and verified. Hence perception is not concerned with awareness of stimulation as such but with observable changes in performance. Just like the neuro-physiological processes are fundamental to sensing and learning, they can account for the phenomenon of perception also. The word "perceive" is often used, as a synonym for "see". But in this connection we must understand that perceiving is not the same as seeing. Perception may involve in any sense modality *i.e.*, hearing, tasting, smelling, and feeling as seeing. Similar to learning it applied to those events coming between input and output called "transformation variables".

Perception is an important mediating cognitive process. Through this complex process, people make interpretations of the stimulus or situation they are faced with. Both selectivity and organisation go into perceptual, interpretations. Externally, selectivity is affected by intensity, size, contrast, repetition, motion and novelty and familiarity. Internally, perceptual selectivity is influenced by the individual's motivation, learning and personality. After the selective process filters the stimulus situation, the incoming information is organized into a meaningful whole. Individual differences and uniqueness are largely the result of the cognitive processes. Although there are a number of cognitive processes, it is generally recognized that the perceptual process is a very important one. It is a process that takes place between the situation and the behaviour and is most relevant to the study of organisational behaviour. For example, the observation that a department head and a subordinate may react quite differently to the same top management directive can be better understood and explained by the perceptual process.

3.1 DEFINITION

Perception can be defined as a process by which individuals organise and interpret their sensory impressions in order to give meaning to their environment. However, what one perceives can be substantially different from objective reality. It need not be, but there is often disagreement. For example, it is possible that all employees in a firm may view it as a great place to work favorable working conditions, interesting job assignments, good pay, an understanding and responsible management but as most of us know, it is very unusual to find such agreement. Perception is a cognitive process that lets a person make sense of stimuli from the environment. These stimuli affect all senses: Sight, touch, taste, smell, and hearing. The stimuli can come from others people, events, physical objects, or ideas. The perceptual process includes both the inputs to the person and the selection of inputs to which the person attends.

A person's perceptual process learns from repeated exposure to stimuli and stores recallable images, which process inputs faster later. A person's perceptual process is a mechanism that helps him adapts to a changing environment. The target of perception emerges over time from its surrounding context, sometimes slowly and sometimes quickly. People discriminate a high-contrast target quickly from its background, but an ambiguous target takes time to see. The degree of contrast can come from the target's size, colour loudness, or smell. Aspect of the person also affects the speed of emergency. People differ in their degree of motivation to attend to stimuli coming from their environment. They attend more quickly to positively valued stimuli than to negatively valued stimuli. For example, an achievement-oriented employee might notice announcements about promotion opportunities faster than an employee with less achievement motivation might In short, perception is the process by which people organize, interpret, experience, process and use stimulus materials in the environment so that they satisfy their needs.

Kolsds defines Perception as the selection and organisation of material which stems from the outside environment at one time or the other to provide the meaningful entity we experience. Perception clarifies the following: People's actions, emotions, thoughts and feelings are triggered by their perceptions of their surroundings. Perceptions are the intellectual process by which a person access the information for the environment, organize it and obtain the meaning from it. Perception is the phase of operation that takes place after the information being received by one that is well high indistinguishable from it. Perception is the basic cognitive or psychological process. The manner in which a person perceives the environment affects his behaviour.

3.2 BASIC PERCEPTUAL PROCESS

Since the rise of experimental psychology in the 19th Century, psychology's understanding of perception has progressed by combining a variety of techniques. Psychophysics quantitatively describes the relationships between the physical qualities of the sensory input and perception. Sensory neuroscience studies the brain mechanisms underlying perception. Perceptual systems can also be studied computationally, in terms of the information they process. Perceptual issues in philosophy include the extent to which sensory qualities such as sound, smell or color exist in objective reality rather than in the mind of the perceiver.

Although the senses were traditionally viewed as passive receptors, the study of illusions and ambiguous images has demonstrated that the brain's perceptual systems actively and pre-consciously attempt to make sense of their input. There is still active debate about the extent to which perception is an active process of hypothesis testing, analogous to science, or whether realistic sensory information is rich enough to make this process unnecessary.

The perceptual systems of the brain enable individuals to see the world around them as stable, even though the sensory information is typically incomplete and rapidly varying. Human and animal brains are structured in a modular way, with different areas processing different kinds of sensory information. Some of these modules take the form of sensory maps, mapping some aspect of the world across part of the brain's surface. These different modules are interconnected and influence each other. For instance, the taste is strongly influenced by its odor.

The process of perception begins with an object in the real world, termed the *distal stimulus* or *distal object*. By means of light, sound or another physical process, the object stimulates the body's sensory organs. These sensory organs transform the input energy into neural activity—a process called *transduction*. This raw pattern of neural activity is called the *proximal stimulus*. These neural signals are transmitted to the brain and processed. The resulting mental re-creation of the distal stimulus is the *percept*. Perception is sometimes described as the process of constructing mental representations of distal stimuli using the information available in proximal stimuli.

An example would be a person looking at a shoe. The shoe itself is the distal stimulus. When light from the shoe enters a person's eye and stimulates their retina, that stimulation is the proximal stimulus. The image of the shoe reconstructed by the brain of the person is the percept. Another example would be a telephone ringing. The ringing of the telephone is the distal stimulus. The sound stimulating a person's auditory receptors is the proximal stimulus, and the brain's interpretation of this as the ringing of a telephone is the percept. The different kinds of sensation such as warmth, sound, and taste are called "sensory modalities".

Psychologist Jerome Bruner has developed a model of perception. According to him people go through the following process to form opinions:

1. When we encounter an unfamiliar target we are open to different informational cues and want to learn more about the target.
2. In the second step we try to collect more information about the target. Gradually, we encounter some familiar cues which help us categorize the target.
3. At this stage, the cues become less open and selective. We try to search for more cues that confirm the categorization of the target. We also actively ignore and even distort cues that violate our initial perceptions. Our perception becomes more selective and we finally paint a consistent picture of the target.

According to Alan Saks and Gary Johns, there are three components to perception.

1. The Perceiver, the person who becomes aware about something and comes to a final understanding. There are three factors that can influence his or her perceptions: Experience, motivational state and finally emotional state. In different motivational or emotional states, the perceiver will react to or perceive something in different ways. Also in different situations he or she might employ a "perceptual defence" where they tend to "see what they want to see".
2. The Target. This is the person who is being perceived or judged. "Ambiguity or lack of information about a target leads to a greater need for interpretation and addition".
3. The Situation also greatly influences perceptions because different situations may call for additional information about the target.

Stimuli are not necessarily translated into a percept and rarely does a single stimulus translate into a percept. An ambiguous stimulus may be translated into multiple percepts, experienced randomly, one at a time, in what is called "multi-stable perception". And the same stimuli, or absence of them, may result in different percepts depending on subject's culture and previous experiences. Ambiguous figures demonstrate that a single stimulus can result in more than one percept; for example, the Rubin vase which can be interpreted either as a vase or as two faces. The percept can bind sensations from multiple senses into a whole. A picture of a talking person on a television screen, for example, is bound to the sound of speech from speakers to form a percept of a talking person. "Percept" is also a term used by Leibniz, Bergson, Deleuze and Guattari to define perception independent from perceivers.

In the case of visual perception, some people can actually see the percept shift in their mind's eye. Others, who are not picture thinkers, may not necessarily perceive the 'shape-shifting' as their world changes. The 'esem-plastic' nature has been shown by experiment: An ambiguous image has multiple interpretations on the perceptual level.

This confusing ambiguity of perception is exploited in human technologies such as camouflage, and also in biological mimicry, for example by European Peacock butterflies, whose wings bear eye markings that birds respond to as though they were the eyes of a dangerous predator. There is also evidence that the brain in some ways operates on a slight "delay", to allow nerve impulses from distant parts of the body to be integrated into simultaneous signals.

Perception is one of the oldest fields in psychology. The oldest quantitative laws in psychology are Weber's law which states that the smallest noticeable difference in stimulus intensity is proportional to the intensity of the reference and Fechner's law which quantifies the relationship between the intensity of the physical stimulus and its perceptual counterpart (for example, testing how much darker a computer screen can get before the viewer actually notices). The study of perception gave rise to the Gestalt school of psychology, with its emphasis on holistic approach.

Perceptual constancy is the ability of perceptual systems to recognise the same object from widely varying sensory inputs. For example, individual people can be recognised from views, such as frontal and profile, which form very different shapes on the retina. A coin looked at face-on makes a circular image on the retina, but when held at angle it makes an elliptical image. In normal perception these are recognised as a single three-dimensional object. Without this correction process, an animal approaching from the distance would appear to gain in size. One kind of perceptual constancy is *color constancy*, for example, a white piece of paper can be recognised as such under different colors and intensities of light. Another example is *roughness constancy*: When a hand is drawn quickly across a surface, the touch nerves are stimulated more intensely. The brain compensates for this, so the speed of contact does not affect the perceived roughness. Other constancies include melody, odor, brightness and words. These constancies are not always total, but the variation in the percept is much less than the variation in the physical stimulus. The perceptual systems of the brain achieve perceptual constancy in a variety of ways, each specialized for the kind of information being processed.

The principles of grouping (*or Gestalt laws of grouping*) are a set of principles in psychology, first proposed by Gestalt psychologists to explain how humans naturally perceive objects as organized patterns and objects. Gestalt psychologists argued that these principles exist because the mind has an innate disposition to perceive patterns in the stimulus based on certain rules. These principles are organized into six categories. The principle of *proximity* states that, all else being equal, perception tends to group stimuli that are close together as part of the same object, and stimuli that are far apart as two separate objects. The principle of *similarity* states that, all else being equal, perception lends itself to seeing stimuli that physically resemble each other as part of the same object, and stimuli that are different as part of a different object. This allows for people to distinguish between adjacent and overlapping objects based on their visual texture and resemblance.

The principle of *closure* refers to the mind's tendency to see complete figures or forms even if a picture is incomplete, partially hidden by other objects, or if part of the information needed to make a complete picture in our minds is missing. For example, if part of a shape's border is missing people still tend to see the shape as completely enclosed by the border and ignore the gaps. The principle of *good continuation* makes sense of stimuli that overlap: When there is an intersection between two or more objects, people tend to perceive each as a single uninterrupted object. The principle of *common fate* groups stimuli together on the basis of their movement. When visual elements are seen moving in the same direction at the same rate, perception associates the movement as part of the same stimulus. This allows people to make out moving objects even when other details, such as color or outline, are obscured. The principle of *good form* refers to the tendency to group together forms of similar shape, pattern, color, etc. Later research has identified additional grouping principles.

Contrast effect: A common finding across many different kinds of perception is that the perceived qualities of an object can be affected by the qualities of context. If one object is extreme on some dimension, then neighboring objects are perceived as further away from that extreme. "Simultaneous contrast effect" is the term used when stimuli are presented at the same time, whereas "successive contrast" applies when stimuli are presented one after another.

The contrast effect was noted by the 17th Century philosopher John Locke, who observed that lukewarm water can feel hot or cold, depending on whether the hand touching it was previously in hot or cold water. In the early 20th Century, Wilhelm Wundt identified contrast as a fundamental principle of perception, and since then the effect has been confirmed in many different areas. These effects shape not only visual qualities like color and brightness, but other kinds of perception, including how heavy an object feels. One experiment found that thinking of the name "Hitler" led to subjects rating a person as more hostile. Whether a piece of music is perceived as good or bad can depend on whether the music heard before it was unpleasant or pleasant. For the effect to work, the objects being compared need to be similar to each other: A television reporter can seem smaller when interviewing a tall basketball player, but not when standing next to a tall building. In the brain, contrast exerts effects on neuronal firing rates but also on neuronal synchrony.

Perception is influenced by characteristics of the object being perceived, by the characteristics of the person and by the situational processes.

- Characteristics of the object include contrast, intensity, movement, repetition and novelty.
- Characteristics of the person include attitude, self-concept and personality.

The details of a particular situation affect the way a person perceives an object; the same person may perceive the same object very differently in different situations. The processes through which a person's perceptions are altered by the situation include selection, organisation, attribution, projection, stereotyping process, and the halo effect process. Among these, selective perception and stereotyping are particularly relevant to organisations.

(a) Selective Perception

Selective perception is the process of screening out information that we are uncomfortable with or that contradicts our beliefs. For example, a manager has a very positive attitude about a particular worker and one day he notices that the worker seems to be goofing up. Selective perception may make the manager to quickly disregard what he observed. For example, a manager who has formed a very negative attitude about a particular worker and he happens to observe a high performance from the same worker. In this case influenced by the selective perception process he too will disregard it. In one sense, selective perception is beneficial because it allows us to disregard minor bits of information. But if selective perception causes managers to ignore important information, it can become quite detrimental.

(b) The Perceiver, The Perceived (Target), and The Setting

A related way to summarize the perception process is to view the key factors as: (1) the perceiver, (2) the perceived or target, and (3) the setting (Fig. 3.1). All three dimensions are inextricably linked. When individuals discuss their plans, decisions, and evaluations about other people and events, they usually assume that their assessments are objective and mostly accurate. However, understanding the process of perception must include the perceiver's subjectivity and therefore requires that the perceiver's most basic assumptions (or her "lens") be understood. First, the perceiver tends to view people, events, and objects from the vantage point of her own personality, needs, moods, desires, and attitudes. These internal factors of the perceiver serve as the perceptual schemata. Perception begins with the perceiver, but we would do well to recall the adage. "When Anil talks about Kumar, he is also talking about Anil".

Perceptual inputs encompass all stimuli that exist in our environment including people, events, objects, information, conversation, etc. In other words, everything in the setting where events occur or which contribute to the occurrence of events can be termed perceptual inputs. Perceptual throughputs or the transformation of perceptual inputs to outputs involves the three processes of selecting, organizing, and interpreting the stimuli that are in the environment. Perceptual outputs encompass all that result from the throughout process. These would include such factors as one's attitudes, opinions, feelings, values and behaviours resulting from the perceptual inputs and throughputs. Perceptual errors adversely affect the perceptual outputs. The lesser our biases in perception, the better the chances of our perceiving "reality" as it exists, or at least perceiving situations with the minimum amount of distortions. This will help us to form the right attitudes and engage in appropriate behavioural patterns, which in turn will be beneficial for attaining the desired organisational outcomes.

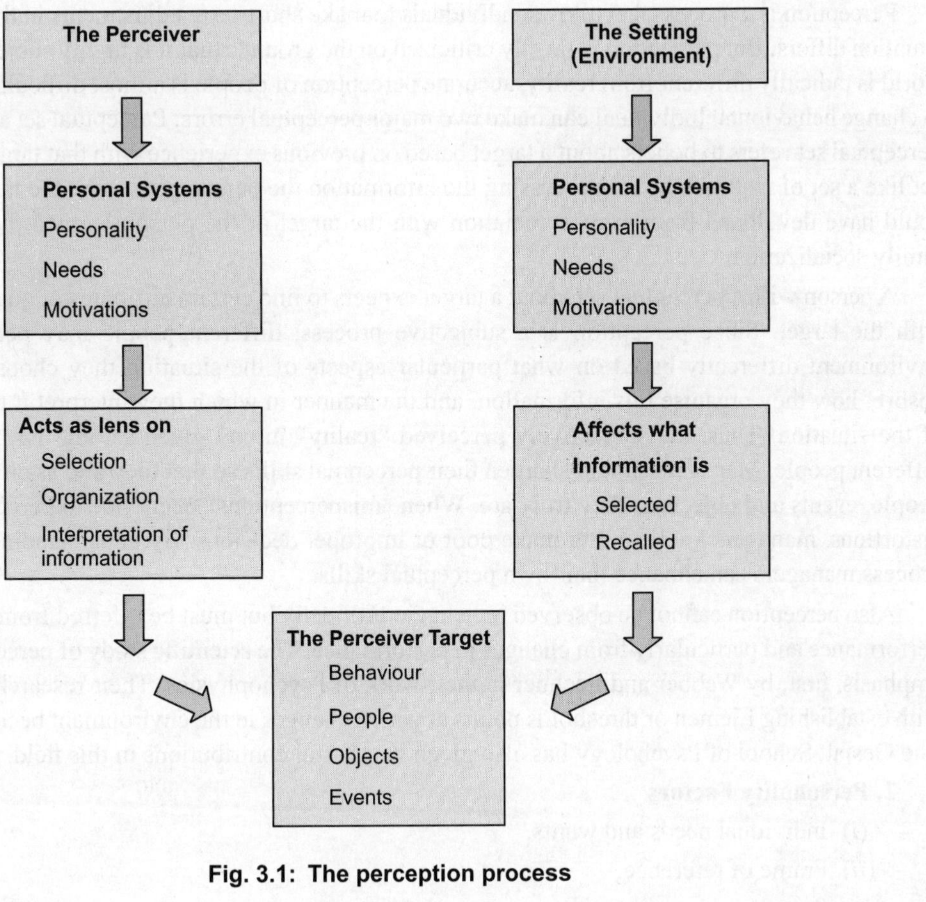

Fig. 3.1: The perception process

1. Role-of-O-Factors: When stimulus situation or object is highly structured, the O-factors (Personal factors) play very little role. But when the situation is unstructured as in protective tests for personality (Rorschach, TAT etc.) perception is highly influenced by the 'want-system'—One would always be projecting one's own needs or wants. Perceptual sensitizations, perceptual defense, or perceptual distortion takes place according to one's own needs and other personality factors. If the situation or object is a pleasant one and enhances one's self respect, then there will be a perception sensitization *i.e.*, to perceive it more quickly and to retain it better. If the object or situation is an obstacle to ones' own needs or unpleasant to the ego, then instead of perceptual sensitization, it leads to perceptual defence. (This is a sort of a mechanism which enables the individual not to perceive it clearly and to forget it immediately) and perceptual distortion.

However, it should be noted that a strong threat to one's self will be perceived quickly, though it happens to be an unpleasant one. Perception of 'self' (individual or group) and perception of 'others' (Individual or group) are important in interpersonal and intergroup interactions. Narrowing down the differences in perception of 'self' and others may reduce the interpersonal and intergroup tensions and conflicts as in Union Management Relations in an industrial organisation. It is of utmost importance to keep in mind that "we perceive people, object, self not as they are but as we are'.

Perception is a process that allows individuals to make short-term adjustments in their behaviour as situation differs. But perception is mostly criticized on the grounds that it is highly subjective, perceived world is radically different from reality, accurate perception of people is almost difficult, and impossible to change behaviours. Individual can make two major perceptual errors: Perceptual set and stereotyping. Perceptual set refers to beliefs about a target based on previous experience with that target. These beliefs act like a set of instructions for processing the information the person gets about the target. The beliefs could have developed from prior association with the target or the person learned them during early family socialization.

A person with a perceptual set about a target expects to find certain attributes or qualities associated with the target. Since perception is a subjective process, different people may perceive the same environment differently based on what particular aspects of the situation they choose to selectively absorb, how they organise this information, and the manner in which they interpret it to obtain a grasp of the situation. Thus, the subjectively perceived "reality" in any given setting may be different for different people. Managers should sharpen their perceptual skills so that they are, as close to perceiving people, events and objects as they truly are. When "misperceptions" occur due to perceptual errors and distortions, managers are bound to make poor or improper decisions. By understanding the perceptual process managers can enhance their own perceptual skills.

Also perception cannot be observed in behaviour directly but must be inferred from observations of performance and particularly from changes in performance. The scientific study of perception was given emphasis, first, by Webber and Fechner in their work of Psychophysics. Their research was concerned with establishing Liemen or thresholds points at which changes in the environment becomes noticeable. The Gestalt School of Psychology has also given wonderful contributions in this field.

2. Personality Factors

(*i*) Individual needs and wants.

(*ii*) Frame of reference.

(*iii*) Set of readings.

(*iv*) Familiarity and past experience.

(*v*) Discrimination and generalization.

3. Sensory Adaptation

(*i*) Dark adaptation (w.r.t. light).

(*ii*) Temp adaptation and so on (w.r.t. temperature).

4. Perception of Movement

(*i*) Projection of wants.

(*ii*) Perception and experience.

(*iii*) Perception of motivation, habits, reduced cues.

(*iv*) Depth perception.

3.3 FACTORS INFLUENCING PERCEPTION

(*a*) ***Physical Features*:** A substantial amount of behavioural research suggest that physical features such as sex, race, dress, facial expression, and body posture, influence both the attention we give to others and the judgements us from about them.

(*b*) ***Work Situation*:** Elements in the surrounding environment or work situation also influence perception in predictable ways. The time at which a message is transmitted can influence attention and interpretation. For example, if an employee has become accustomed to receiving a given report during the first week of every month, he or she may completely ignore the report should it be transmitted at some other time, such as the last week of the months.

(*c*) ***Group Pressure*:** The perception of a person automatically changes when he finds that others do not share his beliefs, attitudes or perception.

(*d*) ***Interaction*:** Interaction among group members helps in improving perception about a person or situation.

(*e*) ***Needs and Desires*:** The needs and desires of the person influence perception. Knott observes that perception of a frustrated individual is entirely different from that of a happy going person.

(*f*) ***Attributes of the Person*:** Probably the most important sources of influence on perception are characteristics of the person, including his or her motives, expectations from the job and personality.

(*g*) ***Status*:** Perception is also influenced by the status of the perceiver. Person at the higher status can exert influence on perception of an employee than a person of low status. For instance, when the general manager and superintendent call the employee at a particular time, the employees first attend the call of the general manager and later to the call of the superintendent.

3.4 NATURE, TYPE OF PERCEPTION AND IT'S IMPORTANCE IN OB

Typically an understanding of the nature of perception and factors involved in it is necessary to predict and control human behaviour in an organisational setup. Different people see things differently. Even 'facts' may be 'seen' and interpreted differently. Since perception is a major determinant of behaviour; it cannot be ignored. We can say now that perception involves attention to start with in sensation and interpretation of sensory data.

Perception which involves attention (which again involves identification, discrimination and interpretation) is the process by which we gain knowledge about the external world. In perception the sensory are interpreted with reference to the totality of one's past experience. As stated earlier perception is always perception of objects and situations and remembers not of stimuli. In other words perception is always meaningful and selectively organized involving signs (cues) and meanings. These meanings attributed to signs or cues are the result of past experiences. The cognitive field of 'appreciation-mass' formed by the cumulative effect of one's past experiences acts as a frame of reference to interpret any news stimulus or one. Above all, perception involves learning, besides it also involves a figure-ground relationship and discrimination and judgement.

A perceptual set, also called ***perceptual expectancy*** or just *set* is a predisposition to perceive things in a certain way. It is an example of how perception can be shaped by "top-down" processes such as drives and expectations. Perceptual sets occur in all the different senses. They can be long term, such as a special sensitivity to hearing one's own name in a crowded room, or short term, as in the ease with which hungry people notice the smell of food. A simple demonstration of the effect involved very brief presentations of non-words such as "sael". Subjects who were told to expect words about animals read it as "seal", but others who were expecting boat-related words read it as "sail".

Sets can be created by motivation and so can result in people interpreting ambiguous figures so that they see what they want to see. For instance, how someone perceives what unfolds during a sports game can be biased if they strongly support one of the teams. In one experiment, students were allocated to pleasant or unpleasant tasks by a computer. They were told that either a number or a letter would flash on the screen to say whether they were going to taste an orange juice drink or an unpleasant-tasting health drink. In fact, an ambiguous figure was flashed on screen, which could either be read as the letter B or the number 13. When the letters were associated with the pleasant task, subjects were more likely to perceive a letter B, and when letters were associated with the unpleasant task they tended to perceive a number 13.

Perceptual set has been demonstrated in many social contexts. People who are primed to think of someone as "warm" are more likely to perceive a variety of positive characteristics in them, than if the word "warm" is replaced by "cold". When someone has a reputation for being funny, an audience is more likely to find them amusing. Individual's perceptual sets reflect their own personality traits. For example, people with an aggressive personality are quicker to correctly identify aggressive words or situations.

One classic psychological experiment showed slower reaction times and less accurate answers when a deck of playing cards reversed the color of the suit symbol for some cards (e.g., red spades and black hearts).

Philosopher Andy Clark explains that perception, although it occurs quickly, is not simply a bottom-up process (where minute details are put together to form larger wholes). Instead, our brains use what he calls ***Predictive coding***. It starts with very broad constraints and expectations for the state of the world, and as expectations are met, it makes more detailed predictions (errors lead to new predictions, or learning processes). Clark says this research has various implications; not only can there be no completely "unbiased, unfiltered" perception, but this means that there is a great deal of feedback between perception and expectation (perceptual experiences often shape our beliefs, but those perceptions were based on existing beliefs).

Perception, as a social information process, includes at least five steps. First, we as individual observe and sense (*i.e.*, select and screen out) external stimuli through internal factors, which include, among other things, out personality traits and our personal systems. Second, this information is interpreted; third, it is categorized (*i.e.*, encoded and simplified) and fourth, information is stored and retained in our memory. Fifth, our judgements and decisions are made by retrieving and responding to this stored information. At the first step, our initial perception *i.e.*, how we sense and see the world in any given situation is affected by our personality, previous learning, level of motivation, moods, attitudes, and cultural conditioning. We do not select information from the environment in a totally objective way. For example, research indicates that authoritarian personality types with a low tolerance for ambiguity screen reality differently than do egalitarian personalities. The former act more directly, taking fewer notes of nuances and differences in the social environment from their perceptions; the latter are more inclusive and participative.

The second and third steps in the process of social information perception are our encoding and simplifying, interpreting, and translating of the raw data into our own cognitive categories or schemata (i.e., mental images and summaries of stimuli and events). It is during these steps that several perceptual distortions and barriers can enter the process. A point to keep in mind here is that we never store data in its first-observed, original form. We frame it through our schemata. Schemata help us to make sense of incoming information. Four general types of schemata include self-schemata, other-person schema, script schema, and person-in-situation schema. Self-schemata refer to the interpretation of information about our behaviour, appearance, and personality. That is, we categorize what we determine to be our best and most effective ways that we view as unacceptable.

The term other-person schemata refer to interpretations of information we have on other's behaviours and modes of thinking. For example, we may form an initial prototype of what constitutes an exceptional performer or a poor performer. Thereafter, we use stereotypes, positive and/or negative, to identify exceptional and poor performers from our prototypical schemata. A third type, script schemata, is used to describe what we consider appropriate steps or sequences of events (i.e., cognitive memory structures that consist of objects, events, roles, conditions, sentiments, and outcomes that happen in sequential patterns in known or familiar tasks and situations). We understand that certain steps should be taken or certain sequences should occur, script schemata enable us to decide whether this is happening and thereby to develop reasonable expectations. Finally, a person-in-situation schema refers to combining categories of self, person, and script schemata. For example, we tend to categories how meetings, encounters, and interactions should proceed and terminate.

The fourth step in the perception process is the storage and retention of observed information in our long-term memory. Long-term memory consists of schemata in which we store information on events, people, and networks of detailed traits and behaviours. How accurately we perceive the information before we store it is always questionable because it is, by definition, subjective. The point here is that research suggests that we store our perceptions in categories and schemata, as just discussed. For instance, physical appearance of people, the topics they speak about, their tone of voice, and even their accent as well as eye contact, facial expressions, body movements, and posture are detailed ways we categorize others to use as interpretative mental references later. Finally, we retrieve information from our long- and short-term memories in response to questions, problems, events and issues. Again, the appropriateness of our response depends in large part on the accuracy of our perceptions and the particular construction of our schemata.

In the process of perception, people receive many different kinds of information through all five senses, assimilate them and then interpret them. Different people perceive the same information differently. Perception plays a key role in determining individual behaviour in organisations. Organisations send messages in a variety of forms to their members regarding what they are expected to do and not to do. In spite of organisations sending clear messages, those messages are subject to distortion in the process of being perceived by organisational members. Hence, managers need to have a general understanding of the basic perceptual process.

(a) Illusions or Normal Perceptual Inaccuracies

When most human beings perceive a particular set of stimuli in an incorrect manner, we say they are responding to an illusion. It may be due to false perceptual cause or due to misinformation.

(b) Subliminal Perception

Perceptions that affect our behaviour without our being aware of it are called subliminal because they apparently take place below perceptual line or threshold (or below the threshold of awareness). This factor is used highly in advertising. The phenomena of subliminal threshold were brought to the attention of the general public by Vicary's in 1956 when he could cause theater patrons to buy certain products.

(c) Extra Sensory Perception (ESP)

Gibson said, "Perception is not sensation". Extra Sensory Perceptions are the perception that takes place without the aid of senses.

1. *Mental Telepathy* : Ability to send and receive thoughts.
2. *Chair Voyance* : To gain awareness of events or objects outside the range of the usual senses.
3. *Telekinesis* : To influence the movement of physical objects without physically contacting them.

(d) Social Perception

Social perception is the process by which people come to know and understand each other's. When forming an impression of a person, a perceiver first observes the persons, the situation surrounding the person, and the person's behaviour. The perceiver may form a quick impression by making a snap judgement about the person, or the perceiver may follow the steps in the center of the figure, making attributions and integrating the attributions to form a final impression. People use three sets of clues when forming their impression of another person. These cure come from the person, the situation surrounding the person, and the observed behaviour of the person.

(e) Projection

When one's own personal attributes are assigned to others, then projection takes place. Self-fulfilling prophecy is the process by which we try to fit our attitudes, beliefs, and expectations to reality. What we perceive could then be governed by what we expect to find.

(f) Self-perception

It is the process by which people a view of themselves. The self-view develops from social interaction within different groups. These groups now include the group encountered on the Internet. Self-perception has three parts: Self-concept, self-esteem, and self-presentation.

1. **Self-concept** is the set of beliefs people have about themselves. It is the view people hold of their personal qualities and attributes. Several factors affect a person's self-concept including the person's observations of his behaviour, his recall of past significant events, and the effect of the surrounding social context.

2. **Self-esteem** is the emotional dimension of self-perception. It refers to the positive and negative judgements people have of themselves. Self-concept is perceptual and cognitive; self-esteem is the feeling a person holds about his self-perception. People degree of self-esteem plays an important role in behaviour. People with low self-esteemed to be unsuccessful and do not adapt well to stressful events. Those with high self-esteem have the opposite experience.
3. **Self-presentation**, the third part of self-perception, includes the behavioural strategies people use to affect how others see them and how they think about themselves self-presentations have two goals. To try to affect other people's impressions to win their approval, to increase the person's influence in a situation, or to ensure that others have an accurate impression of the person. Many people feel strongly motivated to have others perceive them accurately, whether positively or negatively.

(g) Prejudice and Discrimination

Prejudice refers to a person's predetermined negative attitudes toward people based on some group identity. When an individual acts on his negative prejudicial attitudes, discrimination occurs. Discrimination is the result of prejudicial attitudes. Prejudices are generally deeply ingrained, learned beliefs and attitudes passed on by family, regional, and peer cultures. Negative prejudicial attitudes are not based on objective facts or reality but on biased belief systems.

Our needs, past experiences, self-concept, and personality shape the beliefs, feelings, and opinions we hold towards the perceived world. Hellriegel, Slocum, and woodsman (1986) adapt the scheme of Coffey, Athos, and Raynolds (1975) in capturing the five stages in the perceptual process and highlight the following.

1. The observation phase depicts the environmental stimuli being absorbed by the five senses of the perceiver.
2. The selection of the stimuli for further consideration is governed both by factors external to the perceiver, such as the characteristics of the stimulus, and internal to the individual, such as the personality predisposition and motivations of the perceiver.
3. In the organising stage the perceiver is influenced by figure and ground, grouping, and several perceptual errors such as stereotyping, halo effects, projection, and perceptual defense (described later).
4. The interpretation stage is governed by the perceiver's assumptions of people and events and attributions about causes of behaviour.
5. The response of the perceiver takes on both covert and overt characteristic. Covert responses will be reflected in the attitudes; motives and feelings of the perceiver, and overt responses will be reflected in the actions of the individual.

(h) Perceptual Distortions

1. *Stereo typing*: It is a tendency to make generalizations, positive and/or negative about a group or category of people. Stereotyping involves applying, these generalizations to an individual. Stereotyping is the process of categorizing or labeling people on the basis of a single attribute. Perceptions based on stereotypes about people's sex exist more or less in all work places. Typically, these perceptions lead to the belief that an individual's sex determines which tasks he or she will be able to perform. For example, if a woman is sitting behind the table in the office, she will be very often, perceived as a clerk and not an executive at first. But it would induce holding an exactly opposite assumption about a man. Stereotyping consists of three steps: identifying categories of people (like women, politician), associating certain characteristics with those categories (like passivity, dishonesty respectively) and then assuming that anyone who fits a certain category must have those characteristics. For example, if dishonesty is associated with politicians, we are likely to assume that all politicians are dishonest.

2. ***The Halo effect:*** It is another perceptual distortion that occurs when a dominant feature of a person being observed overwhelms the observer's evaluation of the person being observed, resulting in bias. The observer's overall impression of the person for situation is skewed by a single characteristic of the person or situation. First impressions can involve the halo effect; for example, an initial meeting at a work with a newcomer who moves slowly and speaks softly might lead one to judge that person as being lethargic and easy going. In reality, the new comer may be recuperating from an illness or may be highly productive and intense worker who simply thinks carefully before acting. Major distortions are highlighted in Table 3.1.

Table 3.1: Showing major perceptual distortion

Stereotyping	:	Making positive or negative generalizations about a group of category of people, usually based on inaccurate assumptions and beliefs.
Halo effect	:	Developing one's overall impression of an individual or situation from a single characteristic about that individual or based on one situation.
Selective perception	:	Screening out information on objects, people, or events that is inconsistent with one's beliefs, values, and moods.
Projection	:	Attributing one's own feelings, attitudes, or perception to others.
Self-fulfilling prophecy	:	Having expectations about other's behaviours and justifying behavioural outcomes based on those expectations, regardless of the actual behaviours.

***(i) Selective Perception*:** It is a common distortion by which people unconsciously focus on aspects of individuals, events, or situations that are consistent with, or reinforce, their preexisting attitudes, moods, values, needs, or schemata even as they screen out other, relevant information as inconsistent with the pre-held beliefs. For example, a software development manager who values creativity more than productivity may evaluate a lower-level, creative but average software developer positively even though the employee had an unusual number of unexplained absences and poor product designs during the quarter. The manager is screening out the absences and rewarding the average creativity as a result of selective perception. Because of our human limitations, and defense mechanisms, we often tend to single out certain aspects of the environment to become a significant part of our perceptual inputs. Generally, these are the ones that tend to reinforce our values and beliefs, and match our need patterns. In short, we can say that perception is the process of knowing objects and objective facts on the basis of stimuli from the objects, which affect the senses i.e.,

1. We do not perceive stimuli, but objects and facts and situations.
2. Stimuli can be observed if the individual trains himself to attend to the stimuli themselves rather than the objects.
3. Psychology studies the signs (stimuli) by which we perceive the meaning (objective facts). Often we are not aware of the signs, which furnish on the basis of perceptions. Symbols, which are arbitrary names standing for objects.

Signs/Signals-stimuli coming directly from the objects (Are reduced cues, saying sketch of an object).

4. In perception a figure stands out naturally from a ground. Proximity, similarity and continuity and internal factors. Such as familiarity, set and pleasingness will help combine a figure.
5. Camouflage is the concealment of an object by reducing its figural characteristics.
6. The accuracy of perception is measured by tests of discrimination and estimation.
7. Illusions are false perceptions or errors in perception. They illustrate fundamental principles of perceptions. Figure 3.2 summarizes selective perception and stereotyping.

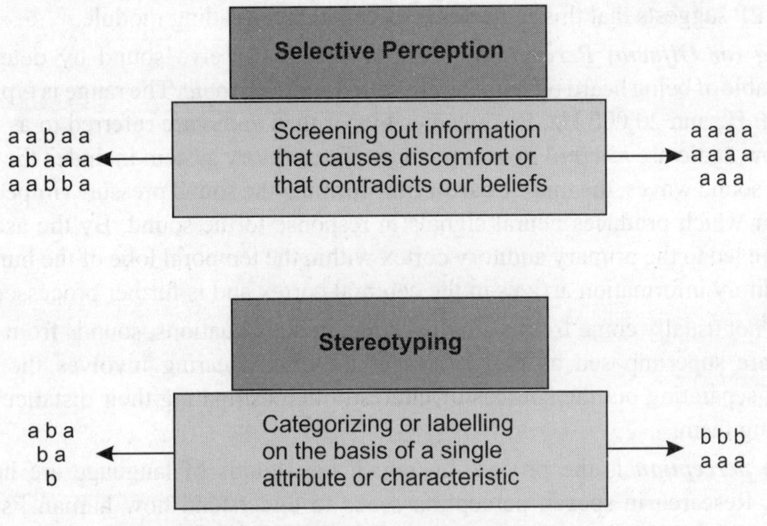

Fig. 3.2: Basic perceptual process

Many philosophers, such as Jerry Fodor, write that the purpose of perception is knowledge, but evolutionary psychologists hold that its primary purpose is to guide action. For example, they say, depth perception seems to have evolved not to help us know the distances to other objects but rather to help us move around in space. Evolutionary psychologists say that animals from fiddler crabs to humans use eyesight for collision avoidance, suggesting that vision is basically for directing action, not providing knowledge.

Building and maintaining sense organs is metabolically expensive, so these organs evolve only when they improve an organism's fitness. More than half the brain is devoted to processing sensory information, and the brain itself consumes roughly one-fourth of one's metabolic resources, so the senses must provide exceptional benefits to fitness. Perception accurately mirrors the world; animals get useful, accurate information through their senses.

Scientists who study perception and sensation have long understood the human senses as adaptations. Depth perception consists of processing over half a dozen visual cues, each of which is based on a regularity of the physical world. Vision evolved to respond to the narrow range of electromagnetic energy that is plentiful and that does not pass through objects. Sound waves provide useful information about the sources of and distances to objects, with larger animals making and hearing lower-frequency sounds and smaller animals making and hearing higher-frequency sounds. Taste and smell respond to chemicals in the environment that were significant for fitness in the EEA. The sense of touch is actually many senses, including pressure, heat, cold, tickle, and pain. Pain, while unpleasant, is adaptive. An important adaptation for senses is range shifting, by which the organism becomes temporarily more or less sensitive to sensation. For example, one's eyes automatically adjust to dim or bright ambient light. Sensory abilities of different organisms often coevolve, as is the case with the hearing of echolocating bats and that of the moths that have evolved to respond to the sounds that the bats make.

Evolutionary psychologists claim that perception demonstrates the principle of modularity, with specialized mechanisms handling particular perception tasks. For example, people with damage to a particular part of the brain suffer from the specific defect of not being able to recognize faces (prospagnosia). EP suggests that this indicates a so-called face-reading module.

(ii) Hearing (or Olfacto) Perception is the ability to perceive sound by detecting vibrations. Frequencies capable of being heard by humans are called audio or *sonic*. The range is typically considered to be between 20 Hz and 20,000 Hz. Frequencies higher than audio are referred to as ultrasonic, while frequencies below audio are referred to as infrasonic. Theauditory system includes the outer ears which collect and filter sound waves, the middle earfor transforming the sound pressure (impedance matching), and the inner ear which produces neural signals in response to the sound. By the ascending auditory pathway these are led to the primary auditory cortex within the temporal lobe of the human brain, which is where the auditory information arrives in the cerebral cortex and is further processed there.

Sound does not usually come from a single source: in real situations, sounds from multiplc sources and directions are superimposed as they arrive at the ears. Hearing involves the computationally complex task of separating out the sources of interest, often estimating their distance and direction as well as identifying them.

(iii) Speech perception is the process by which the sounds of language are heard, interpreted and understood. Research in speech perception seeks to understand how human listeners recognize speech sounds and use this information to understand spoken language. The sound of a word can vary widely according to words around it and the tempo of the speech, as well as the physical characteristics, accent and mood of the speaker. Listeners manage to perceive words across this wide range of different conditions. Another variation is that reverberation can make a large difference in sound between a word spoken from the far side of a room and the same word spoken up close. Experiments have shown that people automatically compensate for this effect when hearing speech.

The process of perceiving speech begins at the level of the sound within the auditory signal and the process of audition. After processing the initial auditory signal, speech sounds are further processed to extract acoustic cues and phonetic information. This speech information can then be used for higher-level language processes, such as word recognition. Speech perception is not necessarily unidirectional. That is, higher-level language processes connected with morphology, syntax, or semantics may interact with basic speech perception processes to aid in recognition of speech sounds. It may be the case that it is not necessary and maybe even not possible for a listener to recognize phonemes before recognizing higher units, like words for example. In one experiment, Richard M. Warren replaced one phoneme of a word with a cough-like sound. His subjects restored the missing speech sound perceptually without any difficulty and what is more, they were not able to identify accurately which phoneme had been disturbed.

(iv) Haptic or Tectonial Perception is the process of recognizing objects through touch. It involves a combination of somato sensory perception of patterns on the skin surface (e.g., edges, curvature, and texture) and proprioception of hand position and conformation. People can rapidly and accurately identify three-dimensional objects by touch. This involves exploratory procedures, such as moving the fingers over the outer surface of the object or holding the entire object in the hand. Haptic perception relies on the forces experienced during touch.

Gibson defined the haptic system as "The sensibility of the individual to the world adjacent to his body by use of his body". Gibson and others emphasized the close link between haptic perception and body movement: Haptic perception is active exploration. The concept of haptic perception is related to the concept of extended physiological proprioception according to which, when using a tool such as a stick, perceptual experience is transparently transferred to the end of the tool.

(v) Taste (or Gustation) is the ability to perceive the flavor of substances including, but not limited to, food. Humans receive tastes through sensory organs called *taste buds*, or *gustatory calyculi*, concentrated on the upper surface of the tongue. The human tongue has 100 to 150 taste receptor cells on each of its roughly ten thousand taste buds. There are five primary tastes: Sweetness, bitterness, sourness, saltiness, and umami. Other tastes can be mimicked by combining these basic tastes. The recognition and awareness of umami is a relatively recent development in Western cuisine. The basic tastes contribute only partially to the sensation and flavor of food in the mouth—other factors include smell, detected by the olfactory epithelium of the nose; texture, detected through a variety of mechanoreceptors, muscle nerves, etc and temperature, detected by thermo receptors. All basic tastes are classified as either *appetitive* or *aversive*, depending upon whether the things they sense are harmful or beneficial.

3.5 LINK BETWEEN PERCEPTION AND DECISION MAKING

Perceiving is a "mind-set", that is, a pattern of seeing and interpreting reality. A mind-set has been described as a predisposition to see the world in a particular way that sets boundaries and provides explanations for why things are the way they are. A filter through which we look at the world.

A 'global' mind-set means that we scan the world from a board perspective, always looking for unexpected trends and opportunities to achieve our personal, professional, or organisational broader perspective as they constantly look for contexts for contexts from which to understand opportunities. They value workforce diversity and multicultural teamwork as the basic form within which to achieve their objectives. They show sensitivity and flexibility in meeting the needs of diverse individuals while attaining project and organisational objectives. They accept life and its complexities as a balance of contradictory forces. They trust organisational processes more organisational structure as a way to manage the unexpected. Individuals with a global mind-set also flow with change and see ambiguity as an opportunity; they continuously search for improvement while being open to others.

(a) Honing Perceptual Skills

Perceptual skills can be enhanced by: (1) knowing and perceiving oneself accurately; (2) being empathic; (3) having positive attitudes; (4) enhancing one's self-concept; (5) making a conscious effort to avoid the possible common biases in perception; (6) communicating with employees to erase incorrect perceptions; and (7) avoiding attributions.

(b) Biases Contributing to Misperceptions

In perceiving the stimuli in our environment, we are likely to make at least seven types of errors, some of which have already been mentioned. They are stereotyping, halo effects, selective perceptions, attributions, distortions, projections, and placing credence on self-fulfilling prophecies. Each of these errors is dysfunctional for good decision-making and management. Stereotyping is the tendency to perceive an individual as belonging to a single class or category and hence attributing favourable or unfavorable characteristics to the individual based upon a widely held generalization about the group. Halo effect is the tendency to perceive all the attributes of a person in a similar manner, based on one characteristic or trait of the individual. A stereotype is a form of perceptual set that holds beliefs and perceived attributes of a target person based on the group to which the target belongs. For example, a study of samples of Russian and American University students found that they held certain images of each other. The Russian students perceived Americans as independent, energetic, and spontaneous. The American students perceived Russians as conservative, orderly, restrained, and obedient.

3.6 LINK BETWEEN PERCEPTION AND WORKFORCE DIVERSITY

Managing a diverse workforce is not easy. Organisational experts and experienced managers agree that managing diversity and working with people who are different is more complex than working with people who share the same attitudes, values, and work behaviours. Effectively integrating diverse workforces can produce a competitive advantage by using individual and group differences to enhance creativity and synergy. In addition to the perceptual distortions and barriers discussed earlier, prejudice and discrimination can also inhibit workforce integration. Sources of prejudice and discrimination include intrapersonal, interpersonal, and societal reinforcement factors.

3.7 LINK BETWEEN PERCEPTION AND ATTRIBUTION

Perception refers to seeing, selecting, and recalling information. Attributions are causes and effects assigned to observed behaviour. Attributions are inferred causes; that is, the cause-and-effect connections are not necessarily based on actual behaviours. Attributions are assigned to other's behaviour based on whether these three factors are high or low in the perceiver's judgement, not necessarily in fact or reality. For example, a perceiver who determines the conditions of the target's behaviours as having high consensus, low consistency, and high distinctiveness, most likely attributes the target's behaviour to external causes.

Perception is also closely linked with another process called attribution. Attribution is a mechanism through which we observe behaviour and then attribute certain causes to it. According to Attribution theory, once we observe behaviour we evaluate it in terms of its consensus, consistency and distinctiveness. Consensus is the extent to which other people in the same situation behave in the same way. Consistency is the degree to which the same person behaves in the same way at different times. Distinctiveness is the extent to which the same person behaves in the same way in other situations. The forces within the person (internal) or outside the person (external) lead to the behaviour.

For instance, if you observe that an employee is much more motivated than the people around (low consensus), is consistently motivated (high consistency), and seems to work hard no matter what the task (low distinctiveness) you might conclude that internal factors are causing that particular behaviour. Another example is of a manager who observes that an employee is late for a meeting. He might realize that this employee is the only one who is laic (low consensus), recall that he is often late for other meetings (high consistency), and subsequently recall that the same employee is sometimes late for work (low distinctiveness). This pattern of attributions might cause the manager to decide that the individual's behaviour requires a change. At this point, the manager might meet the subordinate to establish some disciplinary consequences to avoid future delays. Figure 3.3 explains the basic attribution process as shown below.

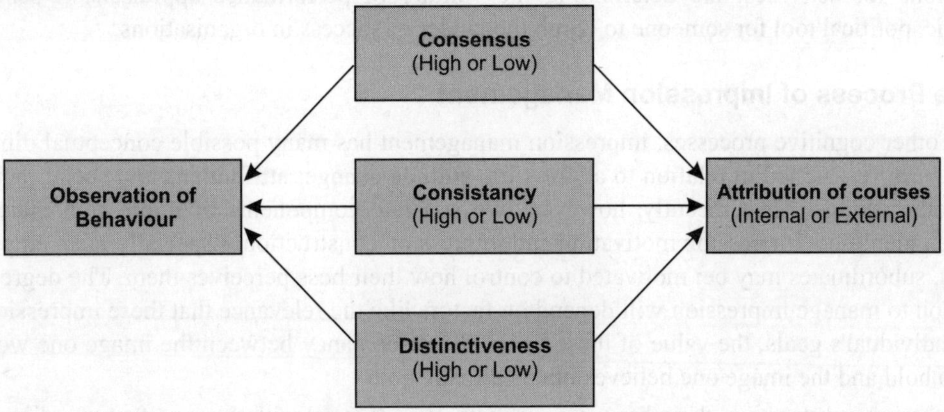

Fig. 3.3: Basic attribution process

Attribution refers to how a person tries to understand behaviour or events by interpreting them as caused by certain other factors. In other words, the person tries to explain why something happened or someone behaved in a particularly way. Our perceptions of what is happening in the environment depend very much on the attributions we make. Attribution explains the ways in which we judge people differently, depending on what meaning we attribute to a given behaviour. Basically, the theory suggests that when we observe an individual's behaviour, we attempt to determine whether it was internally or externally caused. That determination, however, depends largely on three factor: (1) distinctiveness, (2) consensus, and (3) consistency. Distinctiveness refers to whether an individual displays different behaviours in different situations. Is the employee who arrives late today also the source of complaints by co-workers for being a "good-off?" What we want to know is whether this behaviour is unusual? If it is, the observer is likely to give the behaviour an external attribution.

If this action is not unusual, it will probably be judged as internal. If everyone who is faced with a similar situation response in the same way, we can say the behaviour shows consensus. Our late employee's behaviour would meet this criterion if all employees who took the same route to work were also late. From an attribution perspective, if consensus were high, you would be expected to give an external attribution to the employee's tardiness, whereas if other employees who took the same route made it to work on time, your conclusion as to causation would be internal. Finally, an observer looks for consistency in a person's actions. Does the person respond the same way over time? Coming in ten minutes late for work is not perceived in the same way for the employee for whom it is an unusual case (she hasn't been late for several months) as it is for the employee for whom it is part of a routine pattern (she is regularly late two or three times a week). The more consistent the behaviour, the more the observer is inclined to attribute it to internal causes.

3.8 LINK BETWEEN PERCEPTION AND IMPRESSION MANAGEMENT

Social perception is concerned with how one individual perceives other individuals. Conversely, impression management is the process by which the general people attempt to manage or control the perceptions that others form about them. People often tend to present themselves in such a way so as to impress others in a socially desirable manner. Thus, impression management has considerable' implications for activities like determining the validity of performance appraisals. It serves as a pragmatic, political tool for someone to climb the ladder of success in organisations.

(a) The Process of Impression Management

As with other cognitive processes, impression management has many possible conceptual dimensions arid has been researched in relation to aggression, attitude change; attributions and social facilitation, among other things. Most recently, however, two separate components of impression management have been identified, impression motivation and impression construction. Especially in an employment situation, subordinates may be; motivated to control how their boss perceives them. The degree of this motivation to manage impression will depend on factors like the relevance that these impressions have on the individual's goals, the value of these goals, the discrepancy between the image one would like others to hold and the image one believes others already hold.

Impression construction, the other major process, is concerned with the specific type of impression people want to make and how they create it. Although some theorists limit the type of impression only to personal characteristics others include such things as attitudes, physical status, interests, or values. Using this broader approach, five factors have been identified as being especially relevant to the kinds of impression people try to construct: The self-concept, desired and undesired identity images, role constraints, target values and current social image. Although there has been a considerable research done on how these five factors influence the type of impression that people try to make, there is still little known of how they select the way to manage others' perceptions of them.

(b) Employee Impression Management Strategies

There are two basic strategies of impression management that employees can use. If employees are trying to minimize responsibility for some negative event or to stay out of trouble, they may employ a demotion-preventative strategy. On the other hand, if they are seeking to maximize responsibility for a positive outcome or to look better than what they really are, then they lean use a promotion-enhancing strategy.

The demotion-preventative strategy is characterized by the following activities:

- Employees attempt to excuse or justify their actions.
- Employees' apologies to the boss for some negative event.
- Employees secretly tell their boss that they fought for the right thing, but were overruled. Employees using this approach try to disassociate themselves from the group and from the problem.

The promotion enhancing strategies involve the following activities:

- Employees harbor a feeling that they have not been given credit for a positive outcome.
- Employees point out that they did more, but received a lesser credit.
- Employees identify cither personal or organisational obstacles they had to overcome to accomplish an outcome and expect a higher credit.
- Employees ascertain that they are seen with the right people at the right times.

(c) Coping with Individual Differences

Individual differences and people's perception of them affect every aspect of behaviour in organisations. Managers must never underestimate the differences between individuals. Successful managers constantly monitor their own assumptions, perceptions and attributions, trying to treat each individual as a unique person.

3.9 A MANAGERIAL CHECKLIST FOR DIAGNOSING PERCEPTUAL BIASES

Managers can use the following checklist to help prevent perceptual biases. The use of the results from this checklist can also alert individual employees to their biases in decision making.

- What current state of mind and moods generally bias our objective?
- What biases generally influence our perceptions and attributions regarding particular types of decisions?
- What additional information is needed to correct and/or change our potential biases (stereotyping, halo effect, selective perception, projection, and self-fulfilling prophecy) in our decisions?
- What written policies and/or procedures can be designed and used to decrease individual and group biases?
- Are we thinking and acting parochially and/or ethnocentrically in our decisions, or do work think and act globally?
- How do our personality styles influence how ethically or unethically we perceive and assign fair and just causes to events and behaviours?

SUMMARY

Perception is the process we use to screen and interpret reality. It involves selecting external stimuli and then interpreting and categorising the information, storing and retaining it in our memory, and finally retrieving and responding to external stimuli. Some of the common distortions are stereotyping, the halo effect, selective perception, projection and the self-fulfilling prophecy. Attribution is the inferred cause and effect that is assigned to events. Individuals with global mind sets are described as people who view reality with broader, less parochial perspective. Attitudes are a person's complexes of beliefs and feelings about specific ideas, situations, or other people. People who possess positive attitude are optimistic and have an overall sense of well-being and see things in a positive light. Values determine the basis of an action of any individual in the organisation settings.

REVIEW QUESTIONS

1. Explain Perception process.
2. Explain Attribution and its link with perception.
3. What do you mean by selective perception?
4. What do you mean by perceptive distortion?
5. How halo effect will influence the organisational decision making process?
6. How do you manage workforce diversity by minimizing perceptive distortions?

DISCUSSION QUESTIONS

1. How the perception process came into play in IT firms?
2. Imagine you are the CEO of a call centre; how do you limit perceptional distortions?

STUDENT EXERCISE

Visit a relationship banking centre and survey their employees' perception towards their employment and manger's perception on their staff with the help of the theory described in this chapter. Also compare their perceptional distortions between employees and managers within the firms but across departments/ sections as well.

SKILL TEST

ARE YOU MANAGING YOUR TIME?

The key to successful management is the possession of good time-management skills. Find out how well you manage your time by responding to the following statements, and mark the options that are closest to your experience. Be as honest as you can; if your answer is *Never mark option 1*; if your answer is *Always, mark option 4* and so on. Add your scores together, and refer to the Analysis to see how you scored. Use your answers to identify the areas that need most improvement.

OPTIONS

1. Never
2. Occasionally
3. Frequently
4. Always

1. I clear my desk of all paper work.

   1 2 3 4

2. I delegate tasks to colleagues that I could do myself.

   1 2 3 4

3. I follow up on the work I have delegated.

   1 2 3 4

4. I encourage subordinates to limit their reports to one side of paper.

   1 2 3 4

5. I consider who needs to know the information I am circulating.

1	2	3	4

6. I achieve the right balance between thinking-time and action-time.

1	2	3	4

7. I make a list of things to do each day.

1	2	3	4

8. I keep work to a certain number of hours every day and no more.

1	2	3	4

9. The meetings I organise finish on time.

1	2	3	4

10. I open my mail as soon as it arrives on my desk.

1	2	3	4

11. I arrive on time and prepared for meetings.

1	2	3	4

12. I ensure that a clock is visible in the room where meetings are held.

1	2	3	4

13. The meetings I organize achieve their purpose.

1	2	3	4

14. I "skill-read" any relevant newspaper and magazine articles.

1	2	3	4

15. I cross my name off the circulation last for magazines and journals I do not read.

1	2	3	4

16. I read my faxes on the day on which I receive them.

1	2	3	4

17. I am able to complete tasks without interruptions from colleagues.

1	2	3	4

18. I make sure I know about the latest business software package.

1	2	3	4

19. I store e-mail messages in order to read them later on screen.

1	2	3	4

20. I perform housekeeping checks on my computer files.

1	2	3	4

21. I decide how many times I can be interrupted in a day.

1	2	3	4

22. I reserve certain hours for visits from colleagues.

1	2	3	4

23. I close my office door when I want to think strategically.

1	2	3	4

24. I tell telephone callers that I will return their calls, and do so.

1	2	3	4

25. I limit the duration of my telephone calls.

1	2	3	4

26. I allow a colleague or secretary to screen my telephone calls.

1	2	3	4

27. I decide how many telephone calls I can deal with personally in a day.

1	2	3	4

28. I "skim-read" internal memos as soon as I receive them.

1	2	3	4

29. I read internal memos thoroughly later.

1	2	3	4

30. I keep the contents of my in-tray to a manageable size.

1	2	3	4

31. I make an effort to keep in touch with my staff.

1	2	3	4

32. I concentrate on the positive attributes of each of my colleagues.

1	2	3	4

ANALYSIS AND INTERPRETATION

Please tally your score and infer below:

32–64 : Learn to use your time efficiently and reduce the time you spend working in unproductive and labour-intensive ways.

65–95 : You have reasonable time-management skills, but they could improve.

96–128 : You use your time very efficiently; keep looking for new ways to further streamline your work.

If you wish to know more insight on your test score, then you are welcome to contact author via e-mail shaangrila@gmail.com or social media drs.shajahan.7@facebook.com

4

CHAPTER

MOTIVATION

LEARNING OBJECTIVES

This chapter aims at introducing fundamental concepts for explaining the motivation process and its influence in organisational behaviour to the readers:

- *Definition, importance and fundamental concepts of motivation*
- *Theories of motivation Maslow's Hierarchy of Needs Theory, McGregor's Theory X & Y, Herzberg's Motivation–Hygiene Theory, Alderfer's ERG Theory, McClelland's Theory of Needs, Vroom's Expectancy Theory*
- *Motivation process and framework*
- *Money as a motivator and motivation research*

INTRODUCTION

The word motivation is derived from 'motive', which means an active form of a desire, craving or need that must be satisfied. Motivation is the key to organisational effectiveness. The manager in general has to get the work done through others. These 'others' are human resources who need to be motivated to attain organisational objectives. Motivation as the willingness to exert high levels of effort towards organisational goals, conditioned by the effort's ability to satisfy some individual need. While general motivation is concerned with effort towards any goal, we'll narrow the focus to organisational goals in order to reflect our singular interest in work-related behaviour.

The three key elements in our definition are effort, organisational goals, and needs. The effort element is a measure of intensity. When someone is motivated, he or she tries hard. But high levels of effort are unlikely to lead to favourable job-performance outcomes unless the effort is channeled in a direction that benefits the organisation. Therefore, we must consider the quality of the effort as well as its intensity. Effort that is directed towards, and consistent with, the organisation's goals are the kind of effort that we should be seeking. Finally, we will treat motivation as a need-satisfying process. Here we summarise the major motivation theories and also considered the importance of money as a tool for motivating employees. We begin with a general model as shown in Fig. 4.1

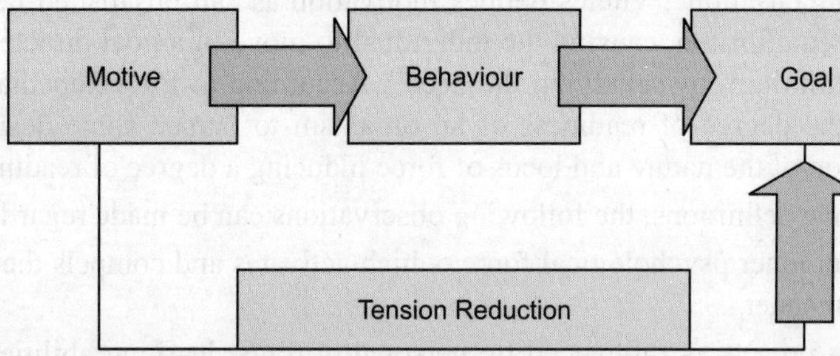

Fig. 4.1: Showing a generalised model of motivation process

1. **Behaviour:** Behaviour is generally motivated by desire to achieve a goal or satisfaction of needs. People watch over from one activity to another activity. As such managers must understand the motives of the people working under them in order to predict and control their behaviour.
2. **Motives:** Motives refer to needs, or drives or wants. Motives prompt people to action. Motives are largely subjective and represent the mental feelings of human beings. They cause behaviour in many ways.
3. **Goals:** Motives are directed towards achievement of goals. Goals are the ends, which provide satisfaction of human wants. Attaining a goal will tend to restore physiological and psychological balance.

The above model presents that individual process in varying host of needs, desires and expectations. All of such needs compete for their behaviour and ultimately the need with the maximum strength at a particular moment leads to activity. When a need is satisfied, it is no longer a motivator of behaviour.

According to Gellerman, the most subtle and most important characteristic of money is its power as a symbol. Its most obvious symbolic power is its market value. It is what money can buy, not money itself that gives it value. But money's symbolic power is not limited to its market value. Since money has no intrinsic meaning of its own, it can symbolize almost any need an individual wants it to represent. In other words, money can mean whatever people want it to mean.

4.1 DEFINITION

Motivation is a psychological feature that induces an organism to act towards a desired goal and elicits, controls and sustains certain goal-directed behaviours. It can be considered a driving force; a psychological one that compels or reinforces an action toward a desired goal. For example, hunger is a motivation that elicits a desire to eat. Motivation is the purpose or psychological cause of an action.

Motivation has been shown to have roots in physiological, behavioural, cognitive, and social areas. Motivation may be rooted in a basic impulse to optimize well-being, minimize physical pain and maximize pleasure. It can also originate from specific physical needs such as eating, sleeping or resting, and sex.

Motivation is an inner drive to behave or act in a certain manner. "It's the difference between waking up before dawn to pound the pavement and lazing around the house all day". These inner conditions such as wishes, desires and goals, activate to move in a particular direction in behaviour.

According to George R. Terry, "Motivation is the desire within an individual that stimulates him or her to action". In the words of Robert Dubin, it is "the complex of forces starting and keeping a person at work in an organisation". Viteles defines motivation as "an unsatisfied need which creates a state of tension or disequilibrium, causing the individual to move in a goal directed pattern towards restoring a state of equilibrium, by satisfying the need". According to Encyclopedia of Management. "Motivation refers to the degree of readiness of an organism to pursue some designated goals and implies the determination of the nature and locus of force inducing a degree of readiness".

On the basis of above definitions, the following observations can be made regarding motivation:

- Motivation is an inner psychological force, which activates and compels the person to behave in a particular manner.
- The motivation process is influenced by personality traits, learning abilities, perception and competence of an individual.
- A highly motivated employee works more efficiently and his level of production tends to be higher than others.
- Motivation originates from the needs and wants of an individual. It is a tension of lacking something in his mind, which forces him to work more efficiently.
- Motivation is also a process of stimulating and channelizing the energy of an individual for achieving set goals.
- Motivation also plays a crucial role in determining the level of performance. Highly motivated employees get higher satisfaction, which may lead to higher efficiency.
- Motivating force and its degree, may differ from individual to individual depending on his personality, needs, competence and other factors.
- The process of motivation helps the manager in analyzing and understanding human behaviour and finding that how an individual can be inspired to produce desirable working behaviour.
- Motivation may be positive as well as negative. Positive motivation includes incentives, rewards and other benefits while negative motivation implies some punishment, fear, use of force etc.

The motivation procedure contributes to and boosts up the morale of the employees. A high degree of motivation may lead to high morale.

4.2 FEATURES OF MOTIVATION

The following are the features of motivation:

- It is an internal feeling and forces a person to action.
- It is a continuous activity.
- It varies from person to person and from time to time.
- It may be positive or negative.

4.3 IMPORTANCE OF MOTIVATION

Motivation is an important part of managing process. A team of highly qualified and motivated employees is necessary for achieving objectives of an organisation because of the following reasons:

- Motivated employees make optimum use of available resources for achieving objectives.
- Motivation is directly related to the level of efficiency of employees.

- Motivated employees make full use of their energy and other abilities to raise the existing level of efficiency.
- Motivated employees make goal-directed efforts. They are more committed and cooperative for achieving organisational objectives.
- Motivated employees are more loyal and sincere to an organisation. These factors help reduce absenteeism and labour turnover.
- Motivation is considered as a backbone of good industrial relations.
- Effectively motivated employees get more job satisfaction and possess high morale.
- Motivation also helps in improving the image of an organisation.

The motivation process begins with identification of individual needs. For example, when an employee feels underpaid then what, then he tries to fulfill his needs by asking for a raise or by working harder to earn a raise or by seeking a new job. He then chooses to pursue one or more of these options for instance, working harder while simultaneously looking for a job. If his hard work resulted in a pay rise, he probably feels satisfied and will continue to work hard. But if no raise has been provided he is likely to try another option. Since people have many different needs, the satisfaction of one need or set of needs is likely to give rise to the identification of other needs. Thus, the cycle of motivation is constantly repeated.

Understanding human motivation is crucial for managing people. Extensive research has been performed to find out what makes people work and how to motivate them. This includes managers, social scientists, behaviourists and psychologists. A number of theories have been developed, even though there is no universally acceptable motivation theory. Understanding these theories facilitates the managers to get a better insight into the human behaviour.

4.4 THE MOTIVATIONAL FRAMEWORK

Motivation is the set of forces that leads people to behave in particular ways. Motivation is important in organisations because, in conjunction with ability and environment, it determines performance. This framework provides a useful way to see how motivational processes occur. When people experience a need deficiency, they seek ways to satisfy it, which results in a choice of goal-directed behaviours. After performing the behaviour, the individual experiences rewards or punishments that affect the original need deficiency. Figure 4.2 showing motivational framework.

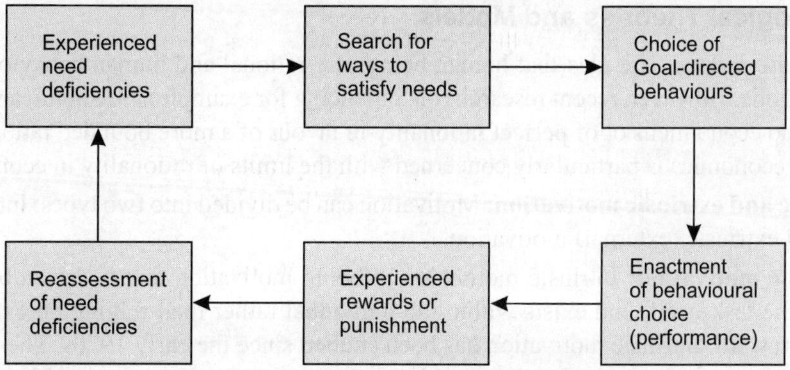

Fig. 4.2: Motivational frame work

4.5 HISTORICAL PERSPECTIVES ON MOTIVATION

Historical views on motivation, although not always accurate, are of interests for several reasons. For one thing, they provide a foundation for contemporary thinking about motivation; an appreciation of their strengths and weaknesses can help managers gain useful insights into employee motivation in the workplace. One early view of motivation was based on the concept of hedonism: The notion that people seek pleasure and comfort and avoid pain and discomfort. Scientific management assumed that employees are motivated by money. The human relations approach to motivation suggested that favorable employee attitudes result in motivation to work hard. Need theories of motivation assume that need deficiencies cause behaviour.

Motivational theories in general are a class of theories about why people do things seeks to reduce the number of factors down to one and explain all behaviour through that one factor. For example, economics has been criticized for using self-interest as a mono-motivational theory. Mono-motivational theories are often criticized for being too reductive or too abstract.

Conscious and unconscious motivations: A number of motivational theories emphasize the distinction between conscious and unconscious motivations. In evolutionary psychology, the "ultimate", unconscious motivation may be a cold evolutionary calculation; the conscious motivation could be more benign or even positive emotions. For example, while it may be in the best interest of a male's genes to have multiple partners and thus break up with or divorce one before moving onto the next, the conscious rationalization could be, "I loved her at the time".

Freud is associated with the idea that human beings have many unconscious motivations that cause them to make important decisions because of these unconscious forces, such as choosing a partner.

(a) Non-Psychological Theories

1. Platonic theory of motivation: In *The Republic*, Plato advances a tri-partite theory of the soul, which consists of three parts: Reason, spirit and appetite. All parts of the soul have desires, however not all desires are the same. Desires take many different forms and have many different responses or results.

2. Machiavellianism : Machiavellianism argues that human beings are motivated to seek power and status above all. Modern research argues that people who are high in this trait do indeed seek power and money, and are willing to use others as instruments towards that end.

(b) Psychological Theories and Models

1. Rational motivations: The idea that human beings are rational and human behaviour is guided by reason is an old one. However, recent research (on Satisficing for example) has significantly undermined the idea of homo economicus or of perfect rationality in favour of a more bounded rationality. The field of behavioural economics is particularly concerned with the limits of rationality in economic agents.

2. Intrinsic and extrinsic motivation: Motivation can be divided into two types: Intrinsic (internal) motivation and extrinsic (external) motivation.

(*i*) Intrinsic motivation: Intrinsic motivation refers to motivation that is driven by an interest or enjoyment in the task itself, and exists within the individual rather than relying on external pressures or a desire for reward. Intrinsic motivation has been studied since the early 1970s. The phenomenon of intrinsic motivation was first acknowledged within experimental studies of animal behaviour. In these studies, it was evident that the organisms would engage in playful and curiosity driven behaviours in the absence of reward. Intrinsic motivation is a natural motivational tendency and is a critical element in cognitive, social, and physical development. Students who are intrinsically motivated are more likely to engage in the task willingly as well as work to improve their skills, which will increase their capabilities. Students are likely to be intrinsically motivated if they:

- Attribute their educational results to factors under their own control, also known as autonomy.
- Believe they have the skills to be effective agents in reaching their desired goals, also known as self-efficacy beliefs.
- Are interested in mastering a topic, not just in achieving good grades.

***(ii)* Extrinsic motivation:** Extrinsic motivation refers to the performance of an activity in order to attain an outcome, whether or not that activity is also intrinsically motivated. Extrinsic motivation comes from outside of the individual. Common extrinsic motivations are rewards (for example money or grades) for showing the desired behaviour, and the threat of punishment following misbehaviour. Competition is in an extrinsic motivator because it encourages the performer to win and to beat others, not simply to enjoy the intrinsic rewards of the activity. A cheering crowd and the desire to win a trophy are also extrinsic incentives.[8]

***(iii)* Comparison of intrinsic and extrinsic motivation:** Social psychological research has indicated that extrinsic rewards can lead to over-justification and a subsequent reduction in intrinsic motivation. In one study demonstrating this effect, children who expected to be (and were) rewarded with a ribbon and a gold star for drawing pictures spent less time playing with the drawing materials in subsequent observations than children who were assigned to an unexpected reward condition. While the provision of extrinsic rewards might reduce the desirability of an activity, the use of extrinsic constraints, such as the threat of punishment, against performing an activity has actually been found to increase one's intrinsic interest in that activity. In one study, when children were given mild threats against playing with an attractive toy, it was found that the threat actually served to increase the child's interest in the toy, which was previously undesirable to the child in the absence of threat.

For those children who received no extrinsic reward, self-determination theory proposes that extrinsic motivation can be internalized by the individual if the task fits with their values and beliefs and therefore helps to fulfill their basic psychological needs.

3. Operant conditioning: Operant conditioning, a term coined by B.F. Skinner, is a method of learning that occurs through rewards and punishments for behaviour. Skinner believed that internal thoughts and motivations could not be used to explain behaviour; instead to look at external, observable causes of human behaviour. His theory explained how we acquire the range of learned behaviours we exhibit each and every day.

4. Drives: A drive or desire can be described as *a deficiency or need that activates behaviour that is aimed at a goal or an incentive*. These drives are thought to originate within the individual and may not require external stimuli to encourage the behaviour. Basic drives could be sparked by deficiencies such as hunger, which motivates a person to seek food whereas more subtle drives might be the desire for praise and approval, which motivates a person to behave in a manner pleasing to others. Another basic drive is the sexual drive which like food motivates us because it is essential to our survival. The desire for sex is wired deep into the brain of all human beings as glands secrete hormones that travel through the blood to the brain and stimulates the onset of sexual desire. The hormone involved in the initial onset of sexual desire is called dihydroepiandosterone (DHEA). The hormonal basis of both men and women's sex drives is testosterone. Men naturally have more testosterone than women do and so are more likely than woman to think about sex, have sexual fantasies, seek sex and sexual variety (whether positions or partners), masturbate, want sex at an early point in a relationship, sacrifice other things for sex, have permissive attitudes for sex, and complain about low sex drive in their partners.

By contrast, the role of extrinsic rewards and stimuli can be seen in the example of training animals by giving them treats when they perform a trick correctly. The treat motivates the animals to perform the trick consistently, even later when the treat is removed from the process.

There are a number of drive theories. The *Drive Reduction Theory* grows out of the concept that people have certain biological drives, such as hunger. As time passes the strength of the drive increases if it is not satisfied (in this case by eating). Upon satisfying a drive the drive's strength is reduced. The theory is based on diverse ideas from the theories of Freud to the ideas of feedback control systems, such as a thermostat.

Drive theory has some intuitive or folk validity. For instance, when preparing food, the drive model appears to be compatible with sensations of rising hunger as the food is prepared and after the food has been consumed, a decrease in subjective hunger. There are several problems, however, that leave the validity of drive reduction open for debate. The first problem is that it does not explain how secondary reinforcers reduce drive. For example, money satisfies no biological or psychological needs, but a pay check appears to reduce drive through second-order conditioning. Secondly, a drive, such as hunger, is viewed as having a "desire" to eat, making the drive a homuncular being—a feature criticized as simply moving the fundamental problem behind this "small man" and his desires.

Drive reduction theory cannot be a complete theory of behaviour, or a hungry human could not prepare a meal without eating the food before he finished cooking it. The ability of drive theory to cope with all kinds of behaviour, from not satisfying a drive (by adding on other traits such as restraint), or adding additional drives for "tasty" food, which combine with drives for food in order to explain cooking render it hard to test.

5. Cognitive dissonance theory: Suggested by Leon Festinger, cognitive dissonance occurs when an individual experiences some degree of discomfort resulting from an inconsistency between two cognitions: Their views on the world around them, and their own personal feelings and actions. For example, a consumer may seek to reassure themselves regarding a purchase, feeling in retrospect that another decision may have been preferable. Their feeling that another purchase would have been preferable is inconsistent with their action of purchasing the item. The difference between their feelings and beliefs causes dissonance, so they seek to reassure themselves.

While not a theory of motivation, per se, the theory of cognitive dissonance proposes that people have a motivational drive to reduce dissonance. The cognitive miser perspective makes people want to justify things in a simple way in order to reduce the effort they put into cognition. They do this by changing their attitudes, beliefs, or actions, rather than facing the inconsistencies, because dissonance is a mental strain. Dissonance is also reduced by justifying, blaming, and denying. It is one of the most influential and extensively studied theories in social psychology.

6. Content Theories of Motivation: Motivation theories can be divided into two approaches: Content and process. Content (or static) theories focus on internal or intrapersonal factors that energize, direct, sustain, and/or prohibit behaviours. These theories explain sources of motivation by focusing on individual needs. Process theories, on the other hand, attempt to identify factors that motivate, energize, sustain, and/or stop behaviours. For example, process theories focus on expectations about effort and performance that affect motivation, expectancies and reinforcements, goals and perceived equity. We begin by explaining the content need theories of Maslow, Alderfer, Herzberg, and McClelland.

7. Need-Based Theories of Motivation: Need-based theories try to answer the question, "what factor(s) motivate people to choose certain behaviours"? Some of the widely known need-based theories are as follows:

4.6 MASLOW'S NEEDS HIERARCHY

Maslow Abraham proposed his theory in the 1940s. This theory, popularly known as the Hierarchy of Needs assumes that people are motivated to satisfy five levels of needs: Physiological, security, belongingness, esteem and self-actualization needs. It's probably safe to say that the most well known theory of motivation is Abraham Maslow's hierarchy of needs. He hypothesized that within every human being there exists a hierarchy of five needs. These needs are:

(*a*) **Physiological:** Includes hunger, thirst, shelter, sex and other bodily needs.

(*b*) **Safety:** Includes security and protection from physical and emotional harm.

(*c*) **Social:** Includes affection, belongingness, acceptance and friendship.

(*d*) **Esteem:** Includes internal esteem factors such as self-respect, autonomy and achievement, and external esteem factors such as status, recognition and attention.

(*e*) **Self-actualization:** The drive to become what one is capable of becoming; includes growth, achieving one's potential and self-fulfillment.

Maslow suggested that the five levels of needs are arranged in accordance with their importance, starting from the bottom of the hierarchy. An individual is motivated first and foremost to satisfy physiological needs. When these needs are satisfied, he is motivated and 'moves up' the hierarchy to satisfy security needs. This 'moving up process continues until the individual reaches the self-actualization level. Physiological needs represent the basic issues of survival such as food, sex, water and air. In organisational settings, most physiological needs are satisfied by adequate wages and by the work environment itself, which provides employees with rest rooms, adequate lighting, comfortable temperatures and ventilation.

Security or safety needs refer to the requirements for a secure physical and emotional environment. Examples include the desire for adequate housing and clothing, the need to be free from worry about money and job security and the desire for safe working conditions. Security needs are satisfied for people in the work place by job continuity, a grievance resolving system and an adequate insurance and retirement benefit package. Belonging or social needs are related to the, social aspect of human life. They include the need for love and affection and the need to be accepted by one's peers. For most people these needs are satisfied by a combination of family and community relationships and friendships on the job. Managers can help ensure the satisfaction of these important needs by allowing social interaction and by making employees feel like part of a team or work group.

Esteem needs actually comprise of two different sets of needs:

- The need for a positive self-image and self-respect.
- The need for recognition and respect from others.

Organisations can help address esteem needs by providing a variety of external symbols of accomplishment such as job titles and spacious offices. At a more fundamental level, organisations can also help satisfy esteem needs by providing employees with challenging job assignments that can induce a sense of accomplishment. At the top of the hierarchy are those needs, which Maslow defines the self-actualization needs. These needs involve realizing one's potential for continued growth and individual development. Since these needs are highly individualized and personal, self-actualization needs are perhaps the most difficult for managers to address. Therefore, an employee should try to meet these needs on his own end.

However, an organisation can help his employee by creating a climate for fulfillment of self-actualization needs. For instance, an organisation can help in fulfillment of these needs by encouraging employee's participation in decision-making process and by providing them with an opportunity to learn new things about their jobs and organisation. This process of contributing to actual organisational performance helps employees experience personal growth and development associated with self-actualizing.

Maslow's hierarchy of needs consists of five basic categories of needs. This Fig. 4.3 illustrates both general and organisational examples of each type of need. Of course, each individual has a wide variety of specific needs within each category.

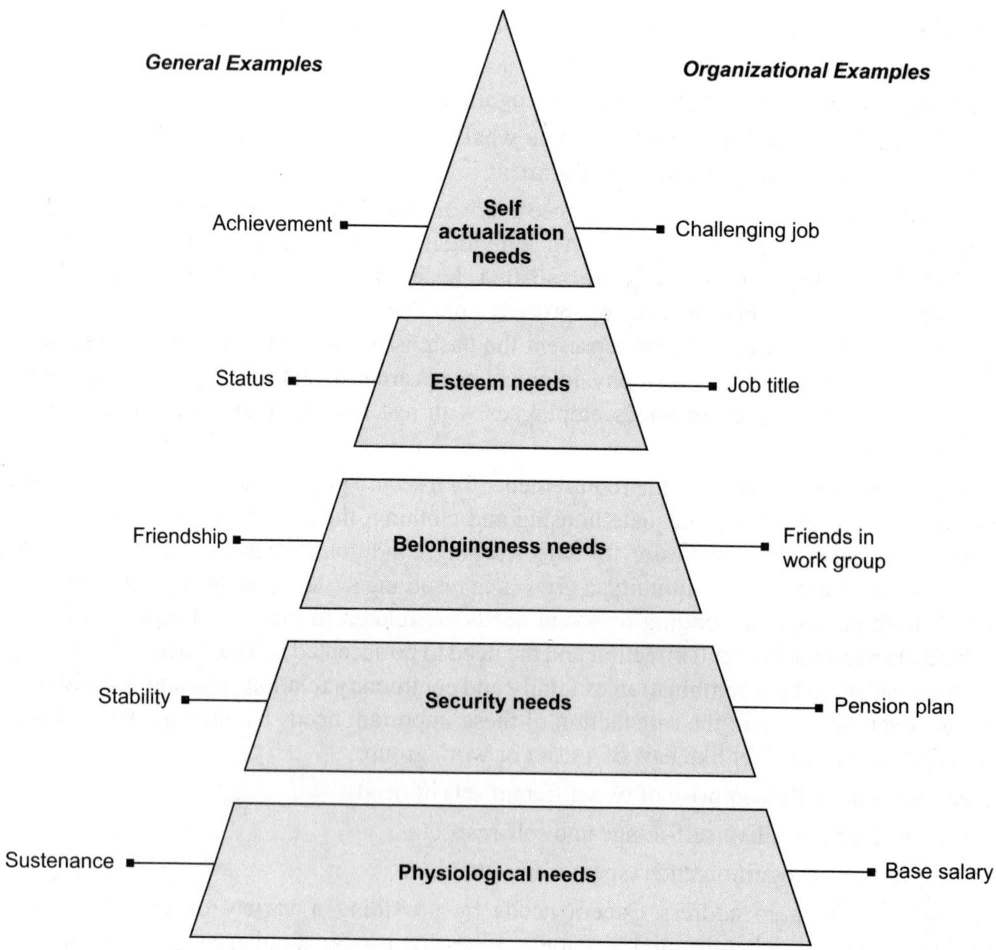

Fig. 4.3: Showing examples of Maslow's Theory

Maslow separated the five needs into higher and lower orders. Physiological and safety needs were described as lower order and social, esteem and self-actualisation as higher order needs. The differentiation between the two orders was made on the premise that higher-order needs are satisfied internally (within the person), whereas lower-order needs are predominantly satisfied externally.

Evaluation of Maslow's Theory

The research studies clearly made clear that Maslow is not the final answer in work motivation. Maslow's need hierarchy provides researchers and practitioners neither with a system that gives do not complete understanding nor one that is invariant in its application, but it does provide a provocative template for the appreciation of the question of why people act as they do or what is motivation? Even in its awkward form, Maslow's model seems to apply to underdeveloped countries. A survey of 200 factory workers in India points out that they give top priority to lower level needs.

Other studies also reveal that Maslow's model applies to managers and professional employees in developed countries like the U.K, and the U.S.A. American philosophers reveal that human needs do not conform to a hierarchy as suggested by Maslow. Hall and Nougaim found that as managers advance in an organisation, their physiological and safety needs tend to decrease in importance, and their needs for affiliation, esteem, and self-actualization tend to increase. Further, Porter's research indicates that managers at all levels had similar security and social needs and that the three higher needs on the hierarchy, developed by Maslow, varied greatly with managerial ranks.

Maslow's concept of the need hierarchy possesses a certain intuitive logic and has been accepted universally by managers. But research has revealed several shortcomings of the theory such as some research has found that five levels of needs are not always present and that the order of the levels is not always the same as assumed by Maslow. Moreover, it is difficult for organisations to use the need hierarchy to enhance employee motivation.

In fact, the natural conclusion to be drawn from Maslow's classification is that in times of economic plenty, almost all permanently employed workers have their lower-order needs substantially met. Litter support was found for the prediction that needs structures are organized along the dimensions proposed by Maslow, that unsatisfied needs motivate, or that a satisfied need activates movement to a new need level.

4.7 MOTIVATION-HYGIENE THEORY

Another popular need-based approach to motivation is the dual-structure approach developed by Frederick Herzberg. This is also known as Two-factor Theory. Herzberg developed this approach after interviewing 200 accountants and engineers in Pittsburg. He asked them to recall such occasions when they had been dissatisfied and less motivated. He found that entirely different sets of factors were associated with satisfaction and dissatisfaction. For instance, an individual who identified 'low pay' as causing dissatisfaction did not necessarily mention 'high pay' as a cause of satisfaction. Instead, several other factors, such as recognition or accomplishment, were cited as causing satisfaction.

This finding suggests that satisfaction and dissatisfaction are at opposite ends of a single scale. Employees would, therefore, be satisfied, dissatisfied or somewhere in between. Herzberg argued that attitudes and motivation consists of a dual structure. One structure involves a set of factors that result in feelings ranging from satisfaction to no satisfaction. The other structure involves a set of factors that result in feelings ranging from dissatisfaction to no satisfaction.

Herzberg identified two sets of factors responsible for causing either satisfaction or dissatisfaction. The factors influencing satisfaction are called motivation factors or motivators, which are related specifically to the job itself and the factors causing dissatisfaction are called hygiene factors, which are related to the work environment in which the job is performed.

Motivators

- Achievement
- Recognition
- Advancement
- The work itself
- The possibility of personal growth
- Responsibility

Hygiene or Maintenance Factors

- Company policies
- Technical supervision
- Interpersonal relations with supervisor
- Interpersonal relations with peers
- Interpersonal relations with subordinates
- Salary
- Job security
- Personal life
- Work conditions
- Status

Based on these findings, Herzberg recommended that managers seeking to motivate employees should first make sure that hygiene factors are taken care of and that employees are not dissatisfied with pay, security and working conditions. Once a manager has eliminated employee dissatisfaction, Hertzberg recommends focusing on a different set of factors to increase motivation, by improving opportunities for advancement, recognition, advancement and growth. Specifically, he recommends job enrichment as a means of enhancing the availability of motivation factors. Figure 4.4 showing motivation and hygiene factors.

According to Herzberg, the factors leading to job satisfaction are separate and distinct from those that lead to job dissatisfaction. Therefore, managers who seek to eliminate factors that create job dissatisfaction can bring about peace, but not necessarily motivation. They will be placating their work force rather than motivating them. As a result, such characteristics as company policy and administration, supervision, interpersonal relations, working conditions, and salary have been characterized by Herzberg as hygiene factors. When they are adequate, people will not be dissatisfied; however, neither will they be satisfied. If we want to motivate people on their jobs, Herzberg suggests emphasizing achievement, recognition, the work itself, responsibility, and growth. These are the characteristics that people find intrinsically rewarding.

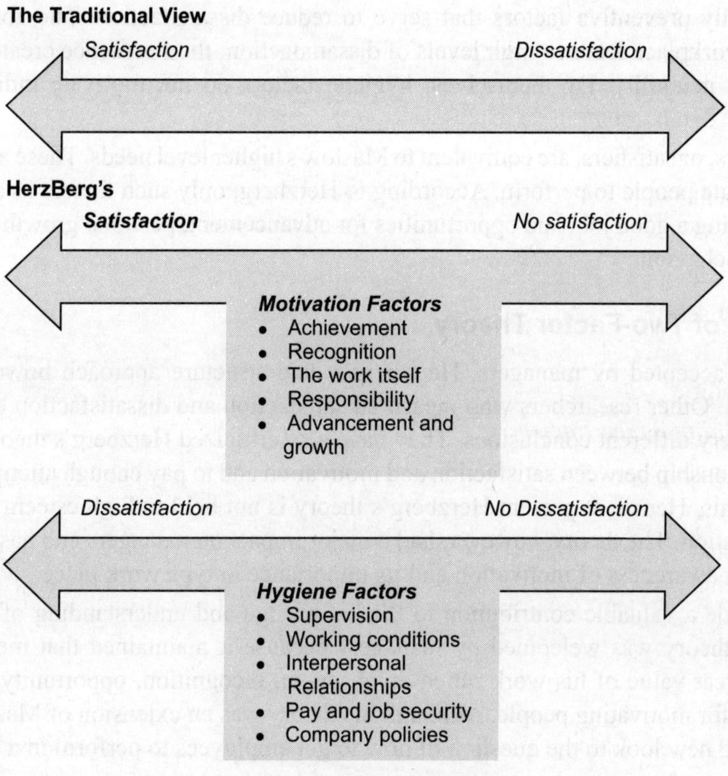

Fig. 4.4: Showing motivation and hygiene factors

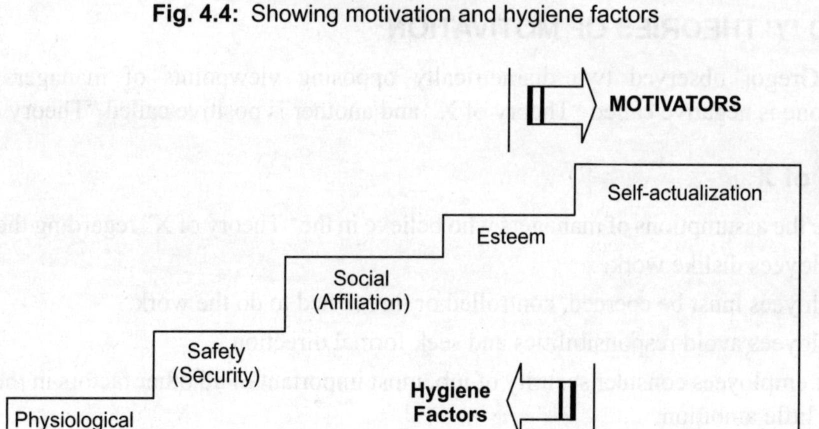

Fig. 4.5: Showing the relationship between the motivation-hygiene theory and Maslow's hierarchy of needs

(a) Herzberg Versus Maslow

Herzberg reduced Maslow's five need levels into two distinct levels of analysis. The hygiene factors, or dissatisfiers, are analogous to Maslow's lower-level needs such as physiological, safety and social.

They are essentially preventive factors that serve to reduce dissatisfaction. The absence of hygiene factors from the workplace leads to high levels of dissatisfaction; their presence creates a state of 'zero dissatisfaction' or neutrality. By themselves, hygiene factors do not motivate individuals to better performance.

The motivators, or satisfiers, are equivalent to Maslow's higher level needs. These are the job-content factors that motivate people to perform. According to Herzberg, only such factors as a challenging job, recognition for doing a good job, and opportunities for advancement, personal growth and development foster motivated behaviour.

(b) Evaluation of Two-Factor Theory

Although widely accepted by managers, Hertzberg's dual structure approach however suffers from certain drawbacks. Other researchers who measured satisfaction and dissatisfaction based on different aspects reached very different conclusions. They have also criticized Herzberg's theory for its inability to define the relationship between satisfaction and motivation and to pay enough attention to differences between individuals. Hence, at present Herzberg's theory is not held in high esteem by researchers in the field of motivation. The theory, however, had a major impact on managers and has played a key role in increasing their awareness of motivation and its importance in type work place.

Herzberg made a valuable contribution to the knowledge and understanding of the nature of job satisfaction. His theory was welcomed by managers because it maintained that money is not a true motivator. The great value of his work relied emphasis on recognition, opportunity for advancement and other factors for motivating people. Although his theory was an extension of Maslow's need-based theory, it provided new look to the question of how to get employees to perform in a better way.

4.8 'X' AND 'Y' THEORIES OF MOTIVATION

Douglas McGregor observed two diametrically opposing viewpoints of managers 'about their employees'; one is negative called "Theory of X" and another is positive called "Theory of Y".

(a) Theory of X

Following are the assumptions of managers who believe in the "Theory of X" regarding their employees.

- Employees dislike work.
- Employees must be coerced, controlled or threatened to do the work.
- Employees avoid responsibilities and seek formal direction.
- Most employees consider security of job, most important of all other factors in the job and have very little ambition.

(b) Theory of Y

Following are the assumptions of managers who believe in the "Theory of Y" regarding their employees.

- Employees love work as play or rest.
- Employees are self-directed and self-controlled and committed to the organisational objectives.
- Employees accept and seek responsibilities.
- Innovative spirit is not confined to managers alone, some employees also possess it.

In short, Douglas McGregor proposed two distinct views of human beings: One basically negative, labeled Theory X, and the other basically positive, labeled Theory Y. After viewing the way in which managers dealt with employees, McGregor concluded that a manager's view of the nature of human beings is based on a certain grouping of assumptions and that he or she tends to mould his or her behaviour towards subordinates according to the assumptions described above.

(c) Applicability of Theories 'X' and 'Y'

Theory 'X' in its applicability, places exclusive reliance upon external control of human behaviour, while theory 'Y', relies heavily on self-control and self-direction.

Theory 'X' points to the traditional approach of management. Literally, this theory of behaviour is related to organisations that lay hard and rigid standards of work-behaviour. Some examples of such organisations are organisations that break down jobs into specialized elements, establish norms of production, design equipment to control worker's pace of work, have rigid rules and regulations, which are sometimes very vigorously enforced.

Theory 'Y', on the other hand, secures the commitment of employees to organisational objectives. This motivational theory places emphasis on satisfaction of employees. While applying this theory, the use of authority, as an instrument of command and control is minimal. Employees exercise self-direction and self-control.

The concepts of 'Job' Enlargement, 'Participation' and 'Management by Objectives' are quite consistent with theory 'Y'.

McGregor supports the applicability of motivational theory 'Y', instead of theory 'X'. Organisation should keep in mind that once theory 'X' is employed for organisational working, it is difficult for the management to shift to theory 'Y', all of a sudden. However, with systematic, judicious and slow steps, shifting in the practical applicability of Theory 'X' to Theory 'Y' usually can be achieved.

Again , Theory X assumes that lower-order needs dominate individuals. McGregor himself held to the belief that Theory Y assumptions were more valid than Theory X. Therefore, he proposed such ideas as participative decision making, responsible and challenging jobs, and good group relations as approaches that would maximise an employee's job motivation. Unfortunately, there is no evidence to confirm that either set of assumptions is valid or that accepting Theory Y assumptions and altering one's actions accordingly will lead to more motivated workers.

4.9 ERG THEORY

Clayton Alderfer of Yale University has reworked Maslow's need hierarchy to align it more closely with the empirical research. His revised need hierarchy is labeled ERG theory. Alderfer argues that there are groups of core need—existence, relatedness, and growth—hence, the label: ERG theory. The existence group is concerned with providing our basic material existence requirements. They include the items that Maslow considered to be physiological and safety needs. The second groups of needs are those of relatedness—the desire we have for maintaining important interpersonal relationships. These social and status desires require interaction with others if they are to be satisfied, and they align with Maslow's social need and the external component of Maslow's esteem classification. Finally, Alderfer isolates growth needs—an intrinsic desire for personal development. These include the intrinsic component from Maslow's esteem category and the characteristics included under self-actualisation.

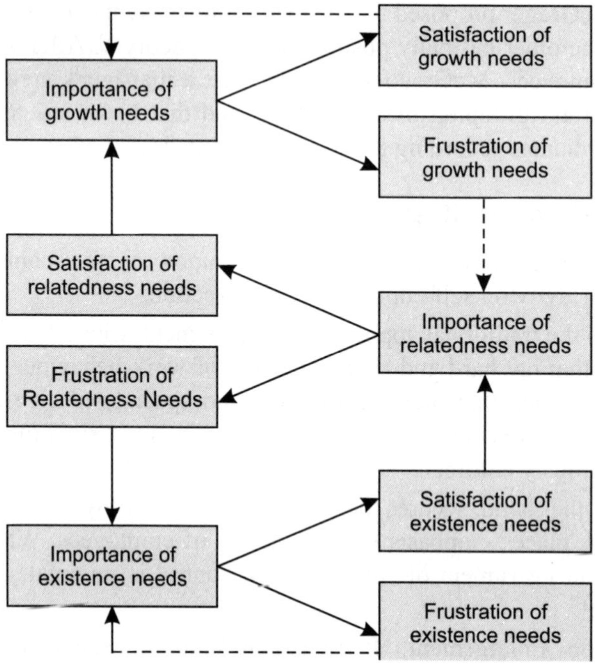

Fig. 4.6: ERG Theory framework

As shown in Fig. 4.6, the ERG theory demonstrates that (1) more than one need may be operative at the same time, and if the gratification of a higher-level need is stifled, the desire to satisfy a lower - level need increases. ERG theory also contains a frustration-regression dimension. Maslow, argued that an individual would stay at a certain need level until that need was satisfied. ERG theory counters by noting that when a higher-order need level is frustrated; the individuai's desire to increase a lower level need takes place. Inability to satisfy a need for social interaction, for instance, might increase the desire for more money or better working conditions. So frustration chanced to a regression to a lower need.

Although ERG Theory assumes that motivated behaviour follows a hierarchy in somewhat the same fashion as suggested by Maslow, there are two important differences. Firstly, ERG theory suggests that more than one kind of need might motivate a person at the same time. For example, it allows for the possibility that people can be motivated by a desire for money (existence); friendship (relatedness), and an opportunity to learn new skills (growth) all at the same time.

Secondly, ERG theory has an element of frustrations-regression that is missing from Maslow's need hierarchy. Maslow maintained that one heed must be satisfied before an individual can progress to needs at a higher level, for example, from security needs to belongingness. This is termed as satisfaction-progression process. Although the ERG theory includes this process, it also suggests that if needs remain unsatisfied at some higher level, the individual will become frustrated, regress to a lower level and will begin to pursue low level needs again. For example, a worker previously motivated by money (existence needs) is awarded a pay rise to satisfy this need. Then he attempts to establish more friendship to satisfy relatedness needs. If for some reason an employee finds that it is impossible to become better friends with others in the workplace, he may eventually become frustrated and regress to being motivated to earn even more money. This is termed as 'frustration-regression' process.

In short, Alderfer, expanding on Maslow's hierarchy of needs, created the *ERG theory*. This theory posits that there are three groups of core need—existence, relatedness, and growth, hence the label: ERG theory. The existence group is concerned with providing our basic material existence requirements. They include the items that Maslow considered to be physiological and safety needs. The second group of needs is those of relatedness—the desire we have for maintaining important personal relationships. These social and status desires require interaction with others if they are to be satisfied, and they align with Maslow's social need and the external component of Maslow's esteem classification. Finally, Alderfer isolates growth needs as an intrinsic desire for personal development. These include the intrinsic component from Maslow's esteem category and the characteristics included under self-actualization.

The ERG theory emphasis on the following key points regarding needs:

- Some needs may be more important than others.
- People may change their behaviour after any particular set of needs has been satisfied.

ERG theory is more consistent with our knowledge of individual differences among people. Variables such as education, family background, and cultural environment can alter the importance or driving force that a group of needs holds for a particular individual. The evidence demonstrating that people in other cultures rank the need categories differently. For instance, natives of Spain and Japan place social needs before their physiological requirements would be consistent with ERG theory.

4.10 SELF-DETERMINATION THEORY

During the early nineties Edward L. Deci and Richard M. Ryan proposed the self-determination theory (SDT). This theory focuses on the degree to which an individual's behaviour is self-motivated and self-determined. SDT identifies three innate needs that, if satisfied, allow optimal function and growth: Competence, relatedness and autonomy. These three psychological needs motivate the self to initiate specific behaviour and mental nutriments that are essential for psychological health and well-being. When these needs are satisfied, there are positive consequences, such as well-being and growth, leading people to be motivated, productive and happy. When they are thwarted, people's motivation, productivity and happiness plummet.

There are three essential elements to the theory.

- Humans are inherently proactive with their potential and mastering their inner forces (such as drive and emotions).
- Humans have an inherent tendency towards growth, development and integrated functioning.
- Optimal development and actions are inherent in humans but they do not happen automatically.

4.11 McCLELLAND'S THEORY OF NEEDS

Achievement motivation is an integrative perspective based on the premise that performance motivation results from the way broad components of personality are directed towards performance. As a result, it includes a range of dimensions that are relevant to success at work but which are not conventionally regarded as being part of performance motivation. The emphasis on performance seeks to integrate formerly separate approaches as need for achievement with, for example, social motives like dominance. Personality is intimately tied to performance and achievement motivation, including such characteristics as tolerance for risk, fear of failure, and others.

Achievement motivation can be measured by The Achievement Motivation Inventory, which is based on this theory and assesses three factors (in 17 separated scales) relevant to vocational and professional success. This motivation has repeatedly been linked with adaptive motivational patterns, including working hard, a willingness to pick learning tasks with much difficulty, and contributing success to effort.

McClelland's Theory of Needs was developed by David McClelland and his associates. The theory focuses on three needs: achievement, power, and affiliation. They are defined as follows:

- ***Need for power***: The need to make others behave in a way that they would not have behaved otherwise.
- ***Need for affiliation***: The desire for friendly and close interpersonal relationships.
- ***Needs for achievement***: The drive to excel, to achieve in relation to a set of standards, to strive to succeed.

(a) Need for Power

According to this theory the need for power, which might be defined as the desire to be influential in a group and to control one's environment is an important motivation factor. Research suggests that people with a strong need for power, are likely to be superior performers and occupy supervisory positions. Such types of individuals generally look for positions of leadership, they act effectively, are outspoken, have a stubborn character and exert authority.

(b) Need for Affiliation

The need for affiliation means the desire for human companionship and acceptance. Those with a high need for affiliation often behave the way they think other people want them to, in an effort to maintain friendship. They prefer a job that entails a good deal of social interaction and offers opportunities to make friends. The principal characteristics of such peoples' traits are as follows:

- Desire to like and be liked.
- Enjoy company and friendship.
- Prefer cooperative situation.
- Excel in group task.
- Star attraction in gathering.
- Leadership qualities.

This need is closely associated with the "social-type" of personality, who are sociable, friendly, cooperative and understanding. Persons with high motivation for power and affiliation have better chances of becoming good managers.

(c) Need for Achievement

People with a high need for achievement, always feel ambitious to be successful; are ever prepared to face challenging situations and set arduous goals for themselves. They are prone to take calculated risks; and possess a high sense of personal responsibility in getting jobs done. These people are concerned with their progress, and feel inclined to put in longer hours of work "Failures never dishearten them and they are always ready to put in their best efforts for excellent performance".

Some people have a compelling drive to succeed. They're striving for personal achievement rather than the rewards of success per se. They have a desire to do something better or more efficiently than it has been done before. This drive is the achievement need. From research into the achievement need, McClelland found that high achievers differentiate themselves from others by their desire to do things better. They seek situations where they can attain personal responsibility for finding solutions to problems, where they can receive rapid feedback on their performance so they can tell easily whether they are improving or not, and where they can set moderately challenging goals.

High achievers are not gamblers; they dislike succeeding by chance. They prefer the challenge of working at a problem and accepting the personal responsibility for success or failure rather than leaving the outcome to chance or the actions of others. Importantly, they avoid what they perceive to be very easy or very difficult tasks. They want to overcome obstacles, but they want to feel that their success is due to their own actions. This means they like tasks of intermediate difficulty.

4.12 CONTENT THEORIES IN PERSPECTIVE

The five content theories of motivation we have discussed are summarized in Table 4.1. Taken together, these theories challenge leaders, managers, and organisational members to the following:

- Gain an understanding of their own needs and the needs of those with whom they work and manage regarding the nature of the work.
- Create learning environments that motivate the needs of individuals and terms to perform more effectively and with quality.

Table 4.1: Showing Needs Theories: A comparison

Maslow's need history	Alderfer's ERG theory	Herzberg's two-factor theory	McClelland's trichotomy
Physiological Safety and Security	Existence	Hygiene	
Belongingness and Love Self-esteem	Relatedness		Affiliation
Self-actualization	Growth	Motivators	Achievement Power

Some of the commonalities of the four theories include a recognition of the role that human needs play in organisation satisfaction, performance, and growth, and the distinction between lower and higher-level needs. Higher-level needs for Maslow include self-actualization, esteem, and belonging; for Alderfer they are growth and relatedness; for Herzberg motivational factors, and for McClelland they are achievement and power. There are important distinctions in the four theories. Maslow held to a hierarchy of five needs; Alderfer constructed a hierarchy of three needs with much more flexibility; Herzberg used two factors that did and did not motivate employees (e.g., dissatisfies). McClelland found that three needs common to all cultures; he viewed all people as learned and capable of being taught. Most of these theories lack sufficient empirical validation, especially from a cross-cultural perspective, but they are a starting point for discussing the role of human needs and motivation in the workplace. They can also be used to discover the effects of organisational change on individual's needs and motivations. Managers can use the vocabulary and concepts of the content theories in employee interviews and dialogues to identify development and training areas in which employee motivation can be improved.

4.13 PROCESS THEORIES OF MOTIVATION

The field of organisational behaviour has generally moved away from the needs theories of motivation. Needs theories are content-oriented, that is, they explain what the causes are leading to motivated behaviours. They do not explain why or how motivated behaviour occurs. These questions relate to behaviours or actions, goals and feelings of satisfaction. These concepts are addressed by various process-based theories to motivation. Process-based theories to motivation are concerned with how motivation occurs. They focus on why people choose to enact certain behavioural options to fulfill their needs and how they evaluate their satisfaction after they have attained these goals. Two of the most useful process-based approaches to motivation are expectancy theory and equity theory. Process theories use external variable to identify individual sources of motivation. Whereas content theories deal with intrapersonal, internal sources (i.e., needs) for motivation, process theories include perceived and actual exogenous, workplace, dimensions, for example, performance, goals, and tasks.

(a) Expectancy Theory

Currently, one of the most widely accepted explanations of motivation is Victor Vroom's expectancy theory. Basically, Vroom's expectancy theory views motivation as a process of governing choices. The expectancy theory tries to explain how and why people choose a particular behaviour over an alternative. The theory suggests that motivation depends on two things: How much an individual desires a particular goal and how likely he thinks he can get it. For instance, a person is looking for a job and reads an advertisement for a position of Marketing Executive with a starting salary of Rs. 3 lakh per year.

Even though he might want the job, he probably does not apply because he is aware that there is little chance of getting it. Next he sees an advertisement is for Field Supervisor for a salary of Re. 1 lakh per year. In this case he realizes that he can probably get the job, but still doesn't apply simply because he doesn't want it. Then he comes across another advertisement for a Management Trainee in a big organisation with a starting salary of Rs. 2 lakh per year. He chooses to apply for this job because he wants it and also thinks that he has a reasonable chance of getting it. The theory, therefore, focuses on three relationships. The strength of a tendency to act in a certain way depends on the strength of an expectation that the act will be followed by a given outcome and on the attractiveness of that outcome to the individual.

- **Effort performance relationship:** The probability perceived by the individual that exerting a given amount of effort would lead to performance.
- **Performance reward relationship:** The degree to which the individual believes that performing at a particular level will lead to the attainment of a desired outcome.
- **Rewards personal goals relationship:** The degree to which organisational rewards satisfy an individual's personal goals or needs and the attractiveness of those potential rewards for the individual.

The expectancy theory rests on four assumptions:

- The theory assumes that behaviour is determined by a combination of forces in the individual and in the environment.
- It assumes that people make decisions about their own behaviour in organisations.
- It assumes that different people have different types of needs, desires and goals.

- It assumes that people make choices from among alternative plans of behaviour based on their perceptions of the extent to which a given behaviour will lead to desired outcomes.

This model suggests that motivation leads to efforts and that effort, when combined with individual ability and environmental factors, result in performance. Performance, in turn, leads to various outcomes—each of which has an associated value called its 'valence'. According to this model, individuals develop some sense of these expectations before they exhibit motivated or non-motivated behaviour.

1. Effort-to-Performance Expectancy: The effort-to-performance expectancy refers to an individual's perception of the probability that effort will result in high performance. When an individual believes that effort will lead directly to high performance, expectancy is quite strong, that is close to 1.00. For instance, if one feels sure that studying hard for an examination (effort) will result in scoring high marks (performance), then his effort-to-performance expectancy is high, that is close to 1.0. When an individual believes that effort and performance are unrelated, the effort-to-performance expectancy is very weak, that is close to 0.0. Usually we are not sure about our expectations, so they fall somewhere between 0.0 and 1.0 with a moderate expectancy.

2. Performance-to-Outcome Expectancy: The performance-to-outcome expectancy means an individual's perception of the probability that performance will result in a specific outcome. For example, an individual who believes that high performance will lead to a pay raise has a high performance-to-outcome expectancy, approaching to 1.00. An individual who believes that high performance may possibly lead to a pay raise has a moderate expectancy between 1.00 and 0. And an individual who believes that performance has no relationship to rewards has a low performance-to-outcome expectancy that is close to 0.

3. Outcomes and Valences: Expectancy theory recognizes that an individual may experience a variety of outcomes as a consequence, of behaviour in an organisational environment. A high performer, for example, may get big pay raises, fast promotions and praise from the boss. However, he may also be subject to a lot of stress and incur resentment from co-workers. Each of these outcomes has an associated value or valence that is,, an index of how much an individual desires a particular outcome. If an individual wants an outcome, its valence is positive. If an individual does not want an outcome, its valence is negative. If an individual is indifferent to an outcome, its valence is zero. It is this advantage of expectancy theory that goes beyond the need-based approaches to motivation.

Thus, for motivated behaviour to occur on the part of any individual, three conditions must be met, which are as follows:

- First, the effort-to-performance expectancy must be greater than zero.
- Second, the performance-to-outcome expectancy must also be greater than zero.
- Third, the sum of the valences for all relevant outcomes must be greater than zero.

Expectancy theory maintains that when all of these conditions are met, the individual is motivated to expand effort. The expectancy theory also has several other important practical implications, which managers should keep in mind. The managers can perform the following activities in relation:

- Determine what outcomes employees prefer.
- Define, communicate and clarify the level of performance that is desired.
- Establish attainable performance goals.
- Link desired outcomes to performance goal achievement.

4. Practical Applicability of Expectancy Theory: If a manager wishes to motivate his employees for increased and better performance, then he has to make sure whether the reward system is highly supportive to hard work or high quality. The manager will particularly see that the specific system, as applicable in their case, is communicated to them, so as to make them feel confident that their energized efforts will be rewarded.

Another important point, which should not be ignored by the manager, is that rewards must correspond to the varying preferences of an individual employee. In conclusion, no doubt 'expectancy' theory has gained much popularity with theorists, but much more work still needs to be put in, before it can be accepted for use as an effective instrument of explanation of 'motivation' with all its implications.

5. The Porter-Lawler Extension: Porter and Lawler have proposed an interesting extension to the expectancy theory. The human relationists assumed that employee satisfaction causes good performance but research has not supported such relationship. Porter and Lawler suggest that there may indeed be a relationship between satisfaction and performance but that it goes in the opposite direction, that is, superior performance can lead to satisfaction.

(b) The Porter-Lawler Model

The Porter and Lawler expectancy model provides interesting insights into the relationships between satisfaction and performance. As illustrated here, this model predicts that satisfaction is determined by the perceived equity of intrinsic and extrinsic rewards for performance. That is, rather than satisfaction causing performance, which many people might predict, and this model argues that it is actually performance that eventually leads to satisfaction.

- Determine the primary outcomes each employee wants.
- Decide what levels and kinds of performance are needed to meet organisational goals.
- Make sure the desired levels of performance are possible.
- Link desired outcomes and desired performance.
- Analyze the situation for conflicting expectancies.
- Make sure the rewards are large enough.
- Make sure the overall system is equitable for everyone.

It is to be remembered always that an individual's initial effort is influenced firstly by his perception regarding the value of reward and the likelihood that the effort will yield a reward. The probability that increased effort will lead to improved performance is affected by an individual's traits, abilities and perception of his role in an organisation. The model also distinguishes between intrinsic and extrinsic rewards. Finally, the Porter-Lawler model borrows from equity theory the idea that the employee's satisfaction depends on the perceived equity of the rewards relative to the effort expended and the level of performance attained.

Implications for Managers: Expectancy theory can be useful for organisations attempting to improve the motivation of their employees. Nadler and Lawler suggest a series of steps for managers in applying the basic ideas of the theory.

1. They should determine the primary outcomes that each employee likely desires.
2. They should decide what kind and levels of performance are needed to meet organisational goals.

3. They should ascertain that the desired levels of performance are attainable.
4. They should ensure that desired outcomes and performance are linked.
5. They should also analyze the complete work situation for conflicting expectancies.
6. They should make sure that the rewards are large enough.
7. They should make sure that the overall system is equitable for everyone.

The expectancy theory has also its limitations. It is quite difficult to apply, for example, application of this theory in the workplace would require to identify all the potential outcomes for each employee, to determine all relevant expectancies and then to balance everything somehow to maximize employee motivation. Expectancy theory also assumes that people are rational, therefore, they will systematically consider all the potential outcomes and their associated expectancies before selecting a particular behaviour. However, few people actually make decisions in such a precise and rational manner.

(c) Equity Theory

J. Stacy Adams developed equity theory of motivation. The equity theory argues that motivations arise out of simple desire to be treated fairly. Equity can be defined as an individual's belief that he is being treated fairly relative to the treatment of others. A person's perception of equity develops through a four-step process as shown below:

1. First an individual evaluates the way he is being treated by an organisation.
2. The next step is for an individual to choose a co-worker who seems to be in a roughly similar situation and to observe how an organisation treats him.
3. In the crucial step of equity theory an individual 'compares' the two treatments.
4. In the fourth step evaluate a sense of equity to see if the two treatments seem similar or if they are different.

Adam suggests that employees make these comparisons by focusing on input and outcome ratios. An employee's contributions or input to an organisation include time, education, effort, experience and loyalty. Outcomes are what an individual receives from an organisation such as, pay, recognition and social relationships. The theory suggests that people view their outcomes and inputs as ratio and then-compare their ratio to the ratio of someone else. This other 'person' may be someone in the work group. The comparison may result in three types of attitudes:

- The individual may feel equitably rewarded.
- Under-rewarded.
- Over-rewarded.

An individual will experience a feeling of equity when the two ratios are equal. If an individual has the feeling of equity then he should maintain the status quo. If he has a feeling of inequity then he is likely to change the input. Equity theory recognizes that individuals are concerned not only with the absolute amount of rewards they receive for their efforts, but also with the relationship of this amount to what others receive. They make judgements as to the relationship between their inputs and outcomes and the inputs and outcomes of others.

Based on one's inputs, such as effort, experience, education, and competence, one compares outcomes such as salary levels, raises, recognition, and other factors. When people perceive an imbalance in their outcome-input ratio relative to others, tension is created. This tension provides the basis for motivation, as people strive for what they perceive as equity and fairness. Specifically, the theory establishes four propositions relating to inequitable pay:

1. Given payment by time, over-rewarded employees will produce more than will equitably paid employees.
2. Given payment by quantity of production, over-rewarded employees will produce fewer, but higher quality, units than will equitably paid employees.
3. Given payment by time, under-rewarded employees will produce less or poorer quality of output.
4. Given payment by quantity of production under-rewarded employees will produce a large number of low-quality units in comparison with equitably paid employees.

The single most important idea for managers to remember about equity theory is that if rewards are to motivate employees, they must be perceived as being equitable and fair. However, managers must remember that different employees have different sense towards basis for a reward and this may result in problems. Hence, the best way to avoid such problems is to make all employees aware of the basis for rewards.

(d) Reinforcement Based Approaches to Motivation

A final approach to the motivation process focuses on why some behaviour are maintained and changed overtime. Reinforcement-based approaches explain the role of those rewards as they cause behaviour to change or remain the same over time. Specifically, reinforcement theory is based on the fairly simple assumption that behaviours that result in rewarding consequences are likely to be repeated, whereas behaviour those results in punishing consequences are less likely to be repeated. There are similarities between expectancy theory and reinforcement theory. Both consider the processes by which an individual chooses behaviours in a particular situation. However, the expectancy theory focuses more on behaviour choices and the latter is more concerned with the consequences of those choices.

(e) Reinforcement Contingencies

Reinforcement contingencies are the possible outcomes that an individual may experience as a result of his or her behaviours. The four types of reinforcement contingencies that can affect individuals in an organisational setting are positive reinforcement, avoidance, punishment and extinction.

Positive Reinforcement is a method of strengthening behaviour. It is a reward or a positive outcome after a desired behaviour is performed. When a manager observes an employee is doing a good job and offers praise then this praise helps in positive reinforcement of behaviour. Other positive reinforces include pay, promotions and awards.

The other reinforcement, contingency that can strengthen desired behaviour is avoidance. This occurs when an individual chooses certain behaviour in order to avoid unpleasant consequences. For instance, an employee may come to work on time to avoid criticism.

Punishment is used by some managers to weaken undesired behaviours. The logic is that the unpleasant, consequence will reduce an undesirable behaviour again, for example, punishing with fine for coming late.

Extinction can also be used to weaken behaviour especially that has previously been rewarded. When an employee tells a vulgar joke and the boss laughs, the laughter reinforces the behaviour and the employee may continue to tell similar jokes. By simply ignoring this behaviour and not reinforcing it, the boss can cause the behaviour to subside which eventually becomes 'extinct'.

Positive reinforcement and punishment are the most common reinforcement contingencies practiced by organisations. Most managers prefer a judicious use of positive reinforcement and punishment. Avoidance and extinction are generally used only in specialized circumstances.

4.14 NEW APPROACHES TO MOTIVATION IN ORGANISATIONS

New approaches are emerging to supplement the established models and theories of motivation. Two of the most promising goals are Setting Theory and the Japanese Approach.

(a) Goal-Setting Theory

This approach to motivation has been pioneered in the USA by Edwin Locke and his associates in 1960s and refined in 1980s. Goal-setting theory suggests that managers and subordinates should set goals for an individual on a regular basis, as suggested by MBO. These goals should be moderately difficult and very specific and of type that an employee will accept and make a commitment to accomplishing them. Rewards should be tied directly to accomplished goals. When involved in goal-settings, employees see how their effort will lead to performance, rewards and personal satisfaction.

Salient features of this theory are as follows:

- Specific goal fixes the needs of resources and efforts.
- It increases performance.
- Difficult goals result higher performance than easy job.
- Better feedback of results leads to better performances than lack of feedback.
- Participation of employees in goal has mixed result.
- Participation of setting goal, however, increases acceptance of goal and involvements.
- Goal setting theory has defined two factors, which influences the performance. These are given below:
  (*i*) Goal commitment.
  (*ii*) Self-efficiency.

The mere act of goal setting does not ensure higher levels of motivation among employees. In fact, there seem to be three important criteria that goals must meet if they are to influence the behaviour of organisation members. They are goal specificity, goal difficulty and goal acceptance.

1. Goal Specificity: Goals must be stated in specific terms if they are to motivate effective performance. Goals must be set in terms of measurable criteria of work performance, *i.e.*, number of units produced, new sales etc., and must specify a time period within which the goal is to be attained. It also gives a sense of personal satisfaction and accomplishment to workers if he is able to meet the specific goal.

2. Goal Difficulty/Challenge: There exists a relationship between goal difficulty and work motivation. The more difficult and challenging the goal is, the higher the level of motivation and performance. However, it is essential that goals are set at realistic levels. Goals that are very difficult to achieve are unable to motivate since it is beyond the capacity of the concerned individual.

3. Goal Acceptance: In order to influence motivation and performance, a goal must be internalized by an individual. In other words, the person has to feel some personal ownership of the goal and must have commitment to achieve it.

4. Goal Setting in Practice: The most obvious implication of goal-setting theory is that managers should be helping subordinates to set goals that are specific and reasonably difficult so that subordinates accept and internalize them as their own goals. Besides this, there are a number of issues that arise in implementing goal setting in practice.

- Though specificity of goal is essential and measurability is desirable, it should not affect in identifying meaningful and valid objective of goal attainment.
- The manager can stimulate goal acceptance in at least three ways:
  (*i*) By involving subordinates in goal-setting process.
  (*ii*) By demonstrating a supportive attitude and approach towards his subordinates.
  (*iii*) By assigning various rewards to the achievement of goals.

Management By Objectives (MBO) is a managerial technique for improving motivation and performance using goal-setting principles.

5. Cognitive Evaluation Theory: A researcher 'Charms' reported in 1960 that extrinsic motivation like pay or rewards for a job, which has an intrinsic-motivation content, which is prior to such rewards. It tends to decrease overall level of motivation. This proposal is called Cognitive Evaluation Theory which has been supported by a large number of research studies conducted subsequently.

(b) Japanese Approach to Motivation

The Japanese approach to motivation has gained increasing popularity around the world during the past few years. This approach is rather a philosophy of management than a theory or model. The basic tenet of the Japanese approach is that managers and workers should perform together as partners. Since both of them see themselves as one group, all members are committed and motivated to work in the best interests of an organisation. No one is called an employee; instead everyone is a team member, team leader or coach and everyone owns the 'share' of an organisation. Like goal-setting meow, the Japanese approach is likely to become more common in businesses throughout the world.

(c) Integration of Motivation Theories

Thus several theories complicate our understanding. Some of these theories are compatible and some are not. The real challenge that a researcher has to face is integration of all or at least some of these together so that their inter and intra-relationships are established. This will also improve the understanding of motivation. Certain attempts are made in USA and elsewhere.

4.15 ENHANCING MOTIVATION IN ORGANISATIONS

Managers trying to enhance the motivation of their employees can, of course, draw on any of the theories described above. They may in practice adopt specific interventions derived from one or more theories or they may influence motivation through the organisation's reward system. The organisation can enhance motivation in following ways:

- ***Humanize the work environment:*** Respect the need to treat each employee as an individual.
- ***Publicize both short and long-term organisational goals:*** Encourage personal and departmental goal setting.
- ***Promote from within:*** It's great for morale and simplifies hiring procedures.
- ***Use incentive programs:*** Inducing the feeling that 'if you're creative enough, you won't have to rely on expensive financial bonuses'.
- ***Establish appropriate deadlines:*** Every project should have a deadline.
- ***Be liberal with praise:*** It's almost impossible to over praise and easy to under praise.
- Be consistent in your own work and in your relations with others.
- ***Show a personal interest in the people who work for you:*** Relations are always smoother between people who know each other on a personal basis than relations between people who merely want something from each other.
- ***Admit mistakes:*** People will respect you for it and will be less likely to hide their own mistakes.
- ***Don't whitewash unpleasant assignments:*** Prepare subordinates for unpleasant assignments well in advance and offer what support you can.

(a) Managerial Approaches for Improving Motivation

A number of approaches can help managers motivate workers, to perform more effectively. The following steps promote intrinsic motivation:

- Workers Participation in Management (WPM).
- Management By Objectives (MBO).
- Organisation Behaviour Modification.
- Job-Redesign.
- Alternative Work Schedules.

Two approaches, however, have been especially effective: linking pay to job performance and quality of work-life programs.

1. Pay and Job Performance: Pay often can be used to motivate employee performance. But a pay plan also must be able to do the following tasks:

- Create the belief that good performance leads to high levels of pay;
- Minimize the negative consequences of good performance; and
- Create conditions in which rewards other than pay are evaluated as related to good performance.

2. Quality of Work Life Programs: Quality of Work Life (QWL) is defined as an attempt through a formal program to integrate employee needs and well being with the intention of improved productivity, greater worker involvement and higher levels of job satisfaction. Programs for QWL improvements range from those requiring minor changes in an organisation to those requiring extensive modifications in structure, personnel and the utilization of resources. There are three types of QWL programs, which are as follows:

(*a*) **Quality Circles:** Quality Circles (QC) are small groups of workers who meet regularly with their supervisor as their 'circle leader' to solve work-related problems. QCs give an employee an opportunity for involvement, social-need satisfaction, participation in work improvement and challenge and opportunity for growth. They are, in essence, vehicles for providing employees with opportunities to satisfy lower and upper-level needs as stated by Maslow, through the motivators described in Herzberg's theory.

(*b*) **Alternative Work Schedule:** Organisations also frequently use the modified 'work-week' as a way to increase employee motivation. A modified 'work-week' can be any work schedule that does not conform to a traditional 8 hours a day or 5 days a week format. The modified 'work-week' helps individual satisfy higher-level needs by providing more personal control over one's work schedule. It also provides an opportunity to fulfill several needs simultaneously.

(*c*) **Job-Redesign:** Job-redesign or changing the nature of people's job is also being used more as a motivational technique. The idea pursued here is that managers can use any of the alternatives job rotation, job enlargement, job enrichment as part of motivational programme. Expectancy theory helps explain the role of work design in motivation.

4.16 LEARNING THEORY AND MOTIVATION

Learning is an integral part of motivation for several reasons. First, expectations needs, and responses that are motivating and demotivating are learned (or not learned). Understanding how we learn and can assist organisation leaders and members in diagnosing motivational levels and finding ways to enhance them second, since rewards and punishments are a vital part of human motivation, understanding how people learn to respond to rewards and punishments can assist organisation leaders and managers in allocating rewards more effectively. Finally, learning has taken on added importance in the process of "continuous improvement". Influenced by the Japanese concept of Kaizen (translated as "continuous improvement"), which focuses not on "quick fixes" to problems or opportunities but on transformational, incremental, and organisation wide learning processes that enhance product and service quality, many successful corporations practice kaizen. Learning how we learn is important to enable self-improvement.

(a) Behaviour Modification

The basic tenet in the behaviour modification approach to learning is that to effect change, behaviours must be addressed, rather than their psychological inferences or causes. Behavioural modification specialists, therefore, approach human problems in organisation by focussing on specific behaviours. A five-step behavioural modification model addresses change as follows:

1. Identify and define specific behaviour(s). Can these be seen? Can they be measured?
2. Establish a baseline. Before attempting to change the behaviour, determine its strength in the present by measuring or counting the occurrences of the behaviour.
3. Analyze the A-B-Cs (antecedents, behaviours, consequences) of the behaviour to determine the source of the problem.
4. Develop and implement an action plan using operant conditioning, strengthen the desirable behaviours, and weaken or extinguish the undesirable one through conditioning techniques.
5. Evaluate the effects of the change using different measurements.

(b) Cognitive Evaluation Theory

The introduction of extrinsic rewards, such as pay. For work effort that had been previously intrinsically rewarding due to the pleasure associated with the content of the work itself would tend to decrease the overall level of motivation. This proposal, which has come to be called the cognitive evaluation theory has been extensively researched, and a large number of studies have been supportive.

Historically, motivation theorists have generally assumed that intrinsic motivations such as achievement, responsibility and competence are independent of extrinsic motivators like high pay. Promotions, good supervisor relations and pleasant working conditions. That is, the stimulation of one would not affect the other. But the cognitive evaluation theory suggests otherwise. It argues that when extrinsic rewards, which are derived from individuals doing what they like, are reduced. In other words, when extrinsic rewards are given to someone for performing an interesting task, it causes intrinsic interest in the task itself to decline. The theory may have limited applicability to work organisations because most low-level jobs are not inherently satisfying enough to foster high intrinsic interest and many managerial and professional positions offer intrinsic rewards. Cognitive evaluation theory may be relevant to that set of organisational jobs that falls in between those that are neither extremely dull nor extremely interesting.

(c) Goal-Setting Theory

Gene Broadwater, coach of the Hamilton High School Cross-country team, gave his squad these last words before they approached the line for the league championship race. "Each one of you is physically ready. Now, get out there and do your best. No one can ever ask more of you than that". In the late 1960s, Edwin Locke proposed that intentions to work toward a goal are a major source of work motivation. That is, goals tell an employee what needs to be done and how much effort will need to be expended. The evidence strongly supports the value of goals. More to the point, we can say that specific goals increase performance; that difficult goals, when accepted, result in higher performance than do easy goals; and that feedback leads to higher performance than does non-feedback. Specific hard goals produce a higher level of output than does the generalized goal of "do your best". The specificity of the goal itself acts as an internal stimulus. If factors like ability and acceptance of the goals are held constant, we can also state that the more difficult the goal, the higher the level of performance. However, it's logical to assume that easier goals are more likely to be accepted. But once an employee accepts a hard task, he or she will exert a high level of effort until it is achieved, lowered, or abandoned.

(d) Reinforcement Theory

A counterpoint to goal-setting theory is reinforcement theory. The former is a cognitive approach, proposing that an individual's purposes direct his or her action. In reinforcement theory, we have a behaviouristic approach, which argues that reinforcement conditions behaviour. Reinforcement theory ignores the inner state of the individual and concentrates solely on what happens to a person when he or she takes some action. Because it does not concern itself with what initiates behaviour, it is not, strictly speaking, a theory of motivation. But it does provide a powerful means of analysis of what controls behaviour, and it is for this reason that it is typically considered in discussions of motivation.

Employees might compare themselves to friends, neighbours, co-workers, colleagues in other organisations, or past jobs they themselves have had. Which referent an employee chooses will be influenced by the information the employee holds about referents as well as by the attractiveness of the referent. This has led to focusing on four moderating variables—gender, length of tenure, level in the organisation, and amount of education or professionalism. Research shows that both men and women prefer same sex comparisons. Based on equity theory, when employees perceive an inequity, they can be presented to make one of six choices.

In conclusion, equity theory demonstrates that, for most employees, motivation is influenced significantly by relative rewards as well as by absolute rewards, but some key issues are still unclear. For instance, how do employees handle conflicting equity signals, such as when unions point to other employee groups who are substantially better off, while management argues how much things have improved? Yet, regardless of these problems, equity theory continues to offer us some important insights into employee motivation.

4.17 MANAGING MOTIVATION AND CHANGE

The scope, radical nature, and fast rate of planned organisational change have been unprecedented in recent times. Mergers, acquisitions, strategic alliances, reengineering and downsizing activities have significantly taken off. The extent to which these levels of organisational change will continue is uncertain; however, it has been predicated that organisational change will become a constant, that is, change will no longer be a single event. Because information technologies are also changing the very nature of work and expertise requirements, employee motivation takes on an even greater importance.

Several practices to enhance motivation in the contemporary workplace have been suggested:

- Ensure that employees' motives and values are appropriate and "fit" the jobs on which they are placed.
- Ensure that jobs, roles and responsibilities are attractive and consistent with employees' values, beliefs and motives.
- Assist employees and ensure that work goals are clear, challenging, attractive, and attainable.
- Provide employees with required personal and material resources that enhance their effectiveness.
- Create and sustain supportive social and working environments.
- Recognize and reinforce performance.
- Ensure that the elements are harmonized and fit into a consistent socio-technical organisational system.

Managing motivation in rapidly and continuously changing organisational settings will require flexibility, focus, experimentation, the skill of balancing paradoxes, openly communicating and testing assumptions, and being open to and skilled in implementing planned change. Motivation is, to a large extent, culturally conditioned and learned. Individual organisation members working with those from different cultures should not assume when the topic is motivations, whether it be needs, expectancies, or satisfiers. These individuals should find out what the basic cultural orientation is, whether it is collectivist, individuals, productivity or quality of life oriented, uncertainty avoidance or comfort with ambiguity. Not everyone from a culture shares all of its basic societal values, but these values can and do influence unspoken beliefs, attitudes, and motivations. A person's own values or motivational assumption and standards should not be accepted as absolute.

The characteristics of a changing, ever-more diverse workforce suggest that managing motivation will be challenging and difficult. The challenge for owners, managers, and organisation members will be to find ways to integrate, not assimilate, the diverse individuals and to address their motivational needs. Integrating and motivating a diverse workforce involves understanding and addressing value differences. Valuing and motivating diverse workforces must be organisational priorities. The scope, radical nature, and fast rate of planned organisational change in recent times have been unprecedented.

Several practices have been suggested to enhance motivation in the contemporary workplace. These include ensuring that employee' motives and values are appropriate and fit the jobs in which they are placed; that jobs, roles and responsibilities are attractive and consistent with employees' values, beliefs, and motives; and that work goals are clear, challenging, attractive, and attainable. Other ways to enhance motivation include providing employees with required personal and material resources that enhance their effectiveness; creating and sustaining supportive social and working environments; recognizing and reinforcing performance; and ensuring that these elements are harmonized and fit into a consistent socio-technical organisational system. Managing motivation in rapidly and continuously changing organisational settings will require flexibility, focus, experimentation, the skill of balancing paradoxes, openly communicating and testing assumptions, and being open to and skilled in implementing planned change. Nature of job content and design are very important in motivating the workers. Hence MPS can be considered

The Motivating Potential Score (MPS) can be calculated, using the following formulae:

$$\text{MPS} = \frac{\text{Skill Variety} + \text{Task Identity} + \text{Task Significance}}{3} \times \text{Autonomy} \times \text{Feedback}$$

Jobs that are high in motivating potential must be high on at least one of the three factors that lead to experienced meaningfulness, and also must be high on both Autonomy and Feedback. If a job has a high MPS, the job characteristics model predicts that motivation, performance and job satisfaction will be positively affected and the likelihood of negative outcomes, such as absenteeism and turnover, will be reduced.

4.18 MONEY AS A MOTIVATOR

Workers in any organisation need something to keep them working. Most of the time, the salary of the employee is enough to keep him or her working for an organisation. An employee must be motivated to work for a company or organisation. If no motivation is present in an employee, then that employee's quality of work or all work in general will deteriorate. People differ on a personality dimension called locus of control. This variable refers to individual's beliefs about the location of the factors that control their behaviour. At one end of the continuum are high internals who believe that opportunity to control their own behaviour rests within themselves. At the other end of the continuum there are high externals who believe that external forces determine their behaviour. Not surprisingly, compared with internals, externals see the world as an unpredictable, chancy place in which luck, fate, or powerful people control their destinies. When motivating an audience, you can use general motivational strategies or specific motivational appeals. General motivational strategies include soft sell versus hard sell and personality type. Soft sell strategies have logical appeals, emotional appeals, advice and praise. Hard sell strategies have barter, outnumbering, pressure and rank. Also, you can consider basing your strategy on your audience personality. Specific motivational appeals focus on provable facts, feelings, right and wrong, audience rewards and audience threats.

The widespread misconception about finance being a motivating factor or motivator in industry has led to the failure of the best-laid incentive plans. The Wire Meld company, USA after a six week, drive the company concluded that awarding war bonds to employees for perfect attendance was not the solution to absenteeism. Habits of the employees were not influenced by the plan. Most of those who had been irregular in attendance before the award system was inaugurated were irregular. There was a bus slow down in New York in it easy 1980's due to the refusal of drivers (bus) to work overtime. They were not interested in more money. They felt they were tired after duty to engage in extra work. An analysis of these drivers indicated an average income of 3200 a year, an income that even then could not be considered very high.

Ever since Taylor's time "experts" have concocted one wage incentive system after another, resulting in a myriad of these. Lytle (1938) gave one of the most comprehensive reviews of wage incentive plans. He believed such plans were important in any cost production problem. He cited two advantages of wage incentive plans as being (1) an increase in production per unit, (2) an increase in employees' earnings. He believed that the advantages of a well-installed and ably managed wage payment plan accrue annually to employees and employers. It is then difficult to demarcate (among) the various incentive systems from the industrial psychologists point of view. Lytle's attempt to classify all financial incentive plans on the basis of production earning characteristics is shown below. It's an idea of the numerous systems that have been promoted. This is a historical method and is least used today.

Class I: Employee takes all gain or loss

Time : Hour, week, or any straight statuary rate, not an extra incentive.

Standard time using two rates, one either side of the task; a two zone multiple time plan.

Multiple time : With arithmetic in rate between production zones (standard time plan).

Multiple time : Geometric steps in rate between production zones.

Class II: Employee takes all gain

Piece or straight commission rate: This sub divides into punitive basic and high, etc.

Class III: Gain shared between employer and employee but day wage guaranteed exception one-third premium.

Class IV: Empirical location of points between two variables, piecework or commission above 100% production.

(a) Theories Concerning Money as an Incentive

Opsahl and Dunnete (1966) list 5 theories in this respect. This attempt to explain the effect or money or job performance.

1. Money as a generalised conditioned rein forcer: Money, due to its association with more basic reinforcers (need satisfiers) acquires the status of a secondary reinforcer. Wolf studies (1936) and Cowles (1937) demonstrated that poker chips acquired requirements value when they could be exchanged for food, *i.e.*, subjects in their experiments worked as hard to get clops which could 'buy' food as they had previously worked for food itself.

2. Money as a conditioning incentive: Money acquires an incentive value due to continued pairing with other incentives of a more basic nature. Despite laboratory data this method is difficult to practice. It is difficult to point out the more basic incentives with which money can be paired.

3. Money as an anxiety reducer: The absence of money is generally associated with anxiety reactions in our society. Therefore lack of money becomes a conditioned stimulus for an anxiety response. Money therefore serves as a reducer of anxiety.

4. Money as a "Hygiene Factor": Hertzberg, Mausner and Synderman in their notion of satisfier and dissatisfies are viewed as being two distinct classes of motivators. Money is a hygiene factor which serves primarily as a dissatisfier *i.e.*, causes dissatisfaction when absent, but contributes a little to satisfaction when present. It is uncertain whether their data supports this hypothesis (Opsahl and Dunnete, 1966).

5. Money as a means of instrumentality: According to Vroom's Theory of Motivation Model, money acquires valance due to its perceived instrumentality for obtaining the desired outcomes e.g., if money were perceived as being instrumental to the positive goal of security, then money would acquire a positive valance. Then the likelihood of a person acting in a way to acquire money would be a function of his need for security multiplied by the expectancy that a particular money-seeking act would result in a specified monetary return. A simple numerical explanation would be

$$L_m = f(s) \times E$$

Where L_m = Likelihood of a person acting in a way to acquire money

S = Need for security

E = Expectancy that a particular money seeking act would result in a specified monetary return.

In their review on the role of financial compensation in industrial motivation; Opsahl and Dunnete, 1966) state: The role of money as reward in modern industry continues to be poorly understood despite our economies being based on a monetary reward system. Although the use of formal incentive pay systems has diminished in recent years in favour of other non-financial incentives, money units will probably always be exchanged for work. Thus, a better knowledge of the dynamics of this exchange process is certainly needed.

(b) Kinds of Incentives

Incentives may be classified financial and non-financial. More aptly co-operative and competitive.

(*i*) **Co-operation incentives:** This involves organising people into groups (meaningful groups) and having them work together for a common goal. This is the latest of kinds of incentives and is practiced in industry as well as educational institutions. This results in more learning at the educational level and greater production at the industrial level. People contribute equal and maximum efforts towards the realisation of common goal.

(*ii*) **Competitive incentives:** These involve the urge of doing better than the next individual. Individual incentives: These are extremely, meaningful if the individual himself introduces them. In industry the incentive is used as a means of spurring an employee towards someone else's goal. He may not be interested in either reduced costs or increased production. But he may be persuaded to achieve his goal by an incentive when the incentive results in equal satisfaction for the employer too when the plant is being successfully operated. The major difficulty with financial incentives has been the facts that fear of a rate cut whether the fear is justified or not. They also fear a lay off. Hence indifference or evasiveness to wage rises.

Both competition and co-operation are not mutually inclusive especially when individuals co-operate in groups to compete with other groups. Industry in the past has placed too much emphasis on competition; only recently have the advantages of co-operative behaviour as an incentive been recognised. The use of co-operation as an incentive holds considerable promise of success.

(c) Maslow's View on Financial Incentives

Maslow's theory of motivation dismisses finance as a motivator. He argued that money satisfies only lower needs (safety and psychological needs) and not the higher order need. In one of his research survey he found that when managers were asked what factors they felt determined their pay they responded training and experience were the most important factors.

SUMMARY

Author has presented a number of motivation theories and applications. While it's always dangerous to synthesize a large number of complex ideas into a few simple guidelines, as stated in the chapter will help managers to motivate their employees in their organisations in the new millennium.

Generally, motivation is conceptualized as either *intrinsic* or *extrinsic*. Classically, these categories are regarded as distinct. Today, these concepts are less likely to be used as distinct categories, but instead as two ideal types that define a continuum.

Intrinsic motivation occurs when people are internally motivated to do something because it either brings them pleasure, they think it is important, or they feel that what they are learning is significant. It has been shown that intrinsic motivation for education drops from grades 3–9 though the exact cause cannot be ascertained. Also, in younger students it has been shown that contextualizing material that would otherwise be presented in an abstract manner increases the intrinsic motivation of these students.

Extrinsic motivation comes into play when a student is compelled to do something or act a certain way because of factors external to him or her (like money or good grades).

At lower levels of Maslow's hierarchy of needs, such as physiological needs, money is a motivator, however it tends to have a motivating effect on staff that lasts only for a short period (in accordance with Herzberg's two-factor model of motivation). At higher levels of the hierarchy, praise, respect, recognition, empowerment and a sense of belonging are far more powerful motivators than money, as both Abraham Maslow's Theory of Motivation and Douglas McGregor's Theory X and Theory Y (pertaining to the Theory of Leadership) demonstrate.

According to Maslow, people are motivated by unsatisfied needs. The lower level needs such as Physiological and Safety needs will have to be satisfied before higher level needs are to be addressed. We can relate Maslow's Hierarchy of Needs Theory with employee motivation. For example, if a manager is trying to motivate his employees by satisfying their needs; according to Maslow, he should try to satisfy the lower level needs before he tries to satisfy the upper level needs or the employees will not be motivated. Also he has to remember that not everyone will be satisfied by the same needs. A good manager will try to figure out which levels of needs are active for a certain individual or employee.

Maslow has money at the lowest level of the hierarchy and shows other needs are better motivators to staff. McGregor places money in his Theory X category and feels it is a poor motivator. Praise and recognition are placed in the Theory Y category and are considered stronger motivators than money.

- Motivated employees always look for better ways to do a job.
- Motivated employees are more quality oriented.
- Motivated workers are more productive.

The average workplace is about midway between the extremes of high threat and high opportunity. Motivation by threat is a dead-end strategy, and naturally staffs are more attracted to the opportunity side of the motivation curve than the threat side. Motivation is a powerful tool in the work environment that can lead to employees working at their most efficient levels of production.

Nonetheless, Steinmetz also discusses three common character types of subordinates: Ascendant, indifferent, and ambivalent that all react and interact uniquely, and must be treated, managed, and motivated accordingly. An effective leader must understand how to manage all characters, and more importantly the manager must utilize avenues that allow room for employees to work, grow, and find answers independently.

The assumptions of Maslow and Herzberg were challenged by a classic study at Vauxhall Motors' UK manufacturing plant. This introduced the concept of orientation to work and distinguished three main orientations: instrumental (where work is a means to an end), bureaucratic (where work is a source of status, security and immediate reward) and solidaristic (which prioritizes group loyalty).

Other theories which expanded and extended those of Maslow and Herzberg included Kurt Lewin's Force Field Theory, Edwin Locke's Goal Theory and Victor Vroom's Expectancy Theory. These tend to stress cultural differences and the fact that individuals tend to be motivated by different factors at different times.

According to the system of scientific management developed by Frederick Winslow Taylor, a worker's motivation is solely determined by pay, and therefore management need not consider psychological or social aspects of work. In essence, scientific management bases human motivation wholly on extrinsic rewards and discards the idea of intrinsic rewards.

In contrast, David McClelland believed that workers could not be motivated by the mere need for money, in fact, extrinsic motivation (e.g., money) could extinguish intrinsic motivation such as achievement motivation, though money could be used as an indicator of success for various motives, e.g., keeping score. In keeping with this view, his consulting firm, McBer & Company, had as its first motto "To make everyone productive, happy, and free". For McClelland, satisfaction lay in aligning a person's life with their fundamental motivations.

Elton Mayo found that the social contacts a worker has at the workplace are very important and that boredom and repetitiveness of tasks lead to reduced motivation. Mayo believed that workers could be motivated by acknowledging their social needs and making them feel important. As a result, employees were given freedom to make decisions on the job and greater attention was paid to informal work groups. Mayo named the model the Hawthorne effect. His model has been judged as placing undue reliance on social contacts within work situations for motivating employees.

William Ouchi introduced Theory Z, a hybrid management approach consisting of both Japanese and American philosophies and cultures. Its Japanese segment is much like the clan culture where organisations focus on a standardized structure with heavy emphasis on socialization of its members. All underlying goals are consistent across the organisation. Its American segment retains formality and authority amongst members and the organisation. Ultimately, Theory Z promotes common structure and commitment to the organisation, as well as constant improvement of work efficacy.

In *Essentials of Organisational Behaviour*, Robbins and Judge examine recognition programs as motivators, and identify five principles that contribute to the success of an employee incentive program:

- Recognition of employees' individual differences and clear identification of behaviour deemed worthy of recognition.
- Allowing employees to participate.

- Linking rewards to performance.
- Rewarding of nominators.
- Visibility of the recognition process.

Motivation is of particular interest to educational psychologists because of the crucial role it plays in student learning. However, the specific kind of motivation that is studied in the specialized setting of education differs qualitatively from the more general forms of motivation studied by psychologists in other fields. Motivation in education can have several effects on how students learn and how they behave towards subject matter. It can:

1. Direct behaviour toward particular goals.
2. Lead to increased effort and energy.
3. Increase initiation of, and persistence in activities.
4. Enhance cognitive processing.
5. Determine what consequences are reinforcing.
6. Lead to improved performance.

Because students are not always internally motivated, they sometimes need *situated motivation*, which is found in environmental conditions that the teacher creates. If teachers decided to extrinsically reward productive student behaviours, they may find it difficult to extricate themselves from that path. Consequently student dependency on extrinsic rewards represents one of the greatest detractors from their use in the classroom.

REVIEW QUESTIONS

1. Explain the motivation cycle and hygiene factor. How it is applicable to a manager?
2. Explain the money as motivator. Is there any exception? Explain.
3. Explain process theories of motivation.
4. Describe briefly the content theories of motivation.
5. How do you explore the motivation as a positive concept for organisation growth and productivity?

DISCUSSION QUESTIONS

1. Is it possible for someone to be unmotivated, or is all behaviour motivated?
2. What similarities exist between the views of human motivation of scientific management theorists and those of human relations theorists? How do they differ?
3. Do you think the hierarchy of needs theory or the ERG model has the greatest value? Explain.
4. Which of the need theories discussed in the chapter has the most practical value for managers? Which one has the least practical value?
5. How do you evaluate yourself in terms of your needs for achievement, affiliation, and power?
6. Besides distinctions between need-based and process-based perspectives, are there any basic differences between the motivation theories discussed in this chapter.
7. Which is likely to be a more serious problem, perceptions of being under rewarded or perceptions of being over rewarded?

8. Do you think expectancy theory is too complex for direct use in organisational settings? Why or why not?

STUDENT EXERCISE

There are two broad theories of motivation: Content Theories and Process Theories. Organisational Behaviour scholars are very interested in whether process theories are culture-bound. There are three popular process theories—expectancy theory, equity theory, and goal setting theory. These theories describe the processes through which need deficiencies (identified in content theories) are translated into behaviour. The origins of these theories are argued to be culture-bound as they were developed and studied in the western, industrialized context. The argument can be made that because of the origins and applications of these theories, they cannot be effectively transferred to other cultures. Identify the elements of Equity Theory. Identify factors that would support Equity Theory of motivation for workers in Saudi Arabia. Do the same analysis for Zambia. Based on observations, do you think that Equity Theory is culture-bound? Explain and provide examples.

SKILL TEST

Are you a Theory X or Y Manager?

The questions below are intended to provide insights into your tendencies towards Theory X or Theory Y management styles. Answer each of the following questions on the scales by circling the number that best reflects your feelings. For example, mark a "5" beside a statement if you strongly agree with it, or a "2" if you disagree with it.

1. Most employees today are lazy and have to be forced to work hard.

5	4	3	2	1
Strongly Agree	Agree	Neither Agree Nor Disagree	Disagree	Strongly Disagree

2. People in organisations are only motivated by extrinsic rewards such as pay and bonus.

5	4	3	2	1
Strongly Agree	Agree	Neither Agree Nor Disagree	Disagree	Strongly Disagree

3. Most people do not like to work.

5	4	3	2	1
Strongly Agree	Agree	Neither Agree Nor Disagree	Disagree	Strongly Disagree

4. Most people today generally avoid responsibility.

5	4	3	2	1
Strongly Agree	Agree	Neither Agree Nor Disagree	Disagree	Strongly Disagree

5. Many employees in big companies today do not accept the company's goals but instead work only for their own welfare.

5	4	3	2	1
Strongly Agree	Agree	Neither Agree Nor Disagree	Disagree	Strongly Disagree

6. Most people are not innovative and are not interested in helping their employers to solve problems.

5	4	3	2	1
Strongly Agree	Agree	Neither Agree Nor Disagree	Disagree	Strongly Disagree

7. Most people need someone else to tell them how to do their job.

5	4	3	2	1
Strongly Agree	Agree	Neither Agree Nor Disagree	Disagree	Strongly Disagree

8. Many people today have little ambition, preferring to stay where they are and not work hard for advancement.

5	4	3	2	1
Strongly Agree	Agree	Neither Agree Nor Disagree	Disagree	Strongly Disagree

If you wish to know more insight on your test score, then you are welcome to contact author via e-mail shaangrila@gmail.com or social media drs.shajahan.7@facebook.com

5 CHAPTER

GROUP BEHAVIOUR AND GROUP DECISION MAKING

LEARNING OBJECTIVES

This chapter aims at introducing fundamental concepts for explaining the group behaviour and its usefulness in making joint and collaborative decision making in an organisation to the readers:

- *Definition, importance and fundamental concepts of groups and group formation*
- *Nature, type and characteristics of groups*
- *Stages of group development, group norms and cohesiveness*
- *Group decision making and problem solving process and techniques*

INTRODUCTION

Are they clowning these executives? The whites with black painted faces and the blacks with white painted faces? Not exactly. This is also a part of the curriculum in giant business schools like Harvard, Boston and the New School of Social Research called "encounter session". It strives to prove differences in a group are only "skin deep!". The world of behaviouralists have a spectrum of names for sessions of this sort like the acid less trip, therapy for normals, the bold biz, a sensitivity session. The socialization of man is gaining a spiral attention for the enhancing of human resources as a group. In other words, group dynamics and group decision making is gathering momentum not only on a theoretical speculation in Research Institutes of Social Sciences but also as a relevant facet in executive lounges, University classrooms and Government circles. Group Dynamics is defined as a field of inquiry dedicated to achieving knowledge about the nature of groups, the laws of their development and their inter-relations with individuals, other groups and larger institutions. It is therefore a blend of sociology, psychology and anthropology. This chapter focuses the groups and their typical characteristics in general.

5.1 DEFINITION OF A GROUP

A group is a two or more individual who interact regularly with each other to accomplish a common purpose or goal. According to Marvin Shaw, "a group comprises, of two or more persons who interact with one another in such a manner that each person influences and is influenced by each other person". The key parts of this definition are the concepts of interaction and influence, which also limit the size of the group. It is difficult for members to interact sufficiently in a large group.

In short, a group is an assemblage, cluster or aggregation of persons considered to be related in some way or united by communities or interests. (Family, recreation occupation etc.) In behavioural science the emphasis is on the interrelationships among members, where the connotation of aggregation is not stressed. The criteria of mutual awareness and interactions suggest that a casual crowd or nationwide organisations are not psychological groups. Groups as defined in Webster Universal Dictionary as Aggregation of persons sharing the same special views, theories, aspirations, beliefs in politics, religion, art, philosophy etc. In fact this is a general definition and does not mention whether these individuals are in active interactions with one another or not. Psychologist uses the teams, psychological or functional group to avoid any possible confusion in the meanings of what they imply.

In general, groups or work teams are the primary tools used by managers. Managers need groups to coordinate individual behaviour in order to reach the organisational goals. Groups can make a manager's job easier because by forming a group, he need not explain the task to each and every individual. A manager can easily coordinate with the work of an individual by giving the group a task and allow them to coordinate with each other. But for a group to work effectively, the interactions between its members should be productive. Therefore, managers must pay attention to the needs of individuals.

Further, a group is a collection of two or more interacting individuals with a stable pattern of relationship between them who share common goal and who perceive themselves as being a group. Hence every individual, at least in our present complex societies, is a member of many different social groups—groups that are vitally significant to be individual welfare. These groups are divided into two categories (*i*) psychological group and (*ii*) social organisation. A psychological group may be defined as two or more persons who meet the following conditions.

1. The relation among the members are interdependent each member's behaviour influences the behaviour of each other.
2. The members share on ideology—a set of beliefs, values, and norms, which regulate their mutual conduct, this ideology keeps the group away from other groups.

The concept of a group in an organisational setting includes a boundary and environments suggesting external relationship with other groups and individuals. Hence groups are open system with a continual input-output flow of material, energy and information. Psychological group as any number of peoples whom

- Interact with one another.
- Are psychologically aware of one another.
- Perceive themselves to be a group.

Groups can provide with or without the conscious knowledge of the members, a means of fulfilling many of the needs of the individuals in them. The more significant needs in them can be categorised as

(*i*) Affiliative need
(*ii*) Egoistic need
(*iii*) Instrumental need
(*iv*) Cognitive needs

The reasons for the need of groups are as follows:

- Management of modern organisations makes mutual efforts to introduce industrial democracy at workplace. They use project teams and work committees where workers get due recognition. They willingly participate in decision making.
- The tasks in modern industries are becoming more complex, tedious arid of repetitive nature. Work committees, work groups and teams are formed to monitor the work. They also make the environment at workplace more lively.
- Groups help in making participative management more effective.
- Groups of all kinds and types help by cooperating in all the matters related to production and human relations to work effectively in the organisation.
- An individual cannot perform each and every task. Group efforts are required for its completion. For example, building a ship, making of a movie, construction of a fly-over, etc. All these require coordinated and unified efforts of many individuals, working in a group.
- A group can judge in a better way as compared to an individual.
- While accomplishing tasks, all members of a group together use their creative and innovative ideas than a single individual.
- In a group, individuals communicate with each other, discuss their work performances and take suggestions from each other to make it better.
- Group efforts affect an individual, his attitude and behaviour and group has the ability to satisfy the needs of its members.

5.2 CHARACTERISTICS OF GROUPS

The definitions of a group stress interdependent relations and interactions among individuals. Different characteristics have been devised to designate groups usually characterised by the highest degree of interdependence and interactions are 'dyads' or two-person groups. "Small group" usually designated from 4–8 people but may be extended to include 20.

Characteristics of groups are summarized below:

Social interaction	:	People who are interacting with one another form a group.
Common goal	:	People, who work together, work for a common goal, which can even involve having a good time.
Shared standards	:	People who observe the same customs, traditions and rules of etiquette would constitute a group.
Self-definition	:	Among collection of people who consider themselves to form a group.
Group size	:	Hyerdalls.
Cohesiveness	:	Attractiveness, which is a function of the group. This is defined as the tenacity with which a group sticks together or the extent to which members would give up membership.

Group may vary in their sociability and in their determination of productivity. Another important variable is the extent to which members are self oriented or goal oriented—dependency, status, dominance, aggression, etc. are important.

5.3 DIFFERENT TYPES OF GROUPS

Variations in site, even within the limits of the small group, have many repercussions. As the number of people in the group increases, the opportunity for face-to-face interaction with every other member decreases. At some point the group becomes unwieldy and subgroups appear. As groups become larger, they tend to become less homogeneous and consensus becomes more difficult to attain. The size variables are important, partly in its own right and partly because variations in the number of members in a group can have profound qualitative effects. The power of a group to modify the attitudes of new members is a function of certain characteristics of group. Characteristics of a group can be broadly classified into structure and relationship with one another and the individual role within the group.

Size of group: As the size of the group increases the potential relationship increases. Whether or not all potential relationships within a group play a significant role in the analysis of the group's behaviour.

Determination of size of group: This is determined by the operation of arbitrary external factors and also the intergroup determinants.

Groups may be classified in many different ways—the basis for differentiation may be purpose of goals, duration and extent of structuring legal organisation or setting. Accordingly there are eight types of groups. In an organisation, there are three types of groups, which are as follows:

(*a*) ***Functional or formal group*:** Functional groups are the groups formed by the organisation to accomplish different organisational purposes. According to A L Stencombe, "a formal group is said to be any social arrangement in which the activities of some persons are planned by others to achieve a common purpose". These groups are permanent in nature. They have to follow rules, regulations and policy of the organisation. A formal organisational group includes departments such as the personnel department, the advertising department, the quality control department and the public relations department. In short, formal groups means groups that have been established under legal and formal authority to achieve a specific end result or to undertake delegated tasks can be called formal groups. They are structured and in that sense are organized with a definite allocation of tasks among members and a clear delineation of duties and relationship among them.

(*b*) ***Task group*:** Tasks groups are the groups formed by an organisation to accomplish a narrow range of purposes within a specified time. These groups are temporary in nature. They also develop a solution to a problem or complete its purpose. Informal committees, task forces and work teams are included in task groups. The organisation after specifying a group membership, assigns a narrow set of purposes such as developing a new product, evaluating a proposed grievance procedure, etc.

(*c*) ***Informal group*:** Informal groups are the groups formed for the purposes other than the organisational goals. Informal groups form when individuals are drawn together by friendship, by mutual interests or both. These groups are spontaneous. According to Keith David, "the network of persons and social relations which is not established or required forms an informal organisation". These are the groups formed by the employees themselves at the workplace while working together. The organisation does not take any active interest in their formation.

In an organisational set-up, an activity that is formally specified on the job probably doesn't occupy the entire attention or satisfy all the needs of the individuals who are operating under the guidelines. Informal groups may be fostered through simple physical factors such as fulfillment of specific needs of a set of individuals. Dalton (1950) identifies three different kinds of informed groups that are found in organisation. They are classified as Horizontal Clique, Vertical Clique and Random Clique.

Informal groups are very effective and powerful. These groups work as an informal communication network forming a part of the grapevine to the organisations. They are also like a powerful force, which an organisation cannot avoid. Some managers consider them to be harmful to the interest of an organisation. They suspect their integrity and consider as a virtual threat. Some managers do not consider them as threat and seek the help of group members in getting the organisational task accomplished. Informal groups are of following types:

- ***Interest group:*** Interest groups are the groups formed to attain a common purpose. Employees coming together for payment of bonus, increase in salary, medical benefit and other facilities are the examples of interest groups.
- ***Membership group:*** Membership groups are the groups of individuals' belonging to the same profession and knowing each other. For example, teachers of the same faculty in a university.
- ***Exclusive and inclusive groups:*** This is based on the membership. In exclusive group, membership is restricted to persons having specified characteristics. The origin can be traced to the attraction among similar. This group can be formed with ulterior motive e.g., Professional and occupational association. In inclusive group, membership is common to all for example, the executive healthcare package membership of Apollo is considered as a common for all senior executives of many corporate in India.
- ***In-groups and out-groups:*** Exclusive groups often create barriers between those who are in and those who are out of them. There is a general tendency among people to be loyal to group of sympathetic and identified with the group to which they belong. This in-group and out-groups are relative terms, which are often useful in describing certain group processes. For example, Apollo Hospital.
- ***Friendship group:*** Friendship groups are the groups of individuals belonging to same age group, having similar views, tastes and opinions. These groups can also be formed outside the plant or office and can be in the form of clubs and associations.
- ***Reference group:*** Reference groups are the group where individuals shape their ideas, beliefs, values etc. They want support from the group. Reference group is one with which he identifies or to which he would like to belong. They may actually be a subsidiary member of a particular group to project the norms of mother group, the group which he refers. The norm of reference group will become more influential in determining behaviour.

Primary and secondary groups: This is based on the nature of interpersonal selection among the members of the group in a primary group; the group exercises a considerable influence on an individual personality. Values, beliefs, and attitudes because of frequent intimate and face to face contacts. On the other hand, in a secondary group, members do not show such frequency and intimacy in the interactions of their members, they are formalised and contractual in nature. It is possible to further classify group as

- Command group,
- Task group,
- Interest group, and
- Friendship group.

Of these first two are dictated by the formal organisation where as the latter two are informal alliances. Command group is composed of the subordinates who report directly to a given manager. Task groups represent those working together to complete a job task. Group often develops because the individual members have one or more common characteristics and is called friendship groups. A group is cohesive when the members of the group are attached to the group's task, to its prestige, and to other members of the group. Members of cohesive groups like to be together, care about each other; and typically known each other well. Cohesive groups also usually perform better than non-cohesive groups, especially if they are small. Group norms are unwritten rules of behaviour for members of a cohesive group. The norms define acceptable behaviour and roles of group members. Norms include levels of performance valued by the group, teamwork within the group, and relationships with managers and other aspects of the formal organisation. New members learn a group's norms from its socialization process. A cohesive group will pressure a new member to conform to those norms.

Behaviour in groups falls into two major classes such as Required and Emergent behaviour. Required behaviour is what a person must do because of membership in the organisation and as part of the person's role in the formal group. Required behaviours include beings at work at a specific time, performing job duties in a certain way, and interacting with specific people in another department to complete a task. Emergent behaviour grows out of the interactions among group members. Such behaviour grows out of the interactions among group members. Such behaviour can focus on work tasks or be purely social. The norms of a group can define emergent behaviour.

5.4 GROUP FORMATION AND DEVELOPMENT

Groups are formed for certain purpose. The important among them are:

- ***For accomplishment of task:*** This is primary requirement for the purpose of existence of formal groups in an organisation. To attain its objectives and goals, organisation will formally bring individuals into a group to complete the set task or tasks. Such groups are designated by the structure of the organisation as production, finance, maintenance, sales and sales promotion, designs, etc.
- ***For the purpose of problem solving:*** This group is also formed for the purpose of achieving some desired goals. Such groups may exist for only a short time, that is, they may be disbanded after the attainment of goals.
- ***For proximity and reward:*** Individuals join together for proximity and attention, if they perform similar problem solving skills. Their group activity may be informal such as having lunch together, taking tea together, making complaints against management together, etc. They may form informal groups because of their proximity in working together and perceive this interaction to be rewarding.
- ***Socio-psychological objectives:*** This objective of a group formation is that an individual need can be better satisfied in a group. Individual needs include physiological, safety, affiliation, esteem and self-actualization.

Groups can form when individuals with similar goals and motives come together. Groups are formed voluntarily. The individuals of a group can join and leave the group any time and they can also change their tasks. Hence, understanding how groups form and develop is important for managers. There are certain motives because of which, the individuals join a group, which are as follows:

- ***Organisational motives to join groups:*** Organisations form functional and task groups because such groups help the organisation in structuring and grouping the organisational activities logically and efficiently.
- ***Personal motives to join groups:*** Individuals also choose to join informal or interest groups for unimportant reasons. Since joining these groups is voluntary, various personal motives affect membership. Some of these are shown in the Fig. 5.1.

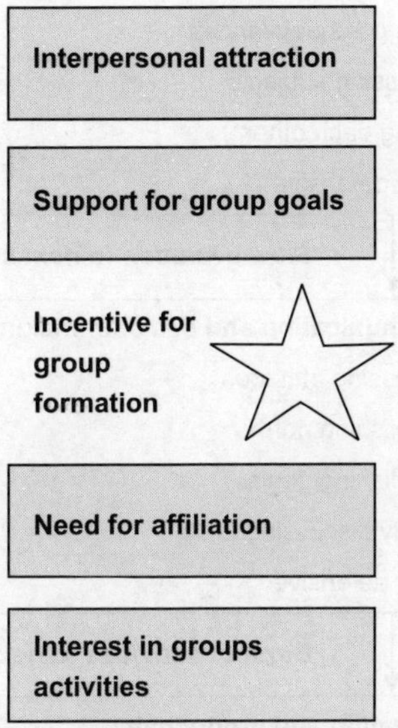

Fig. 5.1: Incentive for group formation

- ***Interpersonal attraction:*** Individuals conic together to form informal or interest group, as they are also attracted to each other. The factors that contribute to interpersonal attraction are sex, similar attitudes, personality and economic standing. The closeness of group members may also be an important factor.
- ***Interest in-group activities:*** Individuals may also be motivated to join an informal or interest group because the activities of the group appeal to them. Playing tennis, discussing current events or contemporary literature, all these are group activities that individuals enjoy.
- ***Support for group goals:*** The individuals may also be motivated goals by the other group members to join. For example, a club, which is dedicated to environmental conservation, may motivate individuals to join. Individuals join groups, such as these in order to donate their money and time to attain the goals they believe in and to meet other individuals with similar values.
- ***Need for affiliation:*** Another reason for individuals to join groups is to satisfy their need for attachment. Retired/old aged individuals join groups to enjoy the companionship of other individuals in similar situation.
- ***Instrumental benefits:*** Group membership sometimes also helpful in providing other benefits to an individual. For example, a manager might join a Rotary/Lions club if he feels that being a member of this club will lead to important and useful business contacts.

(a) Stages of Development

Members of new group are unfamiliar with one another's personalities and hesitant in their interactions. The new group must pass of development, which are depicted in Fig. 5.2.

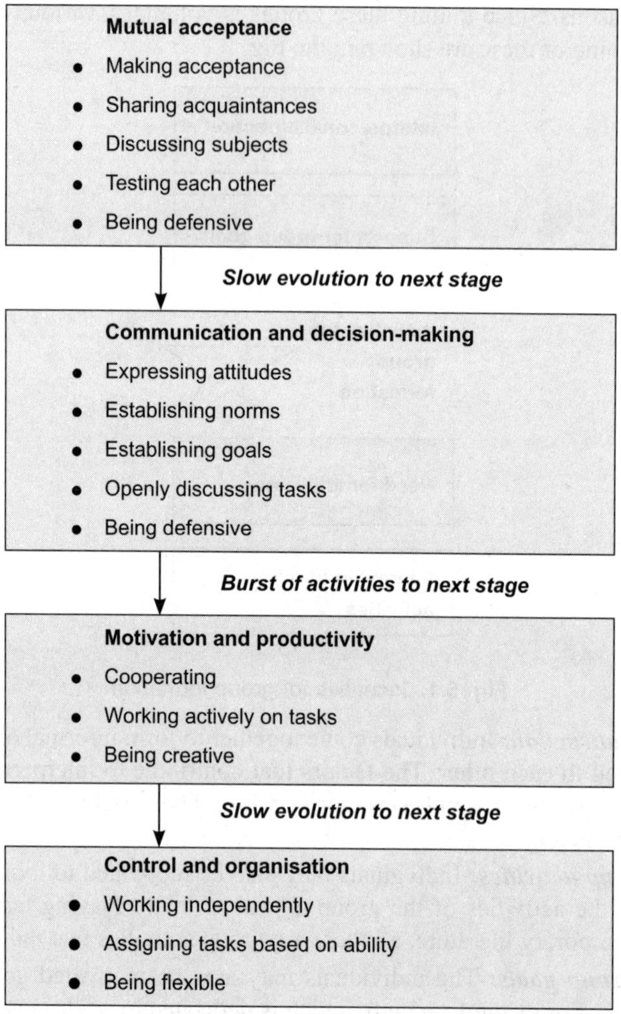

Fig. 5.2: Stages of group development

These different stages of group development are explained as follows:

- ***Mutual acceptance*:** The very first stage of a group development is called "Mutual Acceptance". During this stage, the members of the group get familiar with one another and check, which inter-personal behaviour is acceptable and which is unacceptable by the other members of the group. This helps all the members of a group to know each other better and helps the group to move to the next stage easily.

- ***Communication and decision making***: The second stage of group development is "Communication and Decision making". During this stage, group members share their opinions and formulate the group's goals. Through communication and decision making, the structure becomes clear and the group moves to the third stage.
- ***Motivation and productivity***: The third stage is "Motivation and Productivity", which is characterized by a shared acceptance among members of what the group is trying to do. Each person recognizes and accepts his role as well as to accept and to understand the roles to others. Members also become more comfortable with each other and develop a sense of group identity and unity.
- ***Control and Organisation***: The fourth stage is "Control and Organisation", in which the members perform the roles they have accepted and direct their group efforts towards goal attainment. In reality, this developmental sequence varies from group to group, depending on the time, personal characteristics of group members and frequency of interaction.

(b) Characteristics of Mature Groups

As groups pass through the stages of development to maturity, they begin to show signs of the following four characteristics: A role structure, behavioural norms, cohesiveness and informal leadership.

1. *Role structures*: A role is the part that an individual plays in a group to reach its goals. Some individuals are leaders, some focus on the group's task; some interact with other groups and so on. Role structure is the set of defined roles and interrelationships among those roles that the group members define and accept. The failure in role development result in role ambiguity, role conflict and role overload. Managers have to take steps to avoid role ambiguity, role conflict and role overload.

2. *Behavioural norms*: Although informal groups do not have any specific goals to accomplish, but they must have some goals over a period of time. These goals are temporary and can be changed in accordance with the needs of the group members. The goals can be achieved effectively depending on the following factors:

- The extent of cooperation with management.
- Maintenance of an efficient communication system.
- Satisfaction of the needs of group members.

3. *Informal leadership*: Each informal group has one or more leaders. These leaders come forward on the basis of acceptance of all the group members. Every informal group has one primary leader apart from the secondary leaders. The primary leader has more influence on the group members than the secondary leaders.

4. *Group norms*: Norms are rules that govern specific behaviour and apply to everyone in the group. Norm specifies what must or must not be done when (Steiner 1972). Norms may be explicit and develop through group discussion. On they may develop through practice and they are unwritten and unspecific. They refer to the expected behaviour sanctioned by the system and then have a specific 'ought' or must quality. In this they resemble roles. Values furnish rationale for the normative requirements. They are standards to which reference is made for judging acceptable and unacceptable behaviour of relevance to the system. System norms and ideology furnish cognitive maps for members, which facilitate their work in the system and their adjustment to it. Norms and ideology provide the moral and social justification for system activities both for members and for people formally outside the system. Following are the three criteria, which defines system norms.

Norms refer to group behaviour standard, beliefs, attitudes, traditions and expectations shared by group members. According to Michael Argyle, "Group norms are rules or guidelines of accepted behaviour which are established by a group and used to monitor the behaviour of its members". They are framed to achieve objectives of the group. They can be social and fair in nature. Norms define boundaries between acceptable and unacceptable behaviour. They make the members to identify themselves with the group. Norms play a significant role in disciplining the members of a group to make them to work regularly and properly. This reduces absenteeism and employee turnover. The members of the group are expected follow to the norms strictly. This will make the group more organized.

(a) Types of group norms: There are two types of group norms, which are as follows:

(i) Behaviour norms: Behaviour norms are rules that standardize how individuals act while working on a day to day basis. Examples are "Do not come to committee meetings unless you have read the reports to be "discussed", "greet every customer with a smile", etc. These norms tend to reflect motivation, commitment to the organisation and therefore result in high level of performance.

(ii) Performance norms: Performance norms are rules that standardize employee output and number of hours worked.

(b) Reasons for strong enforcement of norms: Groups don't have the time or energy, to regulate each and every action of the group members. Only those behaviours that sound to be important by group members should be brought under control. Groups, like individuals, try to operate in such a way that they maximize their chances of task success and minimize their chances of task failure. Groups want to facilitate their performance and overcome barriers to reach their goals. Moreover, groups want to increase morale and prevent any interpersonal discomfort to their members. Norms that will help groups meet these aims of performing successfully and keeping morale high are likely to be strongly enforced. Conditions where group norms will be strongly enforced are as follows:

- If the norms facilitate group success or ensure group survival.
- If the norms simplify or predict regarding the behaviour which is expected from group members.
- If the norms emphasize the roles of specific members within a group.
- If the norms help the group to solve the inter-personal problems themselves.

(c) Uniqueness of group norms: The norms of one group cannot be easily mixed with another group. Some differences are primarily due to the difference in structure of the groups. However, even very similar work groups may develop different norms. The members of one group may be friendly with their supervisor whereas those of another group may not.

(d) Norm conformity: Norms have the power to force a certain degree of conformity. There are several factors consist of norm conformity, which are as follows:

- Some groups may exert more pressure for conformity than others because of the personalities of the group members.
- The history of the group and its members also plays a part in conformity. For example, if the group has always been successful by following certain behaviours, new group members are also asked to follow the same. If the group was not successful in the past, a new group member may have greater freedom to exhibit other behaviours.

5. *Group cohesiveness:* Cohesiveness is defined as the attractiveness of group members towards the group. It also emphasizes on the group's ability to satisfy its member's needs. It, therefore, helps the group members to work more consistently and make greater contribution to the achievement of the organisational goals. It is also psychologically more satisfying to all of its members. According to Likert, "cohesiveness is the attractiveness of the members towards the group or resistance of the members leaving it". It refers to the attachment of members with the group. According to K. Aswathappa, "cohesiveness is understood as the extent of liking each member has towards others and how far everyone wants to remain as the member of the group". According to Cartwright there are four principal consequences of cohesiveness, which are as follows:

- Ability of a group to retain its members.
- Power of the group to influence its members.
- Degree of participation and loyalty of members.
- Feeling of security on the part of the members.

Attractiveness is the key to cohesiveness. Cohesiveness is the extent to which group members are loyal and committed to the group and to each other. In a highly cohesive group, the members work well together, support and trust one another and are generally effective at achieving their chosen goals. A group that lacks cohesiveness will not be very much coordinated. Its members will not support one another and they may face difficulty in reaching their goals. Managers should develop an understanding of the factors that increase and reduce group cohesiveness.

Advantages of Group Cohesiveness

The advantages of group cohesiveness are as follows:

- The members of cohesive groups have high morale.
- The members don't have conflicting views, which decreases the chances of in-clash among the views of group members at the workplace or elsewhere.
- Individuals of cohesive groups have no anxiety at the workplace.
- Members of cohesive groups are regular at their work.
- Cohesiveness increases productivity.
- Organisations gain from the members of cohesive group because they communicate better, they share ideologies and respect opinions of fellow employees.

The following factors can increase group cohesiveness:

- Competitiveness with other groups.
- Inter personal attraction.
- Favourable evaluation from outsiders.
- Agreement on goals.
- Frequent interaction.

The following factors decrease cohesiveness:

- Large group size.
- Disagreement on goals.

- Competitiveness within group.
- Domination by one or more members.
- Unpleasant experiences.

5.5 INTERGROUP PROCESSES IN ORGANISATIONS

Intergroup processes happen when members of two or more groups must interact to complete a task. Such processes feature interactions among members of different groups in an organisation, such as manufacturing, quality assurance, finance, marketing, and design engineering. Although behaviour at group interfaces is called intergroup behaviour, groups do not interact directly. Members of groups interact with each other, representing the interests of their group. The basic management issue is the effective coordination of activities, which requires contributions of people from different groups. Cultural differences in-group dynamics suggest one should learn about those differences before talking an assignment in another country.

The pressure to conform to group norms and the value placed on conformity to those norms vary from culture to culture. Culture also differs in how much conflict between groups they will accept. The major ethical issues about groups in organisations center on conformity to group norms and the question of informed free choice. Cohesive groups develop powerful forces of socialization to their norms. Such groups reject deviant members after unsuccessful efforts to get conformity to norms. Productivity typically is lower in large groups than in small ones. Group size has several specific efforts including the following:

- Satisfaction with the group's activities decreases as size increase.
- Participation of members drops as size increases.
- The strength of bonds among group members decreases as group size increases.
- Large groups have more resources for doing the group's task.
- Reaching agreement about a group's activities or making decisions is more difficult in large groups than in small ones.
- A leader is more likely to emerge as group size increases.
- Larger groups make communication and coordination of group members more difficult.
- People in large groups find it difficult to learn about each other. For example, in a three-person group, the number of possible relationship is 6 and in a four-person group, it is 25.

5.6 CERTAIN IMPORTANT TERMINOLOGIES W.R.T. GROUP

(*a*) ***Roles:*** By 'role' we mean a set of expected behaviour patterns attributed to someone occupying a given position in a social unit. The understanding of role behaviour is simplified each of us chose one role and played it regularly and consistently.

(*b*) ***Role identify:*** There are certain attitudes and behaviours consistent with a role and they create the role identify. People have the ability to shift roles rapidly when they recognize that the situation and its demands clearly require major changes.

(*c*) ***Role perception:*** One's view of how one is supposed to act in a given situation. How you behave is determined to a large extent, by the role defined in the context in which you act.

(*d*) ***Role conflict:*** When an individual is confronted by divergent role conflict. This is the most critical role concept in attempting to explain behaviour certainly. Role conflict will increase internal pension and frustration in an organisational set-up.

(*e*) ***Group roles:*** This may vary in several ways in their complexity, in their social function, and in their cultural significance. Each of these variables helps define the role to the individual and to the group. Conformity in-group goals may be determined by individual variables, the rigidity of the group standards, prestige variables and so on. Table 5.1 explains different roles of group in detail.

Table 5.1: Different roles of group

(*a*) Some Typical Roles Found in Groups		
Initiator	:	Offers new ideas about how to do the group's task or resolve its problems.
Information seeker/giver	:	Seeks clarifying information or adds new information to the group's discussions.
Elaborator	:	Extends the information used by the group by offering examples or trying to show the expected results of the group's effort.
Coordinator	:	Helps pull together the activities of group members.
Recorder	:	Keeps a written record of the group's activities.
(*b*) Maintenance Roles		
Encourager	:	Motivates other members to contribute ideas to the group.
Harmonizer	:	Reference conflict among group members.
Compromiser	:	Reduces conflict within the group by finding ways of splitting differences.
Gatekeeper	:	Tries to keep communication links open with important parties outside the group.
Follower	:	Accepts the direction of the group, usually passively.
(*c*) Individual Roles		
Aggressor	:	Acts hostilely towards other group members.
Blocker	:	Resists the direction of the group and opposes the views of others.
Joker	:	Engages in horseplay; tells stories and jokes unrelated to group activities.
Dominator	:	Tries to give direction to other group members and asset own higher status over others.

Source: Benne, K, and P. Sheats. 1948 "Functional Roles of Group Members", Journal of Social Issues 2:

5.7 GROUP DECISION MAKING

People in organisations work in a variety of groups—formal and informal, permanent and temporary. Most of these groups make decisions that affect the welfare of the organisation and the people in it. There are several issues surrounding how groups make decisions: Group polarisation, groupthink and group problem solving. Group polarisation is the tendency for a group''s average post-discussion attitudes to be more extreme than its average pre-discussion attitudes. Groupthink is a mode of thinking that occurs when members of a group are deeply involved in a cohesive in-group and desire for unanimity offsets their motivation to appraise alternative courses of action.

(*a*) An illusion of invulnerability, shared by most or all members, that creates excessive optimism and encourages extreme risk taking.

(*b*) Collective efforts to rationalise or discount warnings that might lead members to reconsider assumptions before recommitting themselves to past policy decisions.

(*c*) An unquestioned belief in the group's inherent morality, inclining members to ignore the ethical and moral consequences of their decisions.

(*d*) Stereotyped views of "enemy" leaders as too evil to warrant genuine attempts to negotiate or as too weak or stupid to counter whatever risky attempts are made to defeat their purposes.

(*e*) Direct pressure on a member who expresses strong arguments against any of the group's stereotypes, illusions or commitments, making clear that such dissent is contrary to what is expected of loyal members.

(*f*) Self-censorship of deviations from the apparent group consensus, reflecting each member's inclination to minimise the importance of his or her doubts and counter arguments.

(*g*) A shared illusion of unanimity, resulting partly from self-censorship of deviations, augmented by the false assumption that silence means consent.

(*h*) The emergence of self-appointed "mind guards", members who protect the group from adverse information that might shatter their shared complacency about the effectiveness and morality of their decisions.

In short, a decision is a choice among alternative actions, made after consideration of the likelihood of various outcomes occurring as a result of the choice, and according to a decision rule that forces the decision to be made in line with the decision maker's objectives or goals. Group decision making is an activity, which permits the coming together of people with heterogeneous characteristics who can understand the problems in a better way and hence, develop creative alternatives leading to effective group performance.

Decision making is the process of choosing from among several alternatives. Managers' decisions usually are guided by a goal. A programmed decision is a decision that recurs often enough for a decision rule to be developed. A decision rule is a statement that tells a decision maker which alternative to choose based on the characteristics of the decision situation. A nonprogrammed decision is a decision that recurs infrequently and for which there is no previously established decision rule. Problem solving is a form of decision making in which the issue is unique and alternatives must be developed and evaluated without the aid of a programmed decision rule. Table 5.2 describes showing characteristics of different type of decisions.

Table 5.2: Showing characteristics of different type of decisions

Characteristics	Programmed Decisions	Nonprogrammed Decisions
Type of decision	Well structured	Poorly structured
Frequency	Repetitive and routine	New and unusual
Goals	Clear, specific	Vague
Information	Readily available	Not available, unclear channels
Organisational level	Minor	Major
Consequences	Lower levels	Upper levels
Time for solution	Short	Relatively long
Basis for solution	Decision rules, set procedures	Judgement and creativity

1. Problem Solving: Problem solving is one of the important functions of leaders. Improved problem solving demands the knowledge of certain important points in the mind of the leader. They include:

- The leader must convene a meeting only when there is good reason for it.
- Rather elaborating the answer to a decision problem, try to define it.
- Create an atmosphere in which all group members participate freely and actively and allow them to express conflicting views.
- Try to elicit ideas from the group members rather than supplying to them.
- Look for best solution to a problem by discussing all the possible alternatives.
- While resolving conflicting problems, try to find out the troublemakers and prevent blow up situations.
- Observe the following rules laid down by A. Jay, in holding the meetings, such as control the garrulous; draw out the silent; protect the weak; encourage the clashes of ideas; watch out for the suggestion-squashing reflex; come to the most senior people last; close on a note of achievement.

2. Problem Solving Techniques: Murnighan has suggested the following techniques, which are helpful to the managers in better decision making and for improved problem solving.

(i) Brainstorming: It means to use the brain to storm a problem. It is an effective technique to improve the problem solving abilities of groups and increasingly applied by almost all the organisations. Under this technique a group is assembled, presented with the problem and encouraged to produce as many ideas and solutions to a problem. No one is allowed to criticise until the group members came out with new suggestions. This technique requires group members to generate as many ideas and alternatives as possible; quickly and without inhibitions. Brainstorming is most useful for simple, well-defined problems. For brainstorming to work effectively, all members must agree to and deliberately follow four rules:

- All criticism is ruled out. No one is allowed to judge or evaluate any ideas until the idea-generation process has been completed.
- "Freewheeling" is welcomed. The emphasis is on creativity and imagination; the wilder or more radical the ideas, the better.
- Quantity is wanted. The more ideas, the more likely that a superior idea will appear.
- Piggybacking is good. Everyone is encouraged to suggest how other's ideas can be turned into new ideas or how to or more ideas can be joined into a new idea.

Brainstorming can be disrupted when members try to dominate the process, or when they argue and get stuck on one point or refuse to contribute openly to the process, or when they attack others. Effective facilitation ensures that all viewpoints are written for all to see and build on, that members listen to each other, and that the focus of the subject is kept on track.

(ii) Nominal Group Technique: Another useful group and team decision making technique is the nominal group technique (NGT). This technique attempts to solicit as much valuable information and perspective as possible from as many members as possible. The nominal group technique (NGT) restricts verbal interaction between members during the decision-making process. The nominal group consists of a number of individuals acting independently a paper work and their actions are added together at the end. The nominal group decision is the pooled outcome of the individual votes. This technique is widely used in industry, education and health, etc. in these days. The NGT works when the team or group is so large that free discussion is difficult or when the members disagree and consensus cannot be reached. In this technique, members get to consensus by following this sequence.

(*a*) ***Members generate the ideas:*** Participants are assigned to groups of five to seven members and are then given a "nominal" question (e.g., when should be done to improve the effectiveness of this work unit?). Usually, this question is stated in writing as part of an individual worksheet. Group participants work silently and independently and respond in writing to the nominal question; they are encouraged to list as many alternatives or ideas as they can.

(*b*) ***They record the ideas:*** With the assistance of a recorder, participants read their responses to the nominal question aloud in round-robin fashion. The recorder writes each response as it is offered; on criticism or discussion of the ideas is allowed.

(*c*) ***They clarify the ideas:*** The recorder asks for questions on each response. This is done in round-robin fashion again, and questions are allowed for clarification only.

(*d*) ***They vote on the ideas:*** Participants are asked to rank the five or seven responses they consider most valuable. The balloting is tallied to rank order each response in the master list.

(*e*) ***They refine the ideas:*** Steps C and D are repeated as needed to refine the list to identify the most preferred response or set of responses.

The ranked lists are collected by the facilitator and used to make additional assignments or refinements in the decision process.

(*iii*) ***Group Interaction:*** This is the general method of holding meeting in which the chairman of the meeting convene it and explains the problem to the group members. The deliberations are somewhat unstructured and social pressures exert influence. In order to have improved decision making abilities of the group, the leader must clarify the input and try to resolve the conflicting views satisfactorily.

3. Precautions to be taken for Ensuring Group Decision Making More Effective: Jains, who developed the concept of groupthinking and decision making, suggests the following guidelines to avoid pitfalls in the process of making decisions:

- Assign the role of critical evaluator to each group member.
- Encourage sharing of objections.
- Insist that the leader avoid seeming partial to one course of action.
- Create subgroups that operate under different leaders but work on the same problem.
- Have group members discuss issues with subordinates and report back on their reactions.
- Invite outside experts to observe group activities and react to group processes and decisions.
- Assign one member of the group to play a "devil's advocate" role at each meeting.
- Write alternative scenarios for the intentions of competing group.
- Hold "Second-chance" meetings on key issues after consensus has apparently been achieved.

SUMMARY

A group consists of a number of individuals working together for a common objective. Groups have significant influence on an organisation and are inseparable from an organisation. They are useful for the organisation as they form foundation of human resources.

The study of group behaviour is essential for an organisation to achieve its goals. Individual and group behaviours vary from each other. In 1920, Elton Mayo and his associates conducted the Hawthorne experiments and came to know that the group behaviour has great impact on productivity. The importance of group behaviour has been realized from time to time.

Human behaviour consists of individuals, who move in groups. The knowledge of group behaviour as well as individual behaviour is necessary for a manager. He must understand group psychology and should also understand individual behaviour in the context of group behaviour. The group in which he moves influences individual work, job satisfaction and effective performance.

The study of groups is important to the manager for a number of reasons such as the group is a key element in the social order of our culture. Groups serve not only as the focal point of social life, but they provide an important source of direction to individuals for understanding social values and norms. Through participation in groups, individuals may satisfy important economic status, safety, security, and friendship needs. The behaviour and performance of groups provide a major mechanism for the achievement or organisational goals.

The students of the Berkeley University now live a co-ed dormitory! Much to the disquietude of elders, the movement towards "living in groups for normalization" is gathering momentum. The Kierkegaard slogan "to be that self which one truly is" is not only the remedy of psychotics but the ideal of normal. This process of knowing oneself is best achieved through a group. This chapter explained the importance of groups in taking the organisation to new heights especially in the present highly competitive global economy.

REVIEW QUESTIONS

1. What do you mean by group formation? How is it important for an organisation?
2. Explain group decision making techniques. How do you ensure the success in that process?
3. Describe various type of groups and group norms with suitable examples of your choice.
4. Explain characteristics of different types of decision making with examples.

DISCUSSION QUESTIONS

1. Some have argued that people, not organisations, make decisions and that the study of "organisational" decision making is therefore pointless. Do you agree with this argument? Why or why not?
2. Describe at least three points in the decision making process at which information plays an important role.
3. Can you think of a time when you satisfied while making a decision? Have you ever suboptimised?

STUDENT EXERCISE

The Decision Making Styles stated in the chapter, can assist a manager in determining when, and to what extent, they should involve employees in decision making. If a manager elects to use a group to make a decision, it usually requires that the group reach a consensus. Consensus is achieved "when all members can say they either agree with the decision or have had their 'day in court' and were unable to convince the others of their viewpoint. In the final analysis, everyone agrees to support the outcome." Discuss the relevance of this selection model in a global context.

SKILL TEST

Test your Equity Sensitivity

The questions that follow are intended to help you better understand your equity sensitivity. Answer each question on the scales by circling the number that best reflects your personal feelings:

1. I think it is important for everyone to be treated fairly.

5	4	3	2	1
Strongly Agree	Agree	Neither Agree Nor Disagree	Disagree	Strongly Disagree

2. I pay a lot of attention to how I am treated, in comparison to how others are treated.

5	4	3	2	1
Strongly Agree	Agree	Neither Agree Nor Disagree	Disagree	Strongly Disagree

3. I get really angry if I think I'm being treated unfairly.

5	4	3	2	1
Strongly Agree	Agree	Neither Agree Nor Disagree	Disagree	Strongly Disagree

4. It makes me uncomfortable if I think someone else is not being treated fairly.

5	4	3	2	1
Strongly Agree	Agree	Neither Agree Nor Disagree	Disagree	Strongly Disagree

5. If I thought I was being treated unfairly, I would be very motivated to change things.

5	4	3	2	1
Strongly Agree	Agree	Neither Agree Nor Disagree	Disagree	Strongly Disagree

6. It doesn't really bother me if someone else gets a better deal than me.

5	4	3	2	1
Strongly Agree	Agree	Neither Agree Nor Disagree	Disagree	Strongly Disagree

7. It is impossible for everyone to be treated fairly all the time.

5	4	3	2	1
Strongly Agree	Agree	Neither Agree Nor Disagree	Disagree	Strongly Disagree

8. When I'm a manager, I'll make sure that all of my employees are treated fairly.

5	4	3	2	1
Strongly Agree	Agree	Neither Agree Nor Disagree	Disagree	Strongly Disagree

9. I would quit my job if I thought I was being treated unfairly.

5	4	3	2	1
Strongly Agree	Agree	Neither Agree Nor Disagree	Disagree	Strongly Disagree

10. Short-term inequities are okay, because things all even out in the long run.

5	4	3	2	1
Strongly Agree	Agree	Neither Agree Nor Disagree	Disagree	Strongly Disagree

ANALYSIS AND INTERPRETATION

Add up your total points. If you scored 35 or above, you are highly sensitive to equity and fairness; 15 or less, you have very little sensitivity to equity and fairness; between 35 and 15, you have moderate equity sensitivity.

If you wish to know more insight on your test score, then you are welcome to contact author via e-mail: shaangrila@gmail.com or social media: drs.shajahan.7@facebook.com

6
CHAPTER

COMMUNICATION PROCESS IN ORGANISATION

LEARNING OBJECTIVES

This chapter aims at introducing fundamental concepts for explaining the importance of effective communication for moulding sustained high performance and organisation for AD 2020 to the readers:

- *Definition, importance and fundamental concepts of communication*
- *Communication process and direction of communication*
- *Schuler's model for organisational communication*
- *Barriers to effective communication and listening*
- *Improving personal communication, Johari Window and transactional analysis*

INTRODUCTION

Communication is one of the most frequently discussed dynamics in the entire field of organisational behaviour. In practice, effective communication is a basic prerequisite for the attainment of organisational goals. Therefore, communication is considered to be the most important and most effective ingredient of the management process. Interpersonal communication is fundamental to all managerial activities. All other management functions involve communication in some form of directions and feedback. Thus, effective management is a function of effective communication.

6.1 DEFINITION OF COMMUNICATION

In modern society, the term communication is frequently and freely used by everyone, including members of the general public, organisational behaviour scholars, and management practitioners. Communication is the process of transmitting information from one person to another. Broadly, it means who says what, to whom, through which channel and with what effect. It is a way of reacting to the other person with ideas, facts, thoughts, feelings and values. Communication experts emphasize the behavioural implications of communication by pointing out that "the only means by which one person can influence another is by the behaviours he shows that is, the communicative exchanges between people provide the sole method by which influence or effects can be achieved". In other words, the behaviours that occur in an organisation are vital to the communication process. This personal and behavioural exchange view of communication takes many forms.

(a) Objectives of Communication

Managements depend upon communication to achieve organisational objectives. Since managers work with and through other people, all their acts, policies, rules, orders and procedures must pass through some kind of communication channel. Also there must be channel of communication for feedback. Accordingly, some of the purposes of communication are:

- To discourage the spread of misinformation, ambiguity and rumors, which can cause conflict and tension.
- To foster any attitude, that is necessary for motivation, cooperation and job satisfaction.
- To develop information and understanding among all workers. This is necessary for group effort.
- To prepare workers for a change in methods of environment by giving them necessary information in advance.
- To encourage subordinates to supply ideas and suggestions for improving the product or work environment and taking these suggestions seriously.
- To improve labor management relations by keeping the communications channels open and accessible.
- To improve social relations among workers by encouraging intercommunication. This would satisfy the basic human need for a sense of belonging and friendship.

(b) Importance of Communication

Interpersonal roles require managers to interact with supervisors, sub-ordinates, peers and others outside the organisation. Thus, for co-ordinated action, communication is necessary. Communication transforms a group of unrelated individuals into a team that knows what its goals are and how it will try to reach them. Communication allows people to co-ordinate with each other by providing them with a way to share information. The first type of information that needs to be shared is what the goals of the organisations are people need to know where they are heading and why. They also need directions for their specific tasks.

Communication is especially important for the task of decision-making. Decision-makers must share their views on what the problem is and what the alternatives are. Once a decision has been made, communication is necessary to implement the decision and to evaluate its results. Changes in market or in customer preferences can lead to uncertainty about whether a product or a marketing strategy needs to be updated or overhauled. The uncertainty resulted from the lack of information, can be reduced by communicating that information. Market researchers, for example, can communicate with other groups about changes in the market place. The greater the uncertainty about a task, the more important the communication of information becomes.

Communication also allows people to express their emotions. Communication of feelings can be very important to employee morale and productivity. Employees who feel that they cannot vent their anger or express their joy on the job may feel frustrated and repressed. On any given day, a manager may communicate for all the purposes described above. Communication goes up, down and across the levels of the hierarchy of an organisation.

6.2 THE COMMUNICATION PROCESS

As a process, communication involves sending and receiving information (messages) through symbols that is, words, nonverbal cues, attitudes, and moods, simply stated, communication involves, Who ... says what, ... in which way..., to whom..., with what effect? A simplified model of the communication process in presented in Fig. 6.1 as shown below.

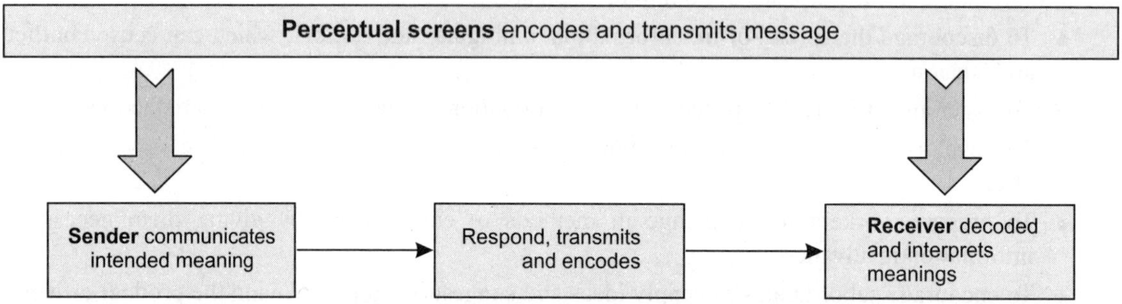

Fig. 6.1: The communication process

However, it may be noted that sending and receiving a message is rarely a straightforward data exchange because of our ever-present perceptual screens and interpretation of meaning based on voice fluctuations, gestures of the sender and context in which the message was send.

Thus, the communication process is a loop that connects the sender and the receiver and operates in both directions. Communication is not complete until the original sender knows that the receiver understands the message. Encoding is the process by which the message is translated from an idea or thought into transmittable symbols. Transmission is the process through which the symbols that represent the message are sent to the receiver. The medium is the channel or path through which the message is transmitted. Decoding is the process by which the receiver of the message interprets the message's meaning. Feedback is the process in which the receiver returns a message to the sender that indicates receipt of the message. Interpersonal communication involves a process that is defined by at least four factors:

- Feelings about oneself.
- Feelings about the other.
- Feelings about the content of what is to be discussed.
- Feelings about the subject being discussed.

The Fig. 6.2 presents a general view of the communication process, as a loop between the source and the receiver. In the simplest kind of communication, both the sender and the receiver perform the encoding and decoding functions automatically.

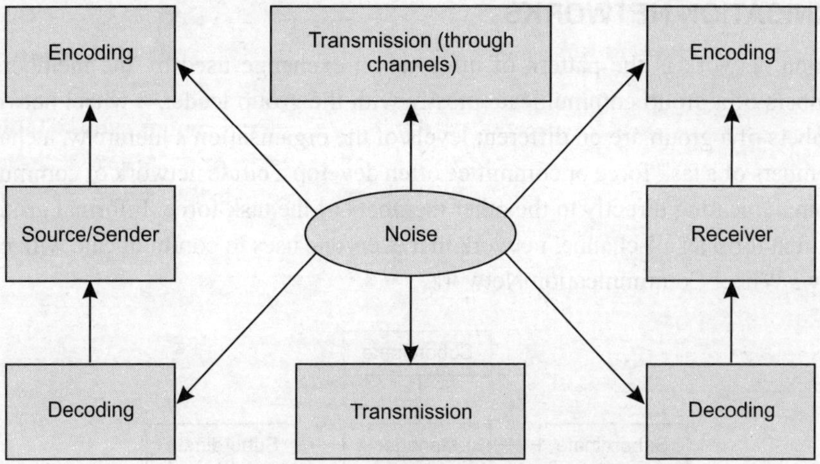

Fig. 6.2: Message sending process

Source or sender: The communication cycle begins when one person called the sender wants to transmit a fact, idea, opinion or other information to someone else. A manager, for instance, might call the research department to send the latest information on a particular market.

Encoding: The second step is to encode the message into a form appropriate to the situation. The encoding might take the form of words, facial expressions, gestures, physical actions and symbols such as numbers, pictures, graphs etc. Indeed, most communication involves a combination of these. The encoding process is influenced by the content of the message, the familiarity of the sender and receiver and other situational factors.

Transmission: After the message has been encoded, it is transmitted through the appropriate channel or medium. Common channels or media in organisations include face-to-face communication using the media of sound waves, light, letters and reports.

Decoding: The person to whom the message is sent, called the receiver interprets the meaning of the message through the process of decoding. This process may be simple and automatic, but it can also be quite complex. Even when you are just reading a letter, you may need to use all your knowledge of the language, your experience with the letter-writer and so on. If the intended message and the received message differ a great deal, there is a communication gap and misunderstanding is likely to follow.

Receiver: The receiver can be an individual, a group, or an individual acting on behalf of a group. The sender has generally little control over how the receiver will deal with the message. The receiver may ignore it, decide not to try to decode, understand it or respond immediately. The communication cycle continues when the receiver responds by the same steps back to the original sender, which is called the feedback.

Noise: In the communication process, noise takes on a meaning slightly different from its usual one. Noise refers to any type of disturbance that reduces the clearness of the message being transmitted. Thus, it might be something that keeps the receiver from paying close attention such as someone coughing, other people talking closely, a car driving by etc. It can be a disruption such as disturbance in a telephone line, weak signal due to bad weather etc. It can also be internal to the receiver such as tiredness or hunger or minor ailments, which may affect the message.

6.3 COMMUNICATION NETWORKS

A communication network is the pattern of information exchange used by the members of a group. When the members of a group communicate mostly with the group leader, a wheel network develops. When the members of a group are on different levels/of the organisation's hierarchy, a chain network is developed. Members of a task force or committee often develop a circle network of communication with each person communicating directly to the other members of the task force. Informal groups that lack a formal leader often form an all-channel network that everyone uses to communicate with everyone else. Figure 6.3 shows Wheel Communication Network.

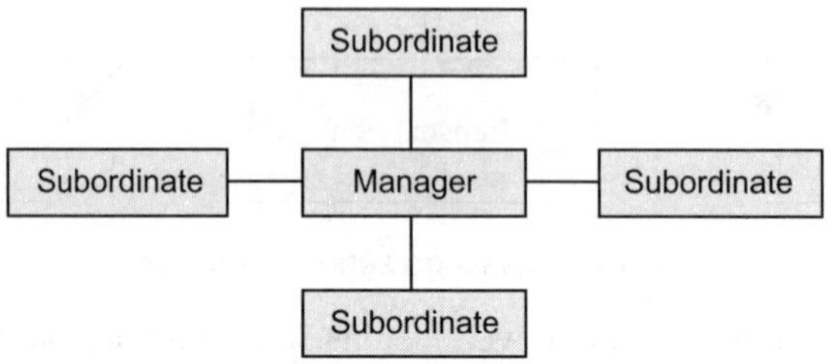

Fig. 6.3: Wheel communication network

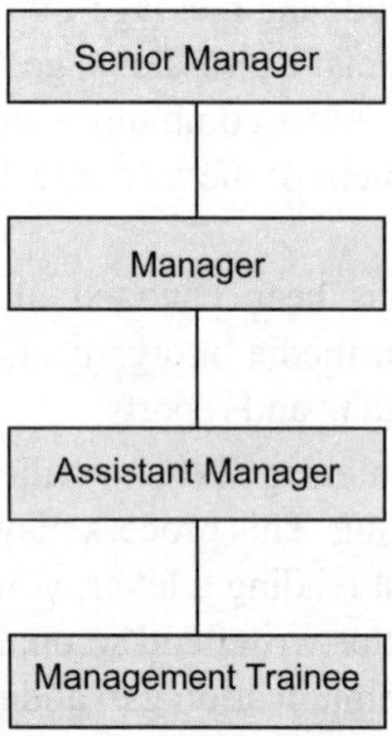

Fig. 6.4: Chain communication network

The density of communication refers to the total quantity of communication among members. The distance between members describes how far a message must travel to reach the receiver. The ease with which members can communicate with others is measured by member's relative freedom to use different paths to communicate. Members' commitment to the group's work is defined by the centrality of the position of the members. All these provide insight into possible communication problems. For instance, a group with high density and distance can expect a lot of noise distortion in its communication, as messages travel a long distance to get to the receivers.

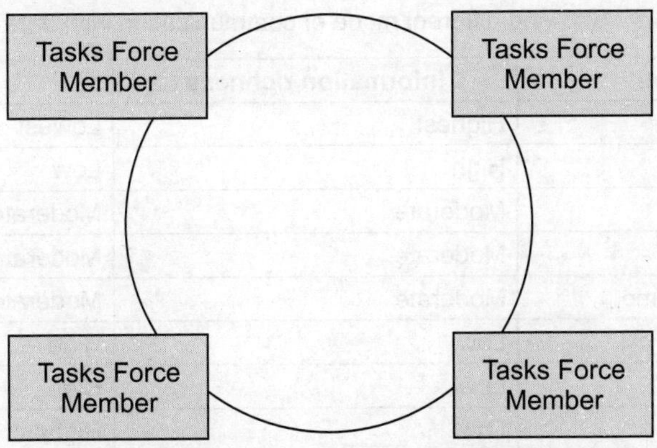

Fig. 6.5: Circle communication network

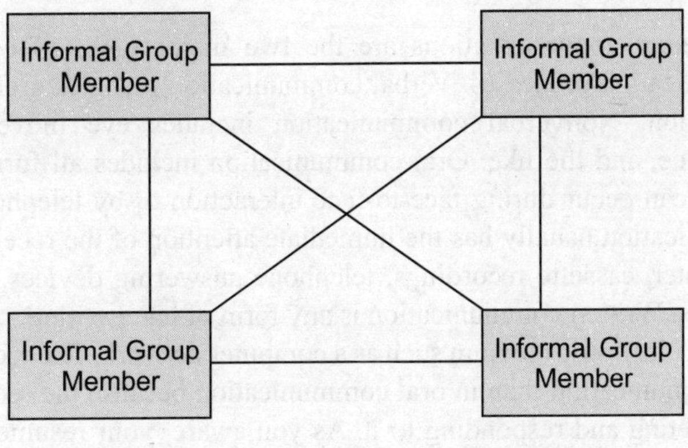

Fig. 6.6: All channel communication network

6.4 MODE OF COMMUNICATION

Communication processes in organisations are continuous and constantly changing. They do not have beginning or an end, nor do they follow a strict sequence. During communication, the sender creates messages from one or more symbols to which he attaches meaning. Messages can be oral, written, or nonverbal; they can also be intentional or unintentional. Messages deal with tasks to be done, maintenance of organisational policies, or information about some state of the organisation. They can go to people inside the organisation or outside. Organisation communication includes the purpose, flow, and direction of messages and the media used for those messages. Such communication happens within the complex, interdependent social systems of organisations. Think of organisational communication as another view of behaviour in organisations. Author describes such behaviour as "message behaviour", behaviour that includes sending, receiving, and giving meaning to messages in the organisational context. Table 6.1 describes Different mode of Communication with data capacity and information richness.

Table 6.1: Showing different mode of communication with data capacity

Communication	Information richness	Data capacity
Face-to-face discussion	Highest	Lowest
Telephone	High	Low
Electronic mail	Moderate	Moderate
Individualized letter	Moderate	Moderate
Personalised note or memo	Moderate	Moderate
Formal written report	Low	High
Flyer or bulletin	Low	High
Formal numeric report	Low	Highest

Source: *R.L. Draft and R.H. Lengal, Information Richness: A New Approach to Managerial Behaviour and Organisational Design in B. Slow and L. Cummings, ed., Research in Organisation Behaviour, vol.6., Greenwich, Conn., JAI Press.1984.*

Verbal and non-verbal communications are the two major types of communication found in organisational communication processes. Verbal communication includes oral, written, and electronic forms of communication. Nonverbal communication includes eye movements, gestures, facial expression, tone of voice, and the like. Oral communication includes all forms of speech between a sender and receiver. It can occur during face-to-face interaction or by telephone, radio, or television. Although oral communication usually has the immediate attention of the receiver, the message can be recorded and played later, cassette recordings, telephone answering devices, and computer-recorded voice mail are examples. Written communication is any form of handwriting, printed memo and report, or message sent over an electronic medium such as a computer network. The receiver's response is more delayed in written communication than in oral communication because the receiver must first read the message before interpreting and responding to it. As you aware, your resume is an important written communication about yourself.

6.5 METHODS OF COMMUNICATION

As modern technology develops, electronic or video communications are becoming increasingly important. Such communication includes e-mail, computer networks, fax machines, computer conferencing, and video conferencing. Those methods offer the advantages of speed, accuracy, and easy dispersal to many locations, direct interaction, and quick feedback. Video conferencing also allows people in different places to see each other while they talk.

There are mainly three primary methods of communication in an organisation, which are written, oral, and non-verbal. These methods of communication are often combined. Considerations that affect the choice of method include the audience whether it is physically present, the nature of the message, and the lost of transmission. The Fig. 6.7 given below shows various forms each method can take.

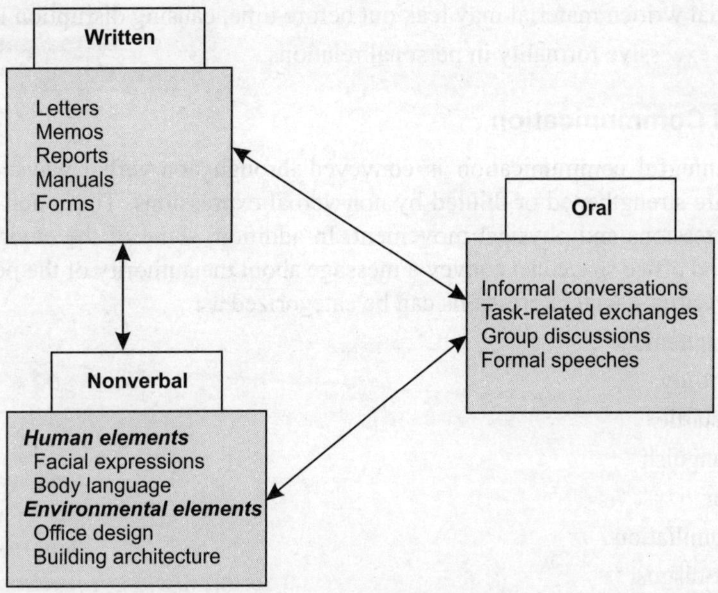

Fig. 6.7: Methods of communication in organisation

(a) Written Communication

A written communication is put in writing and is generally in the form of instructions, letters, memos, formal reports, rules and regulations, policy manuals, information bulletins and so on. These areas have to be covered in writing for efficient functioning of the organisation. It is most effective when it is required to communicate information that requires action in the future and also in situations where communication is that of general informational nature. It also ensures that everyone has the same information.

Advantages

- It serves as an evidence of events and proceedings.
- It provides a permanency of record for future references. The message can be stored for an indefinite period of time.
- It reduces the likelihood of misunderstanding and misinterpretation. The written communications are more likely to be well considered, logical and clear. The message can be checked for accuracy before it is transmitted.
- It can save time when many persons must be contacted at the same time.
- It is more reliable for transmitting lengthy statistical data.
- It appears formal and authoritative for action.

Disadvantages

- It can be very time-consuming, especially for lengthy reports.
- There is no immediate feedback opportunity to be sure that the receiver has understood the message.

- Confidential written material may leak out before time, causing disruption in its effectiveness.
- It leads to excessive formality in personal relations.

(b) Non-Verbal Communication

Some of the meaningful communication is conveyed through non-verbal ways. Even some of the verbal messages are strengthened or diluted by non-verbal expressions. These non-verbal expressions include facial expressions and physical movement. In addition, some of the environmental elements such as building and office space can convey a message about the authority of the person. According to Tompkins and McCarter, facial expressions can be categorized as:

- Interest-excitement
- Enjoyment-joy
- Surprise-startle
- Distress-anguish
- Fear-terror
- Shame-humiliation
- Contempt-disgust
- Anger-rage

Physical movements or body language is known as "kinesics". A handshake is probably the most common form of body language and tells a lot about a person's disposition. Other examples of body language are tilting of head, folding of arms or sitting position in a chair. Our facial expressions can show anger, frustration, arrogance, shyness, fear and other characteristics that can never be adequately communicated through written word or through oral communication itself. Some of the other body language symptoms are shrugging our shoulders for indifference, wink an eye for mischief or intimacy, tap our fingers on the table for impatience and we slap our forehead for forgetfulness. As far as environmental elements are concerned, a large office with luxurious carpeting and expensive furniture conveys a message of status, power and prestige such as that of a chief operating officer. On the other hand, a small metal desk on a corner communicates the status of a low ranking officer in the organisational setting. Accordingly non-verbal actions have considerable impact on the quality of communication.

Typically organisations produce a great deal of written communication of many kinds. A letter is a formal means of communication with an individual, generally someone outside the organisation. Probably the most common form of written communication in organisations is the office memorandum, or a memo. Memos usually are addressed to a person or group inside the organisation. They tend to deal with a single topic and are more impersonal, but less formal than letters. Other common forms of written communication include reports, manuals and forms. Reports generally summarize the progress or results of a project and often provide information to be used in decision-making. Manuals have various functions in organisations. Instruction manuals tell employees how to operate machines; policy and procedure manuals inform them of organisational rules; operations manual describe how to perform tasks and respond to work-related problems. As such, they represent attempts to make communication more efficient and information more accessible. A performance appraisal form is an example.

(c) Oral Communication

Oral communication, also known as face-to-face communication is the most prevalent form of organisational communication. It may be in the form of direct talk and conversation between the speakers and listeners when they are physically present at one place or through telephone or intercom system conversation. Where one-way communication is required, then oral communication may include public address system. Informal rumour mill or grapevine is also a popular form of oral communication. It is most effective for leaders to address the followers via public address system or audio-visual media. Oral communication is particularly powerful because the receiver not only hears the content of the message, but also observes the physical gestures associated with it as well as the changes in tone, pitch, speed and volume of the spoken word. The human voice can impart the message much more forcefully and effectively than the written words and is an effective way of changing attitudes, beliefs and feelings, since faith, trust and sincerity can be much better judged in a face-to-face conversation rather than in written words.

Advantages

Some of the advantages of oral communication are:

- It is direct, simple, time saving and least expensive form of communication.
- It allows for feedback and spontaneous thinking, so that if the receiver is unsure of the message, rapid feedback allows for early detection by the sender so that corrections can be immediately made, if necessary.
- Because the message is conveyed instantaneously, it helps in avoiding delays, red tape and other formalities.
- It conveys personal warmth and friendliness and it develops a sense of belonging because of these personalized contacts.

Disadvantages

- There is no formal record of communication so that any misunderstood message cannot be referred back to what was actually said.
- If the verbal message is passed on, the long hierarchical chain of command, then some distortions can occur during the process. The more people the message is to pass through, the greater is the potential distortion.
- Lengthy and distant communication cannot be conveyed verbally in an efficient way.
- The receiver may receive the message in his own perception and thus misunderstand the intent of the message.
- Spontaneous responses may not be carefully thought about.
- The spirit of authority cannot be transmitted effectively in verbal transactions.
- Organisational Communications.
- More or less or a different meaning might be conveyed by manner of speaking, tone of voice and facial expressions.

6.6 COMMUNICATION PROCESSES IN ORGANISATIONS

The changing marketplace demands that organisations communicate faster, more flexibly, and in more focused ways so the communication process, must be continually examined. Also, since organisations are increasingly forming and reinforcing strategic alliances and networked partnerships, it is important for organisational members to effectively communicate with external stakeholders. Hightech informational exchanges will continue to increase in the twenty-first century. Everyone will be using e-mail, voice mail, cellular phones, the Internet, groups' software, faxes, teleconferencing, and wireless systems not yet invented.

These electronics forms of communication speed the rate at which information is transmitted and connect users up, down, across, inside and outside organisational boundaries as never before. Such hightech forms of communication and information sharing are increasingly in use as timed competition and outsourced organisational resources (*i.e.*, bought, rented, or leased from other sources) is emphasized. The rate at which Hewlett Packard generates information today will be the norm for the organisation of tomorrow. "Every month Hewlett Packard's 97,000 employees exchange 20 millions e-mail message nearly 3 trillion characters of data, such as engineering specifications, and execute more than a quarter of a million electronic transactions with customer and suppliers".

With ever larger volumes of information transmitted electronically, it has become increasingly important for employees to be able to differentiate the types of information they receive and to correctly decide the appropriateness of the communication form, with whom the message should be shared, and the occasion on which is should be transmitted. Being able to manage the flow, the appropriateness, the quantity, and the cost of information is a necessary part of the communication structure in and between organisations.

Managers must make use of all these characteristics and tendencies to help groups communicate and work most efficiently. A manager, who sees that a wheel network is forming around an experienced, trusted employee, might not interfere with the process. If an assertive but irresponsible employee becomes the hub of such a wheel, the manager may need to take action. If the manager relies on a group to help make decisions, the manager may encourage silent group members to speak in order to get the desired decisions.

Type of task: If the task of the group is simple, a chain or wheel network is used. For hard tasks, all channel networks arises.

Environment: Environment including the group's seating arrangement and meeting place also affects communication patterns. For instance, if members always sit around a table, then circle network arises.

Group performance factors: The group performance factors like group's size, composition, norms and cohesiveness also affect the formation of communication networks. For instance, it is much easier to have an all-channel network in a group of eight than in a group of eighty.

(a) Forms of Organisational Communication

Although interpersonal and group forms of communication pertain even at the broadest organisational levels, they do not sufficiently describe the paths of all messages transmitted in organisations. Individuals can send and receive messages across whole organisational levels and departments by means of vertical communication or the informal communication network. Non-verbal communication is also important and can be a part of interpersonal, group and organisational communication.

1. ***Vertical Communication:*** Vertical communication is the communication that flows both up and down the organisational hierarchy. This communication typically takes place between managers and their superiors or sub-ordinates.

2. *Upward Communication:* Upward communication consists of messages moving up the hierarchy from sub-ordinates to superiors. The content of upward communication usually includes requests, suggestions or complaints and information the sub-ordinate thinks is of importance to the superior.

3. *Downward Communication:* Downward communication consists of messages moving down the hierarchy from superiors to sub-ordinates. The content of downward communication often includes directives, assignments, performance feedback and information that the superior thinks are of value to the sub-ordinate.

4. *Transactional Communication:* Wenburg and Wilmont suggest that instead of communication being "upward" or "downward" which is inter-communication, it should be "transactional" communication, which is mutual and reciprocal because, "all persons are engaged in sending and receiving messages simultaneously. Each person is constantly sharing in the sending and receiving process and each person is affecting the other". In the transactional process, the communication is not simply the flow of information, but it develops a personal linkage between the superior and the subordinate.

5. *Electronic Information Processing and Telecommunications:* Changes in the workplace are occurring at an astonishing rate. Many innovations are based on new technologies—computerised information processing systems, new types of telecommunication systems, the Internet, emerging intranets, and various combinations of these technologies. Experts have estimated that performance of new information technology (at the same cost) doubles every eighteen months. Managers can now send and receive memos and other types of communications around the world on their computer terminals, and they can do so in their cars or via their notebook computers and cellular phones. New information-processing and transmission technologies have created new media, symbols, message transmission methods, and networks for organisational communication.

One of these new ways of communicating is idea sharing, or knowledge sharing, by sharing information on what practices work best. A computer-based system is necessary to store, organize, and then make available to others the best practices. In the information age, in which speed and timed competition are criteria for doing business, effective communication still depends on the extent to which information is accurately and emotionally/received, accepted, and acted upon selecting the right medium is a first step in effectively communicating interpersonally, between groups, and inter organisationally. The liaison serve as a bridge between groups, tying groups together and facilitating the communication flow needed to integrate group activities. The cosmopolite links the organisation to the external environment and may also be an opinion leader in the group. The isolate and the isolated dyad tend to work alone and to interact and communicate little with others.

Organisations need to balance information load and information processing capabilities. In other words, they must take care not to generate more information than people can handle. It is useless to produce sophisticated statistical reports that managers have no time to read. Furthermore, the new technologies that are making more information available to managers and decision makers must be unified to produce usable information. Information production, storage, and processing capabilities must be compatible with one another and, equally important, with the needs of the organisation. Organisations need to balance information load and information processing capabilities.

6. *Informal Communication:* Another term for informal communication network is the grapevine. Informal networks are found in all organisations. It is in the form of gossip in which a person spreads a message to as many other people as possible who may either keep the information to themselves or pass it on to others. The content of gossip is likely to be personal information or the information about the organisation itself.

Managers should have some control over the informal network. For example, the grapevine in an organisation may be carrying harmful information, false information or politically motivated information. When these kinds of rumors are being spread, managers may need to intervene. They can hold open meetings and objectively discuss the issues that are being informally discussed already. They may also issue a clearly worded memo or report stating the facts and thereby help minimize the damage that the informal network can do. Managers can also obtain valuable information from the grapevine and use it for decision-making.

7. ***Other Forms of Communication:*** One that has become especially popular is informally labelled as "management by wandering around". The basic idea is that some managers keep in touch with what is going on by wandering around and talking with people such as sub-ordinates, customers, dealers and anyone else involved with the company in any way. This will give managers, new ideas and a better feel for the entire company.

(b) Schuler's Model of Organisational Communication

Schuler's model of organisational communication specifies that organisational communication should be reciprocally related to performance and satisfaction. The idea of reciprocity presented in the model indicated by the arrows leads to some important implications relating to influence of communication on individuals within the organisation. These implications are:

1. The person's role or his interpretation of communication may influence the communication itself.
2. Role perceptions mediate the influence of communication on employee satisfaction and performance.
3. Role perceptions reciprocate with satisfaction and performance.

The communication will be effective only when employees understand, accept and act upon the information that has been transmitted to them. The sender of message must know the various barriers that can impede not only transmission of information but also affecting understanding and acceptance of it. Communication barriers cause breakdown of communication process leading to many managerial problems.

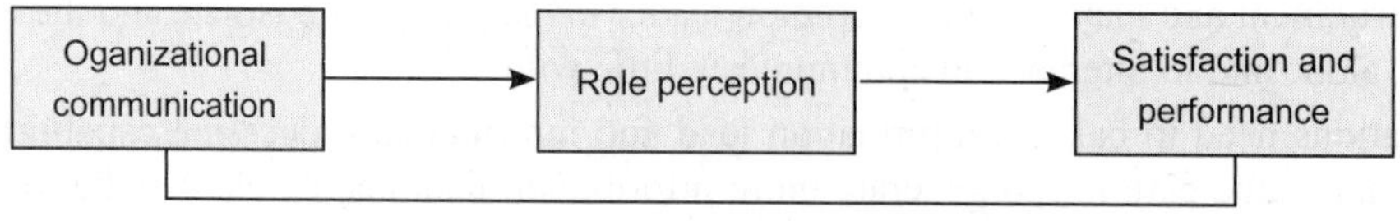

Fig. 6.8: Schuler's model

The modern communication theory presents different models of communication barriers. According to McFarland, the important barriers to communication are: Unsound objectives, organisation of blocks, semantic blocks and human relations problems. Theo Hermann classified them as barriers due to organisational structure; barriers caused by status and position, language and general inclination to resist change.

(c) Communication in the Informal Organisation

Informal organisational networks (friendship circles, grapevines, rumor mills) and emergent relationships are major factors in how and with whom information is discovered, passed on, and finally acted upon, and they will continue to play this role. Because formal structures and decision-making are often slow, ineffective, and inefficient in transmitting critical information, informal social linkages and networks emerge. These linkages are not identified on a formal chart. Asking people how and with whom they talk to obtain answers to their questions is one method for constructing a grapevine and an informal social network. Sociogram were an early method used to identify frequent communication patterns and linkages among members and groups in organisations and are still used for this purpose. Sociogram are constructed by drawing circles around individuals and groups and then drawing arrows pointing to and from these parties to indicate whom they communicate with and who communicates with them and how frequently.

Informal networks and linkages not only speed up and facilitate critical decision-making within and between organisations, but also offer other social functions. They provide a release for tension and stress; convey a sense of belonging, security recognition, and interaction; and so on. In the downside of information communication networks, dysfunctional groups norms and rumor mills can be created and sustained, loyalties can begin to conflict with the larger, official organisation; and coalition building can occur that resists planned organisational changes. Electronic communication is disrupting old ways of managing business.

Formerly closed bureaucracies and command and control systems are being pressured to open up in 2014–15. It is important for leaders and followers to remain focused on the aim of all communication: coordinated action that achieves the organisation's goals and mission. It is clear that with new information technologies, individuals and teams must assume more responsibility for their works, support, and training needs. Interpersonal (high-touch) and hightech skills will be emphasized in future work. Learning environments and cultures that encourage and facilitate change are required.

(d) Non-verbal Communications

Nonverbal communication is behaviour that communicates but does not use written or spoken words. Examples include gestures, posture, seating position, pitch of voice, speed of speech, and the physical environment of the communication interaction. People use these to communicate explicitly or implicitly with each other. Individuals combine verbal and nonverbal communications to create unique communication styles. The functions of organisational communication include information sharing, feedback, integration, persuasion, emotion, and innovation. Communication processes help share information with people both inside and outside the organisation. The information includes descriptions of the organisation's mission, strategy, policies, and tasks. Descriptions of the organisation's mission go to organisation members, to stockholders, and through advertising and other media, to people outside the organisation. Information about task direction and feedback on task performance mainly goes to members of the organisation.

Modern organisations feel they must turn out a continuous stream of innovative services and products to meet competition in both domestic and world markets. The communication process lets an organisation gather information from its external environment and move it to key decision points within the organisation. As managers make innovative decisions, they can move information about those decisions to people both inside and outside the organisation. By supporting innovation, the communication process plays a major role in the adaptation of the organisation to its ever-changing external environment. Many people in the communication profession consider listening a primary skill for success in almost any activity. It is the first skill a person learns as a child, followed by speaking, reading, and writing. Listening is also a big part of human communication activities.

Estimates vary, but they suggest people spend about 50 percent of their time listening. Face-to-face communication has the lowest data capacity but the highest information richness. Information that is highly personal, ambiguous, or complex and that requires persuasion as well as explanation is best transmitted face-to-face. For sending information of this nature, the telephone is the next best medium, followed by electronic mail. Formal reports contain the highest data capacity but are lowest in transmitting information richness. Managers and employees can ask certain questions before sending message inside and outside the organisation. They are as follows:

- What is the nature of the information/message being sent?
- What medium is most appropriate for acceptance of this message?
- What are the likely consequences if the message is transmitted through an inappropriate medium?

(e) Communication Fidelity

Communication fidelity is the degree of correspondence between the message intended by the source and the message understood by the receiver.

Table 6.2: Showing communication problems

Root of the Problem	Type of Problem
Source	Filtering.
Encoding and Decoding	Lack of common experience semantics; jargon medium problems.
Receiver	Selective attention value judgements; lack of source credibility overload.
Feedback	Omission.
Organisational Factors	Noise status differences time pressures overload.

(f) Listening

Listening is mental process of assigning meaning to the sounds. It is also an active process with the listener choosing from among listening behaviours depending on the form and purpose of the listening. The listening process includes both intrapersonal and interpersonal activities. A person receives a message from another person (interpersonal), tries to interpret it (intrapersonal), and responds to the other person to show the meaning given to the message (interpersonal). The process repeats during a communication interaction as both parties try to reach mutual understanding. With active listening, the listener is responsible for the completeness of a speaker's message. A listener's role in the communication process is not one of passively absorbing spoken message and deriving meaning from it. With active listening, the listener is responsible for hearing a speaker's message correctly. It involves accurately hearing the facts in a message and understanding the speaker's feelings about the message. Active listening features a deliberate effort to understand a message from the speaker's viewpoint. Initiators start communications and send more messages than they receive or pass on to someone else. Relayers receive and pass on more message than they start or end. The liaison role is more complicated than either the initiator or relayer. A liaison connects two parts of an organisation but is not a member of either part. A liaison person helps coordinate organisational functions by getting messages from one part of an organisation to another. Liaisons can hinder the flow of messages, however, if they become bottlenecks in a communication network. The last two roles involve more passive communication behaviour. Terminators are at the end of a communication network and mainly yet messages. They infrequently send messages or relay information to others in the organisation. Isolates are usually outside the normal communication process. They send, receive, or relay only a few messages. Several possible communication networks can emerge in an organisation. Communication over the network is often bidirectional. The following discussion of communication networks applies to all forms of communication whether face-to-face, by electronic media, or by video media.

No discussion of communication would be complete without a discussion of nonverbal communications. This includes body movements, the intonations or emphasis we give to words, facial expressions, and the physical distance between the sender and receiver. The academic study of body motions has been labeled kinesics. It refers to gestures, facial configurations, and other movements of the body. It is a relatively new field, and it has been subject to far more conjecture and popularizing than the research findings support. Hence, while we acknowledge that body movement is an important segment of the study of communication and behaviour, conclusions must be necessarily guarded. Recognizing this qualification, let us briefly consider the ways in which body motions convey meaning.

6.7 BARRIERS TO COMMUNICATION

The communication must be interpreted and understood in the same manner as it was-meant to be sent by the sender, otherwise it will not achieve the desired result and a communication breakdown will occur. There are certain external roadblocks to effective communication. In addition, there are personal factors, which affect communication. Some of the organisational barriers and some of the interpersonal barriers to effective communication are discussed below:

(*a*) ***Noise Barriers:*** Noise is any external factor, which interferes with the effectiveness of communication. The term is derived from noise or static effects in telephone conversation or radio wave transmission. It may cause interference in the process of communication by distraction or by blocking a part of the message or by diluting the strength of the communication. Some of the sources contributing towards noise.

(*b*) ***Poor Timing:*** A message sent on poor timing acts as a barrier. For instance, a last minute communication with a deadline may put too much pressure on the receiver and may result in resentment. A message must be sent at an appropriate time to avoid these problems. Hence the manager must know when to communicate.

(*c*) ***Inappropriate Channel:*** Poor choice of channel of communication can also be contributory to the misunderstanding of the message. The manager must decide whether the communication would be most effective if it is in writing or by a telephone call or a face-to-face conversation or a combination of these modes.

(*d*) ***Improper or Inadequate Information:*** Information must be meaningful to the employee and should be precise or to the point. Too little or too much information endangers effective communication. Ambiguity in use of words will lead to different interpretations.

(*e*) ***Physical Distractions:*** Any physical distractions such as telephone interruptions or walk-in visitors can interfere with the effective face-to-face communication process.

(*f*) ***Organisational Structure:*** Communication may be blocked, chaotic or distorted if the channels are not clear or if there are bottlenecks. Hence the organisation structure should be such that the chain of command and channels of communication are clearly established and the responsibility and authority are clearly assigned and are traceable.

(*g*) ***Information Overhead:*** Overload occurs when individuals receive more information than they are capable of processing. The result could be confusion or some important information may be laid aside for the purpose of convenience.

(*h*) ***Network Breakdown:*** Network breakdown may be intentional or due to information overload and time pressures under which a communication has to be acted upon. Some factors contributing to such disruptions are:

- The managers may withhold important negative information.
- The secretary may forget to forward a memo.
- There may be professional jealousy resulting in closed channels.

(*i*) ***Interpersonal Barriers:*** There are many interpersonal barriers that disrupt the effectiveness of the communication process and generally involve such characteristics that either the sender or the receiver can cause communication problems. Some of these are:

1. ***Filtering:*** Filtering refers to intentionally withholding or deliberate manipulation of information by the sender, either because the sender believes that the receiver does not need all the information or that the receiver is better off not knowing all aspects of a given situation. It could also be that the receiver is simply told what he wants to hear. Filtering refers to sender manipulating information so that the receiver will see it more favorably. For example, when a manager tells his boss what he feels his boss wants to hear, he is filtering information. The major determinant of filtering is the number of levels in an organisation's structure. The more vertical levels in the organisation's hierarchy, the more opportunities there are for filtering.

2. ***Semantic Barriers:*** These barriers occur due to differences in individual interpretations of words and symbols. The words and paragraphs must be interpreted with the same meaning as was intended. The choice of a wrong word or a comma at a wrong place in a sentence can sometimes alter the meaning of the intended message. For example, a nightclub advertisement sign, "clean and decent dancing every night except Sunday", could lead to two interpretations. First, that there is no dancing on Sundays and second, that there is dancing on Sundays, but it's not clean and decent.

3. ***Perception:*** We have mentioned selective perception earlier in Chapter 3 of this book. It appears again because the receivers in the communication process selectively see and hear based on their needs, motivations, experience, background, and other personal characteristics. Receivers also project their interests and expectations into communications as they decode them. Perception relates to the process through which we receive and interpret information from our environment and create a meaningful word out of it.

   Different people may perceive the same situation differently. Hearing what we want to hear and ignoring information that conflicts with what we know can totally distort the intent or the content of the message. Some of the perceptual situations that may distort a manager's assessment of people resulting in reduced effectiveness of the communication are:

- A manager may perceive people to belong to one category or another as stereotypes, rather than unique and distinct individuals. For example, he may perceive women to be less efficient managers.
- A manager may make total assessment of a person based on a single trait. A pleasant smile may make a positive first impression.
- A manager may assume that his subordinate's perception about things and situations are similar to his own.

This perception limits the manager's ability to effectively respond to and deal with individual differences and differing views of work situations.

4. ***Cultural Barriers:*** The cultural differences can adversely affect the communication effectiveness, specially for multi-national companies and enterprises.
5. ***Sender Credibility:*** When the sender of the communication has high credibility in the eyes of the receiver, the message is taken much more seriously and accepted at face value. If the receiver has confidence, trust and respect for the sender, then the decoding and the interpretation of the message will lead to a meaning of the sender. Conversely, if the sender is not trusted, then the receiver will scrutinize the message heavily and deliberately look for hidden meanings or tricks and may end up distorting the entire message. Similarly, if the source is believed to be an expert in a particular field then the listener may pay close attention to the message, and believe it specially if the message is related to the field of expertise.
6. ***Emotions:*** The interpretation of a communication also depends upon the state of the receiver at the time when message is received. The same message received when the receiver is angry, frustrated or depressed may be interpreted differently than when he is happy. Extreme emotions are most likely to hinder effective communication because rational judgments are replaced by emotional judgments.
7. ***Language:*** Words mean different things to different people. "The meanings of words are not in the words; they are in us. Age, education, and cultural background are three of the more obvious variables that influence the language a person uses and the definitions he or she gives to words".

   Many organisations have paid attention to communication. Some innovative successful practices have been evolved. For example, BHEL (Bhopal Unit), Management Employee Communication Meeting (MECOMs) has been effectively used. A MECOM as an open forum, in which more than 700 persons participate, has contributed to mutual sharing of information and concerns and better understanding between management and employees. In TISCO, the Chairman maintains communication with his employees by answering every letter that is addressed to him (some 80,000 a year) and holds "dialogues" with large groups, sometimes of 2500 persons.
8. ***Multi-meaning Words:*** Many words in English language have different meanings when used in different situations. Accordingly, a manager must not assume that a particular word means the same thing to all people who use it. Hence, the managers must make sure that they use the word in the same manner as the receiver is expected to understand it; otherwise it will create a barrier to proper understanding of the message. Table 6. 3 showing sources of communication problem in the organisational context.

Table 6.3: Showing sources of communication problem

Source of problem	Examples
Language	1. *Coco cola* in Chinese meant.
	"Bite the head of a dead tadpole"
	2. Idioms cannot be translated literally: "*to murder the king's English*" becomes **"to speak French like a Spanish cow"** in French.
Nonverbal signs	1. *Shaking your head up and down in Greece means no.*
	2. *Swinging it from side to side means yes.*
	3. In most European countries, it is considered impolite not to have both hands on the table.
Colour	**1. Green:** Popular in Muslim countries. Suggests disease in jungle-covered countries. Suggests cosmetics in France, Sweden, and the Netherlands.
	2. Red : Blasphemous in African countries. Stands for wealth and masculinity in Great Britain.
Product	*Coco Cola* had to alter the taste of its soft drink in China when the Chinese described it as **"tasting like medicine".**

Source: Adapted from David A.Ricks, Big Business Blunders: Mistakes in Multinational Marketing Homewood, III : Dow Jones-Irwin, 1983.

9. ***Defensiveness:*** When people feel that they're being threatened, they tend to reach in ways that reduce their ability to achieve mutual understanding. That is why they become defensive-engaging in behaviours such as verbally attacking others, making sarcastic remarks, being overly judgmental, and questioning others motives. When individuals interpret another's message as threatening, they often respond in ways that retard effective communication.
10. ***Feedback Barriers:*** The final source of communication barrier is the feedback or lack of it. Feedback is the only way to ascertain as to how the message was interpreted.

6.8 OVERCOMING COMMUNICATION BARRIERS

It is very important for the management to recognize and overcome barriers to effective communication for operational optimization and this would involve diagnosing and analyzing situations, designing proper messages, selecting appropriate channels for communicating these messages, assisting receivers of messages in correct decoding and interpretation and providing an efficient and effective feedback system. Some of the steps that can be taken in this respect are as follows:

(*a*) ***Feedback:*** Feedback helps to reduce misunderstandings. The information is transferred more accurately when the receiver is given the opportunity to ask for clarifications and answer to any questions about the message. Two-way communication, even though more time-consuming, avoids distrust and leads to trust and openness, which helps in building a healthy relationship contributing to communication effectiveness.

(*b*) ***Improve Listening Skills:*** Good listening habits lead to better understanding and good relationships with each other. Some guidelines for effective listening are:

- Listening requires full attention to the speaker. Do not let your mind wander or be preoccupied with something else; otherwise you will not be able to grasp the meaning of the message in its entirety.
- The language used tone of the voice and emotions should receive proper attention. Listen for feelings in the message content and respond positively to these feelings.
- Ask questions to clarify any points that you do not understand clearly and reflect back to the speaker, your understanding of what has been said.
- Make sure that there are no outside interruptions and interference during the course of conversation.
- Do not prejudice or value the importance of the message due to your previous dealings and experiences with the sender or your perceptions about him, positive or negative.
- Do not jump to conclusions before the message is over and is clearly understood.
- Summarize and restate the message after it is over to make sure about the content and the intent of the message.

(*c*) ***Develop Writing Skills:*** Clearly written messages can help avoid semantic and perception barriers. A well-written communication eliminates the possibility of misunderstanding and misinterpretation. When writing message it is necessary to be precise thus making the meaning as clear as possible so that it accomplishes the desired purpose. Some helpful hints in written communication are suggested by Robert Degise as follows:

Keep words simple: This will reduce your thoughts to essentials and the message will be easier to understand for the receiver. The message will be lost if the words are complex and do not lend to a clear single meaning.

1. ***Do not be Bogart down by rules of composition:*** While the rules of grammar and composition must be respected, they should not take priority over the ultimate purpose of the communication.
2. ***Write concisely:*** Use as few words as possible. Do not be brief at the cost of completeness, but express your thoughts, opinions and ideas in the fewest number of words possible.
3. ***Be specific:*** Vagueness destroys accuracy, which leads to misunderstanding of the meaning or intent of the message. Accordingly, be specific and to the point.

(*d*) ***Avoid Credibility Gaps:*** Communication is a continuing process and the goal of the communication is complete understanding of the message as well as the creation of trust among all members of the organisation. Accordingly, the management must be sincere and should earn the trust of the subordinates. Management should not only be sensitive to the needs and feelings of workers but also its promises should be supported by actions. According to the studies conducted by J. Luft, openness and an atmosphere of trust builds healthy relationship and closes credibility gaps, thus contributing to communication effectiveness.

6.9 IMPROVING PERSONAL COMMUNICATION

Following are the popular techniques employed for improving personal communication:

(a) Johari Window

The framework developed by Luft and Ingham is called the Johari Window (taken from the first names of its authors). The Johari Window is used in our consulting to depict leadership, personality, communication effectiveness. According to this framework, there are some attitudes or behaviours engaged in by people that they themselves know about. This known-to-self area includes their knowledge of the way they are coming across—the impact they are having with the people they are trying to influence. At the same time, part of the managers' personality is unknown to self; that is, in some areas managers are unaware of how they are coming across to others. It may be that their followers have not given them feedback or it may be that a manager has not been alert enough to pick up some of the verbal or nonverbal feedback that actually exists within the environment.

We can also look at a person's personality that includes behaviours and attitudes known to others in a manager's organisational setting, as well as areas unknown to others. In terms of what is known and unknown to self and known and unknown to others, we can create four areas that comprise the total window, as depicted. The arena that is known to self and also known to others in any specific organisational setting is called the public arena—it is known to all (the manager and others; that is, superior, subordinate(s), and peers) within that organisational setting.

	Known to self	**Unknown to self**
Known to others	Public	Blind
Unknown to others	Private	Unknown

Fig. 6.9: The Johari window

The arena that is unknown to self (the manager) but is known to others is referred to as the blind arena. It is unknown to the manager either because subordinates have been unwilling to share feedback with or communicate ("level") to that person, or it may be that the data are there in terms of verbal and nonverbal behaviour but the manager is not able or does not care to "see" them. The arena that is known to self but unknown to others is referred to as the private arena since it is only known to the manager. Again, it may be private because the manager has been unwilling to share or disclose this to others in the organisational setting, or it may be private because the others in the system are not picking up the nonverbal and verbal responses that are available from the manager in the system. The last arena, unknown to self and unknown to others, is called the unknown. In Freudian psychology this would be referred to as the subconscious or unconscious.

1. *Feedback:* There are various processes that affect the shape of the Johari Window (the configuration of the four arenas). This is the extent to which others in the organisational setting are willing to share with the manager. It is the willingness of others to be open and level and to give relevant feedback to the manager. But again, you have to look at it from both perspectives. It is also the extent to which the leader is attempting to perceive the verbal and nonverbal feedback that exists in the system. Treating staff members with respect will lead to a relationship in which they feel free to share and talk. As can be seen, the more relative feedback that takes place within an organisation, the more the public arena of a leader begins to extent into and displaces the blind arena and thus the smaller the blind arena that leader has.

2. *Disclosure:* The other process that affects the shape of the Johari Window is disclosure. This is the extent to which managers are willing to share with others in their organisational setting data about themselves. In the process of disclosure, the more and more organisationally relevant the information that leaders disclose about the way they think or behave, the more the public arena opens into the private arena and the smaller and smaller that arena becomes.

(b) Transactional Analysis (TA)

When people interact there is a social transaction in with one-person responds to another. The study of these social transactions between people is called Transactional Analysis (TA). The transactional analysis was developed by Eric Berne and he was very famous for psychotherapy in the 1950s. Its application to ordinary interactions soon was apparent and was popularized by Berne's book entitled "Games People Play" in 1964 and by Harris, Jongeward, and others. The purpose of TA is to provide better understanding of how people relate to each other, so that they may develop improved communication and human relationships. In the views of Berne, people interact with each other from one of the three psychological positions, known as ego states. These ego states are called Parent, Adult and Child, and a person can operate from any of these three positions.

His parents, older siblings, teachers and religious preachers influence parent ego state of a person. The parent ego state is reflected by these facts; "playing old tap" and utters such sentences "It is wrong", "It is good" or "you should" or "you should not" and so on. There are three main kinds of parent ego states; nurturing parent, critical parent, and instructive or standard setting. They may dogmatically refer to policies and standards with such comments as "You know the rule, Thomas. Now follow it". The adult ego state will appear as rational, calculating, factual and unemotional behaviour. It rises to upgrade decisions by seeking facts, processing data, estimating probabilities, and holding factual discussion. Person with adult ego pick up the emotional content from the child ego and value-laden content from their parent ego state which are checked and verified in the perspective of actualities prevailing in the world. The child ego state reflects the emotions developed in response to childhood experiences. It may be spontaneous, dependent, creative or rebellious. Like an actual child, the child ego state desires approval from others and prefers immediate rewards. It can be identified by its emotional tone, as when an employee comments to the supervisor "you're always picking on me".

1. *Type of Transactions:* Transactions may be: (*i*) complementary or (*ii*) non-complementary. They are complementary when the ego states of the sender and receiver in the opening transaction are simply reversed in the response. When the pattern ego state is charted, the lines are parallel. This relationship is depicted in which the supervisor speaks to an employee as parent to child and the employee responds as child to parent. For example, the superior says "Thomas, I want you to stop what you're doing and hurry to the supply room to pick up a box they have for me". The employee responds, "I don't want to go, because I am busy; but I will since you are the boss". If a supervisor initiates a transaction in parent-to child pattern, the employee tends to respond from a child state. Unfortunately, a supervisor-subordinate relationship tends to lead to parent-child transactions, especially when instructions are given or appraisals are conducted. If the supervisor's behaviour is dominated by this pattern, it may lead to reduce interpersonal and group effectiveness. Non-complementary transactions or crossed transactions occur when the stimulus and response lines are not parallel, as also shown. In this instance, the supervisor tries to deal with the employee on an adult-to-adult basis, but the employee responds on a child-to parent basis.

2. *Life Position:* Each person tends to exhibit one of four life positions. Very early in childhood a person develops a dominant way of relating to people. That philosophy tends to remain with the person for a lifetime unless major experiences occur to change it; hence, it is called a life position. Although one life position tends to dominate a person's transactions, other positions may be exhibited from time to time in specific transactions. That is, a life position dominates, but it is not the only position ever taken. Life positions stem from a combination of two viewpoints, first how do people view themselves? Second, how do they view other people in general? Either a positive response (O.K.) or a negative response (not O.K.) results in four possible life positions, which are:

I'm not O.K. : You're O.K.
I'm not O.K. : You're not O.K.
I'm O.K. : You're not O.K.
I'm O.K. : You're O.K.

The desirable position and the one that involves the greatest likelihood of adult-to-adult transactions are: "I'm O.K. - You're O.K.". It shows healthy acceptance of self and others.

3. ***Benefits of TA:*** Organisations that have used TA report that it has been moderately successful. Training in TA can give employees fresh insights into their own personalities and it also can help them understand why others sometimes respond as they do. A major benefit is improved interpersonal communication. Employees can sense when crossed communication occurs and then can take steps to restore complementary communication, preferably in the adult-to-adult pattern. The result is a general improvement in inter-personal transactions. TA especially is useful in sales and other areas where success depends on customer relations.

6.10 GUIDELINES FOR EFFECTIVE COMMUNICATION

These guidelines are designed to help management improve their skills in communicating so as not only avoid any barriers to effective communication, but also to strengthen the basis for optimum results which depend upon the clear understanding of the desired communication.

The Ideas and Messages should be Clear, Brief and Precise: The ideas to be communicated must be well planned and clearly identified. This will eliminate ambiguity so that the message will not be subject to more than one interpretation. The message must be clear, precise and to the point and free from distortions and noise. It should also be brief so that only necessary and sufficient meanings are provided.

Sense of Timing: The message should not only be timely so that the decisions and actions can be taken in tie and when necessary, but also the timing of the message and the environmental setting in which the message is delivered and received is equally important.

Integrity: The communication must pass through the proper channels to reach the intended receiver. The communication flow and its spread must avoid bypassing levels or people. When these concerned levels are omitted or bypassed, it creates bickering, distrust, confusion and conflict. Accordingly, the established channels must be used as required.

Consult with Others who are Involved in Planning the Communication: If people have participated in the planning process, they would be highly motivated to give active support to such communication. The people who are concerned must know exactly what they need and when they need the communication.

Consider the Receiver's Interest: Take the receivers interests into account, and then the receiver will be more responsive to the communication. The management must clarify any part of the communication that may be necessary and must encourage comments, questions, and feedback. The management must always be helpful in carrying out the intended message of the communication.

Mode of Delivery: While delivering the communication, avoid negative statements like, "I am not sure it will work", but be confident and definitive. The success of the communication also depends upon the tone of the voice if the communication is verbal, expressions and emotions exhibited attentiveness to the receiver and so on. The written communication should be polite and unambiguous.

Use proper Follow-up: All communications need a follow-up to ensure that these were properly understood and carried out. The response and feedback to the communication should determine whether the action to the communication has been prompt, appropriate and accurate.

Communication should be Comprehensive: Communication should be complete so as not only to meet the present demands. It should also fee based on future needs of the organisation as well as individuals. Recently, the nature of managerial and organisational communication has changed dramatically, mainly because of breakthrough of the electronic technology and advent of computers. Now cellular phones, e-mail and Internet have made the communication quick and convenient. It is now even possible for managers from different cities to meet by teleconferencing method without leaving their offices. At the same time, psychologists are beginning to discover some problems associates with these new advances in communication.

SUMMARY

The communication ensures flow of goal-oriented information and messages amongst different individuals and groups through various media. The main purpose of communication is to maximise exchange of appropriate information amongst individuals and group, in all directions, to help them perform their roles more effectively; minimize distortion of information (studies have shown that in downward communication the information loss in terms of original messages is about 40% by the time it reaches GMs, 60% by the time Plant Managers receive it, 70% by the time General Foreman get it, and the loss is as high as 80% by the time it reaches the worker); minimise hierarchical psychological distance; and maximise collaboration amongst individuals and teams of an organisation.

More specifically, the objectives of communication in an organisation are information sharing, feedback, control, influence, problem solving, decision-making, facilitating change, and facilitating group development.

Communication networks are systems of information exchange within organisations. Pattern of communication emerge as information flows from person to person in a group. Managing communication involves understanding the numerous problems that can interfere with effective communication. Infact, communication is the vehicle through which we negotiate, resolve conflicts and improve productivity. Various communication styles, strategies and technologies were discussed in detail.

REVIEW QUESTIONS

1. Explain modern communication methods.
2. Explain organisation communication model. How is it important? State barriers to effective communication.
3. Explain Transaction Analysis. With its practical application to manager of a software company.

4. Explain the importance of nonverbal communication in OB.
5. How do you compare the communication process in an informal organisation with that of a formal organisation?

DISCUSSION QUESTIONS

1. Imagine you as CEO of a software company. What method of communication, will you adopt in your organisation? Why?
2. Discuss the modern communication methods in Indian context.
3. A college classroom is a forum for a typical attempt at communication as the professor tries to communicate the subject to the students. Describe classroom communication in terms of the basic communication process described in this chapter.
4. What types of communication problems will solve by utilizing oral communication?
5. Explain the importance of a communication for retail banker says ICICI to the external and internal customers.

STUDENT EXERCISE

Visit a traditional company like TVS and new generation company like Yes Bank. Compare the communication methods and technique used for their organisational communication by adopting the theory explained in the chapter. Comment on the practicability of various methods of organisation communication on different context.

SKILL TEST

What is your Conflict-Handing Style?

Instructions

For each of the fifteen items, indicate how often you rely on that tactic by circling the appropriate number.

No.	Statement	Rarely	Always
1.	I argue my case with my co-workers to show the merits of my position.	1-2-3-4-5	
2.	I negotiate with my co-workers so that a compromise can be reached.	1-2-3-4-5	
3.	I try to satisfy the expectations of my co-workers.	1-2-3-4-5	
4.	I try to investigate an issue with my co-workers to find a solution acceptable to us.	1-2-3-4-5	
5.	I am a firm in pursuing my side of the issue.	1-2-3-4-5	
6.	I attempt to avoid being "put on the spot" and try to keep my conflict with my co-workers to myself.	1-2-3-4-5	
7.	I hold on to my solution to a problem.	1-2-3-4-5	
8.	I use "give and take" so that a compromise can be made.	1-2-3-4-5	
9.	I exchange accurate information with my co-workers to solve a problem together.	1-2-3-4-5	

10.	I avoid open discussion of my differences with my co-workers.	1-2-3-4-5
11.	I accommodate the wishes of my co-workers.	1-2-3-4-5
12.	I try to bring all our concerns out in the open so that the issues can be resolved in the best possible way.	1-2-3-4-5
13.	I propose a middle ground for breaking deadlocks.	1-2-3-4-5
14.	I go along with the suggestions of my co-workers.	1-2-3-4-5
15.	I try to keep my disagreements with my co-workers to myself in order to avoid hard feelings.	1-2-3-4-5

SCORING KEY

Collaborating		**Accommodating**		**Competing**		**Avoiding**		**Compromising**	
Item	Score	Item	Score	Item	Score	Item	Score	Item	Score
4	–	3	–	1	–	6	–	2	–
9	–	11	–	5	–	10	–	8	–
12	–	14	–	7	–	15	–	13	–
Total	–	Total	–	Total	–	Total	–	Total	–

Your primary conflict handling style is: ____________

(The category with the higher total)

Your backup conflict handling style is: ____________

(The category with the second highest total)

Source: A measure of styles of handing interpersonal conflict (Adaptation) M.A. Rahim, Academy of Management Journal, June 1983.

If you wish to know more insight on your test score, then you are welcome to contact author via e-mail shaangrila@gmail.com or social media drs.shajahan.7@facebook.com

7

CHAPTER

LEADERSHIP

LEARNING OBJECTIVES

This chapter aims at introducing fundamental concepts and theories for explaining the leaderships and its influence in organisational behaviour to the readers:

- *Definition, Importance and fundamental concepts of leadership*
- *Leadership types and skills*
- *Theories of leadership styles such as the trait approach, behavioural theory, the managerial grid, contingency theory: Fiedler's model, the Path-goal theory, the Vroom-Yetton-Jago model and the life cycle model*
- *Effective leadership styles and moulding a global leader*

INTRODUCTION

Leadership is an integral part of management and plays a vital role in managerial operations. It provides direction, guidance, and confidence to the employees and helps in the attainment of goals in much easier way. In business and industrial organisations, managers play the role of leader and acquire leadership of subordinates, their efforts towards the achievement of organisational goals and activate the individuals of an organisation to make them work. Leadership influences behaviour of the individuals. It has an ability to attract others and potential to make them follow the instructions. Individuals can be induced to contribute their optimum towards the attainment of organisational goals through effective leadership. Leadership acquires dominance and the followers accept the directives and control of a leader. Leadership provides direction and vision for future to an organisation. This chapter discusses major theories and issues related with leadership and also give suggestion for developing global leaders in the new millennium.

7.1 DEFINITION

Leadership is a relationship between the individual and the group depending mainly on a certain situation and is very much dynamic in nature. According to Tannenbaum, Waschler and Massarik, "Leadership is interpersonal influence exercised in a situation and directed through the communication process towards the attainment of a specific goal or goals. Hence leadership is the process of influencing the members of the group with respect to goal setting and goal achievement".

In the words of Keith Davis, "Leadership is the ability to persuade others to seek defined objectives enthusiastically. It is the human factor that binds a group together and motivates it towards goals". In the words of Gupta, "Leadership may be defined as a process of influencing the action of individuals as members of a group to achieve the desired goal in a given situation use of force by the leader".

Robbins defines leadership as "the ability to influence a group toward the achievement of goals". Hodge and Johnson are of the opinion that, "leadership is fundamentally the ability to form and mould the attitudes and behaviour of other individuals, whether informal or formal situation and that management relates to the formal task of decision and command" .

Ivancevich, Szilagyi and Wallace, define leadership "as the relationship between two or more people in which one attempts to influence the other toward the accomplishment of some goal or goals". Thus, leadership is a process of influencing other people to mobilise and direct their efforts towards certain goals and to accomplish these goals through them.

Leadership is the art of influencing and inspiring subordinates to perform their duties willingly, competently and enthusiastically for achievement of group's objectives. According to Wendell French, "Leadership is the process of influencing the behaviour of others in the direction of a goal or set of goals or, more broadly, towards a vision of the future".

According to Keith Davis, "Leadership is the process of encouraging and helping others to work enthusiastically towards objectives". According to Koontz and O'Donnell, "Leadership is the art or process of influencing people so that they will strive willingly towards the achievement of group goals". According to Peter Drucker, "Leadership means the lifting of man's visions to higher sights, the raising of man's performance to higher standard, the building of man's personality beyond its normal limitations".

According to Grey and Starke, "Leadership is both a process and a property. As a process, it is used for non-coercive influence to shape up the goals of a group or organisation, to motivate behaviour toward the achievement of those goals and to help define group or organisational culture. As a property, leadership is the set of multi characteristics, attributed to those who are perceived to be leaders". Thus, leaders are people who are able to influence the behaviour of others without recourse to threats or other forms of force towards the individuals. Leaders are the people who are accepted by the other individuals, as a superior person to them. For our purpose, leadership may be classified at 3 levels.

- Top Manager : The Big Boss
- Middle Manager : Simply Boss
- Front line Manager : Foreman and Supervisor

All of them operate on different levels and have different responsibilities and duties having the same problem of dealing with people and leading them.

7.2 IMPORTANCE OF LEADERSHIP

Leadership is the process of influencing behaviour of individuals of an organisation. Leadership uses non-coercive methods to direct and coordinate the activities of the individuals of an organisation. Leadership directs the individuals to attain the tasks assigned to them by following the instructions of their leaders. A leader possesses qualities to influence others. Leadership gives the individuals, a vision for future. Leadership is a group activity. Leader influences his followers and followers also exercise influence over his leader. Leadership is meant for a given situation; given group for a pre-determined period of time. Leadership is a continuous process of influencing behaviour. It encourages liveliness in the group.

Further, a leader should act as a friend of the people whom he is leading. A leader must have the capacity to recognize the potentials of the individuals and transform them into realities. A leader should have the confidence of the individuals of the organisation. A leader must be able to unite the people as a team and build up team spirit. A leader should be able to maintain discipline among his group and develop a sense of responsibility. A leader must be able to build up a high morale among the individuals of the organisation. A leader should motivate his people to achieve goals. A leader should try to raise the morale of the individuals and should maintain ethical standards among the individuals. A leader should act as a link between the work groups and the forces outside the organisation.

Chris Argyris has mentioned the following characteristics of a leader:

- The leader is constantly interacting and commanding.
- The leader makes the organisation a part of his self-image.
- The leader's personal goals, values and feelings are organisationally centered.
- The leader handles the supervisors as individuals.
- The leader controls the transmission of important information.
- The leader emphasis the present.
- The leader sets realistic goals.

Successful leadership requires behaviour that unites and stimulates followers toward defined objectives in specific situations. All these elements leader, followers, and situations are variables that affect each other in determining appropriate leadership behaviour. The interdependence of leader, follower and situation as Greg Hicks from his experience, feels that leadership resides in himself alone; untouched by outside influences. He fails to realize that as his people and environment changes, he needs to change his leadership. This is because that his style of leadership was acceptable about 30 years ago, but it is not acceptable. Leadership is situational; in one situation, action may be the best, but in the other it will be the least.

There may be a number of generally accepted criteria for determining good leadership, like whether the group follows the leader's orders without question, whether the work group has high morale, whether the people in the group respects the leader. At the same time, it is extremely difficult to have objective measures of leadership. One method of objective measurement is to study the productivity of a team or a work group. This method is based upon the premise that productivity is a by-product or a result of good leadership. The behaviour approach to the study of leadership regards leadership as behavioural, situational, or related to the interaction of the leader and the group. It sites that the best way to study and to define leadership is in terms of what leaders do rather than in terms of what traits they possess. In this approach, the critical incidents of good and bad leadership behaviour are collected. This is usually done by interviewing the persons concerned. Each incident is then rated on a scale by experts on the basis of judging as to how "good" or how "bad" each behaviour is. On the basis of this information a checklist type questionnaire is developed. This questionnaire can then be used to check off which of these behaviours have been exhibited by each leader or supervision. A leadership "score" can then be computed by using the medium scale value, of the behaviours, which have been checked.

(a) Functions of a Leader

Leader is an executive, planner, policy, maker and expert, punishing authority, arbitrator, mediator and the rewarding authority. He is also looked up on as an example, a father figure, an ideologist, symbol of the group and also a scape goat at times. Historically the concept of leadership has had two distinct phases differing considerably in their philosophy. The first phase namely the Scientific Management phase originated in the early 1890's by Taylor. In this system the manager's sole purpose was to expedite the goals of the organisation and the management was completely impersonal. The personal interactions were ruled out.

Bennis (1966) said that the philosophy of Scientific Management was that the only road to efficiency and productivity was to surrender man's needs to the services of a blood less machine. The second phase was the Human Relation phase. The Hawthorne studies marked the beginning of the end of scientific management.

If Taylorism implied organisation without considering the human element taken the extreme form of human relation notion implied people without any organisational constraints. Such extreme views are futile. Any useful and meaningful model of leadership must certainly include both the aspects and must admit that the organisational structure goals and objectives are also as important as the interpersonal relationship between employee and supervisors.

Following are the essentials of a leadership:

1. ***Self-confidence:*** They have complete confidence in their judgement and ability.
2. ***A vision:*** This is an idealized goal that proposes a future better than the status quo. The greater the disparity between this idealised goal and the status quo, the more likely that followers will attribute extraordinary vision to the leader.
3. ***Ability to articulate the vision:*** They are able to clarify and state the vision in terms that are understandable to others. This articulation demonstrates an understanding of the flower's needs and, hence, acts as a motivating force.
4. ***Strong convictions about the vision:*** Charismatic leaders are perceived as being strongly committed, and willing to take on high personal risk, incurs high costs, and engage in self-sacrifice to achieve their vision.
5. ***Behaviour that is out of the ordinary:*** Those with charisma engage in behaviour that is perceived as being novel, unconventional and counter to norms. When successful, these behaviours evoke surprise and admiration in followers.
6. ***Perceived as being a change agent:*** Charismatic leaders are perceived as agents of radical change rather than as caretakers of the status quo.
7. ***Environment sensitivity:*** These leaders are able to make realistic assessment of the environmental constraints and resources needed to bring about change.

(b) Type of Leadership Skills

Leaders use three types of skills—technical, human and conceptual.

- ***Technical skill:*** It refers to a person's knowledge and ability in any type of process or technique. For example, the skills learned by chartered accountants, engineers, etc. This skill is the distinguishing feature of job performance at the operating level; but an employee is promoted to leadership responsibilities, his technical skill becomes less important. Conversely, he increasingly depends on the technical skills of subordinates.

- ***Human skill:*** It is the ability to work effectively with people and to build teamwork. No leader can escape from human skill. It is the major part of the leadership behaviour.
- ***Conceptual skill:*** This is the ability of the leader to think in terms of models, framework and broad relationships such as long-term plans. Conceptual skill deals with ideas while human skill concerns people and technical skill is with things.

A review of literature of major researchers reveals that leadership is the process of influencing the activities of an individual or a group in efforts toward goal achievement in a given situation. From this definition of leadership, it follows that the leadership process is a function of the leader (l), the follower (f) and other situational variable(s) which is shown as $L = f(l, f, s)$.

Table 7.1: Traits and skills found most frequently to be characteristics of successful leaders

Traits	Skills
Adaptable to situations	Clever (intelligent)
Alert to social environment	Conceptually skilled
Ambitious and achievement-oriented	Creative
Assertive	Diplomatic and tactful
Cooperative	Fluent in speaking
Decisive	Knowledgeable about group task
Dominant (desire to influence others)	Organized (administrative ability)
Energetic (high activity level)	Persuasive
Persistent	Socially skilled
Self-confident	
Tolerant of stress	
Willing to assume responsibility	

Table 7.1 explained clearly traits and skills found most frequently to be characteristics of successful leaders in detail. Further, Yukul identified four common traits or areas of competence shared by all ninety leaders.

- **Management of attention:** The ability to communicate a sense of outcome, goal, or direction that attracts followers.
- **Management of meaning:** The ability to create and communicate meaning with clarity and understanding.
- **Management of trust:** The ability to be reliable and consistent so people can count on them.
- **Management of self:** The ability to know one's self and to use one's skills within limits of strengths and weaknesses.

Bennis suggests leaders empower their organisations to create an environment where people feel significant, learning and competence matter, people are part of the community or team, and work is exciting. It is also an environment where quality matters and dedication to work energizes effort.

(c) Leadership Versus Management

Leaders focus more on enterprise wide, strategic, long-term, eventful, and value-added roles and competencies. Managers, on the other hand, are concerned more with implementation-oriented, routine, short to mid-term predictable tasks and technical detail. Table 7.2 compares these dimensions: (1) Agenda creation: Leaders establish direction; managers plan and budget; (2) Network development for agenda achievement: Leaders align people; managers organize and staff; (3) Execution: Leaders motivate and inspire; managers control and solve problem; (4) Outcomes: Leaders produce often dramatic and useful change; managers produce predictable (on-time, within budget ordered results that are expected of stakeholders.)

In short, leading and managing go together but some differences exist between the two. The following are the differences between the leadership and the management can be summarized as follows. Management takes rational and logical decisions while leadership takes decision on expectations of the followers. Leadership has an emotional appeal while management acts on rationality. The management establishes relationship through a lawful authority while leadership establishes relationship through power. Managers have formal authority but the leaders have no such authority. All leaders are not managers and all managers are leaders. Management is a process of planning, organizing, directing and controlling the activities of others to attain the organisational objectives. Leadership on the other hand, is a process of influencing the behaviour of the people to attain their assigned tasks. A successful manager must possess both the managerial and leadership qualities.

Table 7.2: Kotter's comparison of leadership and management

Dimension	Leader	Manager
Agenda creation	**Establish direction** 1. Develop future vision (often very distant). 2. Develop change strategies to achieve vision.	**Plan and budget** 1. Develop detailed steps and timetables for results. 2. Allocate necessary resources.
Network development for agenda achievement	**Align People** 1. Communication directly by words and deeds to those whose co-operation is needed. 2. Influence creation of coalition and teams that understand and accept vision and strategies.	**Organise and staff** 1. Develop necessary planning, staffing, and delegation structures. 2. Provide policies and procedures for guidance and methods and systems for monitoring.
Execution	**Motivation and inspire** 1. Energy to overcome barriers (e.g., political, resources, bureaucratic) to change by satisfying basic needs.	**Control and problem solve** 1. Monitor results vs plan in detail. 2. Identify results and plan deviations and plan and organize to correct.
Outcomes	**Tend to produce** 1. Change, often dramatic. 2. Provide potential for very useful change (e.g., new products, etc.).	**Tend to produce** 1. Order and predictability. 2. Key results expected by stakeholders. (e.g., on time, within budget).

Source: A Force for change: How Leadership Differs from Managements by John. P. Koller.

7.3 TYPE OF LEADERSHIP STYLES

Following are the main types of leadership styles:

(a) Autocratic or Authoritarian

In this type of leadership, there is a complete centralization of authority in the leader, *i.e.*, authority is centered in the leader himself. He has all the powers to make decisions. He uses coercive measures and adopts, negative methods of motivation. He wants immediate obedience of his orders and instructions. Any negligence on the part of subordinates results in punishment. There is no participation from the subordinates in decision-making. A leader thinks that he is the only competent person in the organisation.

According to Edwin B. Filippo, there are three types of leaders in autocratic style under:

1. ***Hard Boiled or Strict Autocrat:*** Leader, under such type uses negative influence and expects that the employees should obey his orders immediately. Non-compliance of his orders results in punishment. He makes all decisions and does not disclose anything to anyone. He is quite rigid on performance.

2. ***Benevolent Autocrat:*** Benevolent autocrat leader uses positive influences and develops effective human relations. He is known as paternalistic leader. He praises his employees if they follow his orders and invites them to get the solutions of the problems from him. He feels happy in controlling all the actions of his subordinates.

3. ***Manipulative Autocrat:*** Leader, under such type is manipulative in nature. He creates a feeling in the minds of his subordinates and workers that they are participating in decision-making processes. But he makes all decisions by himself. Non-compliance of his orders also results in punishment.

An Autocratic leader centralises power and decision making in him. Such a leader considers human values as irrelevant. He considers that most people are in need of strong direction and control as they are self-centered, uncooperative, indolent and naturally dependent. He is intolerant of conflict in subordinates and tries to suppress it by not listening to it. He perceives his team as a productive and economic entity and matches manpower with methods, machines, materials, and money. He has too much reliance on authority to control his junior and constantly ignore consideration and respect, mounting pressure all the time. At the same time, he feels himself on the satisfaction of his ego like the alcoholic clinging to his bottle or the performer bunkering after applause. As a natural reaction to such a leader, questioning and resistance emerges in the group at the earliest opportunity through non-cooperation.

(b) Democratic or Participative

The other style of leadership, namely, the democratic style, assumes that the employees are intelligent and educated adults capable of managing their own affairs in a responsible manner and they react positively to opportunities for expressing their natural human attributes and negatively to deprivation of such opportunities. In a democratic system, every one cannot have his way; he can only have his say. As long as in small face-to-face meeting people, have the opportunity to say what they feel, there is a great deal of satisfaction derived by the participants, differences are resolved through consensus and dissidents usually keep back their views in support of group goals.

Democratic or Participative leadership is also known as group centered or consultative leadership. In this type of leadership, leaders consult their groups and consider their opinion in the decision making process. Leaders encourage discussion among the group members on the problem under consideration and arrive at a decision depending on their consent. Participation or involvement of the employees in the decision making process is also rewarded. Exchange of ideas among subordinates and with the leader is given encouragement. Leaders give more freedom to their group members, who feel that, their opinions are honoured and they are given importance. It develops a sense of confidence among subordinates and they derive job satisfaction. It improves quality of decision as it is taken after due consideration of valued opinions of the talented group members. The demerit of this type of leadership is that it takes more time to arrive at a decision, as a lot of time is wasted while taking the views from the employee. It is, therefore, very time consuming.

(c) Laissez-faire or Free Rein

In this type of leadership, there is virtual absence of direct leadership. It is, therefore, known as "no leadership at all". There is complete delegation of authority to subordinates so that they can make decisions by themselves. Absence of leadership may have both positive and negative effects. Free rein leadership may be effective if members of the group are highly committed to their work. The negative aspect shows that the leader is not competent enough to lead his group effectively. Members may feel insecure and develop frustration for lack of decision making authority.

(d) Bureaucratic

This type of leadership emphasizes the rules and regulations of an organisation. The behaviour of a leader is determined by the rules, regulations and procedure to be followed under his leadership. The leader and the subordinates both follow these rules and regulations. Therefore, there is no difference between the management and the administration in this type of leadership. The employees, themselves cannot do anything in this regard. It is the rules that determine their performance.

(e) Manipulative

This type of leadership manipulates the employees to attain their assigned tasks. A manipulative leader is quite selfish and exploits the aspirations of the employees for his gains. He knows very well the needs and desires of the employees but he does very little to fulfill them. Due to such attitude, he has to face the hatred of the employees at times.

(f) Paternalistic

The paternalistic leadership believes in the concept that the happy employees work better and harder. It maintains that the fatherly attitude is the right one for better relationship between the manager and the employees. Everyone within the organisation should work together like a family.

(g) Expert Leadership

The expert leadership emerged as a result of complex structure of modern organisations. This type of leadership is based on the ability, knowledge and competence of the leaders. He handles the situation skillfully with his talent. The employees feel relieved as they are working under a person who is expert and can handle the situation without any problem.

In modern organisations, human resources vary in terms of skill, knowledge and competences. They differ in quality, determination and their attitude towards the organisation. They exhibit different behaviours as they differ in attitude and outlook also. The leader must understand their behaviour and accordingly can make use of the various types of leaderships. The manager should assess the situation and adopt that type of leadership, which suits that situation. He should remember that leadership is situational. If situation changes, the use of leadership among its various types also changes. A successful leader is the one who assesses the situation, studies the psychology of the subordinates and adopts the most useful type of leadership to lead the people at work to accomplish the organisational goals.

7.4 THEORIES OF LEADERSHIP STYLES

A number of theories and approaches to study leadership styles have been developed. There are broadly three categories of leadership style theories. They are as follows:

- Trait Theory,
- Behaviour Theory, and
- Contingency Theory.

(a) Trait Theory

This theory of studying leadership is taken into consideration to analyze the personal, psychological and physical traits of strong leaders. The assumption made in this theory was that some basic traits or set of traits differentiates leaders from non-leaders. For example, the leadership traits might include intelligence, assertiveness, above average height, self-confidence, initiative and understanding of interpersonal human relations. The existence of these traits determines the importance of leadership. Possession of these traits helps the individuals to gain possession of leadership. Since all individuals do not have these qualities, only those who have them would be considered potential leaders.

Much leadership research has focused on finding a set of leadership traits that were the qualities of a successful leader (or that distinguished leaders from followers). The traits investigated were physical factors, such as height and weight; social characteristics, such as interpersonal skills and status; and personality characteristics. Leaders were intelligent, aware of their situations, and able public speakers. Leaders had higher Intelligent Quotients than their followers but were not successful if they were much more intelligent than their followers were. Leaders with knowledge that applied to their situation and who knew how to get things done could move people to high levels of achievement. Leaders carried out their responsibilities. They were self-confident, took the initiative, and persisted when rough times occurred. Leaders had high energy and showed a high level of physical and social activity. They were cooperative and were able to persuade group members to cooperate. Leaders were adaptable and were able to change with changing situation.

Some of the weaknesses of this theory are:

- All the traits are not identical with regard to essential characteristics of a leader.
- Some traits may not be inherited, but can only be acquired by training.
- It does not identify the traits that are most important and that are least important for a successful leader.
- It does not explain the leadership failures, in spite of the required traits.
- It has been found that many traits exhibited by leaders are also found among followers without explaining as to why followers could not become leaders.
- It is difficult to define traits in absolute terms.
- Thus, the trait theory has been criticized for lack of conclusiveness and predictability.

(b) Behaviour Theory

The behavioural theory assumed that effective leaders behaved differently from ineffective leaders. It also identified the need of consistency of behaviour of good leaders. This theory can be more clearly understood with the help of following case studies.

1. ***The University of Michigan Studies:*** Researchers at the University of Michigan, led by Rensis Likert, began studying leadership in the late 1940s. Depending on broad discussions with both the managers and subordinates, the Michigan studies identified two forms of leadership behaviour. They are discussed as below:

(*i*) ***Job centered leadership behaviour:*** The first was called job-centered leadership behaviour, which focuses on performances and efficient completion of the assigned tasks. A job-centered leader interacts with group members to explain task procedures and oversee their work.

(*ii*) ***Employee centered leadership behaviour:*** The second behaviour was identified as employee centered leadership behaviour, which focuses on, high performance standards to be accomplished. This can be done by developing a cohesive work group and ensuring that employees are satisfied with their jobs. Thus, the leader's primary concern is the welfare of the ordinates. The Michigan researchers thought a leader could show signs of one kind of behaviour, but not both.

The University of Michigan Studies conceptualizes the above two dimensions of leadership behaviour. Production centered leaders focused on the tasks that had to be done pressured subordinates to perform, and had little concern for people. Such leaders did not trust people to work on their own, and therefore they closely supervised others. Production centered leaders had little understanding or appreciation for the social system within their work units. They did not set high performance goals.

Employee centered leader focused on the people, their personal success, and the quality of the social system that formed within the work unit. Such leaders had high performance goals for their work units and communicated their performance expectations to their subordinates. Employee centered leadership combined a strong concern for the social aspects of the work unit with high performance expectations. The Michigan researchers felt that their research showed employee centered leadership more likely led to higher work unit performance than production centered leadership. They also felt that production centered leadership could do high productivity but had several latent dysfunction. The dysfunctions were poor employee attitudes with resulting higher turnover or absenteeism, little group loyalty, and high levels of distrust between subordinates and their leaders.

The University of Michigan had an effective and productive program in leadership behaviour and this was carried out by people such as Likert, Katz, Maccoby, Kahn and Seashore at the Survey Research Centre. The initial study was conducted by Katz, Maccoby and Morse (1950). The study was done in the home office of the Prudential Insurance Company and was matched with reference to the kind of people, the number of people, and the type of work performed. Each pair was so formed that one section in a pair was a high productivity section and the other section in the same pair was a low productivity section.

The level of productivity of each section, whether high or low, was determined from prior work records. The heads of each section were then compared. The comparison was made on a number of variables to see if there was any significant difference between that of a high productivity section supervisor and a low productivity section supervisor.

The Michigan studies were different from the Hawthorne studies. In Michigan studies a systematic measurement was made of the perceptions and attitudes of supervisors and workers whereas in Hawthorne studies the researches failed to develop quantitative measures for variables affecting supervisors and workers. In Michigan studies, factors such as type of work, working conditions and work methods were controlled.

When a comparison was made between the productivity of the two section it was found that with regard to demographic variables like age, sex and marital status there was no difference between the high and low supervisors. But when the attitudes and orientation were studied it was found that supervisors in charge of high producing section were found to be employee centered in term of their attitudes, i.e., they had concern for employees as uppermost in their minds. On the other hand, supervisors in charge of low producing section were found to be production centered in their orientation, i.e., concern for production, was uppermost in their minds, and this was often at the cost of concern for employees. This clearly shows that the attitude of the supervisor appears to be closely related to the productivity of the work group.

In short, the Michigan studies found that for effective supervision the following four factors are essential:

1. More time should be spent on planning the work.
2. There should be greater degree of delegation of authority.
3. The attitude of the supervisor should be employee oriented rather than production oriented.
4. There should be a feeling of group pride amongst the members of the group.

Table 7.3 showing the link between supervisor's attitude and productivity as under:

Table 7.3: Showing the link between supervisor's attitude and productivity

	Employee Centered	Production Centered	Not Ascertained	Total
Heads of high producing sections	6	1	5	12
Heads of low producing sections	3	7	2	12

Source: Research study @MIT , USA.

The Michigan studies also listed the following characteristics of a high producing group.

- They are under less close supervision from their own supervisors.
- They place less direct emphasis upon production as a goal.
- They encourage employee participation in the making of decisions.
- They are more employee centered.
- They spend more of their time in supervision and less in straight production work.
- They have a greater feeling of confidence in their supervisory roles.
- They feel that they know where they stand with the company.

It can be inferred from the results of the Michigan studies that high productivity depends upon supervisors adopting an employee centered approach and are dependant upon behavioural, situational and group-leader interaction rather than personal trait characteristics. In these studies, the following factors were not taken into account for the purpose of the study.

1. Responsibility level
2. Level of authority
3. Delegation of authority
4. Goal and Achievement index
5. Consideration
6. Initiating structure
7. Perceptual flexibility
8. Employee orientation.

In conclusion, the results of these studies indicate that leadership characteristics are behavioural, situational and depend upon interaction with the group. Hence, it would be more appropriate to train people to become leaders rather than looking for "born" leaders.

2. *The Ohio State University Leadership Studies:* At about the same time, a group of researchers at Ohio State also began studying leadership. The Ohio State Leadership Studies also identified two major kinds of leadership behaviours or styles, which are as follows:

(i) ***Initiating-structure behaviour:*** In initiating-structure behaviour, the leader clearly defines the leader-subordinate roles so that everyone knows what is expected. The leader also establishes formal lines of communication and determines how tasks will be performed.

(ii) ***Consideration behaviour:*** In consideration behaviour, the leader shows concern for subordinates feelings' and ideas. He attempts to establish a warm, friendly and supportive.

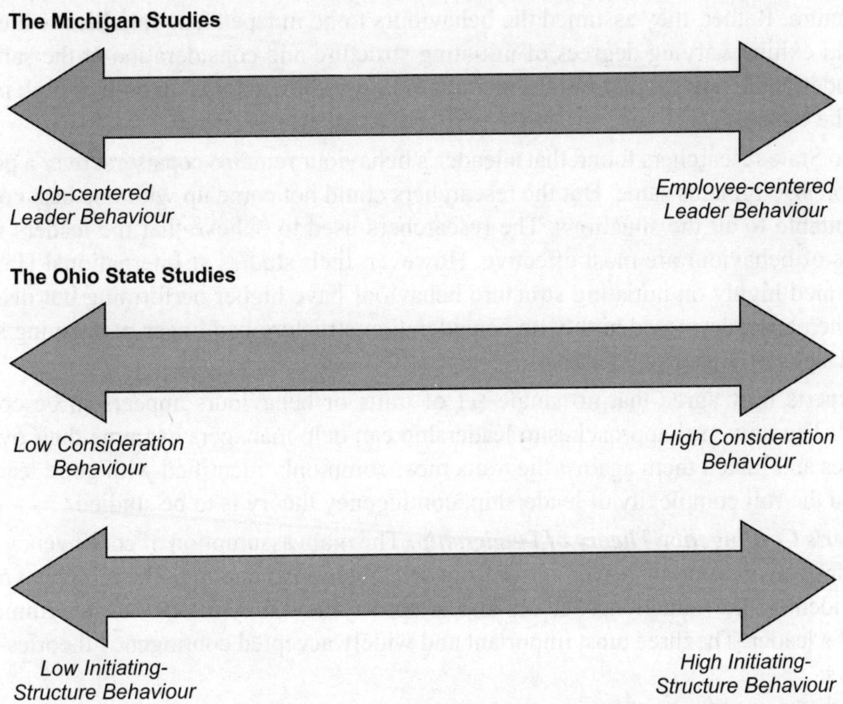

Fig. 7.1: Early behavioural approaches to leadership

Leaders high in initiating structure make individual task assignments, set deadlines, and clearly lay out what needs to be done. They act decisively without asking for their subordinates suggestions and ideas. Leaders low in initiating structure tends not to take the initiative. These leaders practice "hands off" management, leaving people alone and letting them defines the tasks and deadlines.

Excessively high initiating structure, especially when combined with strong elements of coercion, is associated with high turnover, high grievance rates, and low satisfaction. A moderate amount of initiating structure can help get good task performance in situations where people are not trained or face high task ambiguity. Initiating structure also had positive relationship with project quality and schedule in industrial development teams.

Consideration is the people-oriented dimension of leadership behaviour. Leaders high in consideration show concern for members of their group. They are empathic, interpersonally warm, and interested in developing relationships and opinions of their subordinates and accept and carry out that suggestion. Leaders low in consideration often publicly criticizes a subordinate's work. They lack concern for the feeling of others and have little interest in the quality of their interpersonal interactions. High consideration is associated with high job satisfaction, low turnover, and group cohesion. The last two factors can help maintain a group's level of performance. Consideration also had positive relationship with project quality and schedule in industrial development teams. Employees working or supervisors high on both dimensions had more positive work attitudes than employees working for supervisors with other combinations of the dimensions did.

The most obvious difference between Michigan and Ohio State studies as shown in Figure 7.1 that the Ohio State researchers did not position their two forms of leader behaviour at opposite ends of a single continuum. Rather, they assumed the behaviours to be independent variables, which means that a leader could exhibit varying degrees of initiating structure and consideration at the same time i.e. a particular leader could have higher ratings on both measures, low ratings on both or high ratings on one and low on the other.

The Ohio State researchers found that a leader's behaviour remains consistent over a period of time, if the situation also remains same. But the researchers could not come up with one best combination of behaviour suitable to all the situations. The researchers used to believe that the leaders in possession of both types of behaviour are most effective. However, their studies at International Harvester found that leaders rated highly on initiating structure behaviour have higher performing but dissatisfied sub-ordinates, whereas leaders rated highly on consideration structure had lower-performing sub-ordinates who showed signs of higher satisfaction

Most experts now agree that no single set of traits or behaviours appears to be common to all good leaders. The universal approaches to leadership can help managers examine their own leadership characteristics and match them against the traits most commonly identified with good leaders. In order to understand the full complexity of leadership, contingency theory is to be studied

3. *Fiedler's Contingency Theory of Leadership:* The main assumption of contingency theory is that the behaviour of an appropriate leader varies from one situation to another. The motive of a contingency theory is to identify key situational factors and to specify how they interact to determine appropriate behaviour of a leader. The three most important and widely accepted contingency theories of leadership are as follows:

The LPC theory: The first contingency theory of leadership is Fred Fielder's Least Preferred Co-worker (LPC) Model. Fielder identified two types of leadership: task-oriented and relationship-oriented.

Fielder believes that a leader's tendency to be task-oriented or relationship oriented remains constant. In-other words, a leader is either task-oriented or relationship-oriented while leading his group members. Fielder used the Least Preferred Co-worker (LPC) scale to measure the type of leadership. A leader is asked to describe characteristics of the person with whom he or she is least comfortable while working. They can do this by marking in a set of sixteen scales at each end, by a positive or negative adjective. For example, three of the scales Fielder uses in the LPC are:

Helpful	**:**	**Frustrating**	**8 7 6 5 4 3 2 1**
Tense	**:**	**Relaxed**	**1 2 3 4 5 6 7 8**
Boring	**:**	**Interesting**	**1 2 3 4 5 6 7 8**

The leader's LPC score is then calculated by adding up the numbers below the line checked on each scale. A high total score is assumed to reflect a relationship orientation and a low score, a task orientation by the leader. The LPC measure is controversial because researchers disagree about its validity. This is because some of the LPC measures show whether the score is an index of behaviour, personality or some other unknown factor.

According to Fielder, the contingency factor favours the situation from the leader's point of view. This factor is determined by leader-member relations, task-structure and position-power, which are discussed as below:

(*i*) ***Leader-member relations:*** A leader-member relation refers to the nature of relationship between the leader and his work group. If the leader and the group enjoy mutual trust, respect, confidence and they like one another, relations will remain good. If there is little trust, respect or confidence and if they do not like one another, relations will remain bad. Good relations are assumed to be favourable and bad relations unfavourable.

(*ii*) ***Task-structure:*** Task-structure is the degree to which the group's task is clearly defined. When the task is routine, easily understood, and unambiguous and when the group has standard procedures, the structure is assumed to be high. When the task is non-routine, ambiguous, complex, with no standard procedures and precedents, structure is assumed to be low. High structure is more favourable for the leader and low structure is unfavourable. If the task structure is low, the leader will have to play a major role in guiding and directing the group's activities. If the task structure is high, the leader will not have to pay much attention.

(*iii*) ***Position-power:*** Position-power is the power vested in the position of a leader in an organisation. If the leader has the power to assign work, administer rewards and punishment, recommend employees for promotion or demotion, position-power is assumed to be strong. If the leader does not have required powers, the position-power is weak. From the leader's point of view, strong position power is favourable and weak position power is unfavourable.

Fielder and his associates conducted various studies highlighting if a situation favours the leadership and group effectiveness or not. When the situation includes good relations, high structure and strong power, a risk oriented leader to lie most effective. However, when relations are good but task structure is low and position-power is weak, LI relationship-oriented leader is considered to be most effective. A final point about LPC theory is that, Fielder argues that any particular type of leadership, which is measured by the LPC is inflexible and cannot be changed. In other words a leader cannot change his behaviour to fit a particular situation. Fielder's contingency theory has been criticized on the ground that LPC measure lacks validity and that the assumption about the inflexibility of the leader's behaviour is unrealistic.

Table 7.4: Showing Fiedlers contingency theory

	Situation is favourable for leader						Situation is unfavourable for leader	
Leader-Member Relation	Good	Good	Good	Good	Poor	Poor	Poor	Poor
Task Structure	Structured	Structured	Un-structured	Un-structured	Structured	Structured	Un-structured	Un-structured
Position Power	Strong	Weak	Strong	Weak	Strong	Weak	Strong	Weak
Reco-mmended leadership orientation	**Task oriented**		**Relationship oriented**					**Task-oriented**

Leader-member relations the degree of confidence, trust, and respect subordinates have in their leader. Tasks structure the degree to which job assignments are procedurized. Position powers influence derived from one's formal structural position in the organisation; includes power to hire, fire, and discipline, promote, and give salary increases. Fiedler states the better the leader-member relations, the more highly structured the job, and the stronger the position power and the more control or influence the leader has.

For example, a very favourable situation might involve a payroll manager who is well respected and whose subordinates have confidence in her (good leader member relations), where the activities to be done—such as wage computation, check writing, report filing—are specific and clear (high task structure), and the job provides considerable freedom for her to reward and punish her subordinates. On the other hand, unfavorable situation might be the disliked chairperson of a voluntary United Way Fund-raising team. In this job, the leader has very little control. Altogether, by mixing the three contingency variables, there are potentially eight different situations or categories in which leaders could find them.

4. *Houses's Path-Goal Theory of Leadership:* The path-goal model of leadership was introduced by Martin Evans and Robert House. Path-goal theory says that a leader can motivate subordinates by influencing their expectations. Leaders can motivate subordinates by making clear what they have to do to get the reward they desire. The path-goal model assumes that leaders can change their style or behaviour to meet the demands of a particular situation. This model identifies four kinds of leader behaviour: directive, supportive, participative and achievement oriented. According to this model managers can adjust their behaviour to include any four kinds of leadership behaviour mentioned above.

For instance, while leading a new group of subordinates, the leader may be directive in giving guidance and instructions to them. He may also adopt supportive behaviour to encourage group cohesiveness, to look after their needs and ensuring that they get the rewards and benefits. As the group becomes more familiar with the task and as new problems are taken into consideration, the leader may use participative behaviour by which he can participate with employees in making decisions and take their suggestions as well. Finally, the leader may use achievement oriented behaviour to encourage continued high performance of subordinates.

Environmental characteristics are factors, which are beyond the control of subordinates. It includes task structure, the primary work group and the formal authority system. For instance, when structure is high, directive leadership is less effective than when structure is low. Subordinates do not usually need their boss to repeatedly tell them how to do a routine job. According to the path-goal theory, these environmental factors can create uncertainty for employees. A leader who helps employees reduce such uncertainty can motivate them. The Fig. 7.2 shows the path goal model of leadership. Leaders do not always have control over environmental factors, but the theory emphasizes that leaders can use the control they want, to adjust the environment and to motivate subordinates.

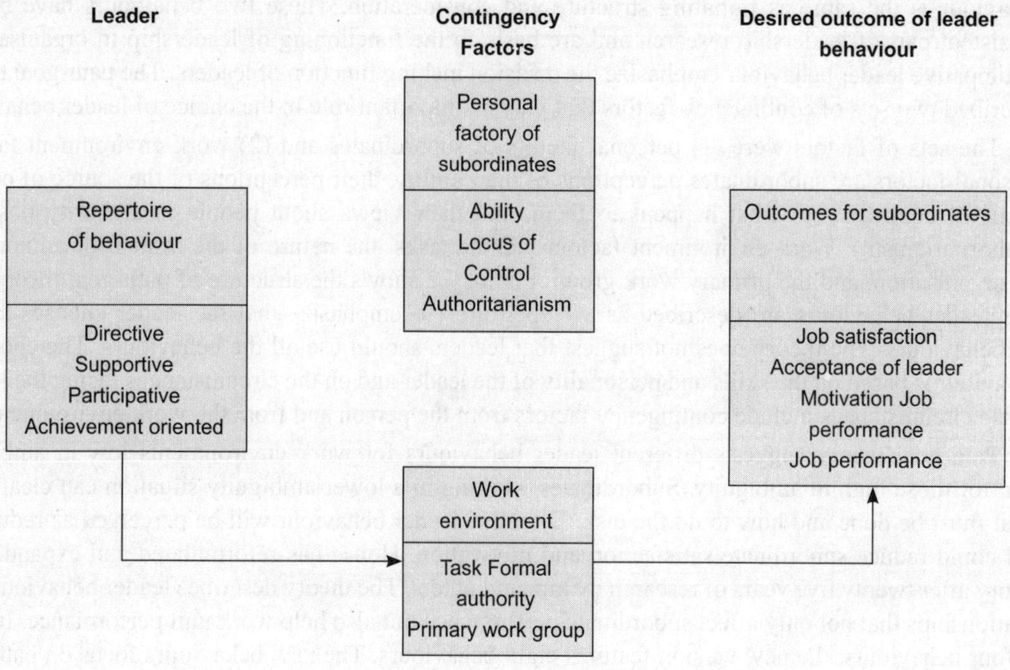

Fig. 7.2: Showing Path-goal theory

Path-goal theory sees the leader's role as one of affecting a subordinate's motivation to reach desired goals. The leader affects a subordinate's motivation by using rewards when she reaches desired goals, being supportive while the subordinate is trying to reach the goals, making task assignments that are inherently motivating, and cleaning barriers to goal accomplishment. The name of the theory summarizes what a leader does—clearing subordinate's paths so they can reach desired goals. The leader's behaviour can enhance a subordinate's motivation and increase a subordinate's job satisfaction. Acceptance of the leader by the subordinate should also increase. Path-goal theory proposed the following four leader behaviours:

Directive : Directive leader behaviour focuses on what must be done, when it must be done, and how it must be done. This behaviour clarifies performance expectations and the role of each subordinate in the work group.

Supportive : Supportive leader behaviour includes concern for subordinates as people and the needs they are trying to satisfy. Supportive leaders are open, warm, friendly, and approachable.

Participative : Participative leader behaviour includes consultation with subordinates and serious consideration of subordinate's ideas before making decisions.

Achievement oriented: Achievement oriented leader behaviour emphasizes excellence in subordinate performance and improvements in performance. An achievement oriented leader sets high performance goals and shows confidence in people's abilities to reach those goals.

The four behaviours of path-goal theory have several important qualities. Directive and supportive behaviour is the same as initiating structure and consideration. These two behaviours have been a consistent part of leadership research and are basic to the functioning of leadership in organisations. Participative leader behaviour emphasize the decision making function of leaders. The path-goal theory described two sets of contingency factors that play an important role in the choice of leader behaviour.

The sets of factors were (1) personal factors of subordinates and (2) work environment factors. Personal factors are subordinates perceptions of their ability, their perceptions of the source of control (locus of control) over what happens to them, and their views about people in authority positions (authoritarianism). Work environment factors include tasks, the nature of the system of authority in the organisation, and the primary work group. Figure 7.2 shows the structure of path-goal theory. The four leader behaviours are described as a "repertoire" to emphasize that the leader chooses among the behaviours. The theory does not suggest that leaders should use all the behaviours. The choice of behaviour is based on the skills and personality of the leader and on the circumstances facing the leader. Those circumstances include contingency factors from the person and from the work environment.

Path-goal theory suggests different leader behaviours for work environments low in ambiguity than for those high in ambiguity. Subordinates working in a lower-ambiguity situation can clearly see what must be done and how to do the task. Directive leader behaviour will be perceived as redundant and could reduce subordinate satisfaction and motivation. House has reformulated and expanded the theory after twenty five years of research by him and others. The theory describes leader behaviours and relationships that not only affect subordinate performance but also help work unit performance. Instead of four behaviours, the new version features eight behaviours. The new behaviours focus on path-goal clarification, social interaction within the work group, the political behaviour necessary to increase the group's power, and the leaders' charismatic behaviour. These behaviours add to the behaviour repertoire noticed earlier. This expanded version of path-goal theory has not yet been empirically tested.

The following are some examples of hypotheses that have evolved out of path-goal theory:

- Directive leadership leads to greater satisfaction when tasks are ambiguous or stressful than when they are highly structured and well laid out.
- Supportive leadership results in high employee performance and satisfaction when subordinates are performing structured tasks.
- Directive leadership is likely to be perceived as redundant among subordinates with high-perceived ability or with considerable experience.
- The more clear and bureaucratic formal authority relationships, the more leaders should exhibit supportive behaviour and deep emphasize directive behaviour.

- Directive leadership will lead to higher employee satisfaction when there is substantive conflict within a work group.
- Subordinates with an internal locus of control will be more satisfied with a participative style.
- Achievement oriented leadership will increase subordinates' expectancies that effort will lead to high performance when tasks are ambiguously structured.

5. *Cognitive Resource Theory:* More recently, Fiedler and an associate, Joe Garcia, reconceptualised the former's original theory to deal with some serious oversights that need to be addressed. Specifically, they are concerned with trying to explain the process by which a leader obtains effective group performance. They call this as reconceptualisation cognitive resource theory.

The essence of the new theory can be boiled down to three predictions: (1) Directive behaviour results in good performance only if linked with high intelligence in a supportive, (2) non-stressful leadership between job experience and performance, and (3) the intellectual abilities of leaders correlate with group performance in situations that the leader perceives as non-stressful. Situational leadership uses the same two leadership dimensions that Fiedler identified: task and relationship behaviours. However, Hersey and Blanchard go a step further by considering each as either high or low and then combining them into four specific leader behaviours: telling, selling, participating and delegating. They are described as follows:

- ***Telling:*** The leader defines roles and tells people what, how, when, and where to do various tasks. It emphasizes directive behaviour.
- ***Selling:*** The leader provides both directive behaviour and supportive behaviour.
- ***Participating:*** The leader and follower share in decision making, with the main role of the leader being facilitating and communicating.
- ***Delegating:*** The leader provides little direction or support.

6. *The Leaders Mystique:* EE Jennings' leadership mystique is a set of ideas, values and beliefs that Jennings feels is the essence of leadership. The leadership mystique has three dimensions.

- A sense of missing
- A capacity for power
- A will to survive and to preserve.

A leader has a sense of mission—a vision of some future state for the organisation. The vision is more than a strategic plan; rather it is a dream about something that the leader wants to create. A capacity for power is the ability to get and use power to pursue the mission. Leaders have no fear of power, nor do they believe having power is undesirable. Power is undesirable. Power and the capacity to get it is basic to achieving the mission. Leaders are often frustrated in their pursuit of their mission. They must have a will to survive and preserver in reaching their mission. Transformational leaders strive for major increases in performance beyond that needed to reach immediate organisation goals. They bring excitement to the work place and build strong emotional bonds between themselves and their subordinates. Transformational leader work towards what they believe is right and good for the organisation, not for its present direction. They often bring dramatic changes to an organisation's culture and are remembered long after they are gone.

In addition to these three major theories, there are other contingency models or theories developed in recent years. The other models are as follows:

(i) Vertical Dyad Linkage Model: This model stresses the fact that leaders actually have different kinds of working relationship with different subordinates. Each manager-subordinate relationship represents one vertical dyad. The Vertical Dyad Linkage model suggests that leaders establish special working relationships with some subordinates based on some combination of respect, trust and liking. These people constitute the 'in-group'. Other subordinates remain in the 'out-group's, who receive less of leader's time and attention. Those in the 'in-group' receive more of the manager's time and attention and are better performers. Research shows that people in the 'in-group' are more productive and more satisfied with their work than 'out group' members.

(ii) Life Cycle Model: The life cycle model suggests that appropriate leader behaviour depends on the maturity of the followers. In this context, maturity includes motivation, competence and experience. The model suggests that as followers become more mature, the leader needs to move gradually from high to low task orientation. Simultaneously, the leader's employee-oriented behaviour should start low, increase at a moderate rate and then decline again. Many leaders are familiar with the life cycle theory because it is both simple and logical. However, it has received little scientific support from researchers.

(iii) The Vroom-Yetton-Jago Theory (VYJ): The Vroom-Yetton-Jago model was first introduced by Vroom and Yetton in 1973 and was revised by Vroom and Jago in 1988. This model has a much less focus than the path-goal theory. It helps a leader to determine the extent, to which employees should participate in the decision-making processes. The VYJ theory argues that decision-effectiveness is best judged by the quality of decision and by the acceptance of that decision on the part of employees. Decision acceptance is the extent to which employees accept and are loyal to their decisions. To maximize decision effectiveness, the VYJ theory suggests that leaders adopt one of five decision-making leaderships. The appropriate leadership depends on the situation. As summarized in the following Table 7.5, there are two autocratic types of leadership, which are AI and AII, two consultative types of leadership, which are CI and CII and the other one is group GII.

Table 7.5: Decision-making styles in the VYJ model

Decision Style	*Description*
AI	Manager makes the decision alone.
AII	Manager asks for information from subordinates but makes the decision alone. Sub ordinates may or may be informed about what the situation is.
CI	Manager shares the situation with individual subordinates and asks for information and evaluation. Subordinates do not meet as a group and the manager alone makes the decision.
CII	Manager and subordinates meet as a group to discuss the situation but the manager makes the decision.
GII	Manager and subordinates meet as a group to discuss the situation and the group makes the decision.

A = Autocratic; C = Consultative; G = Group

The situation is defined by a series of questions about the characteristics or attributes of the problem under consideration. To address the questions, the leader uses one of the four decisions. Two of them are used when the problem affects the entire group. For example, a decision about the facilities to be given to employees in a new office affects the entire group and the other two are appropriate when the decision affects a single individual only. For example, a new office for that individual only.

Moreover, one of each is to be used when the decision has to be made quickly because of some urgency and the others are to be used when the decision can be made more slowly and the leaders wants to use the opportunity to develop subordinates' decision-making abilities. The VYJ model was criticized because of its complexity. Computer software has been developed to aid leaders in defining the situation, answering the questions about the problem attributes and developing a strategy for decision-making participation. Although the VYJ model is too new to have been thoroughly tested, evidence so far indicates that this model can help leaders to choose the most effective way to include the subordinates in decision-making.

(c) Other Leadership Theories

Let us now summarize some of the empirical and humanistic theories in brief.

According to Stogdil (1915) , there are three critical factors which are most important in leadership. They are as follow:

- Status and functions of the position occupied by the individual.
- Demands made up on the individual by his group.
- Perception of the group members concerning the kind of person the individual is. Leadership can emerge out of any one or all of these three factors.

Successful leadership must involve the process of employee's participation. Democratic supervision is suggested as facilitating the involvement of the worker in the decision making process influenced by Michigan. According to them three critical dimensions are:

(*a*) The personal relations of a leader with his group.

(*b*) The degree of structure in the task which the group must perform.

(*c*) The power and authority inherent in the leadership position.

Blake designed a theory of effective management known as the managerial grid. According to him two critical dimensions of effective leadership are:

(*a*) Concern for production (Task orientation), and

(*b*) Concern for people.

Blake says that these two dimensions are independent. A manager can be high on both, (9, 9) low on both, (1, 1) high on one (1, 9 or 9, 1) or low on the other as shown under Figure 7.3.

McMurray (1959) argues for leaders who are benevolent autocrats. This model goes away from the human relation notions towards the goal of the organisation. This premise is that democratic procedures are just not practical or possible in most of the bureaucratic organisations. He doesn't think that one can convince the top management that democratic leadership is the only way to run a business. One can solve the "Human Relation" aspect of leadership by having the leader benevolent and the structure aspect by making him an autocrat.

Argyris is of the opinion that the needs of the individual and his goals are not compatible with the needs and the goals of the organisation. He says that the organisation will often make unreasonable demands on the individual. To him leadership should be that which fosters the development and growth of the individual. He depends greatly on Maslow's notion of need structure and would have unbeliever that the best leadership is that which permits the worker to self-actualise. He suggests:

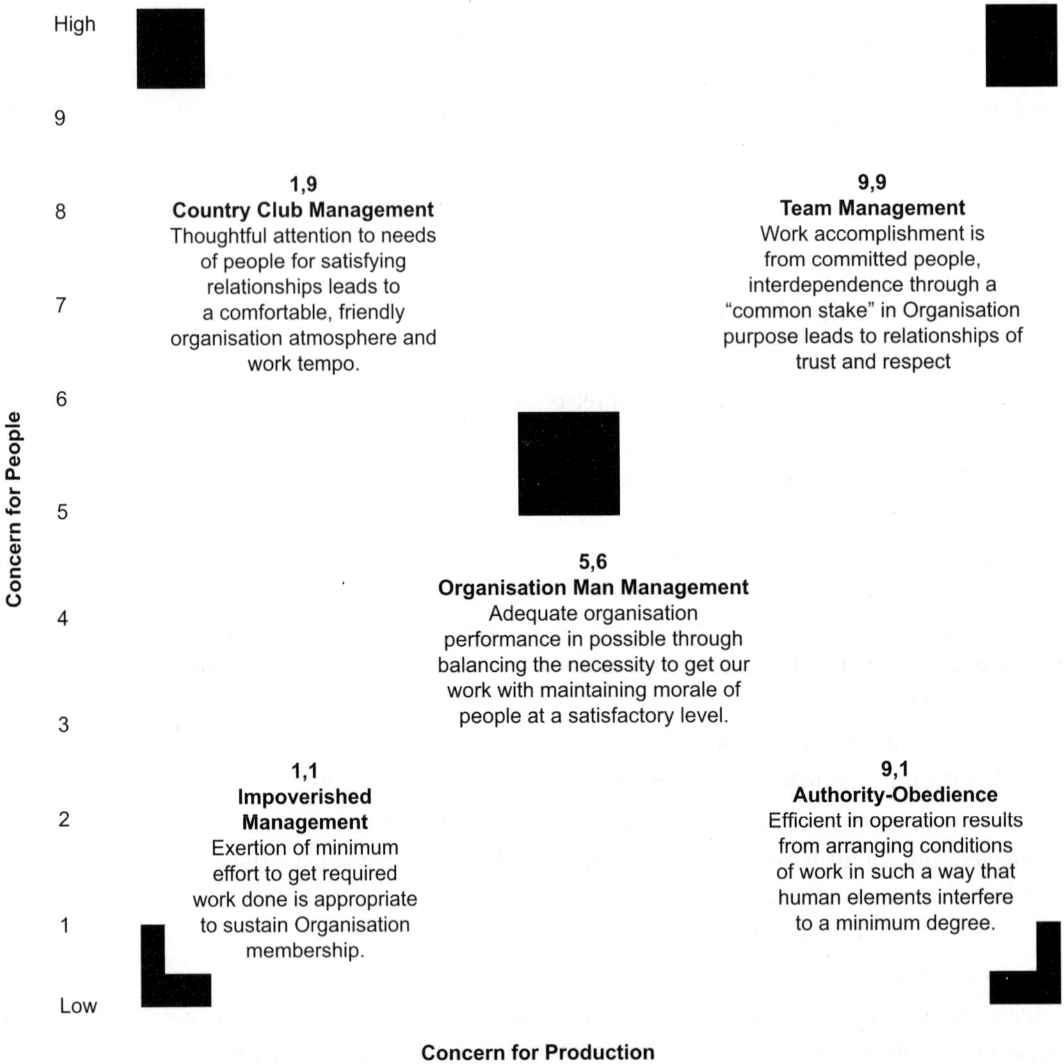

Fig. 7.3: The managerial grid

Source: R.R. Blake, J.S. Mouton, L.B. Barmes, and L.E. Grenier, "Breakthrough in Organisation Development", Harvard Business Review, Nov–Dec. 1964.

- Job enlargement,
- Employee-centered leadership, and
- Reality leadership.

McGregor through Theory-X—Emphasis on the goals of the organisation and Theory-Y—on the individual. An advocate of the theory 'Y' he proposes that the key to success is the concept of integration is the goals of the organisations are integrated with that of the individual. Another concept in effective leadership for McGregor is collaboration. For achieving integration collaboration between superior and subordinate is a necessary condition.

Tannen Baum probably the one most oriented toward individual goals and least concerned with organisational structure and goals of the enterprise. According to them a primary requirement for effective leadership is flexibility. Hence according to them leadership is interpersonal relation exercised in a situation and directed through communication process toward the attainment of the specified goal or goals. Leadership involves attempts on the part of a leader (influencer) to affect (influence) the behaviour of a follower (influence) or followers in a situation. Super leadership is "leading others to lead themselves". Super leadership "empowers others to stand on their own two feet and to feel ownership of their job". In this sense, super leadership begins with self-leadership: "The influence we exert on ourselves to achieve the self-motivation and self-direction we need to perform".

7.5 EMERGING PERSPECTIVES ON LEADERSHIP IN ORGANISATIONS

The new perspectives that have attracted attention are the concepts of substitutes for leadership and transformational leadership.

(a) Substitutes for Leadership

The existing leadership theories and models try to specify what kind of leader's behaviour is appropriate for different situations. They do not take into consideration, the situations where the leadership is not needed. The substitute concept identifies the situations where the characteristics of the subordinates, the task and the organisation replace leaders' behaviours. For example, when a patient is admitted to an emergency room in a hospital, nurses, doctors and attendants act immediately without waiting for directive or supportive behaviours of leaders in an emergency ward. Several characteristics of the subordinate may serve to replace or change the behaviour of the leaders. For example, employees with much ability and experience may not need to be told what to do. Similarly, a strong need for independence by the subordinate may result in ineffectiveness of leaders' behaviour.

Characteristics of the task that may substitute the leadership include the availability of feedback and intrinsic satisfaction. For example, when the job is routine and simple, the subordinate may not need direction. When the task is challenging, the subordinate may not need or want support. Organisational characteristics that may substitute for leadership include formalization group cohesion, inflexibility and a rigid reward structure. For example, when policies are formal and rigid, leadership may not be needed.

(b) Transformational Leadership

Another new concept of leadership goes by a number of labels: Charismatic leadership, inspirational leadership, symbolic leadership and transformational leadership. This is a leadership that transmits a sense of mission, increases teaming experiences and inspires new ways of thinking. Charisma is a form of interpersonal attraction. Charismatic people attract followers and this type of leader has great power over his or her followers. Charismatic leaders are self-confident and can influence others. The followers of a charismatic leader identify with the leader's beliefs, accept, trust and obey the leader without questioning him and thereby contribute towards the success of the organisational goals.

(c) Effective Leadership

Often leadership and management and erroneously considered synonymous and the function of leadership is labeled as planning, organising, directing staff, controlling, evaluating and rewarding.

What then constitutes leadership? What is special about it? Who can become a leader? What kind of leader is effective? Are leaders born or made? These are some of the questions that are raised quite often. In our search for the appropriate kind of leadership, it will be essential to scrutinise the characteristics of different styles of leadership that have been used in various parts of the world over time.

There are differences in the ways leaders approach people to motivate them, if the approach emphasizes rewards economic or otherwise for followers, the leader uses positive leadership. If emphasis is on penalties, he is applying negative leadership. The stronger a penalty, the more negative it is. The same reasoning applies to rewards.

Style is related to one's model or organisational behaviour. The autocratic model tends to produce a negative style; the custodian model is somewhat positive, and the supportive and collegial models are clearly positive. Negative leadership gets acceptable performance in many situations, but it has high human costs. Negative leaders are domineering and act superior to people. To get work done, they hold over their personnel such penalties as loss of job, reprimand in the presence of others, and a few days off without pay.

The art of creative leadership is the art of institution building the reworking of human and technological, material, to fashion an organisation that embodies new and enduring values. To elaborate, it involves educating the group, interpreting the role and character of the enterprise, setting models of thought and behaviour consisting of participants loyalty to the organisation and sensitive awareness of its guiding principles. Apart from day-to-day behaviour, from a long-range angle, it includes the assignment of high prestige to certain operations so as to create a myth. Creativity not only requires perception and determination to see the necessity of the myth, but also the successful formulation and creation of the environment that will sustain the ideals expressed. Creative leadership necessitates large-scale delegation all along the line up to the bottom level, each level in turn being given opportunities for exerting personal influence and contributing creatively a true synthesis of individualism and social conformity.

An important aspect of modern management is its size and complexity. The senior management decisions in strategic areas have a long term impact on the organisation and as such, vision. The leader is responsible for future progress, growth and reputation are assured. Managerial role in modern organisations is increasingly shifting towards the executive coordinator type of leadership. As the management becomes more and more information based, the managerial effectiveness will depend increasingly on his skill in collection, collection and communication of information and in ensuring its optimum use in coordination with people. Whatever the colour or style, a leader should motivate his team, creating the resources to help it perform well and achieve. In doing so, he should recognise and arouse the subordinate's urge for outcomes by counseling and gentle direction.

Empirical research has usually shown positive relationships between transformational leadership and organisational performance. All three dimensions of transformational leadership had positive relationship with organisational performance, Chairman, however, evoked the stronger positive relationship. Looking beyond the present situation includes scanning the environment for new market opportunities, predicting changes in markets and technologies, and looking for ways to keep their organisation aligned with its outside environment. Charismatic leaders are impatient with present conditions and press their organisations to continuously improve. They push their organisation towards a new state by creating dissatisfaction with the present. Empirical research shows a positive relationship between charisma and organisational performance.

(d) Leadership Skills

There is now recognition in both leadership theory and practice of the importance of skills, how leaders should behave and perform effectively. Although there are many skills, such as cultural flexibility, communication, HRD, creativity, and self-management of learning, the research based skills identified by Whetten and Cameron seem to be most valuable. Their personal skills model, involving developing self-awareness, managing stress and solving problems creatively; the interpersonal skills model, involving communicating supportively, gaining power and influence, motivating others and managing conflict, are especially comprehensive and useful. Finally, the widely recognized organisational behaviour techniques such as, training, job design and leaders can also effectively use behavioural management.

7.6 DEVELOPING GLOBAL LEADERS*

In June 2001 as the business world watched expectantly, General Electric (GE) promoted three key executives. Each would report to one of the three potential candidates to succeed CEO Jack Welch. Thus, if one of the latter moves into Welch's office, another seasoned GE professional will be ready to assume his role. Where do GE leaders come from? They do not spring up out of the earth overnight. For many years the company has worked hard to develop ongoing sources of leadership talent not only to prepare for Welch's retirement next year, but also to enrich every level of the organisation with strong leaders. When Ronald Reagan was spokes person for GE, their slogan was "Progress is our most important product". Today the mantra could be, "Leaders are our most important product".

Leaders who keep learning may be the ultimate source of sustainable competitive advantages. With that understanding, many companies are investing in leadership development. As early as 1993, Business Week estimated that $17 billion was being spent annually by globe companies on helping managers develop the thought processes and company specific skills that could enable them to move up and lead their business areas. Training magazine estimates that in 1998 US companies spent $60.7 billion on training. But spending isn't the only commitment. World class executives are investing significant amounts of their time personally guiding and mentoring future leaders. In January 1998, the main profit research group American Productivity and Quality Center, the American Society for Training and Development, Virginia and developed a study to investigate best practices in leadership development, in 1999, they expanded the study to explore the challenge of developing leaders at all levels of an organisation.

(a) The Strategies Perspective

Most significance: Best-practice partners reported that they tied leadership development closely to business strategy and that they invested financial resources in it. CEOs did not support the programs out of a respect for education but from a conviction that such programs can assist in aligning functional areas with corporate strategy. Johnson & Johnson, for one, revised succession planning and performance-management systems to reflect the qualities anticipated by a leader of the future exercise in a leadership-development conference.

Increasingly, programs that focus on developing future leaders are seen as a source of competitive advantage. GE's CEO, Jack Welch, described the company's Leadership Development Institute in, New York, as a "staging ground for corporate revolutions". In fact, innovative ideas such as the Six-Sigma quality-improvement program and GE's expansion into emerging economies have come from

---

* *Courtesy*: SRM Management Digest 2001 and Mr. Senthil Kumar Faculty Member

presentations made at leadership-development events. Tremendous growth, reductions in the number of GE employees worldwide and significant delaying of the organisation in the 1980s and 1990s caused an enormous cultural shift. With fewer vertical promotions and hence fewer opportunities to practice being leaders. A new approach was called for today in the human resource department's "Session C" meetings, senior executives assess key GE personnel. After an initial meeting in March, there are two or three additional meetings and a wrap-up session in June or July to select employees who will attend the executive-development curses. At the end of the year, corporate leadership development, like all corporate functions, is measured by whether it was able to support GE initiatives.

Ralph Larsen, Chairman and CEO of Johnson & Johnson, champions J & J's Executive Conference. Faithful to the company's decentralization tenets, he leaves the program's details to subordinates around the world but takes the time to suggest program themes. At Arthur Andersen, the mission of the Partner Development Program (PDP) is "to help partners worldwide acquire and build the knowledge, skills and behaviours required to be valued and trusted business advisors in an ever-changing market place". To meet the needs of a business that continues to diversify and globalize, managers aim to keep the program closely linked with Arthur Andersen's evolving business strategy. Hewlett-Packard, under the leadership of CEO Carly Fiorina, is rushing to reclaim its status as a top high-tech innovator. Fiorina must convince the public and HP employees that HP is the hottest new company of the Internet era—without losing the old-time commitment to quality and integrity. Past HP glory led many excellent engineers to focus on what used to be important, instead of on the future. Once HP started to improve leadership development, the company could make better business decisions.

Today HP's senior executive actively participates in leadership development. Fiorina uses management meetings and leadership development programs to articulate her vision of making the company "represent the next decade rather than the past one'. Her predecessor, Lewis E. Platt, showed his support for leadership development by making personal appearances at all HP Accelerated Development Programs, opening and closing them with an opportunity for participants to have a dialogue with him. Cor Herkstroter, the former chairman of the Royal Dutch/Shell Group once asked his top 60 leaders to suggest improvements in the company's financial performance. Shell's committee of managing directors decided that a new leadership-development process could be a catalyst for organisational change and Shell's Leadership and Performance (LEAP) program was created. After the program showed measurable returns in the United States and elsewhere, Shell made it corporate wide. When James Wolfensohn joined the World Banks as president in 1995, he created a mission statement that continued the bank's longstanding commitment to dispersing knowledge and financial resources but placed a stronger emphasis on the goal of reducing poverty worldwide.

(b) Methods to Spot a Leader

- Self-reporting method
- Observation method
- Nominating method.

(c) Tests for Selection

1. Intelligence tests
2. Empathy tests

3. Personality tests
4. Vocational interest test
5. Nominating method.

A leader should have fair treatment for all, give sufficient delegation of authority, should be available to all and should discuss the problem with all. However he must refrain from depending too much on his authority simulation of knowledge, interference with work, favouritism and discrimination and public reprimand. One can also become a leader under the following situations:

- By the information that he possesses.
- By his initiative to motivate a group.
- By his sheer courage.

(d) The Five Critical Steps

Pronouncing a strategic vision is not enough to bring about change or to tie leadership development to the company's goals. Research studies suggest that there are five critical steps to achieving those ends.

1. ***Awareness:*** The need for a process to build leadership skills has best-practice organisations looking both inside and outside their organisations for approaches that work. The foundation of such companies, leadership-development is awareness—awareness of external challenges, emerging business opportunities and strategies, internal developmental needs and the ways other leading organisations handle development. Arthur Andersen uses both internal and external data to determine the learning and development needs of the partners in the firm. Internal data come from client satisfaction and employees satisfaction surveys upward communication and analysis of what the firm calls 450 degree feedback (360 degrees feedback plus client evaluations). Arthur Andersen wants to know how its partners are perceived in terms of their technical competence and their responsiveness to customers.

External data about new financial and managerial tools or about challenges in the business environment come from market research, business trends and leading edge thinkers. The partner development program also exploits the research Arthur Andersen does while serving clients and the conversations on emerging trends partners routinely have with leading thinkers in management education and business practice. The PDP also make use of the literature on new concepts in leadership-development. To ensure that its leadership and performance program does not simply react to the immediate needs of the business, Shell's LEAP team has an ongoing conversation with the committee of managing directors about corporate transformation. LEAP staff members negotiate an agreement with the executive of the business unit and the critical players who will go through the program. Together they create budgets for the team project and set time expectations and goals.

To gather external perspectives, Shell has joined the Global Research Consortium; a group of transnational companies that sponsor's research. The consortium gives its members the opportunity to hear and discuss the latest on leadership and learning. Like other best practice companies, Shell also works with consultants and professors to stay abreast of the latest in leadership research. There is greater awareness today that best practice organisations' corporate leadership development function is specifically for strategic issues; more - tactical management skills and business specific challenges are usually left to business units. That seems to work well corporate leadership programs concentrate on helping decision-makers become more effective at using those skills. All the best-practice leadership programs top leaders with extensive line experience. At Arthur Andersen, Johnson & Johnson and Shell, the heads of the leadership-development process have senior level business experience. The use of business leaders is based on a belief that participation from executives will help ensure buy in from the businesses and will keep the programs practical. GE and Shell International bring in high potential individuals on two-year rotational assignments to oversee leadership development. HP recruits key people from line positions for the same purpose. In addition to drawing on the business units, best practice organisations access the experience of individuals in corporate education, human resources and academia. The director of GE's Crotonville center came from a university setting, and the head of World Bank's EDP has a background in corporate education.

2. *Anticipation:* Although business cases traditionally focus on the past and best-practice reviews focus on the present, the best leadership development programs emphasize the future. Top leadership development companies use anticipatory learning tools: Focus groups that explore potential challenges or the impact of emerging technologies; decentralized strategic planning; analysis of future scenarios; and the Delphi method. Strategy guru Gary Hamel recommends decentralized planning because revolutions are beneficial and they "seldom start with the monarchy". The participative and future-centered Merlin Process is an example of decentralized planning. Managers imagine the organisation a decade from the present and describe what it would look like if totally successful. In contrast to more conventional, top-down strategic planning the Merlin Process has groups throughout the organisation describe their ideal and input for senior executives and lead to more formal planning sessions.

From 1993 to 1996, J&J followed that pattern. During its second set of Executive Conferences, executives from around the world worked together for a week with outside consultants to create a vision for a decade later. Participants challenged conventional wisdom about the evolution of the health care industry and focused on actions their divisions could take to create their future. J&J 2002, an extended scenario developed from future focused interviews with more than 100 executives in six countries and from published predictions about the future of health care projected multiple trends and discontinuities. Using a modified Delphi approach, participants assessed the probability and impact of 14 hypothetical developments. An integrative exercise called the Merlin Exercise was used to tie the various aspects of the program together participant groups made formal presentations of the desired future to the CEO or the Vice Chairman. For some organisations, anticipation involves developing a list of the competencies that the company will need.

3. *Action:* Action, not knowledge, is the goal of best practice leadership-development processes. Best practice groups bring the world into the classroom, applying real time business issues to skill development. The answers to tough questions are not in the instructor's head; learners must discover them on the spot. And with program participants implementing their own recommendations, the learning experience benefits both the organisation and the learner. Such action learning can be complicated and costly, however. That is why Arthur Andersen, for example, uses a modified approach, that still includes pre-work and post-work. Before the course begins, the firm gives participants criteria for selecting a client with a business problem and a protocol for interviewing that client. Learners work in a team to develop client recommendations. After the course, the team must make a presentation to the actual client or the program sponsor.

At GE, Welsh he has been the one to choose the action-learning topics for each of the three annual business management courses and for the annual executive development course. Participants in both courses are highly motivated to carry out projects, important as they are to the company's direction. Recommendations made by the participant teams are usually implemented. Students in one management course went to Russia and developed proposals for GE's operations there. A quality report from an individual in another course led to corporate wide adoption of the Six-Sigma an initiative, a quality assurance program designed to eliminate defects from all products.

GE also supports what it calls the Change Acceleration Process (CAP), a systematic attempt to turn managers into professional change agents by disseminating GE's accumulated knowledge about how to initiate; accelerate and secure change. If CAP is successful, says Welch, people who are comfortable as coaches and facilitators will be the norm at GE and the other people won't get promoted. At Johnson & Johnson, the purpose of the third group of Executive Conferences, which started in 1997, was to emphasize J & J's Standards of Leadership and to tie the standards to specific business issues through action learning. The principal session lasted five days, with pre-work and follow-up extending the experience. Before the core session, each operating unit discussed the business topic it would focus on.

Different J & J executives in the various businesses "sponsor" each conference session. Those who choose the topic are asked to pick one that can have significant or transformational impact. Past program topics have included top-line growth, product development cycles, new market entries and leadership development. Once the topic is defined, the executive sponsor chooses 50 to 130 program participants, who do additional preparation, such as gathering data and interviewing people in the company who might have some relevant insight. Participants go through the program and return later for a day to report on implementation results. Typically, the process takes six to nine months. J&J's Executive Conference approach includes work teams from the business area that is experiencing the problem being studied. The company's action-learning approach at the middle management level, however, brings together high potential individuals from all parts of J & J to tackle a more broad based issue. The Executive Conference issues aim more at organisational development, whereas middle management programs focus more on development of individuals' skills.

4. ***Alignment:*** Because best-practice organisations recognize the importance of alignment between leadership-development and other corporate functions, they often tie educational efforts to formal succession planning. At J & J, all development functions use 360 degree feedback evaluations as a part of leadership-development. Facilitators assess a multiple choice behavioural questionnaire, in which participants rate their performance in many areas and get ratings from supervisors, peers and subordinates. Plans may be made for participants to be coached later or to engage in activities to strengthen weak areas as part of the program, but the facilitators' assessments are not typically fed directly into succession planning.

Most of the studies pointed out that the best companies are beginning to integrate and align assessment, development, feedback, coaching and succession planning. In the integrated model, leadership-development becomes an important part of maintaining a steady flow of information throughout an organisation and ensuring that top talent is tracked and continues to grow. GE openly ties leadership development to succession planning. All employees are rated in a nine-block system for the annual Session C review. The review includes discussion about people's performance and their adherence to the values in GE's value statement. The system is an approximation of a typical competency model but was created quickly, simply and with GE self-confidence from a comment by Welch and elaboration by his HR team. It features a chart on which an employee's bottom line performance is rated on one axis, with adherence to GE values on the other axis. Those who don't make their performance numbers but do adhere to GE values are given a chance to improve those numbers and get a higher rating. Those who make their numbers but don't demonstrate the GE values are rated low in the four level models, which gauge promotion suitability. Those who do neither are rated lowest. It is commonly said that, at GE, the corporate headquarters owns the top 500 people in the company and just rents them out to the business. To encourage the sharing of business talent, GE includes a negative variable in its performance appraisals for managers who hold back talented employees. Outstanding business performance and development of leaders go hand in hand.

Hewlett-Packard provides myriad opportunities for emerging leaders to develop and grow. Platt, the former CEO, recognized that many people who grew up with the founders were retiring and that their immediate successors looked a little too much like one another. He saw that as the company became more global, it would need more diversity of ethnicity and gender. Having a female CEO now may help change perceptions about who is leadership material. And HP's leadership development process is clearly supportive of diversity goals, providing stretch assignments for the most promising people and making accelerated programs available for individual contributors and first level managers. Best-practice organisations use the goals of their leadership development program as guides to putting the right people in the right programs. The goal of Shell's LEAP program is to create leaders at all levels, so the programs are open to anyone within the organisation. GE and HP are more selective about entrance because they want to focus only on those individuals with the potential to move quickly through the ranks.

5. ***Assessment:*** Best-practice organisations always assess the impact of their leadership development process. To collect information on the perceived value, the best-practice partners use a number of tools and techniques. The Kirkpatrick Four-Level Model of Evaluation is typical. Participants, human resource development staff, consultants and in some instances, financial staff, do the assessments—the later weighing program expenditures' return on investment. Best-practice partners use an assessment method called the Kirkpatrick levels to quantify the effect of leadership programs on business results. But both the study sponsors and best-practice partners use other metrics, too including corporate performance, customer satisfaction and employee satisfaction. In general, best-practice partners were more aggressive than sponsors about measuring and evaluating program effectiveness were.

Of all the best practice organisations, Arthur Andersen is probably the most dedicated to assessment and has reaped the benefits. The vast amounts of data the firm collects not only demonstrate the partner development program's correlation with improved business results but also show where the organisation needs to head. Although measurement is expensive and some time tricky, its benefits cannot be discounted. Arthur Andersen combines impact research with participants' course evaluations. Program attendees fill out evaluation forms before they take the class, immediately after the class is finished and three months later. The forms contain questions about the knowledge participants believe they have gained.

The impact research consists of comparing, course by course, partners who have attended PDP with those who have not. The results show that attendance increases both client satisfaction and per hour billings. Impact research is done in a two-year cycle, with information gathered on partners a year before the program and a year after. The use of both participants satisfaction and impact research measures helps provide a balanced set of results. Arthur Andersen found that one of its programs was not getting a high participant satisfaction rating, but an impact analysis showed that the program was having a greater effect than any of PDP's other courses. Another key factor in determining satisfaction is whether program participants have similar levels of familiarity with the topic. What may be an exciting concept for one person could be old news to another. Arthur Andersen believes that moving to a problem based course design will help it address different levels of participant knowledge.

To Shell's LEAP staff, a program adds value only if the team project generates revenues at least 25 times greater than the project's cost. During the initial contracting process, a LEAP staff member and the leader of the business unit determine the desired project outcomes, including financial targets. The business leader expresses his or her objectives in sending the candidate to the program; in many cases that defines the program and problem the team or individual will address. You get what you pay for best-practice companies do consider costs, but their main focus is on the value the program can provide. When asked to rank the importance of various criteria in selecting an outside vendor, the companies put fees near the bottom of the list. Arthur Andersen invests approximately 6 percent of total revenues in education. If course offerings achieve their objective to improve business results, support is likely to continue. Cost for each participant in the executive development program at the World Bank is $22000, which includes travel, lodging and business school fees for three modules and for the Grass Roots Immersion Program. The cost is not charged back to the business groups but funded centrally through the bank's $12 million annual executive education budget.

7.7 THE NEW STRATEGIC REALITY OF LEADERSHIP DEVELOPMENT

Globalization, deregulation, e-commerce and rapid technological change are forcing companies to reevaluate the way they operate. Approaches that have worked for years are no longer effective. Development of leaders who think strategically is increasingly a source of sustainable competitive advantage. Hence observations of companies known for excellent leadership development practices can be invaluable.

Development groups such as Arthur Andersen are PDP and the one at GE's Crotonville site emphasizes diligent crafting or programs, careful listening, constant monitoring and frequent communication. That helps senior executives understand how a leadership development process can shape and disseminate an organisation's culture, overcome resistance to change and achieve strategic goals. At GE, the corporate leadership-development group endeavors to maintain buy in. It interviews company leaders around the world on a regular basis to gauge future business needs and the characteristics future leaders should have. Additionally the group at Crotonville identifies early adopters of a given development initiative and leverages their support.

Hewlet Packard has generated support for its leadership development process by having both the CEO and senior managers participate in its programs. The executives serve as mentors, faculty and supporters in leadership-development design and programs. Senior level support for Johnson & Johnson's executive conferences is evidenced by the fact that either the chairman or a member of the company's executive committee participates in each session, articulating J&J's credo and values and the program's link to business success. Although the best practice firms differ in their emphasis on making leadership development strategic, the development program of each includes elements of the five critical steps.

1. Building awareness of external challenges, emerging strategies, organisational needs and what leading firms do to meet the needs.
2. Employing anticipatory learning tools to recognize potential external events, envision the future and focus on action the organisation can take to create its own future.
3. Taking action by tying leadership development programs to solving important, challenging business issues.

4. Aligning leadership development with performance assessment, feedback, coaching and succession planning; and
5. Assessing impact of the leadership-development process on individual behavioural changes and organisational success.

Indian Scenario

HCL Infinet:

As per HCL infinet's model of leadership, a leader should adhere to a few basics, governance to the present business environment

- ***Teamwork is in:*** Good leaders need to understand the true potential of a team and consciously work towards building one.
- ***Coach, do not lead:*** Top-down leadership is passe. Today, you need to be a mentor fostering team spirit and coordination.
- ***Do not micro manage your teams:*** True leaders do not manage the micros. Instead, they take the bird's eye view on strategy and environment to create a team that delivers.
- ***Treat colleagues as equals:*** A leader should be approachable for every single individual in the organisation. Age, seniority and position should not count when you need to relate to people.
- ***Communicate; good leadership actually assures clarity of goals and objectives:*** It stems from ease in communication, both formal and informal.
- ***Walk the talk:*** A cliche no doubt, but a powerful thought. Leading from the front works.

Though it is difficult to distill and use these maxims on the job, yet a true leader should never call it quits. The role of a leader is essentially architectural. This role has four components.

Creating a foundation: the kind of values the organisation stands for, the shared loyalty it generates, the element of inter personal trust its constituents exhibit, and the personal credibility of the leader both with people within the organisation and those without are an integral part of creating a proper foundation. Building a foundation is a time consuming process. A leader should lay it brick by brick. People look for signals that are the tone for them to replicate the leader's behaviour elsewhere in the organisation. Creating space: Every individual values his personal space, where he or she is at his or her best. The task of a leader is to create that space. By creating space, you are giving an individual the freedom to take decisions, to make mistakes, and to learn from them. You also make him, or her, accountable. It eliminates a sense of paranoia—the undoing of most corporate. Creating height: this means setting goals at the individual and the organisational level, to stretch one's limits. A leader should create an atmosphere in which everyone looks up, and is driven by things beyond one's current capabilities. A leader should also ensure an alignment between a company's goals and the goals of individual employees. Creating a staircase: It is about channeling and encouraging the entrepreneurial instincts with the organisation through mentoring, career building and so on.

It is realised from the above that leadership is not achieved only by individuals and managers. In fact, without followers, leaders cannot lead. Effective followers are team players who partner with organisation leaders to create the organisation's vision and to implement goals and suggestions. Effective followers have some similar characteristics to leaders as Table 7.6 shows. A major difference between high-performance followers and leaders is their role perception and enactment.

Table 7.6: Effective followership competencies

1. Ability to self-manage
2. Organisational commitment
3. Integrity, credibility and honesty
4. Competence and focus
5. Versatility
6. Job and task ownership
7. Critical problem-solving skills
8. Team player
9. Energetic and empowered

SUMMARY

In this section we summarise traditional leadership theories, many of which are widely used. In practice, many of these theories apply to managers, supervisors and top-level organisational officers and leaders. Since leadership style and effectiveness depend on their environment, followers, tasks and other contextual variables, this section presents the evolution of leadership studies and illustrates how leadership styles are contingent on other dimensions. It is interesting to note how changing environment, competition, and business practices influence management theory.

Classical leadership theories summarized here include (1) The trait approach, (2) Behavioural theory: The managerial grid, (3) Contingency theory: Fiedler's model, (4) The path-goal theory, (5) The Vroom-Yetton-Jago model and (6) The life-cycle model.

Some reviews of past research have found the traits of intelligence, dominance, self-confidence, energy and task-relevant knowledge to be consistently associated with leadership. Leaders are bright, self-confident, high-energy people who know something about the situation they are trying to affect and take control when they must.

The desire to lead and honesty/integrity expanded the list of traits. Leaders want to affect the behaviour of others. Effective leaders also are honest and have integrity, which helps gain the trust of their followers. Two complementary behavioural theories of leadership were designed to describe that behaviour that distinguished leaders of effective and ineffective work group. One set of researchers was at the University of Michigan; the other set was at Ohio State University.

A review of leadership research identified these six traits as consistently associated with leadership: Drive, the desire to lead, honesty/integrity, self-confidence, cognitive ability, and knowledge of the business". Three traits were found in both reviews: Self-confidence; cognitive ability, which includes intelligence; and knowledge of the business, which is similar to task-relevant knowledge.

REVIEW QUESTIONS

1. Define leadership. How a leader differs from a manager?
2. Explain various contingency theories of leadership.
3. How do you develop leadership in high performance resilient global company?
4. State important characteristics of an effective leader. How does he differ for an effective follower?

DISCUSSION QUESTIONS

Imagine you as a leader plan a venture capital company with 50 software consultants and functional experts. What trait do you think will qualify you as an effective leader to lead the company?

1. Review leadership theories in the present global context. How changes in professional management practices and modern leadership styles affected the performance of so called family owned Indian companies? Comment in the context of leadership changes in Tata group of companies.
2. Reliance Industries Ltd. is now managed by Mukesh Ambani. What do you think about his leadership style w.r.t the founder Ambani? Also compare Mukesh's leadership style with Anil Ambani, his brother in other Reliance Group of companies. What leadership theory is applied in this case?

STUDENT EXERCISE

Visit a software company and find out the techniques and qualities CEO that have an impact on his subordinates. What leadership theories do you think are more suitable in Indian context for service sector firm having a CEO of age less than 30 years with more than 3000 employees?

SKILL TEST

Are you a Charismatic Leader?

Instructions: The following statements refer to the possible ways in which you might behave toward others when you are in a leadership role. Please read each statement carefully and decide to what extent it applies to you. Then encircle the appropriate number as per the table given below:

To a very great extent	1
To a considerable extent	2
To a moderate extent	3
To a sight extent	4
To little or no extent	5

1.	Pay close attention to what others say when they are talking.	**1**	**2**	**3**	**4**	**5**
2.	Communicate clearly.	**1**	**2**	**3**	**4**	**5**
3.	Are trustworthy?	**1**	**2**	**3**	**4**	**5**

4.	Care about other people.	**1**	**2**	**3**	**4**	**5**
5.	Do not put excessive energy into avoiding failure.	**1**	**2**	**3**	**4**	**5**
6.	Make the work of others more meaningful.	**1**	**2**	**3**	**4**	**5**
7.	Seem to focus on the key issues in a situation.	**1**	**2**	**3**	**4**	**5**
8.	Get across your meaning effectively, often in unusual ways.	**1**	**2**	**3**	**4**	**5**
9.	Can be relied on to follow through on commitments?	**1**	**2**	**3**	**4**	**5**
10.	Have a great deal of self-respect.	**1**	**2**	**3**	**4**	**5**
11.	Enjoy taking carefully calculated risks.	**1**	**2**	**3**	**4**	**5**
12.	Help others feel more competent in what they do.	**1**	**2**	**3**	**4**	**5**
13.	Have a clear set of priorities.	**1**	**2**	**3**	**4**	**5**
14.	Are in touch with how others feel.	**1**	**2**	**3**	**4**	**5**
15.	Rarely change once you have taken a clear position.	**1**	**2**	**3**	**4**	**5**
16.	Focus on strengths, of yourself and of others.	**1**	**2**	**3**	**4**	**5**
17.	Seem most alive when deeply involved in some project.	**1**	**2**	**3**	**4**	**5**
18.	Show others that they are all part of the same group.	**1**	**2**	**3**	**4**	**5**
19.	Get others to focus on the issues you see as important.	**1**	**2**	**3**	**4**	**5**
20.	Communicate feelings as well as ideas.	**1**	**2**	**3**	**4**	**5**
21.	Let others know where you stand.	**1**	**2**	**3**	**4**	**5**
22.	Seem to know just how you "fit" into a group.	**1**	**2**	**3**	**4**	**5**
23.	Learn from mistakes, do not treat errors as disasters, but as learning.	**1**	**2**	**3**	**4**	**5**
24.	Are fun to be around?	**1**	**2**	**3**	**4**	**5**

ANALYSIS AND INTERPRETATION

The questionnaire measures six facets of charismatic leadership. Your score can range from four to twenty for each section. Each question is stated as a measure of the extent to which you engage in the behaviour or elicit the feelings. The higher your score, the more you demonstrate charismatic leader behaviours.

PART 1: ***Management of Attention*** (1, 7, 13, 19). Your score ______. You pay especially close attention to people with whom you are communicating. You are also "focused in" on the key issues under discussion and help others to see clearly these key points. You have clear ideas about the relative importance or priorities of different issues under discussion.

PART 2: ***Management of Meaning*** (2, 8, 14, 20). Your score ______. This set of items centers on your communication skills, specifically your ability to get the meaning of a message across, even if this means devising some quite innovative approach.

PART 3: ***Management of Trust*** (3, 9, 15, 21). Your score _______. The key factor is your perceived trustworthiness as shown by your willingness to follow through on promises, avoid "flip-flop" shifts in position, and willingness to take clear positions.

PART 4: ***Management of Self*** (4, 10, 16, 22). Your score _______. This index concerns your general attitudes toward yourself and others and their feelings, as well as for "taking care of" feelings about yourself in a positive sense (e.g., self-regard).

PART 5: ***Management of Risk*** (5, 11, 17, 23). Your score _______. Charismatic leaders are deeply involved in what they do not do not spend excessive amounts of time or energy on plans to "protect" themselves against failure. These leaders are willing to take risks, not on a hit-or-miss basis, but after careful estimation of the odds of success or failure.

PART 6: ***Management of Feelings*** (6, 12, 18, 24). Your score ______. Charismatic leaders seem to consistently generate a set of positive feelings in others. Others feel that their work becomes more meaningful and that they are the "masters" of their own behaviour, that is, they feel competent. They feel a sense of community, a "we-ness" with their colleagues and co-workers. Charismatic leaders articulate a vision, show concern for group members, communicate high expectations, and create high-performing organisations. This assessment exercise measures your charismatic potential.

If you wish to know more insight on your test score, then you are welcome to contact author via e-mail: shaangrila@gmail.com or social media: drs.shajahan.7@facebook.com

8

CHAPTER

ORGANISATIONAL POLITICS

LEARNING OBJECTIVES

This chapter aims at introducing fundamental concepts for explaining the positive organisational politics for moulding sustained high performance organisation for AD 2020 to the readers:

- *Definition, importance and fundamental concepts of organisational politics*
- *Factors contributing organisational politics*
- *Sources of politics and political behaviour*
- *Techniques of acquiring a political base*
- *Preventing and controlling dysfunctional politics*

INTRODUCTION

Many people regard organisational politics as something negative (e.g., pursuing self-interests at the expense of others) and something to be minimized. Consequently, although most people know that organisational politics are common, they avoid saying so when it concerns one's own behaviour. It is more common to talk about politics when complaining about a loss to a friend than it is in the context of one's own political maneuvering. When we win on an issue, we call it leadership; when we lose, we call it politics. In many organisations, politics is a taboo subject, which makes it difficult for individuals to deal with this crucially important aspect of organisational reality.

The author believes that a leader must skillfully use organisational politics to acquire and retain power and to accomplish major goals. Therefore, it would be a mistake to pretend that politics does not exist or to fantasize that a leader can be effective without appropriate use of politics. As Pericles wrote over 2500 years ago, "Just because you do not take an interest in politics doesn't mean politics won't take an interest in you". I regard organisational politics as neither good nor bad, per se, although it is important for us to distinguish between ethical and unethical political behaviour.

Everyone in an organisation has varying degrees of power. Without power, people cannot plan and achieve goals; they cannot motivate themselves or others, manage their careers effectively, mobilise resources, or protect their rights. Without power, organisations cannot compare effectively in national and global markets. Power in and of itself is neither bad nor evil. The motivations underlying power and its uses determine how functional or dysfunctional, moral or immoral. This chapter focuses the importance of organisational politics and explains how it can be channelize for the growth of an organisation.

8.1 DEFINITION

A number of definitions of the term 'Politics' in organisation could be found in the management literature. Some scholars define politics as the management of influence to obtain ends sanctioned by the organisation. Tushman defines "Politics refers to the structure and process of the use of authority and power to effect definition of goals, direction and the other major parameters of the organisation. Decisions are not made in a rational or formal way but rather through compromise, accommodation and bargaining". Again, Pfeiffer defines politics as involving "those activities taken within organisations to acquire develop, and use power and other resources to obtain one's preferred outcomes in a situation in which there is uncertainty or dispenses about choices".

Tushman defined politics, "as the structure and process of the use of authority and power to affect definition of goals, directions and the other major parameters of the organisation". Dubrin, (2001) defined organisational politics as "informal approaches to gaining power through means other than merit or luck". It could be argued that politics are used primarily to achieve power, either directly or indirectly, e.g., by being promoted, receiving a larger budget or other resources, or gaining desirable assignments. Thus, politics are intentional acts of influencing others through the acquired power to enhance self-interest and advancement.

According to Morgan (1986), it is useful to remember the definition of politics in its original meaning, the idea of politics stems from the view that, where interests are divergent, society should provide a means of allowing individuals to reconcile their differences through consultation and negotiation. In ancient Greece, Aristotle advocated politics as a means of reconciling the need for unity in the *Greek polis* (city-state) with the fact that the *polis* was an "*aggregate of many members*". Politics, for him, provided a means of creating order out of diversity while avoiding forms of totalitarian rule. Political science and many systems of government have built on this basic idea, advocating politics, and the recognition and interplay of competing interests that politics implies, as a means of creating a non-coercive form of social order.

However, power and politics are inextricably interwoven with the fabric of an organisation's life. In any organisation, at any given moment, a number of people are seeking to gain and use power to achieve their own ends. This pursuit of power is political behaviour. Organisational politics refers to the activities carried out by people to acquire, enhance and use power and other resources to obtain their preferred outcomes in a situation where there is uncertainly or disagreement.

It may be noted that power is the capacity of one party to influence other parties to act as the first party wants. People can act from legitimate, reward, coercive, informational, expert and referent power bases. Power can influence behaviour through compliance, identification, and internationalization. Power is a function of lies of mutual dependence in social relationship. Power is the ability of one to control the actions of others. Power, at the individual level in an organisation, is the ability of A to influence B to do something that A desires. At the organisational level, power is the ability of a leader or a dominant coalition to use resources to achieve stated goals.

8.2 CHARACTERISTICS OF ORGANISATIONAL POLITICS

Political action takes place when an actor recognizes that the achievement of his goals is influenced by the behaviour of others. Politics involve the management of influence to obtain ends not sanctioned by the formal organisation. Any behaviour by organisational member that is self-serving may be termed 'Political'. Organisational politics exists wherever people work together. Politics takes place in varying degrees in all organisations. All behaviour cannot be treated as political. For example, demanding for a pay rise by an employee is not a political behaviour, but the use of threat to increase in pay would be a political act.

Organisational politics are a natural result of the fact that people think differently and want to act differently. This diversity creates a tension that must be resolved through political means. There are many ways in which this can be done, for example: Autocratically ("We'll do it this way"); bureaucratically ("We're supposed to do it this way"); technocratically ("It's best to do it this way"); or democratically ("How shall we do it?"). In each case the choice between alternative paths of action usually hinges on the power relations between the actors involved. According to Morgan, An organisation's politics is most clearly manifested in the conflicts and power plays that sometimes occupy center stage, and in the countless interpersonal intrigues that provide diversions in the flow of organisational activity. Politics occurs on an ongoing basis, often in a way that is invisible to all but those directly involved.

8.3 SOURCES OF POLITICS AND POLITICAL BEHAVIOUR

The potential complexity of organisational politics is mind-boggling, even before we take account of the personalities and personality clashes that usually bring roles and their conflicts to life. Sometimes the conflicts generated will be quite explicit and open for all to see, while at other times they will lie beneath the surface of day-to-day events.

For example, relations in meetings may be governed by various hidden agendas of which even the participants are unaware. In some organisations disputes may have a long history, decisions and actions in the present being shaped by conflicts, grudges, or differences that others believe long forgotten or settled. The manager of a production department may align with the marketing manager to block a proposal from the production engineer not because he disagrees with the basic ideas, but because of resentments associated with the fact that he and the production engineer have never gotten along. Though such resentments may seem petty, they are often powerful forces in organisational life.

Uncertainty is usually a source for political activity as well as for an opportunity to accrue power. Certain situations provide especially fertile growing ground for uncertainty, which provides opportunities for individuals and units to define their interests. These include lack of an organisational vision and mission, unclear organisational goals and objectives, poorly defined performance metrics and measures, poorly coordinated teams and units, or major change programs that are poorly planned. Unproductive and even destructive political behaviour and competition between groups and individuals can occur when leaders do not see and correct these sources of uncertainty. On the other hand, organisational members and groups who seek to constructively define areas of uncertainty for the good of the organisation can accrue power in politically responsible systems. A summary of a research studies provided an insight into the general nature of the sources of the organisational politics.

- Sixty percent of the managers said organisational politics was a frequent occurrence.
- The larger the organisation, the greater the perceived political activity.

- Ambiguous roles and goals and increased conflict were associated with increased political activity.
- Marketing staffs and members of corporate boards of directors were rated as the most political, while production, accounting, and finance personnel were viewed as the least political.
- Reorganisations and personnel changes prompted the most political activity.

8.4 FACTORS INFLUENCING POLITICAL BEHAVIOUR

People use political behaviour in organisations in response to the following five main factors:

1. ***Ambiguous Goals:*** When the goals of a department or the entire organisation are ambiguous then there is more room available for playing politics. Some people may use the ambiguity to manipulate the situation for their benefit.
2. ***Scarce Resources:*** When resources are scarce, people have the tendency to use political behaviour to make sure that they get the biggest possible share of the resource.
3. ***Technology and Environment:*** Organisational effectiveness is largely a function of the organisation's ability to appropriately respond to external environment which is highly dynamic and generally unpredictable as well as adequately adopt to complex technological developments. Thus, political behaviour is increased when the internal technology is complex and when external environment is highly volatile.
4. ***Non-programmed Decisions:*** Sometimes, the companies have to make a lot of non-programmed decisions on certain issues. These decisions are not based on clear standards and precedents, because such issues involve many factors and variables that are complex in nature. Hence decisions are taken on intuition, bunch and guesses and all these subjective feelings can be affected by political behaviour.
5. ***Organisational Change:*** Whenever there are changes in the organisational structure and policies, people in powerful positions have the opportunity to play politics. These changes may include restructuring of a division or creating a division, personnel changes, introducing a new product line and all these changes influence political behaviour when various individuals and groups try to control the given situation. It is widely accepted that managers have to be politicians in order to maintain their positions in the organisational hierarchy as well as serve the interests of their units.

According to Dubrin (2001) the following individual and organisational factors contribute to political behaviour:

(*i*) ***Pyramid-shaped organisation structure:*** A pyramid concentrates power at the top. Only so much power is therefore available to distribute among the many people who would like more of it. Each successive layer on the organisation chart has less power than the layer above. At the very bottom of the organisation, workers have virtually no power. Since most organisations today have fewer layers than they previously had, the competition for power has become more intense.

(*ii*) ***Subjective standards of performance:*** People often resort to organisational politics because they do not believe that the organisation has an objective and fair way of judging their performance and suitability for promotion. Similarly, when managers have no objective way of differentiating effective people from the less effective, they will resort to favouritism.

(iii) ***Environmental uncertainty and turbulence:*** When people operate in an unstable and unpredictable environment, they tend to behave politically. They rely on organisational politics to create a favourable impression because uncertainty makes it difficult to determine what they should really be accomplishing. The uncertainty, turbulence, and insecurity created by corporate mergers or downsizing is a major contributor to office politics.

(iv) ***Emotional insecurity:*** Some people resort to political maneuvers to ingratiate themselves with superiors because they lack confidence in their talents and skills.

(v) ***Manipulative tendencies:*** Some people engage in political behaviour because they want to manipulate others, sometimes for their own personal advantage.

(vi) ***Disagreements that prevent rational decision making:*** Many executives attempt to use rational criteria when making major decisions, but rational decision making is constrained by major disagreements over what the organisation should be doing. Unless strategy and goals are shared strongly among key organisational members, political motivation is inevitable in organisational decision making.

8.5 USE OF ORGANISATIONAL POLITICS

Organisational politics (the use of power and influence) happens all the time: individuals and groups strive to exert their interpretations and preferences over organisational goals; groups compete over resources, rewards, and recognition; ambiguous information is used for strategic ends; "facts" are used for difference interests. Politics, defined as the need and ability to have use power, is a natural phenomenon. Politics, like power, can become dysfunctional, destructive, and even immoral when individuals or groups use power to supersede organisational goals for their own private ends. Self-interests and organisational interests must always be weighed and balanced. Political behaviour works against the organisation when self-interests are not aligned with those of the organisation. Bill Gates has effectively understood and used his knowledge as power to build Microsoft Corporation, which might be the world's most successful software technology company. Figure 8.1 explains use of Political Behaviour with Reasons, Techniques and Results in detail below.

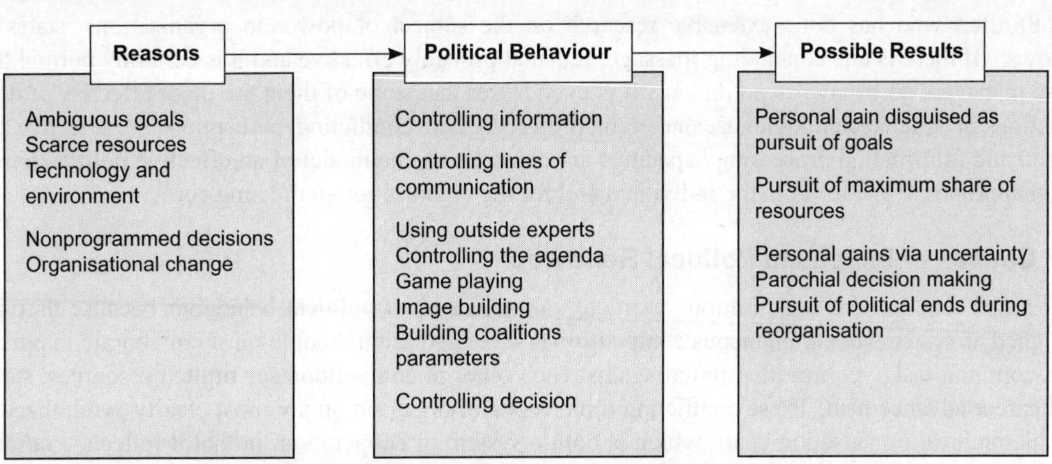

Fig. 8.1: Use of political behaviour: Reasons, techniques and results

Organisational politics are plans, tactics and strategies for seizing, holding, extracting and executing power in organisations. Politics are used by individuals and groups to achieve their respective goals. There is a relationship between power and politics. In the words of Pfeffer, "if power is a force, a store of potential influence through which events can be affected politics involves those activities or behaviours through which power is developed and used on organisational settings. Power is a property of the system at rest: Politics is the study of power in action".

It may be noted further that one does not have to be consciously cunning or deviously political to end up playing organisational politics. Political behaviour is a fairly natural response to the tensions created between individuals and their organisations. The setting of budgets and work standards, the day-to-day supervision and control of work, as well as the pursuit of opportunity and career, is often characterized by sophisticated forms of gamesmanship.

Take, for example, the situations that reveal the guile with which factory workers are able to control their pace of work and level of earnings, even when under the close eye of their supervisors or of efficiency experts trying to find ways of increasing productivity. The workers know that to maintain their positions they have to find ways of beating the system, and do so with great skill and ingenuity. Individuals who systematically wheel and deal their way through organisational affairs merely illustrate the most extreme and fully developed form of a latent tendency present in most aspects of organisational life.

Organisational politics may include the following:

- Behaviour that is outside the normal legitimate system of influence may become illegitimate.
- Behaviour that is designed to benefit the individual or group at the expense of the organisation.

Behaviour that is intentional and designed to acquire and maintain power, has conflictive means.

(a) Managing Political Behaviour

The very nature of political behaviour makes it difficult to manage or even approach in a rational and systematic manner. However a manager who understands why people use political behaviour and the techniques people usually employ has the best chance to manage political behaviour successfully.

Pfeiffer, who has done extensive research on the subject of power in organisations, states as follows: "If there is one concluding message, it is that probably effective and it is certainly normal that these managers do behave as politicians. It is even better that some of them are quiet effective at it. In situations in which technologies are uncertain, preferences are conflicting, perceptions are selective and biased and information processing capacities are constrained, the model of an effective politician may be an appropriate one for both the individual and for the organisation in the long-run".

(b) Causes of Increased Political Behaviour

It is a fact that modern organisations promote various kinds of political behaviour because they are designed as systems of simultaneous competition and collaboration. People must collaborate in pursuit of a common task, yet are often pitted against each other in competition for limited resources, status and career advancement. These conflicting dimensions of organisation are most clearly symbolized in the hierarchical organisation chart, which is both a system of cooperation, in that it reflects a rational subdivision of tasks and a career ladder up which people are motivated to climb. The fact that there are more jobs at the bottom than at the top means that competition for the top places is likely to be keen, and that in any career race there are likely to be far fewer winners than losers. Along with the fact that different individuals and groups are mandated to exercise authority and influence over others, the hierarchy more or less ensures the kinds of competitive struggle on which organisational politics thrives.

Political behaviour would probably emerge when someone or something upsets the status quo of the organisation that is when some change occurs. The causes of political behaviour includes the following:

1. ***Technological and environmental change:*** This is one of the frequently mentioned causes of increased political behaviour. The introduction of computers, automation, changes in government regulations and increased competition, etc. can cause increased political behaviour.
2. ***Personnel changes:*** Personnel changes generally involve promotions, transfers, etc. at the executive levels. New people bring with them uncertainty, differing opinions, and possibly a change in the make-up of groups and coalitions. This may also cause increased political behaviour.
3. ***Structural change:*** Structural or organisational change aims at the core of power and authority relationships and therefore, can be expected to induce political behaviours. When reorganisations occur, no one expect change in jobs, duties, responsibilities and authority.
4. ***Interdepartmental coordination activities:*** These can also facilitate political behaviours. This is because those relations between interacting groups are sometimes not well defined, requiring a set of coordinating mechanisms. When these mechanisms, for example, rules, task, etc. are not used or are improperly used, political behaviours may be utilised to define boundaries and to reduce uncertainty.
5. ***Resource allocation:*** Political behaviours can initiate particularly when there is a scarcity of resources. When the resources are limited, some units will take advantage and some will lose the advantage as a result of allocations process.

8.6 METHOD OR TECHNIQUES OF BUILDING OR ACQUIRING A POLITICAL BASE

According to Mintzberg there are at least six ways of building a political power base depending on the particular focus: Superiors, peers, subordinates, resources, knowledge and authority. Other popular methods are as follows:

Sponsorship: In sponsorship the person attaches to one who is already in a high position (superior). This is the boss of someone in the immediate chain of command. This strategy assumes that a certain set of rules will be followed. These rules include being totally committed, loyal and obedient to the other person and frequently expressing gratitude to the sponsor for attention.

Alliance Building: The focus here turns to one's peers. By forming alliances, coalitions or networks, it is expected that the group and individuals in the group, will benefit from collective action. The process of alliance buildings varies in different organisation, but the general pattern followed is: An idea is promoted; supporters are sought out; an informal leader is identified; the group becomes an interest group within the organisation; in appropriate time it assumes greater power.

Empire Building: Building a political base with subordinates is called empire building. The manager, seeks to surround himself with people or functions that can act to increase one's importance. Two strategies are followed in empire building. First, the manager attracts rewards and retains highly skilled people and allows them the freedom to perform. In this process, sometimes, the manager will not permit good subordinates to progress their efforts leading to be promoted. The second strategy is to acquire excellent subordinates through assuming responsibility for other units, which is called power grabbing.

Budgeting: This is one of the best strategy for political power-building. The purpose is to give control of important resources (financial) so as to improve one's position.

Expertise: This concept is based on the principle that knowledge is powerful in today's organisations. With this approach the individual's skills and knowledge are emphasized and the importance of the unit to the total organisation is stressed. The introductions of computer system, management information system etc. are good example to this.

Lording: This approach is a game in which legitimate authority is misutilised. In other words, the manager uses bluff, faking etc. to influence others far in excess of what is authorised to him. For example, a purchasing agent of a large manufacturing company tells sales representatives from supplying firms that he is the only person makes the decisions on what is purchased, from whom and how much? In reality the actual decision is taken by the director or someone authorized to it.

8.7 TECHNIQUES OF POLITICAL BEHAVIOUR

The most commonly used techniques of political behaviour are controlling information, controlling lines of communication, controlling agenda, using outside experts, game playing, image building and building coalitions.

The main technique of political behaviour is to control the dissemination of critical information to others. The more critical the information and fewer the people who have it, the stronger is political power base of those who possess these information.

Controlling lines of communication is another political technique related to the flow of information. People who have some control over lines of communication can yield considerable political power. For example, the secretary may have considerable power in deciding who sees the boss and who does not at a given time. She may use this power in favouring those whom she likes and frustrating those against whom she may have it grudge.

Controlling the agenda also gives a person power over information. The person who controls a meeting's agenda, for instance, may consistently put a particular item last on the list and then take up time so that meeting adjourns before considering the item.

The opinions of outside experts and consultants often curry much weight in organisations and many consultants can be swayed by political interests. Consultants know who is paying them and even honest consultants are likely to give opinions consistent with those of their employer. Hence, hiring an outside consultant can be a clever political move.

Game playing can range from fairly innocent to very manipulative. It involves people doing something insincere, but not outright illegal or unethical to gain political ends. For instance, a manager who does not want to answer a committee's tough questions may, for instance, avoid meeting by going out of the town on the day of meeting.

Image building is creating positive impression reflected by the personality, appearance and style. Some of the factors that enhance a preferred image consist of being well dressed, having a pleasant smile, being attractive, honest, sociable and loyal to the organisational interests. In addition, always project an image of competence and self-assurance.

Building coalitions or alliance is another technique of gaining political power. It is necessary to have the alliance with the right people. Coalition building can become simply a matter of quid pro quo: I will support you if you will support me.

8.8 MANAGING POLITICAL BEHAVIOUR

Though it is virtually impossible to eliminate political behaviour in organisations, it is possible to reduce it, if a manager understands the reasons for it and the techniques of political behaviour. Politics when carried to the extreme can damage morale, create enemies, destroy loyalty, damper co-operative spirit and much time and energy is spent planning attacks and counter attacks which are detrimental to organisational health. Accordingly, combating politics must be undertaken by the top management and some of the steps that can be undertaken are open communication, reduction of uncertainty and creating awareness.

Open communication can reduce the political activity if all employees know how and why an organisation allocates resources; the employees will be likely to put their energy into meeting the stated criteria for gelling resources rather than into political activity. If the organisation is open about why it made particular decision, then employees will be less likely to think that the decisions were political and less likely to use political techniques to try to influence the next decision. Uncertainty in the form of ambiguous goals and changes that affect the organisation tends to increase the use of political activity. Reducing such uncertainty can, therefore, reduce the political behaviour. Open communication is one of the ways an organisation can reduce uncertainty. For instance, laying down clear criteria and making it transparent to the employees who will be laid off, in case of lay off the organisation can reduce political behaviour.

Finally, managers who develop an ability to recognize and predict political activity are in the best position to limit its effects. Managers with this awareness will expect an increase in political activity during times of organisational change and will learn how to handle it.

8.9 POLITICAL STRATEGIES AND TACTICS

To make effective use of organisational politics, leaders must be able to make appropriate use of specific political strategies and tactics. Remember that ethical behaviour is regarded as an important requirement for effective leadership. As one of many guidelines, The Center for Business Ethics at Bentley College has developed six questions to help evaluate the ethics of a specific decision. Before engaging in a particular influence act or political tactic, they recommend that a person seek answers to the following questions:

- Is it right? (Based on absolute principles of moral rights)
- Is it fair? (Based on absolute principles of justice)
- Who gets hurt? (The fewer the better)
- Would you be comfortable if the details of your decision or actions were made public in the media or through electronic-mail? (Based on the principle of disclosure)
- What would you tell your child, sibling, or young relative to do? (Based on the principle of reversibility)
- How does it smell? (Based on common sense and intuition)

Let's look at a representative group of political tactics and strategies, categorized in the following two sections as ethical or unethical, although many of the strategies and tactics could fall into either category, depending on motivations and methods of implementing them. Used with tact, diplomacy, and good intent, ethical influence tactics can be quite effective. Sequencing of tactics is another important consideration. In general, it is best to begin with the most positive or least abrasive, tactic. If you do not gain the advantage you seek, proceed to a stronger tactic. Also, begin with low-cost, low-risk tactics.

(a) Essentially Ethical Political Strategies and Tactics

This section describes a sampling of ethical political behaviours, divided into three related and overlapping groups: Strategies and tactics aimed at (*i*) directly gaining power, (*ii*) building relationships with superiors and co-workers, and (*iii*) avoiding political blunders. All of these approaches help a leader gain or retain power. They also help the leader cope with the fact that organisations are not entirely rational.

(*i*) Strategies and Tactics Aimed Directly at Gaining Power: It could be argued that all political tactics are aimed at acquiring and maintaining power, if we consider power in a broad scope. Tom Peters says that, although power can often be abused, it can also be used to benefit many people, "and as a career building tool, the slow and steady (and subtle) amassing of power is the surest road to success".

1. ***Develop Power Contacts and Relationships:*** After powerful people have been identified, alliances with them must be established. Cultivating friendly, cooperative relationships with powerful organisational members and outsiders can make the leader's cause much easier to advance. These contacts can benefit a person by supporting his or her ideas in meetings and other public forums. One way to develop these contacts is to be more social, for example, throwing parties and inviting powerful people, although they may not be available.
2. ***Make an Early Showing:*** A display of dramatic results can help gain acceptance for one's efforts. Once a person has impressed management with his or her ability to solve an important problem, that person can look forward to working on problems that will bring greater power.
3. ***Keep Informed:*** It is politically important to keep informed. Successful leaders develop a network to help them keep abreast, or ahead, of developments within the firm. For this reason, a politically astute individual befriends key staff members and executive administrative assistants, for example.
4. ***Control Vital Information:*** Power accrues to those who control vital information. For example, many former government or military officials have found power niches for themselves in industry as a Washington representative of a firm that does business with the government. The vital information they control is knowledge of whom to contact to shorten some of the complicated procedures in getting government contracts approved.
5. ***Control Lines of Communication:*** Related to controlling information is controlling lines of communication, particularly access to key people. Administrative assistants and staff assistants frequently control an executive's calendar. Both insiders and outsiders must curry favour with the conduit in order to see an important executive. Although many people attempt to contact executives directly through e-mail, some executive delegates the responsibility of screening e-mail messages to an assistant.

(*ii*) Strategies and Tactics Aimed at Building Relationships: Much of organisational politics involves building positive relationships with network members who can be helpful now or later. This network includes superiors, subordinates, other lower-ranking people, co-workers, external customers and suppliers. The following are several representative strategies and tactics:

6. ***Provide Favours and Develop Ingratiation:*** A skillful leader always has a positive balance of favours given, and can draw on that balance when something is needed in return.
7. ***Display Loyalty:*** A loyal worker is valued because organisations prosper more with loyal than with disloyal employees. Blind loyalty—the belief that the organisation cannot make a mistake—is not called for; most rational organisations welcome constructive criticism. An obvious form of loyalty to the organisation is longevity, although its value varies.
8. ***Develop a Reputation as a Subject Matter Expert:*** Expertise is one of the major sources of power. Others come to and ask help from an expert.
9. ***Rational Persuasion:*** Using this form of influence helps create an impression that you are reasonable and fair, and also avoids creating resentment that can result from heavy-handed influence tactics.
10. ***Manage Impressions of You:*** Impression management includes behaviours directed at enhancing one's image by drawing positive attention to oneself. Although this can deal with clothing and grooming, it also deals with deeper aspects of behaviour, such as speaking well and presenting one's ideas coherently. Another part of impression management is to tell people about your success or imply that you are an "insider".
11. ***Bring in Outside Experts for Support:*** To help legitimate their positions, executives will often hire a consultant to conduct a study or cast an opinion. One possible problem to avoid is that, consciously or unconsciously, some consultants may slant things to support the executive's position. This tactic would be considered unethical if the executive is intentionally seeking a non-objective opinion.
12. ***Consult With and Ask Advice of Others:*** Consulting with others, even when not required, helps build support for a decision or action. Consulting and asking advice on work-related topics builds relationships with other employees. Asking another person for advice—someone whose job does not require giving it—will usually be perceived as a compliment, and asking advice transmits a message of trust in the other person's judgment.
13. ***Ask Satisfied Customers to Contact your Boss:*** A favourable comment by a customer receives considerable weight because customer satisfaction is a top corporate priority. If a customer says something nice, the comment will carry more weight than one from a co-worker or subordinate.
14. ***Be Courteous, Pleasant, and Positive:*** It has been argued that courteous, pleasant, and positive people are the first to be hired and the last to be fired (assuming they also have other important qualifications).
15. ***Send Thank-you Notes to Large Numbers of People:*** One of the most basic political tactics, sending thank-you notes profusely, is simply an application of sound human relations. Many successful people take the time to send handwritten notes to employees and customers to help create a bond with those people.
16. ***Flatter Others Sensibly:*** Flattery in the form of sincere, specific praise can be an effective relationship builder. By being generous in your positive feedback and comments, you can build relationships with work associates and make them more receptive to your ideas.

17. ***Develop Coalitions:*** Sometimes coalitions are initiated by less powerful actors who seek the support of others. At other times they may be developed by the powerful to consolidate their power. Whether formal or informal, confined to the organisation or extended to include key interests outside, coalitions and interest groups often provide important means of securing desired ends.

***(iii)* Avoiding Political Blunders:** A strategy for retaining power is to refrain from making power eroding blunders. Committing such politically insensitive acts can also prevent one from attaining power. Several leading blunders to avoid are described next.

18. ***Embarrassing or criticizing the boss in a public forum:*** One of the oldest saws in human relations is to "praise in public and criticize in private". Yet, in a moment of anger or stupidity, we may blurt out something that can be costly.
19. ***Surprising the boss:*** Surprises, particularly negative ones, are not appreciated.
20. ***Bypassing the boss:*** Protocol is still highly valued in a hierarchical organisation. Going around the boss to resolve a problem is therefore hazardous. You might be able to accomplish the bypass, but your career could be damaged and your recourses limited.
21. ***Declining an offer from top management:*** Turning down top management, especially more than once, is a political blunder. You thus have to balance your other interests against the blunder of refusing a request from someone powerful in the organisation. An increasing number of managers and professionals today decline opportunities for promotion when the new job requires geographic relocation. For these individuals, family and lifestyle preferences are more important than gaining political advantage on the job.

(b) Potentially Unethical Political Strategies and Tactics

Any technique of gaining power can be unethical if practiced in the extreme and with negative intentions. For example, a person who supports a boss by feeding him or her insider information that could affect the price of company stock is being unethical. Some approaches are almost unequivocally unethical, such as those described next. In the long run they can erode a leader's effectiveness by lowering his or her credibility.

1. ***Back Stabbing:*** The ubiquitous back stab requires that you pretend to be nice, but all the while plan someone's demise. A frequent form of back stabbing is to initiate a conversation with a rival about the weaknesses of a common boss, encouraging negative commentary and making careful mental notes of what the person says. When these comments are passed along to the boss, the rival appears disloyal and foolish. E-mail has become a medium for back stabbing. The sender of the message documents a mistake made by another individual and includes key people on the distribution list. A sample message sent by one manager to a rival began as follows, "Hi, Sam. I'm sorry you couldn't make our important meeting. I guess you had some other important priorities. But we need your input on the following major agenda item we tackled..."
2. ***Purge All But Loyalists:*** The ancient strategy of purge those you have conquered suggests that you remove from the organisation rivals who suffered past hurts through your efforts; otherwise the wounded rivals might retaliate at a vulnerable moment. This kind of strategy is common after a hostile takeover or even a Amerger of equals, e.g., the purge of former Chrysler Corporation executives by the former Daimler-Benz executives after the merger to form Daimler Chrysler.

3. ***Set a Person Up for Failure:*** The object of a setup is to place a person in a position where he or she will either fail outright or look ineffective. For example, an executive whom the CEO dislikes might be given responsibility for a troubled division whose market is rapidly collapsing. The newly assigned division president cannot stop the decline and is then fired for poor performance.
4. ***Exert Undue Pressure:*** Even if you have the power to do this, it would be unethical if used to further your interests at the expense of others. In any case, it may have longer-term repercussions.
5. ***Divide and Conquer:*** An ancient military and governmental strategy, this tactic is also used in business. The object is to have peers struggle among themselves, therefore yielding the balance of power to another person. If team members are not aligned with one another, there is an improved chance that they will align with a common superior. One way of getting subordinates to fight with one another is to place them in intense competition for resources.
6. ***Play Territorial Games:*** Also referred to as turf wars, territorial games involve protecting and hoarding resources that give one power, such as information, relationships, and decision-making authority. A relationship is "hoarded" in such ways as not encouraging others to visit a key customer, or blocking a high performer from getting a promotion or transfer. Other examples of territorial games include monopolizing time with clients, scheduling meetings so someone cannot attend and shutting out co-workers from joining you on an important assignment.

(c) A Caveat

There is a danger when becoming sensitized to political behaviour that one begins to see everything as political, to develop a Machiavellian interpretation that suggests that everyone is trying to outwit and outmaneuver everyone else. We begin to see politics everywhere, and to look for hidden agendas even where there are none. Rather than use politics to generate new insights and understandings that can help deal with divergent interests, there is a temptation to reduce the concept to a tool to be used to advance our own personal interests.

This kind of manipulative stance is reflected in many contemporary writings on the politics of organisation, which have a tendency to emphasize the cynical, selfish, ruthless, get-ahead-at-all-costs mentality that so often turns organisations into corporate jungles. These writings sell through statements such as: "Find out where the real power is and use it" and "Win through intimidation;" This use of a political metaphor breeds mistrust and encourage the idea that organisation involves a zero-sum game where there must be winners and losers. While there may be a measure of truth in this, in that many organisations are dominated by competitive relations, the effect is to reduce the scope for genuine openness and collaboration.

8.10 PREVENTING AND CONTROLLING DYSFUNCTIONAL POLITICS

Although necessary, organisational politics can hurt an organisation and its members when carried to excess. Too much politicking can result in lower morale, higher turnover, and wasted time and effort, thereby lowering performance: To avoid these negative consequences, leaders should combat political behaviour when it is excessive and dysfunctional. Some steps that can help accomplish this follow:

(*a*) To control politics, organisational leaders must be aware of its causes and techniques. For example, during a downsizing, the CEO can be on the alert for instances of back stabbing and transparent attempts to please him or her.

(*b*) Open communication also can constrain the impact of political behaviour. For instance, open communication can let everyone know the basis for allocating resources, thus reducing the amount of political behaviour. When communication is open, it also makes it more difficult for some people to control information and pass along gossip as a political weapon.

(*c*) Avoiding favouritism is a potent way of minimizing politics within a work group. If group members believe that getting the boss to like them is much less important than good job performance in obtaining rewards, they will try to impress the boss through task-related activities.

(*d*) Setting good examples at the top of the organisation can help reduce the frequency and intensity of organisational politics. When leaders are nonpolitical in their actions, they demonstrate in subtle ways that political behaviour is not welcome. It may be helpful for the leader to announce during a staff meeting that devious political behaviour is undesirable and unprofessional.

(*e*) Another way of reducing the extent of political behaviour is for individuals and the organisation to have *goal congruence*, i.e., share the same goals, with thorough understanding of what they mean. If political behaviour will interfere with the company and individuals achieving their goals, workers with goal congruence are less likely to play office politics excessively.

(*f*) Politics can sometimes be constrained by a threat to discuss questionable information in a public forum. People who practice devious politics usually want to operate secretly and privately. They are willing to drop hints and innuendoes and make direct derogatory comments about someone else, provided they will not be identified as the source. An effective way of stopping the discrediting of others is to offer to discuss the topic publicly.

In short, every organisation differs in the specific nature of its politics. The dimensions offered here are board categories that can be used to mitigate unconstructive political activity. Strategies for reducing, preventing, and managing dysfunctional aspects of organisational politics include the following actions:

1. ***Reduce System Diversity***
   - Make clear what the bases for evaluation are.
   - Differentiate rewards among high and low performers.
   - Make sure the rewards are as immediately and directly related to performance as possible.
2. ***Reduce Competition***
   - Try to minimize resource competition among managers.
   - Replace resource competition with externally oriented goals and objectives.
3. ***Break Existing Political Group***
   - When highly cohesive political empires exist, break them apart by removing or splitting the most dysfunctional subgroups. If you are an executive, be keenly sensitive to managers whose mode of operation is the personalization of political patronage. First, approach these persons with a directive to "stop the political maneuvering". If it continues, remove them from the positions and, preferably, the company.

4. *Prevent Future Politisation*

- Make one of the most important criteria for promotion an apolitical attitude that puts organisation ends ahead of personal power ends. Finally, there are strategies for managing the politics and paradoxes of transformation in planned organisational change programs.

The following should be kept in mind as an organisation steers its way through transformation. Everyone must have a voice, but cynics must be silenced. Those individuals with the most to lose from change will be the loudest opponents. Diffusing their arguments will help keep the change moving forward. Without taking their eyes off the horizon, leaders must watch where they step. In order to achieve an organisation's vision, the leaders must ensure that all actions taken by their followers are necessary to achieve desired results. Change in scary, but people volunteer for dangerous tasks only when they feel safe. People will feel safe when they know their future. By giving them responsibility for the implementation and results of the transformation, the new way becomes their future.

SUMMARY

After reflecting on the realities of political dynamics and behaviours in organisations, it seems appropriate to reevaluate the myth of a highly rational, objective, non-political organisation. The idea of rationality seems to be invoked to overcome the contradictions inherent in the fact that an organisation is simultaneously a system of competition and a system of cooperation. An emphasis on rationality could lead us to construct an organisation that does not manage the diversity of interests present and, therefore, is ineffective and unstable.

Power, for an individual, is the ability to influence someone else to do something that he or she wants. At the organisation level, power is the ability of those in control over resources to impact stated goals. The power dependency analysis is a method for diagnosing power in organisations. It involves mapping the major players between the individual and/or an organisation and its constituencies. The meaning of empowerment and the management of power differs across culture and countries. Uncertainty is usually a source for political activity as well as for an opportunity to accrue powers.

Author believes that skillful and appropriate use of organisational politics is necessary for a leader to acquire and retain power and to accomplish major goals. Although political behaviour can be unethical and destructive, it also can and should be ethical and contribute to a balanced set of interests. Perhaps we can join Aristotle in viewing organisational politics as a means of reconciling differences through consultation and negotiation, and as a means of creating order out of diversity while avoiding abuses. As Adolf Berle wrote in 1969 "Your democratic institutions... must foster, defend, and enlarge institutions by which knowledge can be made greater and choices wider and more certain. ...The real function of power and the order it creates... is the liberation of men and women to think and be and make the most of themselves".

REVIEW QUESTIONS

1. Define organisational politics. Explain how important it is that for an organisation?
2. Explain the sources of politics. How can we acquire political-base ethically?
3. Define dysfunctional organisation politics and explain various method of resolving dysfunctional politics.
4. How do you mange organisational politics?

DISCUSSION QUESTIONS

1. Imagine you as a CEO of a social welfare institution. How do you acquire political-base in that organisation for supporting your leadership and agenda?
2. Explain various methods resorted to different people of yours in acquiring political-base unethically in any organisation.

STUDENT EXERCISE

Acquiring Power presents a constant challenge for managers. Politics occurs on a variety of levels within and beyond the organisation. Types of politics that a manager must effectively confront include interpersonal, cross-cultural, and inter-group. The latter category, inter-group, can sometimes be observed between representatives of employees (i.e., unions) and representatives of the organisation (managers) or government agencies. Discover whether there are similarities or differences between countries in handling organisational politics. It encompasses a broad range of issues. A certain level of organisational politics is necessary for change to occur. Differences in culture are more than just a source of power and politics. Global managers have the capacity and ability to influence organisational events on a large scale. Evaluate the extent to which cultural background shapes and/or influences the political styles and abilities of global managers. What do you see as similar trends across these global leaders and managers? What are the differences? Can you identify characteristics that are unique to particular cultures?

SKILL TEST

I Speak your Language

Instructions

It is not possible to get right or wrong answers on this questionnaire. Basically, this is a survey that enables you to describe the underlying strengths you use in your relationships with others. You will be presented with a number of self-descriptive statements, each of which will be followed by four different endings. Your area to indicate the order in which you feel each ending is characteristic of yourself. On the answer sheet to the right of each ending, fill in the number (4, 3, 2 or 1) according to which alternative is most like you. Use number 4 for the ending most like you; 3 next most like you; 2 next most; and number 1 least like you.

1. I am likely to impress others as:
   (*a*) Practical and direct.
   (*b*) Emotional and somewhat stimulating.
   (*c*) Astute and logical.
   (*d*) Intellectually oriented and difficult to understand.
2. In the way I approach my work, I:
   (*a*) Want it to be stimulating and involve lively interaction with others.
   (*b*) Concentrate to make sure the work is systematically or logically developed.

(*c*) Want to be sure the work has a tangible benefit that will justify spending my time and energy on it.

(*d*) Am most concerned as to whether the work is innovative or advances knowledge.

3. In communicating with other, I may:

(*a*) Appear to lost interest with talk that is too detailed.

(*b*) Convey impatience with those who express ideas that are obviously not complete.

(*c*) Show little interest in thoughts and ideas that show little or no originally.

(*d*) Usually ignore those who talk about the future and direct my attention to what needs to be done right now.

4. When circumstances prevent me from doing what I want, I find it most useful to:

(*a*) Review any weakness in my approach and modify it accordingly.

(*b*) Re-think all that has happened and develop a new hypothesis or model for action.

(*c*) Keep in mind the basics, identify the key obstacle or obstacles, and modify my plan.

(*d*) Analyse the motivations of others and develop a new awareness of the situation.

5. Sometimes I think I may appear to others as being:

(*a*) Too emotional or too intense.

(*b*) Almost too controlled or perhaps too logical

(*c*) Too concerned with specifics and matters related to how to do the task.

(*d*) Very concerned with ideas and not showing my feelings.

6. When I write to an individual I do not know, I usually try to:

(*a*) Clarify the reasons for the contact and related this to my purpose in writing.

(*b*) Highlight in plain language what I want, need, or expect of the other person.

(*c*) Show how my main points fit into a broader perspective.

(*d*) Reveal some aspect of my style and myself.

7. When confronted by others with a different point of view, I can usually make progress by:

(*a*) Getting at least one or two specific commitments on which we can build later.

(*b*) Trying to put myself in someone else's place.

(*c*) Keeping my composure and helping others to see things simply and logically.

(*d*) Relying on my basic ability to conceptualize and pull ideas together.

8. In terms of the dimension of time, I probably concentrate most on:

(*a*) Whether what I'm doing or planning to do is going to hurt or disturb others.

(*b*) Making sure that any actions I take is consistent and part of a systematic progression.

(*c*) My immediate actions and involvements and whether they make sense today.

(*d*) Significant long-range actions I plan to take and how they relate to my life's direction.

9. In reacting to individuals whom I meet socially, I am likely to consider whether:

(*a*) They can contribute ideas and challenge.

(*b*) They seem thoughtful and reflective.

(*c*) They are interesting and fun to be with.

(*d*) They know what they're doing and can accomplish things.

10. In speaking to groups with whom I have little regular contact, I would hope to leave the impression of being:

(*a*) A systematic thinker who can analyse the kind of problems the particular group is concerned about.

(*b*) An individual capable of making some innovative contribution.

(*c*) A pragmatic and resourceful individual who could help the group define it concerns and who could assist in solving their problems.

(*d*) A lively and effective individual who was sensitive to their moods and needs.

11. In stressful interactions with others, I may occasionally:

(*a*) Be too open, expressing feelings that might have been better left unsaid.

(*b*) Be overly cautious and avoid some contacts that might have proved rewarding.

(*c*) Become so concerned with a given facet of a person that I fail to see other less obvious, but important characteristics.

(*d*) Be influenced by others who are gifted, but who perhaps lack specific direction.

12. If I am not careful, others may at times feel that I am:

(*a*) Highly unemotional and inclined towards being impersonal or detached.

(*b*) Superficial our self-centered.

(*c*) Snobbish, superior, or condescending.

(*d*) Moody, excitable, or unpredictable.

13. I feel satisfied with myself when I:

(*a*) Get more accomplished than I planned.

(*b*) Understand the underlying feelings of others and react in a helpful way.

(*c*) Solve a problem by using a logical or systematic method.

(*d*) Develop feasible new thoughts or ideas.

14. I find it easy to be convincing when I am:

(*a*) Sensitive to my own feelings and those of others.

(*b*) Logical, patient, and forbearing.

(*c*) Practical and direct.

(*d*) Intellectually in control of things and take all relevant factors into account.

15. I enjoy it when others see me as:

(*a*) Intellectually gifted and having wisdom.

(*b*) An individual who knows where he or she is going and has competence to get there.

(*c*) Creative and stimulating.

(*d*) A dependable individual who gets things done and is reliable.

16. When things are not going well, I feel it is preferable to:

(*a*) Maintain an approach that has proved effective before, even though by taking risks I might with more victories.

(*b*) Be respected as original even if it costs me something in the short term.

(*c*) Concentrate on getting what I want accomplished right now even if it does not leave a memorable impression.

(*d*) Be spontaneous and say what I really think.

17. When others pressure me, I am:

(*a*) Overly emotional, impulsive or inclined to lose control of my feelings.

(*b*) Too inclined toward being analytical and critical of them.

(*c*) Too concerned with proving me with immediate action.

(*d*) Inclined to step back into my own world of thought.

18. In considering my approach to difficult situations, it is possible that I become overly involved:

(*a*) An intellectual arguments.

(*b*) Getting and doing as I wish in the current issue.

In the world of concepts, values, and ideas.

(*c*) About the feelings of others.

Source: Education Institute of American Hotel and Motel Association, Chicago, USA 2002 & MIT, USA courseware. Courtesy: Prof. Simon-Director of TQM Programme.

9

CHAPTER

CONFLICT MANAGEMENT, BARGAINING AND NEGOTIATION

LEARNING OBJECTIVES

This chapter aims at introducing fundamental concepts for explaining the conflict management, bargaining, negotiation strategies and process for moulding sustained high performance organisation for AD 2020 to the readers:

- *Definition, importance and fundamental concepts of the conflict management, bargaining and negotiation*
- *Traditional vis-a vis modern view of conflict management*
- *Functional and dysfunctional conflict and conflict process*
- *Negotiation strategies and negotiation process*
- *Bargaining strategies*

INTRODUCTION

Conflict is an expressed struggle between at least two interdependent parties who perceive incompatible goals, scare resources, and interference from others in achieving their goals. Behavioural scientists widely recognize that conflict in organisations is a basic process that needs to be carefully managed. Some conflicts (mostly positive in nature), many scholars argue that it is vital to continuous improvement in organisations and that conflict management is crucial to the sustained growth and continued success of any high performance resilient new age organisations. Many managers, though, believe they should eliminate conflict from their organisations. Social scientists who have studied conflict also have usually focused on its negative results. Although this chapter's observations are supported by the results of much conflict research, you will find parts of this chapter unsetting if you have a negative view of conflict.

Conflicts are always resolved in the workplace. Conflict between groups can be resolved by collective bargaining, negotiation, mediation, and arbitration while conflict between a boss and a subordinate can be managed by collaboration and accommodation. Conflict accelerates change in an organisation, especially in small businesses, where it is easy to formulate and implement new policies.

Conflict prompts modification of policies and operation procedures in the organisation. Conflict forces the organisation's leadership to realign its objectives towards common goals in order to foster teamwork amongst competing parties.

Conflict that results into healthy competition cultivates innovation and inventiveness amongst employees. When an organisation spends much of its time dealing with conflict, members take time away from focusing on the core goals they are tasked with achieving. Conflict sometimes has a destructive effect on the individuals and groups involved. At other times, however, conflict can increase the capacity of those affected to deal with problems, and therefore it can be used as a motivating force toward innovation and change.

Conflict in organisations is a fascinating subject in its own right and something that any manager needs to understand thoroughly. This chapter also focuses the importance of negotiation and bargaining among the internal and external customers for realizing the objectives of an organisation as a part of conflict management is also discussed towards the end of the chapter.

9.1 CONFLICT MANAGEMENT

Conflict is a battle, contest of opposing forces, discord, antagonism existing between primitive desires and instincts and moral, religious, or ethical ideals. Conflict occurs when two or more people oppose one another because their needs, wants, goals, or values are different. Conflict is almost always accompanied by feelings of anger, frustration, hurt, anxiety, or fear. Conflict arises from difference of opinion between the group members while attaining the organisational goals. An organisation is an interlocking network of groups, departments, sections or work teams. In organisations everywhere, conflict among groups of different interests is unavoidable. According to recent research, managers spend an estimated 20 per cent of their time dealing with group conflicts. The success of an organisation depends upon the harmonious relations among all independent groups. Managers may either directly resolve the conflicts or they may act as mediators between two or more employees. In either case, knowledge and understanding of conflict and the methods of resolving it are important. Inter-group conflicts result from the ways in which organisations coordinate the work of different groups and distribute rewards among those groups.

The potential for conflict exists whenever and wherever people have contact. As people are organized into groups to seek a common goal, the probability of conflict greatly increases. Conflict situations appear with frequency in daily, public, and private life. These conflicts may be on a small or large scale, they may occur within and among groups, communities, or nations; and they may be triggered by ethnic, racial, religious, or economic differences, or arise from differences in values, beliefs, and attitudes regarding issues.

Conflict is a natural disagreement resulting from individuals or groups that differ in attitudes, beliefs, values or needs. It can also originate from past rivalries and personality differences. Conflict is defined as a disagreement through which the parties involved perceive a threat to their needs, interests, or concerns (www.ohrd.wisc.edu). Conflict tends to be accompanied by significant levels of misunderstanding that exaggerate the perceived disagreement considerably. Conflicts occur when people perceive that as a consequence of a disagreement, there is a threat to their needs, interests, or concerns.

Although conflict is a normal part of organisation life, providing numerous opportunities for growth through improved understanding and insight, there is a tendency to view conflict as a negative experience caused by abnormally difficult circumstances. A conflict is more than a mere disagreement—it is a situation in which people perceive a threat (physical, emotional, power, status, etc.) to their well-being.

Conflict management focuses on maintaining conflict at functional levels for a department, work unit, or an entire organisation. Conflict management does not mean the complete elimination of conflict nor does it refers only to conflict reduction. It means maintaining conflict at the right level to help the department, work unit or organisation reaches its goals. Basic to the process of conflict management is the selection of a desired level of conflict. The desired level of conflict varies according to the perceived conflict requirements of the unit. Several factors affect the choice of the desired level of conflict, organisational culture place differing values on debate, disagreement and conflict itself. Managers in organisational cultural that support debate, doubt, and questioning may perceive a higher desired level of conflict than chose who do not. The nature of the organisation's products or service also affects the desired level of conflict. Creative and innovative products or services require a higher level of conflict than more routine and predictable products and services.

Organisations facing fast-changing external environments require higher conflict levels for successful adaptation than organisations facing stable external environments. Suppression and withdrawal are two symptoms of dysfunctionally low conflict. Suppression includes denial of different and a desire to perceive similarities between parties that do not exist. Repressing controversial information and prohibiting disagreements about legitimate issues also are signs of suppression. Withdrawal includes reduced communication to avoid interactions that could lead to controversy, the belief in "peace at any price", and walking away from a disagreeable interaction. Because of the growing complexities of organisational life and the demands made upon individuals and groups, conflicts is more likely to be a usual occurrence than a rarity in contemporary organisations.

(a) Theory of Conflict Management

Conflict is generally defined as "a clash between hostile or opposing elements or ideas." As applied to human behaviour it is a disagreement between individuals, which can vary from a mild disagreement to a win/lose, emotion-packed confrontation.

Conflict is actual or perceived opposition of needs, values, and interests. A conflict can be internal (within one self) to individuals. Conflicts as a concept can explain many aspects of social life such as social disagreement, conflicts of interests, and fights between individual, group, or organisations. In political terms, conflict can refer to wars, revolutions or other struggles, which may involve the use of force as in the term armed conflict. Without proper social arrangement or resolution, conflicts in social settings can result in stress or tensions among stakeholders. When an interpersonal conflict does occur, its effects is often broader than two individuals involved, and can affect many associate individuals and relationships, in more or less adverse, and sometimes even way. Organisational conflict is a state of discord caused by the actual or perceived opposition of needs, values and interests between people working together.

There are two basic, but opposing, views of conflict, the traditional and the modern. The traditional view sees conflict as being primarily negative. In this view, conflict is caused by troublemakers; it is bad; and it should be avoided. The manager who views conflict in this way avoids admitting that it exists, keeps it under cover and tries to suppress it.

Hence traditional view always says that conflict is avoidable. Conflict is caused by management and it disturbs the organisation. The task of the management is to eliminate conflict and optimal organisational performance demands removal of conflict at all levels.

The contemporary view sees conflict in a more positive light. According to this view, conflict is inevitable. It is a natural result of change and is frequently beneficial to the manager if properly managed. In particular, an atmosphere of tension, and hence conflict, is essential in any organisation committed to developing or working with new ideas, for innovation is simply the process of bringing together differing ideas and perspectives into a new and different synthesis. This latter view is much more realistic in modern organisations.

Hence modern view always says conflict is inevitable. Conflict arises from many causes, error including organisational structure or by trouble differences in goals, in perceptions and is unavoidable. Conflict contributes and detracts from prevents optimal performance. Organisational performance in varying degrees and task of management is to manage the level of conflict and its resolution for optimal org. performance and it requires a moderate level of conflict.

In today's environment, conflict is inevitable because of the various competing unit objectives, personal goals, uses for resources, and divergent viewpoints that exist and must be integrated towards the organisation's objectives. It is how the individual manager views and deals with conflict that makes it constructive or destructive for the organisation. From the authors' perspective, the primary aim is to manage conflict constructively to achieve the organisation's goals. In order to do this, it is necessary to understand the conditions leading to conflict, the potential results of conflict, and the various methods of dealing with conflict in an organisational setting.

Table 9.1: Conflict management

Traditional view	Modern view
Caused by trouble makers	Inevitable between people
Very bad	Often beneficial
Should be avoided	Natural result of change
Must be suppressed	Can and should be managed

There are jurisdictional disagreements among individuals, departments and between unions and management. There are subtler forms of conflict involving rivalries, jealousies, personality clashes, role definitions, and struggles for power and favour. Conflict management involves doing things to limit the negative aspects of conflict and to increase the positive aspects of conflict. The aim of conflict management is to enhance learning and group outcomes, including effectiveness or performance in organisational setting. Properly managed conflict can improve group outcomes.

(b) Sources of Organisational Conflict

The most common origin of conflict include the following: (1) Scarcity of resources (finance, equipment, facilities, etc.), (2) Different attitudes (rigid or flexible), (3) Disagreements about needs, goals, priorities and interests, (4) Poor communication, (5) Poor or inadequate organisational structure, (6) Lack of teamwork, (7) Lack of clarity in roles and responsibilities, (8) Differing ideas (creative or mundane), (9) Differing agendas (sometimes hidden ones), (10) Differing circumstances, (11) Differing perspectives (limited or broad, domestic or international), and (12) Differing values (conservative or progressive minded).

9.2 TYPES OF CONFLICT

The levels of group conflict are as follows:

(a) Personal Conflict

They are the conflicts that arise among employees, individuals because of their competitive roles. People have differing styles of communication, ambitions, political or religious views and different cultural backgrounds. In our diverse society, the possibility of these differences leading to conflict between individuals is always there, and we must be alert to preventing and resolving situations where conflict arises.

Signs of Conflict between Individuals: In the organisation, leaders and members should be alert to signs of conflict between colleagues, so that they can be proactive in reducing or resolving the conflict by getting to the root of the issue. Typical Signs are Colleagues not speaking to each other or ignoring each other and contradicting and bad-mouthing one another, and deliberately undermining or not cooperating with each other, to the downfall of the team.

(b) Group Conflict

They are the conflicts arising within two or more groups due to difference in their attitudes and behaviour. Conflict arises in groups because of the scarcity of freedom, position, and resources. People who value independence tend to resist the need for interdependence and to some extent, conformity within a group. People who seek power therefore struggle with others for position or status within the group. Rewards and recognition are often perceived as insufficient and improperly distributed, and members are inclined to compete with each other for these prizes. True interdependence among members leads automatically to conflict resolution in the group. Interdependence recognizes that differences will exist and that they can be helpful. Hence, members learn to listen and to value openness, and they learn to share a mutual problem solving attitude to ensure the exploration of all facets of a problem facing the group.

Whenever people form groups, they tend to emphasize the things that make their group "better than" or "different from" other groups. This happens in the fields of sport, culture, religion and the workplace and can sometimes change from healthy competition to destructive conflict. ***Signs of conflict between Groups of People*:** Similarly, leaders and members can identify latent conflict between groups of people in the organisation or the community and plan action before the conflict becomes open and destructive. The possible signs include (1) Cliques or factions meeting to discuss issues that affect the whole organisation separately, (2) One group being left out of organising an event which should include everybody, and (3) Groups using threatening slogans or symbols against the others to show that their group is right and the others are wrong.

(c) Intra-organisational Conflict

They are the conflict arising between various levels of an organisation, which are of two types. Vertical conflict arises between higher and lower level of management. Horizontal conflict arises among the employees at same level.

Now we look at various categories of organisational conflict based on the nature or parties involved in the conflict.

1. *Constructive and Destructive Conflict:* There are two types of conflict in an organisation: Positive and negative or constructive and destructive conflict. Constructive conflict is not identified on the loudness or intensity of people's voices when arguing or on the glaring look of people's faces. The outcome of constructive conflict is productive.

Characteristics of constructive agreements include strengthening relationships, restoring equality, recognizing the other parties as legitimate, using benefits/promises rather than threats/coercion and finding mutually acceptable solutions. Conflict is actually solved. Characteristics of constructive escalation includes interaction changes often flexible goals/objectives and guided by belief that all parties can win constructive conflicts.

On the contrary, destructive conflict is inevitable, yet it can be controlled and minimized. How an individual or a group responds to conflict and the behaviour towards the situation determines the negative or positive outcome of the disagreement. If conflict is mishandled or not properly managed by the parties involved, then an unproductive and unlikely result will be generated in another round of destructive conflict.

Characteristics of destructive agreements includes damages relationships and promotes inequality. Characteristics of destructive escalation includes both parties become less flexible, goals are narrowly defined and rigid, primary goal is to defeat the other party–assumes the other side must lose. It becomes protracted, intractable and power imbalance , outcomes are imposed unilaterally, often requires redress or revenge and outcomes are more often oppressive to one side and it does not solve any problem.

2. *Functional and Dysfunctional Conflict:* Functional conflict works towards the goals of an organisation or a group. Dysfunctional conflict blocks an organisation or a group from reaching its goals. Conflict is dysfunctional when it is either higher than needed by a group to teach its goals or so low that a group is less effective than it could be in reaching its goals. Because the boundary between functional and dysfunctional conflict is often fuzzy, deciding what level of conflict is functional requires a manager to understand both the positive and negative results of conflict. A knowledgeable manager then tries to manage conflict to keep it within functional bounds.

Conflict that is functional in one group can be dysfunctional in another group. A process analysis team that is trying to solve a difficult quality problem, for example, might need more conflict than a group doing routine tasks. The conflict requirements of a group or an entire organisation can also change with time. Conflict that is functional at one point can be dysfunctional at another point. Organisations or groups that have enjoyed an unchanging environment may need more conflict to help adapt to a turbulent environment. Dysfunctionally high conflict can produce excessive levels of tension, anxiety and stress. It can drive out people who could be valuable to the group but cannot tolerate such a high level of conflict. Dysfunctional high conflict can also reduce trust, leading to continual antagonistic interactions. As a result, one or more parties to the conflict may withhold or distort information. Poor quality decision making can result when conflict reaches a dysfunctional level. The conflict can also become the focus of management's attention, diverting valuable resources from other tasks. Dysfunctionally low conflict is the opposite of functional conflict. The organisation or group does not encourage new idea or tolerate different points of view. Decisions are made with poor information. The organisation encourages traditional approaches, although the external environment requires innovation and change. This description of dysfunctional conflict may strike you as strange because of the widespread idea that conflict is bad for organisations.

3. ***Latent Conflict:*** Latent conflict refers to factors in the person, group or organisation that might lead to conflict behaviour. These conditions are the antecedents to conflict and are a potential for conflict in an organisation.

4. ***Perceived Conflict:*** Even when latent conflict factors are present, those potentially in conflict may not perceive conflict. Two mechanisms limit the perception of conflict. People can block out mild conflict by suppressing their awareness of it. If many conditions exist for conflict in an organisation, individuals may focus on them selectively, letting them successfully manage the conflict.

5. ***Felt Conflict:*** Felt conflict is the emotional part of a conflict episode. At least one individual personalizes the conflict and focuses on the parties involved, losing sight of the underlying issues. Some conflict episodes never enter the felt conflict stage. Two individuals disagree but neither feels any hostility towards the other. They treat the disagreement as an issue to settle that has nothing to do with them personally.

6. ***Manifest Conflict:*** Manifest conflict is the actual conflict behaviour between the parties to the conflict episode. It can be oral, written, or physical aggression. Oral manifestations are the arguments we often see either between ourselves and another person or between other people. Written manifest conflict is the exchange of memoranda or other documents designed to make a point or win an argument. Physical aggression is strongly negative conflict behaviour intended to injure an opponent.

9.3 CONFLICT FRAMES

People can approach conflict episodes with different perceptual frames. They also can have different conflict orientations that can affect their behaviour during the episode. If you must manage conflict, understanding these frames and orientations can help your diagnosis of the conflict. Conflict frames are the perceptual sets that people bring to conflict episodes. They act as perceptual filters removing some information from the episode and emphasizing other information. Research has identified conflict frames that vary along three dimensions.

Relationship-Task : A relationship emphasis focuses on the party's interpersonal relation. A task emphasis focuses on material aspects of an episode, such as a monetary budget.

Emotional-Intellectual : An emotional emphasis focuses on fallings in the episode (felt conflict). An intellectual emphasis focuses on observed behaviour (manifest conflict).

Cooperate-Win : A cooperation focus emphasizes the role of all parties to the conflict. A party with a winning focus wants to maximize personal gain.

9.4 CONFLICT ORIENTATIONS

The five conflict orientations are dominance, collaborative, compromise, avoidance, and accommodative. The following describes each orientation:

1. **Dominance:** Person wants to win the conflict episode and overwhelm the other party; views conflict episodes as battles to fight and win.
2. **Collaborative:** Person want to satisfy the wishes of all parties to the conflict and sincerely wants to find a solution that satisfies.

3. **Compromise:** Person splits the difference so each party gets only part of what he wants. Conflict episodes feature "house-trading", giving something to get something.
4. **Avoidance:** Person backs away from a conflict episode, possibly because of low tolerance for conflict.
5. **Accommodative:** Person focuses on needs and desires of the other party to the conflict, ignoring his own needs and desire.

Research evidence strongly shown that a collaborative orientation to conflict yields more positive long-term benefits for organisations than the other four orientations. Benefits include better decisions, increased trust and an increased satisfaction with the results of a conflict episode.

Intra-organisation Conflict

Intra-organisation conflict includes all types of conflict occurring within an organisation. This type of conflict happens at the interfaces of organisation functions created by the design of the organisation. Such conflict can occur along the vertical and horizontal dimensions of the organisation. Vertical conflict develops between managers and subordinates. Horizontal conflict occurs between departments and work groups. Intergroup conflict is conflict among members of a group. Conflict within a group is likely to be highest during the early stages of group development when there are strong differences among members. Intergroup conflict is conflict between two or more groups in an organisation. This type of conflict often has its roots in the design of the organisation. Interpersonal conflict is conflict between two or more people, such as between a customer and a sales clerk or between two people within an organisation. Interpersonal conflict is the most basic form of conflict behaviour in organisation. Intrapersonal conflict is conflict that occurs within an individual. The conflict arises because of a threat to the person's basic values, a feeling of unfair treatment by the organisation or from multiple and contradictory sources of socialization. Inter-organisation conflict is conflict between two or more organisations that results from relationship between them. For example, an organisation may become highly dependent on its suppliers or distributors, increasing the potential for conflict over delivery times or other agreements.

(i) Conflicts at the Intergroup Level: In-group relations, where interdependence is required for the accomplishment of tasks, conflicts can arise for any number of reasons. There may be unresolved differences in defining goals or methods or reaching the goals, or in the perceptions concerning the distribution of rewards to each group. Conflict can be exciting, engaging, and organisationally significant. The conflict can, in fact, produce reactive problem solving and collaboration among persons. As long as contact is maintained and individuals (or groups) are earnestly aiming for the best creative achievement, the conflict can be productive. The more sharply they differ, and the more intense the feelings, the more likely they are to produce a collective solution which is better than the individual or group solution. Conflicts in an organisation exist at all levels of the system. In some ways it is possible to conceptualize a theory or organisational development and its subsequent technology, in terms of conflict resolution. This is so because one of the primary problems in organisations is achieving the degree and quality of collaboration necessary for overall system effectiveness. It has been argued that conflict within an organisation can be best understood as a dynamic process underlying a wide variety of organisational behaviours. The term conflict refers neither to its antecedent conditions, nor individual awareness of it, nor certain affective states, nor it over manifestations, or its residues of feelings, precedent, or structure, but to all of these taken together as the history of a conflict episode.

Conflict is not necessarily bad or good, but must be evaluated in terms of its individual and organisational functions and dysfunctions. In general, conflict generates pressures to reduce conflict, but chronic conflict persists and is endured and under certain conditions, and consciously created and managed by the politically astute administrator. Conflict resolution techniques may be applied at any of several pressure points. Their effectiveness and appropriateness depends on the nature of the conflict and on the administrator's philosophy of management.

The tension model leads to creation of safety-valve institutions and the semantic model to the promotion of open communication. Although these may be perfectly appropriate for certain forms of imagined conflict, their application to real conflict may only exacerbate the conflict. A general theory of conflict has been elaborated in the context of each of three conceptual models: (1) a bargaining model which deals with interest groups in competition for resources; (2) a bureaucratic model, which deals with authority relations and the need to control; and (3) a system models, which deals with functional relations and the need to coordinate.

(ii) Conflicts at the Interpersonal Level: Interpersonal conflicts often arise in organisations. Sometimes they are the result of differing value systems, sometimes of unresolved differences in personal style or work methods. There are occasions when individuals interpret situations as competitive rather than collaborative; there are others when issues of trust and acceptance are critical in work relationships. Role ambiguity, for example, can often result in intense conflict within work teams.

(iii) Reasons for Conflict: There are many reasons for conflicts among groups and its members. Some of them are related to limited resources, communication problems, differences in interests and goals, different perceptions, attitudes and lack of clarity about responsibilities. The reasons for group conflicts are as follows:

1. ***Communication problems:*** Groups often become very involved with their own areas of responsibility. They tend to develop their own unique vocabulary. Paying attention to an area of responsibility is a worthy endeavour, but it can result in communication problems. The receiver of information should be considered when a group communicates an idea, a proposal, or a decision. Misinformed receivers often become irritated and then hostile.
2. ***Incompatible goals:*** Inter-group conflict arises because of goal incompatibility. In other words, goal attainment by one group may reduce the level of goal attainment by other groups. This may be due to horizontal differentiation and task specialization. The conflict between production and marketing departments, line and staff departments, union and management are few examples of inter-group conflicts that arise because of incompatibility of goals.
3. ***Task interdependence:*** Task interdependence means to what extent a work, group relies on other organisational groups to complete its tasks. In simple words, it refers to the dependence of one group on another for resources or information. It can be said in general that as interdependence increases, the potential for conflict increases. *According to J. Thompson, there are three types of interdependence among groups, which are as follows*:

   (*a*) **Pooled interdependence:** It arises when groups have little interaction with each other but are affected by each other's activities. For example, a branch in Delhi does not need to interact with a branch in Chennai. The only linkage between the two is that they share financial resources from a common pool and the success of each branch contributes to the success of the organisation.

(*b*) **Sequential task interdependence:** It arises when one group is unable to commence its work until the work of other group gets completed. In sequential task interdependence, the output of one group becomes the input of another group. In such situations, the potential for conflict is greater. Life and staff groups often have conflicts resulting from this type of interdependence.

(*c*) **Reciprocal interdependence:** It arises between the groups, which depend on each other for their respective task such as production department and quality department. The production department provides the goods to the marketing department to sell and the marketing department prepares the orders and estimates on the basis of the volume produced by the production department. Inter-group conflict arises from reciprocal task interdependence over difference in performance expectations. Each group is dissatisfied with the quality or quantity of work received; from the other group.

4. *Task ambiguity:* The lack of clarity over job responsibilities is called task ambiguity and it frequently leads to aggression between groups. Inter-group conflict also arises when it is not clear which group is responsible for certain activities. Task ambiguity often arises where the organisation is growing quickly or the organisation's environment is changing rapidly. A good examplc of task ambiguity is inter-group conflict arising in the recruitment of new employees. It may be the responsibility of either the personnel department or any of the functional departments such as marketing, finance. The confusion may also arise regarding who has the final authority to execute the final decisions.

5. *Resource sharing:* The relation between two groups can be affected by the degree to which they make use of a common pool of resources and the degree to which this common pool of resources is adequate to meet the demands of both the groups. Thus, conflict of this nature; arises because of the differences between aggregate demand of a group and available resources to meet them. Each party of the conflict competes with each other to get a larger share. The conflict between management and the labour union is the best example. Such conflicts take place in the quantum of wages, amenities, working conditions and other related matters.

6. *Difference in work orientation:* The ways in which employees do their work and deal with others vary widely with the functional areas of an organisation. First, functional groups differ in their time perspectives. For example, R&D scientists have a longer-range of goals than manufacturing groups. The range of work of manufacturing group is evaluated on how quickly it can manufacture high-quality products while the range of R&D scientists can be evaluated on the basis of product development and testing after a long period of time. Secondly, the goals of different functional groups vary to a large extent.

The goals of manufacturing groups are more specific and clear-cut than the goals of R&D groups. The greater the differences in goal and time between two groups, the more likely it is that conflict will arise between them while coordinating their work efforts. These differences between groups result in frustration, misinterpretation of the behaviours and activities of other groups.

7. *Conflicting reward systems:* Sometimes the ways in which reward systems in organisations are designed to create a situation in which one group can only accomplish its goal at the expense of other groups. For example, staff departments may be rewarded for cutting costs and personnel while line departments are rewarded for increasing the amount of products sold or services provided.

To increase the amount of products sold, the line group may have to depend even more heavily on staff groups such as advertising. However the staff groups are being rewarded for cutting costs and personnel provided the types of services asked for by line groups can prevent them from meeting their own goals. Conflicting reward systems inevitably result in poor inter-group relations.

8. ***Different perceptions and attitudes:*** The attitudes, values and perceptions of members of various groups towards each other can be a cause and a consequence of the nature of their relationship. If the group relations begin with the attitudes of distrust, competitiveness, secrecy and closed communications, there is a possibility of conflicts, disagreements in their views and among themselves. This can affect the success of a group to accomplish their work in an effective manner.

(iv) Dynamics of Inter Group and Intra Group Conflict: The following major points are covered in the dynamics of an inter-group conflict:

(*a*) ***Changes within each group:*** When there is inter-group conflict in an organisation, systematic changes take place in the perceptions, attitudes and behaviours of the participants. They are as follows:

The group demands more loyalty from individual members while facing an external threat. In the face of an external threat, past differences and difficulties between group members are forgotten and group cohesiveness increases.

In an inter-group conflict, it is important for a group to respond quickly and in a unified manner to the activities of other groups. In an inter-group conflict, the organisation and structure of the work group becomes more rigid. It leads to more coordination of activities, allocution of responsibilities to different group members.

(*b*) ***Changes in relation between groups:*** The nature of the relationships between groups also changes markedly during inter-group conflicts. Union Management relationships during contract negotiations are one of the examples of the group dynamics. It becomes difficult for each group to see the positive behaviour and attitude of the other group. Each party undervalues the interests of the other group. The changes that occur are as follows:

- There are distortions of perception about one's own group and about the other group.
- The interaction and communication between groups' decreases.
- There is a shift among the groups from a problem solving motive to a win-lose motive.
- There is increased ill feeling towards the rival group.

(v) Group Strategies to Gain Power: There are several strategies that various groups use to gain power in an inter-group conflict situation. Some of these strategies allow cooperation and sharing between groups while other strategies are more competitive and increase the power of one group at the expense of others.

- ***Contracting:*** It refers to the negotiation or an agreement between two groups. Each group makes some compromises so that there can be some predictability and stability in their relationships. For example, contracting occurs between labour and management at the time of collective bargaining.
- ***Co-opting:*** It occurs when a group gives some of its leadership positions to members of other groups or includes them in its policy making committees. For example, representatives from financial institutions are included in the Board of Directors of a Company to participate in decision-making activities.
- ***Forming association:*** In forming an association, two or more groups cooperate or combine their resources in order to increase their power over other groups. Members of groups co-operate

with each other in order to compete more effectively with members of other groups.

- ***Influencing decision criteria:*** Groups can also sometimes exert power to change criteria for decision-making that are selected as the basic for resource distribution.
- ***Controlling information:*** Gaining access to sensitive information and then limiting other group's access to it increases the power of the information-rich group and other subunits.
- ***Pressure tactics:*** These are applied to force others to use the most competitive strategy a group can use to gain power. For instance, a union might threaten to strike to pressurize management.

Management reaction to disruptive inter-group conflict can take many different forms. But management usually tries to minimize the conflict indirectly and if this fails, become directly involved.

(vi) Methods to Solve Inter-group Conflict Indirectly: The various methods to solve inter-group conflicts indirectly are as follows:

- ***Avoidance:*** It is an indirect method often used by the managers. It includes avoidance of direct approaches on the part of managers to solve among groups. But avoidance does not always minimize the problem. Matters can get worse if nothing is done and the groups can become more aggressive and unfriendly.
- ***Encouragement:*** This is another indirect method to solve the group conflicts. It includes encouragement on the part of managers to the groups so that they will be able to meet and discuss their differences. By doing so, they can find out a solution without the involvement of management.
- ***Bargaining:*** This is the indirect method, in which the groups agree as to what each of them will get and give others regarding their work. This makes the accomplishment of the assigned task much easier. For example, one group may agree to give the other, a quick turnaround time on the repairs of needed equipment only if the second group agrees to bring complaints about the quality of repairs to it before going to management. Bargaining between two groups is successful if both groups are comfortable with the agreement between them.
- ***Persuasion:*** This is the indirect method, in which the groups find the areas of common interests among themselves. The groups try to find out those interests levels where they have the same say. Afterwards, the groups try to show how important it is to each of them in attaining organisational goals. But persuasion is possible only if there are no clashes between the groups and its members.

(vii) Methods to Solve Intra-group Conflict: The various methods to solve intra-group conflicts directly are as follows:

- ***Ignoring the conflict:*** This is a direct method used by the managers to solve inter-group conflicts. Ignoring the conflict is characterized by the absence of behaviour wherein the members of the groups avoids dealing with the dysfunctional aspects of the conflict. In this, a group simply refuses to attack the other group. But the disadvantage of this method is that it ignores the causes of conflicts and as a result, the conflict situation frequently continues or gets worse over time.
- ***Domination by the management:*** This method of solving inter-group conflicts emphasizes on improving the inter-group relations. To improve the inter-group relations, greater integration or collaboration among groups is needed. Management can use domination to minimize the conflicts by exercising its authority and power over the groups and their members.

- ***Removing the key figures in the conflict:*** This is another direct method to solve the inter-group conflicts. If a conflict arises because of personality differences between two individuals, removing them is a possible solution. It includes the removal of the key figures in the conflict. The key figures that are to be removed may be leaders of the groups and removing them could lead to greater conflict. It is also difficult to pinpoint accurately the individuals who are the root cause of conflicts.
- ***Problem solving:*** Management can also establish a task force with representatives from groups in conflict to work on problems. The task force develops the ideas and procedures for improving group interaction and thereby attempt to solve the conflicts arising between the groups.

Appealing to super ordinate goals: The final method to minimize the conflicts is to find super-ordinate goals. These are goals desired by two or more groups that can only be accomplished through the cooperation of the groups. When conflicting groups have to cooperate to accomplish a goal, conflict can be minimized. For example, a wide profit-sharing plan of a company may encourage groups to work together. If the profits of a company are distributed among employees at the end of the year, the conflicts among groups can reduce.

The super ordinate goals are as follows: The assignment and coordination of work among groups should be clarified so that the daily disputes over minor issues can be avoided. Managers should monitor reward systems to eliminate any win-lose conflicts among groups. The use of cooperative approaches among groups in organisations often leads to more positive results than does the use of competitive approaches. Managers can establish rules and standard procedures to regulate conflict in more constructive and effective ways.

9.5 CONFLICT MANAGEMENT: GENERAL STRATEGIES

Blake and Mouton (1964) were among the first to present a conceptual scheme for classifying the modes or styles for handling interpersonal conflict into five types: Forcing (competition), withdrawing (avoidance), smoothing (accommodating), compromising and problem solving.

Conflict management minimizes the negative outcomes of conflicts and promotes the positive outcomes of conflict (Rahim, 2002). Conflict management is something that companies and managers need to deal with. Conflict significantly affects employee morale, turnover and litigation, which affects the prosperity of a company, either constructively or destructively (Lang, 2009).

The conflict management common strategies are summarized below.

(a) Collaboration

This results from a high concern for your group's own interests, matched with a high concern for the interests of other partners. The outcome is "win/win." This strategy is generally used when concerns for others are important. When consensus and commitment of other parties is important. When a high level of trust is present. When a long-term relationship is important. When you don't want to have full responsibility. It is also generally the best strategy when society's interest is at stake. This approach helps build commitment and reduce bad feelings. It reinforces mutual trust and respect. It builds a foundation for effective collaboration in the future. It leads to solving the actual problem. The drawbacks are that it takes time and energy. In addition, some partners may take advantage of the others' trust and openness. Generally regarded as the best approach for managing conflict, the objective of collaboration is to reach consensus.

(b) Compromise

This strategy results from a high concern for your group's own interests along with a moderate concern for the interests of other partners. The outcome is "win some/lose some." This strategy is generally used to achieve temporary solutions, to avoid destructive power struggles or when time pressures exist. Compromising looks for an expedient and mutually acceptable solution which partially satisfies both parties. Compromising is used when the goals are moderately important and not worth the use of more assertive or more involving approaches, such as competition and collaboration. To reach temporary settlement on complex issues. To reach expedient solutions on important issues. When collaboration or competition do not work. Compromising can provide a temporary solution while still looking for a win-win solution. It lowers the levels of tension and stress resulting from the conflict. It may result in a situation when both parties are not satisfied with the outcome; it does not contribute to building trust in the long run.

(c) Competition

This strategy results from a high concern for your group's own interests with less concern for others. The outcome is "win/lose." Competition is used when basic rights are at stake or to set a precedent. When you need to stand up for your own rights, resist aggression and pressure. When a quick solution is required and using force is justified. As a last resort to resolve a long-lasting conflict. However, it can cause the conflict to escalate and losers may try to retaliate.

(d) Accommodation

This result from a low concern for your group's own interests combined with a high concern for the interests of other partners. Accommodation is accommodating the concerns of other people first of all, rather than one's own concerns. The outcome is "lose/win." This strategy is generally used when the issue is more important to others than to you. When you accept that you are wrong. When continued competition would be detrimental. It is a "goodwill gesture. The drawbacks are that your own ideas and concerns don't get attention. You may also lose credibility and future influence.

(e) Avoidance

These results from a low concern for your group's own interests coupled with a low concern for the interests of others. Avoiding or withdrawing occurs when a person does not pursue his/her own concerns or those of the opponent. The outcome is "lose/lose". This strategy is generally used when the issue is trivial or other issues are more pressing. When confrontation has a high potential for damage or more information is needed. When you need time to think and collect information before you act. When it is not the right time or place to confront the issue. When you are unable to handle the conflict. The drawbacks are that important decisions may be made by default.

9.6 CONFLICT RESOLUTION

Conflict resolution involves the reduction, elimination or termination of all forms and types of conflict through bargaining, negotiation, mediation and arbitration

(a) Collective Bargaining: In workplace situations, it is necessary to have agreed mechanisms in place for groups of people who may be antagonistic to collectively discuses and resolve issues. This process is often called "collective bargaining" because representatives of each group come together with a mandate to work out a solution collectively. Experience has shown that this is far better than avoidance or withdrawal, and puts democratic processes in place to achieve "integrative problem solving", where people or groups who must find ways of co-operating in the same organisation do so within their own agreed rules and procedures.

(b) Conciliation: The dictionary defines conciliation as "the act of procuring goodwill or inducing a friendly feeling". The process of conciliation occurs whereby groups who are in conflict and who have failed to reach agreement can come together once again to attempt to settle their differences. This is usually attempted before the more serious step of a strike by workers or a lockout by management is taken, and it has been found useful to involve a facilitator in the conciliation process.

(c) Negotiation: This is the process where mandated representatives of groups in a conflict situation meet together in order to resolve their differences and to reach agreement. It is a deliberate process, conducted by representatives of groups, designed to reconcile differences and to reach agreements by consensus. The outcome is often dependent on the power relationship between the groups. Negotiations often involve compromise: One group may win one of their demands and give in on another. In workplaces, unions and management representatives usually use negotiations to solve conflicts. Political and community groups also often use this method.

(d) Mediation: When negotiations fail, parties often call in an independent mediator. This person or group will try to facilitate settlement of the conflict. The mediator plays an active part in the process, advises both or all groups, acts as intermediary and suggests possible solutions. Mediators act only in an advisory capacity, they have no decision-making powers and cannot impose a settlement on the conflicting parties. Skilled mediators are able to gain trust and confidence from the conflicting groups or individuals.

(e) Arbitration: This means the appointment of an independent person to act as an adjudicator (or judge) in a dispute to decide on the terms of a settlement. Both parties in a conflict have to agree about who the arbitrator should be, and that the decision of the arbitrator will be binding on them all. Arbitration differs from mediation and negotiation in that it does not promote the continuation of collective bargaining, the arbitrator listens to and investigates the demands and counter-demands and takes over the role of decision-maker. People or organisations can agree on having either a single arbitrator or a panel of arbitrators whom they respect and whose decision they will accept as final, in order to resolve the conflict. Table 9.2 shows various Conflict Resolution Techniques.

Table 9.2: Conflict resolution techniques

Problem solving	:	Face-to-face meeting of the conflicting parties for the purpose of identifying the problem and resolving it through open discussion.
Superordinates goals	:	Creating a shared goal that cannot be attained without the cooperation of each of the conflicting parties.
Expansion of resources	:	When a conflict is caused by the scarcity of a resource–say, money, promotion opportunities, office space-expansion of the resource can create a win-win solution.
Avoidance	:	Withdrawal from or suppression of the conflict.
Smoothing	:	Playing down differences while emphasizing common interests between the conflicting parties.

Compromise	:	Each part to the conflict gives up something of value.
Authoritative command	:	Management uses its formal authority to resolve the conflict and communicates its desires to the parties involved.
Altering the human variable	:	Using behavioural change techniques such as human relations training to alter attitudes and behaviours that cause conflict.
Altering the structural variables	:	Changing the formal organisation structure and the interaction patterns of conflicting parties through job redesign, transfers, creation of coordinating positions, and the like.
Conflict Stimulation Techniques		
Communication	:	Using ambiguous or threatening messages to increase conflict levels.
Bringing in outsiders	:	Adding employees to a group whose backgrounds, values, attitudes, or managerial styles differ from those of present members.
Restructuring the organisation	:	Realigning work groups, altering rules and regulations, increasing interdependence and making similar structural changes to disrupt the status up.
Appointing a devil's advocate	:	Designating a critic to purposely argue against the majority positions held by the group.

Source: Based on S.P. Robbins, Managing Organisational Conflict: A Non-traditional Approach (Upper Saddle River, NJ: Prentice Hall, 1974, pp.59–89.

9.7 THE EFFECTS OF CONFLICT

In general, conflict may be stressful and harmful to individuals or groups, have positive results, help define and sharpen community issues to improve decisions, help gain recognition for a group, increase bitterness, alienation and divisiveness, increase unity, cohesion, and solidarity within a group, strengthen group boundaries, aid in the formation of a new group, weaken or destroy a group, increase tension within or between groups, result in restructuring a group, lead to alliances with other groups, disrupt normal channels of cooperation, and become destructive.

In short, conflict accelerates change in an organisation, especially in small businesses, where it is easy to formulate and implement new policies. Conflict prompts modification of policies and operation procedures in the organisation. Conflict forces the organisation's leadership to realign its objectives towards common goals in order to foster teamwork amongst competing parties. Conflict that results into healthy competition cultivates innovation and inventiveness amongst employees. When an organisation spends much of its time dealing with conflict, members take time away from focusing on the core goals they are tasked with achieving. Conflict sometimes has a destructive effect on the individuals and groups involved. At other times, however, conflict can increase the capacity of those affected to deal with problems, and therefore it can be used as a motivating force towards innovation and change.

9.8 NEGOTIATION

The word "negotiation" originated from the Latin expression, "negotiatus", past participle of negotiare which means "to carry on business". "Negotium" (from "Nec Otium") means literally "not leisure". Negotiation is a dialogue between two or more people or parties, intended to reach an understanding, resolve point of difference, or gain advantage in outcome of dialogue, to produce an agreement upon courses of action, to bargain for individual or collective advantage, to craft outcomes to satisfy various interests of two people/parties involved in negotiation process. Negotiation is a process where each party involved in negotiating tries to gain an advantage for themselves by the end of the process. Negotiation is intended to aim at compromise.

Negotiation is a specialized and formal version of conflict resolution most frequently employed when important issues must be agreed upon. Negotiation is necessary when one party requires the other party's agreement to achieve its aim. The aim of negotiating is to build a shared environment leading to long-term trust and often involves a third, neutral party to extract the issues from the emotions and keep the individuals concerned focused. It is a powerful method for resolving conflict and requires skill and experience. Zartman defines negotiation as "a process of combining conflicting positions into a common position under a decision rule of unanimity, a phenomenon in which the outcome is determined by the process".

Negotiation occurs in business, non-profit organisations, government branches, legal proceedings, among nations and in personal situations such as marriage, divorce, parenting, and everyday life. The study of the subject is called negotiation theory. Professional negotiators are often specialized, such as union negotiators, leverage buyout negotiators, peace negotiators, hostage negotiators, or may work under other titles, such as diplomats, legislators or brokers.

Due to globalization and growing business trends, negotiation in the form of teams is becoming widely adopted. Teams can effectively collaborate to break down a complex negotiation. There is more knowledge and wisdom dispersed in a team than in a single mind. Writing, listening, and talking, are specific roles team members must satisfy. The capacity base of a team reduces the amount of blunder, and increases familiarity in a negotiation.

(a) Basic Principles

There are minimum 2 parties involved in the negotiation process. There exists some common interest, either in the subject matter of the negotiation or in the negotiating context that puts or keeps the parties in contact. Though the parties have the same degree of interest, they initially start with different opinions and objectives which hinder the outcome in general. In the beginning, parties consider that negotiation is a better way of trying to solve their differences. Each party is under an impression that there is a possibility of persuading the other party to modify their original position, as initially parties feel that they shall maintain their opening position and persuade the other to change. During the process, the ideal outcome proves unattainable but parties retain their hope of an acceptable final agreement. Each party has some influence or power–real or assumed–over the other's ability to act. The process of negotiation is that of interaction between people–usually this is direct and verbal interchange. In short, features of negotiation includes minimum two parties, predetermined goals, expecting an outcome, resolution and consensus, Parties willing to modify their positions and finally parties should understand the purpose of negotiation.

(b) Why Do We Negotiate?

There are many reasons for our negotiation. To name a few are (*a*) To reach an agreement, (*b*) To beat the opposition, (*c*) To compromise, (*d*) To settle an argument and (*e*) To make a point. Negotiations differ from mere coercion, in that negotiating parties have the theoretic possibility to withdraw from negotiations. It is easier to study bilateral negotiations, as opposed to multilateral negotiations.

(c) Characteristics of an Effective Negotiator

He should be a good learner and observer and should know the body language of the people at the negotiation process. He should be open and flexible and yet firm, exercise great patience, coolness and maturity. He should possess leadership qualities. He should control emotions and not show his weaknesses and should bargain from the position of strength. He should know and anticipate the pros and cons of his each move and its repercussions.

Again, he should know how to create the momentum for the negotiations and must know when to exit and where to exit by closing the talks successfully. He should build trust and confidence and should be confident and optimist too. He should have clear-cut goals and objectives; if necessary, he should provide a face saving formula for his counter party. Moreover he should be able to grasp the situation from many dimensions and should know human psychology and face reading as well. Further he should not be a doubting personality and should plan and prepare thoroughly with relevant data and information to avoid blank mind in the process during negotiation. He also should radiate energy and enthusiasm and must be in a position to empathize with his opponents. And finally he should be a patient listener.

(d) Negotiation Strategies

Negotiation can take a wide variety of forms, from trained negotiator acting on behalf of a particular organisation or position in a formal setting, to an informal negotiation between friends. Negotiation can be contrasted with mediation, where a neutral third party listens to each side's arguments and attempts to help craft an agreement between the parties. It can also be compared with arbitration, which resembles a legal proceeding. In arbitration, both sides make an argument as to the merits of their case and the arbitrator decides the outcome. This negotiation is also sometimes called positional or hard-bargaining negotiation.

Tactics are always an important part of the negotiating process. But tactics don't often jump up and down shouting "Here I am, look at me". If they did, the other side would see right through them and they would not be effective. More often than not they are subtle, difficult to identify and used for multiple purposes. Tactics are more frequently used in distributive negotiations and when the focus in on taking as much value off the table as possible. Many negotiation tactics exist. Negotiation theorists generally distinguish between two types of negotiation. Different theorists use different labels for the two general types and distinguish them in different ways:

1. Distributive negotiation: Distributive negotiation is also sometimes called positional or hard-bargaining negotiation. It tends to approach negotiation on the model of haggling in a market. In a distributive negotiation, each side often adopts an extreme position, knowing that it will not be accepted, and then employs a combination of guile, bluffing, and brinkmanship in order to cede as little as possible before reaching a deal. Distributive bargainers conceive of negotiation as a process of distributing a fixed amount of value.

In this negotiation, Parties compete over the distribution of a fixed sum of value. The key question in a distributed negotiation is, "Who will claim the most value?" A gain by one side is made at the expense of other. The Seller's goal is to negotiate as high a price as possible and the Buyer's goal is to negotiate as low a price as possible. Thus, the deal is confined and there are not many opportunities for creativity or for enlarging the scope of the negotiation.

The term distributive implies that there is a finite amount of the thing being distributed or divided among the people involved. Sometimes this type of negotiation is referred to as the distribution of a "fixed price". There is only so much to go around, but the proportion to be distributed is variable. Distributive negotiation is also sometimes called win-lose because of the assumption that one person's gain results in another person's loss. A distributive negotiation often does not involve people who have never had a previous interactive relationship, nor are they likely to do so again in the near future. Simple everyday examples would be buying a car or a house.

2. Integrative negotiation: Integrative negotiation is also sometimes called interest-based or principled negotiation. It is a set of techniques that attempts to improve the quality and likelihood of negotiated agreement by providing an alternative to traditional distributive negotiation techniques. While distributive negotiation assumes there is a fixed amount of value (a "fixed price") to be divided between the parties, integrative negotiation often attempts to create value in the course of the negotiation ("expand the price"). It focuses on the underlying interests of the parties rather than their arbitrary starting positions, approaches negotiation as a shared problem rather than a personalized battle, and insists upon adherence to objective, principled criteria as the basis for agreement.

The word integrative implies some cooperation. Integrative negotiation often involves a higher degree of trust and the forming of a relationship. It can also involve creative problem-solving that aims to achieve mutual gains. It is also sometimes called win-win negotiation.

In integrative negotiation, parties cooperate to achieve maximize benefits by integrating their interests into an agreement. This is also known as a win-win negotiation. The key question is how the resource best can be utilized. Integrative negotiations tend to occur in following situations like, structuring of complex, long-term strategic relationships or other collaborations. Also, when the deal involves many financial and non-financial terms. In an integrative negotiation, there are many items and issues to be negotiated and the goal of each side is to "create" as much value as possible for itself and the other side.

Following are some of the strategies used during international negotiation:

(i) ***Highball/Lowball:*** Depending on whether selling or buying, sellers or buyers use a ridiculously high, or ridiculously low opening offer that will never be achieved. The theory is that the extreme offer will cause the other party to re-evaluate his or her own opening offer and move close to the resistance point (as far as you are willing to go to reach an agreement). Another advantage is that the person giving the extreme demand appears more flexible he or she makes concessions towards a more reasonable outcome. A danger of this tactic is that the opposite party may think negotiating is a waste of time.

(ii) ***The Nibble:*** Nibbling is asking for proportionally small concessions that haven't been discussed previously just before closing the deal. This method takes advantage of the other party's desire to close by adding "just one more thing".

(iii) ***Snow Job:*** Negotiators overwhelm the other party with so much information that he or she has difficulty determining which facts are important, and which facts are diversions. Negotiators may also use technical language or jargon to mask a simple answer to a question asked by a non-expert. More such strategies are going to discuss under negotiation tactics in detail.

(e) Negotiation Tactics

There are many different ways to categorize the essential elements of negotiation.

One view of negotiation involves three basic elements: *Process, behaviour* and *substance*. The process refers to how the parties negotiate: the context of the negotiations, the parties to the negotiations, the tactics used by the parties and the sequence and stages in which all of these play out. Behaviour refers to the relationships among these parties, the communication between them and the styles they adopt. The substance refers to what the parties negotiate over: the agenda, the issues (positions and more helpfully interests), the options, and the agreement(s) reached at the end.

Another view of negotiation comprises four elements: *Strategy, process*, *tools*, and *tactics*. Strategy comprises the top level goals—typically including relationship and the final outcome. Processes and tools include the steps that will be followed and the roles taken in both preparing for and negotiating with the other parties. Tactics include more detailed statements and actions and responses to others' statements and actions. Some add to this *persuasion* and *influence*, asserting that these have become integral to modern day negotiation success, and so should not be omitted.

1. Adversary or partner: The two basically different approaches to negotiating will require different tactics. In the distributive approach each negotiator is battling for the largest possible piece of the pie, so it may be quite appropriate within certain limits to regard the other side more as an adversary than a partner and to take a somewhat harder line. This would however be less appropriate if the idea were to hammer out an arrangement that is in the best interest of both sides. A good agreement is not one with maximum gain, but optimum gain. This does not by any means suggest that we should give up our own advantage for nothing. But a cooperative attitude will regularly pay dividends. What is gained is not at the expense of the other, but with him.

2. Employing an advocate: A skilled negotiator may serve as an advocate for one party to the negotiation. The advocate attempts to obtain the most favourable outcomes possible for that party. In this process the negotiator attempts to determine the minimum outcome(s) the other party is (or parties are) willing to accept, then adjusts their demands accordingly. A "successful" negotiation in the advocacy approach is when the negotiator is able to obtain all or most of the outcomes their party desires, but without driving the other party to permanently break off negotiations, unless the best alternative to a negotiated agreement (BATNA) is acceptable.

Skilled negotiators may use a variety of tactics ranging from negotiation hypnosis, to a straightforward presentation of demands or setting of preconditions, to more deceptive approaches such as cherry picking. Intimidation and tactics may also play a part in swaying the outcome of negotiations.

Another negotiation tactic is bad guy/good guy. Bad guy/good guy is when one negotiator acts as a bad guy by using anger and threats. The other negotiator acts as a good guy by being considerate and understanding. The good guy blames the bad guy for all the difficulties while trying to get concessions and agreement from the opponent. Another negotiation is leaning back and whispering. This establishes a dominant physical position thus intimidating your counterpart.

Below are a few commonly used tactics.

(i) ***Auction:*** The bidding process is designed to create competition. When multiple parties want the same thing, pit them against one another. When people know that they may lose out on something, they will want it even more. Not only do they want the thing that is being bid on,

they also want to win, just to win. Taking advantage of someone's competitive nature can drive up the price.

(*ii*) ***Brinksmanship:*** One party aggressively pursues a set of terms to the point at which the other negotiating party must either agree or walk away. Brinksmanship is a type of "hard nut" approach to bargaining in which one party pushes the other party to the "brink" or edge of what that party is willing to accommodate. Successful brinksmanship convinces the other party they have no choice but to accept the offer and there is no acceptable alternative to the proposed agreement.

(*iii*) ***Bogey:*** Negotiators use the bogey tactic to pretend that an issue of little or no importance to him or her is very important. Then, later in the negotiation, the issue can be traded for a major concession of actual importance.

(*iv*) ***Chicken:*** Negotiators propose extreme measures, often bluffs, to force the other party to chicken out and give them what they want. This tactic can be dangerous when parties are unwilling to back down and go through with the extreme measure.

(*v*) ***Defence in Depth:*** Several layers of decision-making authority is used to allow further concessions each time the agreement goes through a different level of authority. In other words, each time the offer goes to a decision maker, that decision maker asks to add another concession in order to close the deal.

(*vi*) ***Deadlines:*** Give the other party a deadline forcing them to make a decision. This method uses time to apply pressure to the other party. Deadlines given can be actual or artificial.

(*vii*) ***Flinch:*** Flinching is showing a strong negative physical reaction to a proposal. Common examples of flinching are gasping for air or a visible expression of surprise of shock. The flinch can be done consciously or unconsciously. The flinch signals to the opposite party that you think the offer or proposal is absurd in hopes the other party will lower their aspirations. Seeing a physical reaction is more believable than hearing someone saying, "I'm shocked".

(*viii*) ***Good Guy/Bad Guy:*** The good guy/bad guy approach is typically used in team negotiations where one member of the team makes extreme or unreasonable demands, and the other offers a more rational approach. This tactic is named after a police interrogation technique often portrayed in the media. The "good guy" will appear more reasonable and understanding, and therefore, easier to work with. In essence, it is using the law of relativity to attract cooperation. The good guy will appear more agreeable relative to the "bad guy". This tactic is easy to spot because of its frequent use.

(f) Negotiation Styles

R.G. Shell identified five styles/responses to negotiation. Individuals can often have strong dispositions towards numerous styles; the style used during a negotiation depends on the context and the interests of the other party, among other factors. In addition, styles can change over time.

1. **Accommodating:** Individuals who enjoy solving the other party's problems and preserving personal relationships. Accommodators are sensitive to the emotional states, body language and verbal signals of the other parties. They can, however, feel taken advantage of in situations when the other party places little emphasis on the relationship.

2. **Avoiding:** Individuals who do not like to negotiate and don't do it unless warranted. When negotiating, avoiders tend to defer and dodge the confrontational aspects of negotiating; however, they may be perceived as tactful and diplomatic.
3. **Collaborating:** Individuals who enjoy negotiations that involve solving tough problems in creative ways. Collaborators are good at using negotiations to understand the concerns and interests of the other parties. They can, however, create problems by transforming simple situations into more complex ones.
4. **Competing:** Individuals who enjoy negotiations because they present an opportunity to win something. Competitive negotiators have strong instincts for all aspects of negotiating and are often strategic. Because their style can dominate the bargaining process, competitive negotiators often neglect the importance of relationships.
5. **Compromising:** Individuals who are eager to close the deal by doing what is fair and equal for all parties involved in the negotiation. Compromisers can be useful when there is limited time to complete the deal; however, compromisers often unnecessarily rush the negotiation process and make concessions too quickly.

(g) Types of Negotiators

The basic kinds of negotiators have been identified by researchers involved in The Harvard Negotiation Project. These types of negotiators are: Soft bargainers, hard bargainers, and principled bargainers.

1. ***Soft:*** These people see negotiation as too close to competition, so they choose a gentle style of bargaining. The offers they make are not in their best interests, they yield to others' demands, avoid confrontation, and they maintain good relations with fellow negotiators. Their perception of others is one of friendship, and their goal is agreement. They do not separate the people from the problem, but are soft on both. They avoid contests of wills and will insist on agreement, offering solutions and easily trusting others and changing their opinions.
2. ***Hard:*** These people use contentious strategies to influence, utilizing phrases such as "this is my final offer" and "take it or leave it". They make threats, are distrustful of others, insist on their position, and apply pressure to negotiate. They see others as adversaries and their ultimate goal is victory. Additionally, they will search for one single answer, and insist you agree on it. They do not separate the people from the problem (as with soft bargainers), but they are hard on both the people involved and the problem.
3. ***Principled:*** Individuals who bargain this way seek integrative solutions, and do so by sidestepping commitment to specific positions. They focus on the problem rather than the intentions, motives, and needs of the people involved. They separate the people from the problem, explore interests, avoid bottom lines, and reach results based on standards (which are independent of personal will). They base their choices on objective criteria rather than power, pressure, self-interest, or an arbitrary decisional procedure. These criteria may be drawn from moral standards, principles of fairness, professional standards, tradition, and so on.

   Researchers from the Harvard Negotiation Project recommend that negotiators explore a number of alternatives to the problems they are facing in order to come to the best overall conclusion/solution, but this is often not the case (as when you may be dealing with an individual utilizing soft or hard bargaining tactics (Forsyth, 2010).

(h) Best Alternative to a Negotiated Agreement (BATNA)

In negotiation theory, the Best Alternative to a Negotiated Agreement or BATNA is the course of action that will be taken by a party if the current negotiations fail and an agreement cannot be reached. BATNA is the key focus and the driving force behind a successful negotiator. A party should generally not accept a worse resolution than its BATNA. Care should be taken, however, to ensure that deals are accurately valued, taking into account all considerations, such as relationship value, time value of money and the likelihood that the other party will live up to their side of the bargain. These other considerations are often difficult to value, since they are frequently based on uncertain or qualitative considerations, rather than easily measurable and quantifiable factors.

The BATNA is often seen by negotiators not as a safety net, but rather as a point of leverage in negotiations. Although a negotiator's alternative options should, in theory, be straightforward to evaluate, the effort to understand which alternative represents a party's BATNA is often not invested. Options need to be real and actionable to be of value, however without the investment of time, options will frequently be included that fails on one of these criteria. Most managers overestimate their BATNA whilst simultaneously investing too little time into researching their real options. This can result in poor or faulty decision making and negotiating outcomes. Negotiators also need to be aware of the other negotiator's BATNA and to identify how it compares to what they are offering.

BATNA was developed by negotiation researchers Roger Fisher and William Urey of the Harvard Program on Negotiation (PON), in their series of books on Principled negotiation that started with *Getting to YES*, unwittingly duplicating the game theory concept of a disagreement point from bargaining problems pioneered by Nobel Laureate John Forbes Nash decades earlier.

Equilibrium theory explains that, if in a group of players, each player has in consideration the other player's decisions, and then no one will benefit from altering their decisions, if the other players haven't either. For example, Amy and Phil are in Nash Equilibrium, if Amy is making the best decision she can, taking into account Phil's decision, and Phil is making the best decision he can, taking into account Amy's decision. Likewise, a group of players are in Nash Equilibrium if each one is making the best decision that he or she can, taking into account the decisions of the others.

A ruthless, aggressive and cold blooded negotiation style is the framework approach most people have when it comes to negotiation, a theoretical example of that is Adversarial Approach Style Negotiation.

But in reality, as mentioned by experts and researchers such as Fisher and Urey it doesn't have to be that way. As the world moves to more sophisticated platforms of communication, negotiation follows the trend and Problem-Solving Approach is in a way, the "antidote" of Adversarial Approach Style Negotiation.

Getting to YES suggest an Interest-Based Model for the use of Problem-Solving Approach. Interest-Based Model focuses on separating the person (positional) from the problems (resolution) and then concentrates on the resolution. This lets each party attain its goals in a distributive way.

Attractive alternative is needed to develop a very strong BATNA. In Getting to YES, the authors gives 3 suggestions of how you can accomplish this:

1. Inventing a list of actions you might take if no agreement is reached.
2. Converting some of the more promising ideas and transforming them into tangible and partial alternatives.

3. Selecting the alternative that sounds best.

In negotiations involving different cultures, all parties need to account for cultural cognitive behaviours and not allow judgments and biases to affect the negotiation. The individual should be separate from the objective. Hence BATNA is not disclosed unless it's beneficial.

Negotiation Process: Firstly we will describe various categories and stages in the process before getting exactly into negotiation process:

(a) Bad Faith Negotiation

When a party pretends to negotiate, but secretly has no intention of compromising, the party is considered to be negotiating in bad faith. Bad faith is a concept in negotiation theory whereby parties pretend to reason to reach settlement, but have no intention to do so. For example, one political party may pretend to negotiate, with no intention to compromise, for political effect.

(b) Dispositional Effect

Dispositional affects affect the various stages of the negotiation process: Which strategies are planned to be used, which strategies are actually chosen, the way the other party and his or her intentions are perceived, their willingness to reach an agreement and the final negotiated outcomes. Positive affectivity (PA) and negative affectivity (NA) of one or more of the negotiating sides can lead to very different outcomes.

1. Positive affect in negotiation: Even before the negotiation process starts, people in a positive mood have more confidence, and higher tendencies to plan to use a cooperative strategy. During the negotiation, negotiators who are in a positive mood tend to enjoy the interaction more, show less contentious behaviour, use less aggressive tactics and more cooperative strategies. This in turn increases the likelihood that parties will reach their instrumental goals, and enhance the ability to find integrative gains. Indeed, compared with negotiators with negative or natural affectivity, negotiators with positive affectivity reached more agreements and tended to honour those agreements more.

Those favourable outcomes are due to better decision making processes, such as flexible thinking, creative problem solving, respect for others' perspectives, willingness to take risks and higher confidence. Post negotiation positive affect has beneficial consequences as well. It increases satisfaction with achieved outcome and influences one's desire for future interactions. The PA aroused by reaching an agreement facilitates the dyadic relationship, which result in affective commitment that sets the stage for subsequent interactions.

PA also has its drawbacks: It distorts perception of self performance, such that performance is judged to be relatively better than it actually is. Thus, studies involving self reports on achieved outcomes might be biased.

2. Negative affect in negotiation: Negative affect has detrimental effects on various stages in the negotiation process. Although various negative emotions affect negotiation outcomes, by far the most researched is anger. Angry negotiators plan to use more competitive strategies and to cooperate less, even before the negotiation starts. These competitive strategies are related to reduce joint outcomes. During negotiations, anger disrupts the process by reducing the level of trust, clouding parties' judgment, narrowing parties' focus of attention and changing their central goal from reaching agreement to retaliating against the other side.

Angry negotiators pay less attention to opponent's interests and are less accurate in judging their interests, thus achieve lower joint gains. Moreover, because anger makes negotiators more self-centered in their preferences, it increases the likelihood that they will reject profitable offers.

Opponents who really get angry (or cry, or otherwise lose control) are more likely to make errors: make sure they are in your favour. Anger does not help in achieving negotiation goals either: it reduces joint gains and does not help to boost personal gains, as angry negotiators do not succeed in claiming more for themselves. Moreover, negative emotions leads to acceptance of settlements that are not in the positive utility function but rather have a negative utility.

However, expression of negative emotions during negotiation can sometimes be beneficial: Legitimately expressed anger can be an effective way to show one's commitment, sincerity, and needs. Moreover, although NA reduces gains in integrative tasks, it is a better strategy than PA in distributive tasks (such as zero-sum). In his work on negative affect arousal and white noise, Seidner found support for the existence of a negative affect arousal mechanism through observations regarding the devaluation of speakers from other ethnic origins. Negotiation may be negatively affected, in turn, by submerged hostility towards an ethnic or gender group.

3. Conditions for emotion affect in negotiation: Research indicates that negotiator's emotions do not necessarily affect the negotiation process. Albarracın et al. (2003) suggested that there are two conditions for emotional affect, both related to the ability (presence of environmental or cognitive disturbances) and the motivation:

(*a*) Identification of the affect: Requires high motivation, high ability or both.

(*b*) Determination that the affect is relevant and important for the judgement: Requires that the motivation, the ability or both are low.

According to this model, emotions are expected to affect negotiations only when one is high and the other is low. When both ability and motivation are low the affect will not be identified, and when both are high the affect will be identified but discounted as irrelevant for judgement. A possible implication of this model is, for example, that the positive effects PA has no negotiations (as described above) will be seen only when either motivation or ability are low.

4. The effect of the partner's emotions: Most studies on emotion in negotiations focus on the effect of the negotiator's own emotions on the process. However, what the other party feels might be just as important, as group emotions are known to affect processes both at the group and the personal levels. When it comes to negotiations, trust in the other party is a necessary condition for its emotion to affect and visibility enhances the effect. Emotions contribute to negotiation processes by signaling what one feels and thinks and can thus prevent the other party from engaging in destructive behaviours and to indicate what steps should be taken next: PA signals to keep in the same way, while NA points that mental or behavioural adjustments are needed.

Partner's emotions can have two basic effects on negotiator's emotions and behaviour: Mimetic/ reciprocal or complementary. For example, disappointment or sadness might lead to compassion and more cooperation. In a study by Butt et al. (2005) which simulated real multi-phase negotiation, most people reacted to the partner's emotions in reciprocal, rather than complementary, manner.

Specific emotions were found to have different effects on the opponent's feelings and strategies chosen:

(*i*) ***Anger*** caused the opponents to place lower demands and to concede more in a zero-sum negotiation, but also to evaluate the negotiation less favourably. It provoked both dominating and yielding behaviours of the opponent.

(ii) ***Pride*** led to more integrative and compromise strategies by the partner.

(iii) ***Guilt** or **regret*** expressed by the negotiator led to better impression of him by the opponent, however it also led the opponent to place higher demands. On the other hand, personal guilt was related to more satisfaction with what one achieved.

(iv) ***Worry or disappointment*** left bad impression on the opponent, but led to relatively lower demands by the opponent.

(c) Non-verbal Communication in Negotiation Process

Communication is a key element of negotiation. Effective negotiation requires that participants effectively convey and interpret information. Participants in a negotiation will communicate information not only verbally but non-verbally through body language and gestures. By understanding how nonverbal communication works, a negotiator is better equipped to interpret the information other participants are leaking non-verbally while keeping secret those things that would inhibit his/her ability to negotiate.

1. ***Non-verbal anchoring:*** In a negotiation, a person can gain the advantage by verbally expressing his/or her position first. By "anchoring" your position, you establish the position from which the negotiation will proceed. In a like manner, one can "anchor" and gain advantage with non-verbal (body language) ques.

(i) ***Personal space:*** The person at the head of the table is the apparent symbol of power. Negotiators can repel this strategic advantage by positioning allies in the room to surround that individual.

(ii) ***First impression:*** Begin the negotiation with positive gestures and enthusiasm. Look the person in the eye with sincerity. If you cannot maintain eye contact, the other person might think you are hiding something or that you are insincere. Give a solid handshake.

2. ***Reading non-verbal communication:*** Being able to read the non-verbal communication of another person can significantly aid in the communication process. By being aware of inconsistencies between a person's verbal and non-verbal communication and reconciling them, negotiators will be able to come to better resolutions. Examples of incongruity in body language include:

(i) ***Nervous laugh:*** A laugh not matching the situation. This could be a sign of nervousness or discomfort. When this happens, it may be good to probe with questions to discover the person's true feelings.

(ii) ***Positive words but negative body language:*** If someone asks their negotiation partner if they are annoyed and the person pounds their fist and responds sharply, "what makes you think anything is bothering me?"

(iii) ***Hands raised in a clenched position:*** The person raising his/her hands in this position reveals frustration even when he/she is smiling. This is a signal that the person doing it may be holding back a negative attitude.

If possible, it may be helpful for negotiation partners to spend time together in a comfortable setting outside of the negotiation room. Knowing how each partner non-verbally communicates outside of the negotiation setting will help negotiation partners to sense incongruity between verbal and non-verbal communication within the negotiation setting.

3. ***Conveying receptivity:*** The way negotiation partners position their bodies relative to each other may influence how receptive each is to the other person's message and ideas.

- ***Face and eyes:*** Receptive negotiators smile, make plenty of eye contact. This conveys the idea that there is more interest in the person than in what is being said. On the other hand, non-receptive negotiators make little to no eye contact. Their eyes may be squinted, jaw muscles clenched and head turned slightly away from the speaker.
- ***Arms and hands:*** To show receptivity, negotiators should spread arms and open hands on table or relaxed on their lap. Negotiators show poor receptivity when their hands are clenched, crossed, positioned in front of their mouth, or rubbing the back of their neck.
- ***Legs and Feet:*** Receptive negotiators sit with legs together or one leg slightly in front of the other. When standing, they distribute weight evenly and place hands on their hips with their body tilted toward the speaker. Non-receptive negotiators stand with legs crossed, pointing away from the speaker.
- ***Torso:*** Receptive negotiators sit on the edge of their chair; unbutton their suit coat with their body tilted towards the speaker. Non-receptive negotiators may lean back in their chair and keep their suit coat buttoned.

Receptive negotiators tend to appear relaxed with their hands open and palms visibly displayed.

(d) Preparing for a Successful Negotiation

Depending on a scale of disagreement, the level of preparation might be appropriate for conducting the successful negotiation. For a small disagreement, excessive preparation could be counter-productive because it does takes time which is better focused in reaching the team goals. If the major disagreement needed to be resolved, preparing thoroughly for that is required, and worthwhile.

Think through following points before you could start negotiating:

1. *Goals*

What you want to get out from the negotiation?

What do you expect from the other person?

What you and the other person have which you can trade?

What do you and the other person have so that the other wants it?

What might you both be prepared to give away?

2. *Alternatives*

If you do not reach the agreement with him/her, what alternatives you have?

Are these things good or bad alternatives?

How much it matters if you do not reach the agreement?

Will the failure to reach the agreement cut out future opportunities?

What alternatives may the other person have?

3. *The relationship*

What is the history of relationship?

Can or should this history impact negotiation?

Will there be any of the hidden issues that might influence negotiation?

How you will handle these?

4. *Expected outcomes*

What outcome would people be expecting from the negotiation?

What was the outcome in the past and what precedents been set?

5. *The Consequences*

What are the consequences of winning or losing this negotiation by you?

What are the consequences of winning or losing by the other person?

6. *Power*

Who has the power in the relationship?

Who do control the resources?

Who stands to lose most if agreement is not been reached?

What power does other person have to deliver which you do hope for?

7. *Possible Solutions*

Based on all considerations, what possible compromises might be there?

8. *Negotiating and building long-term Relationships*

Good negotiators are the people who understand.

How to build key relationships and how to identify what people need as well?

How to give them what they need and how to get what they want in return, all in a way that seems effortless.

(e) Issues in Negotiation

1. ***The Role of Mood & Personality Traits in Negotiation:*** Positive moods positively affect negotiations. Traits do not appear to have a significantly direct effect on the outcomes of either bargaining or negotiating processes (except extraversion, which is bad for negotiation effectiveness).
2. ***Gender Differences in Negotiations:*** Women negotiate no differently from men, although men apparently negotiate slightly better outcomes. Men and women with similar power bases use the same negotiating styles. Women's attitudes towards negotiation and their success as negotiators are less favourable than men's globally but there are many exceptions as CEO of General Motors and Pepsi, the world's best negotiating large corporates, are women in 2014.
3. ***Negotiation Strategies:*** Most of the negotiation literature focuses on two strategies, although they call them by different names. One strategy is interest-based (or integrative, or cooperative) bargaining, while the other is positional (or distributive or competitive) bargaining.
4. ***Interest-based Bargaining/Win-win Bargaining:*** Integrative bargaining in which parties collaborate to find a "win-win" solution to their dispute. This strategy focuses on developing mutually beneficial agreements based on the interests of the disputants. Interests include the needs, desires, concerns, and fears important to each side.
5. ***Positional Bargaining:*** Positional bargaining is one that involves holding on to a fixed idea, or position, of what you want and arguing for it and it alone, regardless of any underlying interests.

(f) Techniques for Better Negotiation

1. ***Prepare, Prepare, Prepare:*** Pay attention to timing. Timing is important in any negotiation. Sure, you must know what to ask for. But be sensitive to when you ask for it. There are times to press ahead, and times to wait. When you are looking your best is the time to press for what you want. But beware of pushing too hard and poisoning any long-term relationship.
2. ***Pay Attention to Timing:*** Timing is important in any negotiation.
3. ***Leave Behind your Ego:*** The best negotiators either don't care or don't show they care about who gets credit for a successful deal. Their talent is in making the other side feel like the final agreement was all their idea.
4. ***Ramp up your Listening Skills:*** The best negotiators are often quiet listeners who patiently let others have the floor while they make their case. They never interrupt. Encourage the other side to talk first. That helps set up one of negotiation's oldest maxims: Whoever mentions numbers first, loses. While that's not always true, it's generally better to sit tight and let the other side go first. Even if they don't mention numbers, it gives you a chance to ask what they are thinking.
5. ***If You don't Ask, you don't Get:*** Another tenet of negotiating is "Go high, or go home". As part of your preparation, define your highest justifiable price. As long as you can argue convincingly, don't be afraid to aim high. But no ultimatums, please. Take-it-or-leave-it offers are usually out of place.
6. ***Anticipate Compromise:*** You should expect to make concessions and plan what they might be. Of course, the other side is thinking the same, so never take their first offer. Even if it's better than you'd hoped for, practice your best look of disappointment and politely decline. You never know what else you can get.
7. ***Offer and Expect Commitment:*** The glue that keeps deals from unraveling is an unshakable commitment to deliver. You should offer this comfort level to others. Likewise, avoid deals where the other side does not demonstrate commitment.
8. ***Don't Absorb their Problems:*** In most negotiations, you will hear all of the other side's problems and reasons they can't give you what you want. They want their problems to become yours, but don't let them. Instead, deal with each as they come up and try to solve them. If their "budget" is too low, for example, maybe there are other places that money could come from.
9. ***Stick to your Principles:*** As an individual and a business owner, you likely have a set of guiding principles—values that you just won't compromise. If you find negotiations crossing those boundaries, it might be a deal you can live without.
10. ***Close with Confirmation:*** At the close of any meeting—even if no final deal is struck—recaps the points covered and any areas of agreement. Make sure everyone confirms. Follow-up with appropriate letters or emails. Do not leave behind loose ends.

(g) Handling Difficult Negotiators

Speak more quietly than them and have more space in between your words than them. If they interrupt, pause for a few seconds after they finish. Be critical of foul language and do not rise to bait if they attack or blame you. Finally ignore all threats raised during negotiation process.

(h) Effective Negotiation

Successful relationships are built on communication and trust. Lack of trust leads to "win-lose" or "lose-lose" result. Negotiation is one way of creating trust or deciding whether trust is justified.

Skills for effective negotiation.

Preparation and planning skill.

Knowledge of the subject.

Ability to think clearly and rapidly under pressure and uncertainty.

Ability to express thoughts verbally.

Listening skill, patience and general problem-solving and analytical skills

Ask the following questions and be confident of moving towards the negotiation table:

1. During pre-negotiation (preparatory stage)

1. Firstly understand what it is you want?
2. What do you think your opponent wants?
3. What would happen if you didn't do a deal?
4. Do you know your stakeholders?
5. Do you know who the decision maker is? Are you negotiating with them? If not what affect does that have?
6. Are there concessions you can build into the negotiation?
7. Know your product/service inside out? What standards are there in the market place?
8. Know your price points?
9. What issues do you think you'll need to overcome?
10. Prioritize!
11. Practice!

2. Information Sharing During Negotiation (mid and last stage)

1. Company activities and market position.
2. Opinion on entry points.
3. What elements are clearly off the table or not up for discussion and why?
4. Opponents attitude and commitment.
5. Motivational factors ("I want this price because…").
6. Stakeholders and importantly decision makers.
7. Problems, issues or risk.
8. An order/structure for proceedings.

3. Bargaining has two basic parts: Debating and Proposing

(i) Debating

To be successful in negotiation you must build relationships and trust. You need to avoid the following:

- Point scoring: "Your company is always late with deliveries so I'm not paying that!"
- Insults: "If you insist on that price you must be stupid".

- Provocation: "Keep talking like that and see where it gets you!"
- Threats: "You just wait until your other customers hear about this".
- Instead try building a relationship: It will make your negotiation much easier.
- Sticking to an agreed agenda: This will help avoid destructive discussions.
- Share information and ask questions: What do you want – what do they want?
- Try and be positive and listen: What do they want and why – look for areas of win/win or easy compromise.

(ii) Proposing

When proposing your offer consider the following:

- Consider both your entry and exit: This could include all or some of your wants, and your opponents' entry and exit points.
- Consider how you will phrase your proposal.
- Consider what will motivate your opponent into making the deal.
- Consider the likely response: Think about the "if I do that then they will do that".
- Are there alternative proposals? Once an initial response has been made are you happy or do you need to offer up something new.
- Remember the key thing is to propose—don't argue and try and remain realistic, and invite a response from your opponent.

4. Finalizing the Deal

So when closing the deal consider

Do you have what you want?

Do they have what they want?

Can you signify to your opponent that if certain terms were met the deal could be done?

Do you both understand the potential non deal by not closing or reaching agreement?

Document the agreement quickly and share it with your opponent and get agreement on the details of the deal. Do not offer further concessions! And agree the measures that will be applied to record fulfillment of the deal.

5. Tips for successful bargaining

Promises—keeping them is hard, builds reputation, more trust means more wins and never compromise on integrity. It may be remembered that success is measure over time and people always give the most consideration, the best deals, to those people they like and trust.

(i) A Practical Guide for Effective Win-Win Negotiations

The foundations of negotiation theory are decision analysis, behavioural decision making, game theory, and negotiation analysis. Another classification of theories distinguishes between Structural Analysis, Strategic Analysis, Process Analysis, Integrative Analysis and Behavioural Analysis of negotiations. Individuals should make separate, interactive decisions; and negotiation analysis considers how groups of reasonably bright individuals should and could make joint, collaborative decisions. These theories are interleaved and should be approached from the synthetic perspective.

Effective negotiation helps you to resolve situations where what you want conflicts with what someone else wants. The aim of win-win negotiation is to find a solution that is acceptable to both parties, and leaves both parties feeling that they've won, in some way, after the event.

There are different styles of negotiation, depending on circumstances. For resolving disputes with people with whom you have an ongoing relationship: If one person plays hardball, then this disadvantages the other person–this may, quite fairly, lead to reprisal later. Similarly, using tricks and manipulation during a negotiation can undermine trust and damage teamwork. While a manipulative person may not get caught out if negotiation is infrequent, this is not the case when people work together routinely. Here, honesty and openness are almost always the best policies.

1. Preparing for a successful negotiation: Depending on the scale of the disagreement, some preparation may be appropriate for conducting a successful negotiation. Before people can even begin the process of negotiation, they must first be committed to a fair process.

(i) In preparation for being fair the parties must be ready to:

- Listen.
- Reach a mutually satisfying resolution.
- Hear things they disagree with or find painful without reacting abusively or defensively.
- Accept that something with change.

For small disagreements, excessive preparation can be counter-productive because it takes time that is better used elsewhere. It can also be seen as manipulative because, just as it strengthens your position, it can weaken the other person's. However, if you need to resolve a major disagreement, make sure you prepare thoroughly.

(ii) Think through the following points before you start negotiating:

- **Goals:** What do you want to get out of the negotiation? What do you think the other person wants?
- **Trades:** What do you and the other person have that you can trade? What do you each have that the other wants? What are you each comfortable giving away?
- **Alternatives:** If you don't reach agreement with the other person, what alternatives do you have? Are these good or bad? How much does it matter if you do not reach agreement? Does failure to reach an agreement cut you out of future opportunities? And what alternatives might the other person have?
- **Relationships:** What is the history of the relationship? Could or should this history impact the negotiation? Will there be any hidden issues that may influence the negotiation? How will you handle these?
- **Expected outcomes:** What outcome will people be expecting from this negotiation? What has the outcome been in the past, and what precedents have been set?
- **The consequences:** What are the consequences for you of winning or losing this negotiation? What are the consequences for the other person?
- **Power:** Who has what power in the relationship? Who controls resources? Who stands to lose the most if agreement isn't reached? What power does the other person have to deliver what you hope for?

Possible solutions: Based on all of the considerations, what possible compromises might there be?

Setting some rules: Begin by reviewing these rules and adding any that you mutually decide are important:

- No yelling.
- Don't bring up unrelated issues.
- No threats or intimidation.
- No mind games.
- Is a time limit needed for this discussion?
- Is a third party needed to help with this discussion?

Defining the problem:

- What are we negotiating?
- Is this negotiable?
- How does each person experience and define the problem? (This will be different for each person).
- Who else is affected and how?

Identifying goals:

- **Short term:** Name the things that need to be included in an immediate solution.
- **Long term:** Name the things that need to be included in a final solution.

Finding solutions:

- What would each person propose as an immediate and long term solution that addresses the things each person has said needs to be considered?
- Is compromise necessary, can both parties be enhanced?
- If compromise is necessary, list several fair solutions.

(iii) Style is critical: For a negotiation to be 'win-win', both parties should feel positive about the negotiation once it's over. This helps people keep good working relationships afterwards. This governs the style of the negotiation – histrionics and displays of emotion are clearly inappropriate because they undermine the rational basis of the negotiation and because they bring a manipulative aspect to them.

Despite this, emotion can be an important subject of discussion because people's emotional needs must fairly be met. If emotion is not discussed where it needs to be, then the agreement reached can be unsatisfactory and temporary. Be as detached as possible when discussing your own emotions–perhaps discuss them as if they belong to someone else.

Negotiating successfully. The negotiation itself is a careful exploration of your position and the other person's position, with the goal of finding a mutually acceptable compromise that gives you both as much of what you want as possible. People's positions are rarely as fundamentally opposed as they may initially appear - the other person may have very different goals from the ones you expect!

In an ideal situation, you will find that the other person wants what you are prepared to trade, and that you are prepared to give what the other person wants. If this is not the case and one person must give way, then it is fair for this person to try to negotiate some form of compensation for doing so—the scale of this compensation will often depend on the many of the factors we discussed above. Ultimately, both sides should feel comfortable with the final solution if the agreement is to be considered win-win. Only consider win-lose negotiation if you don't need to have an ongoing relationship with the other party as, having lost, they are unlikely to want to work with you again. Equally, you should expect that if they need to fulfill some part of a deal in which you have "won", they may be uncooperative and legalistic about the way they do this.

9.9 BARGAINING

Bargaining or haggling is a type of negotiation in which the buyer and seller of a good or service dispute the price which will be paid and the exact nature of the transaction that will take place and eventually come to an agreement. Bargaining is an alternative pricing strategy to fixed prices. Optimally, if it costs the retailer nothing to engage and allow bargaining, he can divine the buyer's willingness to spend.

It allows for capturing more consumer surplus as it allows price discrimination, a process whereby a seller can charge a higher price to one buyer who is more eager (by being richer or more desperate). Haggling has largely disappeared in parts of the world where the cost to haggle exceeds the gain to retailers for most common retail items. However, for expensive goods sold to uninformed buyers such as automobiles, bargaining can remain commonplace.

Dickering refers to the same process, albeit with a slight negative (petty) connotation. Bargaining is also the name chosen for the third stage of the Kübler-Ross model (commonly known as the stages of dying), even though it has nothing to do with price negotiations. Not all transactions are open to bargaining. Both religious beliefs and regional custom may determine whether or not the seller is willing to bargain.

(a) Regional Differences

In North America and Europe bargaining is restricted to expensive or one-of-a-kind items (automobiles, jewellery, art, real estate, trade sales of businesses) and informal sales settings such as flea markets and garage sales. In other regions of the world bargaining may be the norm even for small commercial transactions.

In Indonesia and elsewhere in Asia where locals haggle for goods and services everywhere from street markets to hotels, haggling is a strong cultural tradition that even children learn from a young age. Participating in that tradition can make foreigners feel accepted. Haggling for food items is strongly discouraged in Southeast Asia and is considered an insult, because food is seen a common necessity that is not to be treated as a tradable good.

In almost all large complex business negotiations, a certain amount of bargaining takes place. One simplified 'western' way to decide when it's time to bargain is to break negotiation into two stages: Creating value and claiming value. Claiming value is another phrase for bargaining. Many cultures take offence when they perceive the other side as having started bargaining too soon. This offence is usually as a result of their wanting to first create value for longer before they bargain together. The Chinese culture by contrast places a much higher value on taking time to build a business relationship before starting to create value or bargain. Not understanding when to start bargaining has ruined many an otherwise positive business negotiation.

In areas where bargaining at the retail level is common, the option to bargain often depends on the presence of the store's owner. A chain store managed by clerks is more likely to use fixed pricing than an independent store managed by an owner or one of owner's trusted employees.

The store's ambiance may also be used to signal whether or not bargaining is appropriate. For instance, a comfortable and air-conditioned store with posted prices usually does not allow bargaining, but a stall in a bazaar or marketplace may. Super markets and other chain stores almost never allow bargaining. However, the importance of ambiance may depend on the cultural commitment to bargaining. In Israel, prices on day-to-day items (clothing, toiletries) may be negotiable even in a western style store manned by a clerk. In India, a sign posted with the phrase fixed price indicates that bargaining is not allowed, although quite often this is not the case.

(b) Theoretical Framework for Bargaining

Following are the major theories for bargaining:

1. Behavioural theory: The personality theory in bargaining emphasizes that the type of personalities determine the bargaining process and its outcome. A popular behavioural theory deals with a distinction between hard-liners and soft-liners. Various research papers refer to hard-liners as warriors, while soft-liners are shopkeepers. It varies from region to region. Bargaining may take place more in rural and semi-urban areas than in a metro city.

2. Game theory: Bargaining games refer to situations where two or more players must reach agreement regarding how to distribute an object or monetary amount. Each player prefers to reach an agreement in these games, rather than abstain from doing so; however, each prefers that agreement which most favours his interests. Examples of such situations would be the bargaining involved in a labour union and the directors of a company negotiating wage increases, the dispute between two communities about the distribution of a common territory or the conditions under which two countries can start a program of nuclear disarmament. Analyzing these kinds of problems looks for a solution specifying which component in dispute will correspond to each party involved.

Players in a bargaining problem can bargain for the objective as a whole at a precise moment in time. The problem can also be divided so that parts of the whole objective become subject to bargaining during different stages. In a classical bargaining problem the result is an agreement reached between all interested parties, or the status quo of the problem. It is clear that studying how individual parties make their decisions is insufficient for predicting what agreement will be reached.

However, classical bargaining theory assumes that each participant in a bargaining process will choose between possible agreements, following the conduct predicted by the rational choice model. It is particularly assumed that each player's preferences regarding the possible agreements can be represented by a von Neumann–Morgenstern utility theorem function.

Nash [1950] defines a classical bargaining problem as being a set of joint allocations of utility, some of which will correspond to what the players would obtain if they reach an agreement, and another which represents what they would get if they failed to do so. A bargaining game for two players is defined as a pair (F, d) where F is the set of possible joint utility allocations (possible agreements), and d is the disagreement point.

For the definition of a specific bargaining solution it is usual to follow Nash's proposal, setting out the axioms this solution should satisfy. Some of the most frequent axioms used in the building of bargaining solutions are efficiency, symmetry, independence of irrelevant alternatives, scalar invariance, monotonicity, etc.

The Nash bargaining solution is the bargaining solution which maximizes the product of an agent's utilities on the bargaining set. The Nash bargaining solution, however, only deals with the simplest structure of bargaining. It is not dynamic (failing to deal with how Pareto outcomes are achieved). Instead, for situations where the structure of the bargaining game is important, a more mainstream game theoretic approach is useful. This can allow players' preferences over time and risk to be incorporated into the solution of bargaining games. It can also show how the details can matter. For example, the Nash bargaining solution for Prisoners' Dilemma is different from the Nash equilibrium.

3. Procession theory: This theory isolates distinctive elements of the bargaining chronology in order to better understand the complexity of the negotiating process. Several key features of the processual theory include:

- Bargaining range
- Critical risk
- Security point.

4. Integrative theory: Integrative bargaining (also called "interest-based bargaining", "win-win bargaining') is a negotiation strategy in which parties collaborate to find a "win-win" solution to their dispute. This strategy focuses on developing mutually beneficial agreements based on the interests of the disputants. Interests include the needs, desires, concerns, and fears important to each side. They are the underlying reasons why people become involved in a conflict.

Integrative refers to the potential for the parties' interests to be combined in ways that create joint value or enlarge the pie. Potential for integration only exists when there are multiple issues involved in the negotiation. This is because the parties must be able to make trade-offs across issues in order for both sides to be satisfied with the outcome.

5. Narrative theory: A very different approach to conceptualizing bargaining is as co-construction of a social narrative, where narrative, rather than economic logic drives the outcome.

(c) Bargaining and Posted Prices in Retail Markets

Retailers can choose to sell at posted prices or allow bargaining: Selling at a public posted price commits the retailer not to exploit buyers once they enter the retail store, making the store more attractive to potential customers, while a bargaining strategy has the advantage that it allows the retailer to price discriminate between different types of customer. In some markets, such as those for automobiles and expensive electronic goods, firms post prices but are open to haggling with consumers. When the proportion of haggling consumers goes up, prices tend to rise.

(d) Automated Bargaining

When a bargaining situation is complex, finding Nash equilibrium will be difficult using game theory. Evolutionary computation methods have been designed for automated bargaining, and demonstrated efficient and effective for approximating Nash equilibrium.

(e) Anchor Pricing

Anchor price is the first call that is made during a bargain. Due to the first call a condition of biased pricing is set which tilts the bargain towards the first caller.

SUMMARY

Conflict is an integral part of organisational life. Understanding the sources of conflict and the different resolution methods enhances both communication skills and management ability in contemporary organisations. Various types of conflict and approaches for resolving conflict were discussed. A free flow of information to the CEO of the organisation is essential for the company's success.

Following is the sequence in which a conflict can arise:

- ***Latent conflict:*** Is a situation when the conditions for conflict arise. For example, two groups competing for scarce resources.
- ***Perceived conflict:*** Is a situation when both the groups realize that there exists conflict between them.
- ***Felt conflict:*** Is a situation when members involved in the conflict feel tense or anxious.
- ***Manifest conflict:*** Is a situation when both the group tries to frustrate each other.
- ***Conflict outcome:*** Is a situation or consequence arising after the conflict is eliminated.

Most theories of negotiations share the notion of negotiations as a process, but they differ in their description of the process. Negotiating is the process of communicating back and forth, for the purpose of reaching a joint agreement about differing needs or ideas. A negotiator may be a buyer or seller, a customer or supplier, a boss or employee, a business partner, a diplomat or a civil servant. On a more personal level, negotiation takes place between spouse's friends, parents or children.

Bargaining or haggling is a type of negotiation in which the buyer and seller of a good or service dispute the price which will be paid and the exact nature of the transaction that will take place, and eventually come to an agreement. Bargaining is an alternative pricing strategy to fixed prices. It allows for capturing more consumer surplus as it allows price discrimination, a process whereby a seller can charge a higher price to one buyer who is more eager (by being richer or more desperate).

REVIEW QUESTIONS

1. Define conflict? How is it helping the organisation?
2. Explain conflict resolving methods with suitable example of your choice.
3. Explain various negotiation strategies and tactics suitable for a banking company.
4. Describe various bargaining methods for a customer to set right price from a fashion retailer .

DISCUSSION QUESTIONS

1. Explain the conflict resolving technique by which you are familiar with. Compare its merit over other techniques.
2. Comment on the practicability of the techniques in forming group and also for solving conflict in the group? What technique, which you will resort to for making decisions?
3. Discuss suitable bargaining and negotiation tactics and strategies for a computer manufacturing firm with trade unions and stockists.

STUDENT EXERCISE

1. Management is the process of working with and through others to achieve organisational objectives. Effective managers are team players who actively support others through empowerment and other means. Despite claims to the contrary in the popular press, effective female and male managers do not have significantly different skill profiles. While this is true for the Indians, it may not be as true for other cultures. Evaluate the statement in the context of cultural factors in India and in China. What factors in these two countries may have an impact on gender differences in management? How do you set-up separate conflict management team along with negotiation process and bargaining tactics in such circumstances?
2. Visit a leading corporate house like Infosys, or ICICI via Internet and chat with their leader N.R. Narayana Murthy or Chandan Kochar. Find out what made/motivate them to set a team for the new millennium for managing organisational conflict along with negotiation process and bargaining tactics based on the theory, which we described in the chapter.

SKILL TEST

What is your Conflict-handling Style?

Instructions

For each of the fifteen items, indicate how often you rely on that tactic by circling the appropriate number.

No.	Statement	Rarely	Always
1.	I argue my case with my co-workers to show the merits of my position.	1–2–3–4–5	
2.	I negotiate with my co-workers so that a compromise can be reached.	1–2–3–4–5	
3.	I try to satisfy the expectations of my co-workers.	1–2–3–4–5	
4.	I try to investigate an issue with my co-workers to find a solution acceptable to us.	1–2–3–4–5	
5.	I am firm in pursuing my side of the issue.	1–2–3–4–5	
6.	I attempt to avoid being "put on the spot" and try to keep my conflict with my co-workers to myself.	1–2–3–4–5	
7.	I hold on to my solution to a problem.	1–2–3–4–5	
8.	I use "give and take" so that a compromise can be made.	1–2–3–4–5	
9.	I exchange accurate information with my co-workers to solve a problem together.	1–2–3–4–5	
10.	I avoid open discussion of my differences with my co-workers.	1–2–3–4–5	
11.	I accommodate the wishes of my co-workers.	1–2–3–4–5	
12.	I try to bring all our concerns out in the open so that the issues can be resolved in the best possible way.	1–2–3–4–5	
13.	I propose a middle ground for breaking deadlocks.	1–2–3–4–5	
14.	I go along with the suggestions of my co-workers.	1–2–3–4–5	
15.	I try to keep my disagreements with my co-workers to myself in order to avoid hard feelings.	1–2–3–4–5	

Scoring key

Collaborating		Accommodating		Competing		Avoiding		Compromising	
Item	Score	Item	Score	Item	Score	Item	Score	Item	Score
4	–	3	–	1	–	6	–	2	–
9	–	11	–	5	–	10	–	8	–
12	–	14	–	7	–	15	–	13	–
Total	–	Total	–	Total		Total	–	Total	–

Your primary conflict handling style is: __________

(The category with the higher total)

Your backup conflict handling style is: __________

(The category with the second highest total)

Source: A measure of styles of handling interpersonal conflict (Adaptation) M.A. Rahim, Academy of Management Journal, June 1983.

If you wish to know more insight on your test score, then you are welcome to contact author via e-mail shaangrila@gmail.com or social media drs.shajahan.7@facebook.com

10

CHAPTER

ORGANISATIONAL DESIGN, CLIMATE, ORGANISATIONAL CULTURE AND OB MODELS FOR AD 2020

LEARNING OBJECTIVES

This chapter aims at introducing fundamental concepts for explaining the positive organisational design, climate and culture for moulding sustained high performance organisation for AD 2020 to the readers:

- *Definition, importance and fundamental concepts of organisational design, organisational climate and organisational culture*
- *Various organisational structures and their effects on human behaviour*
- *Factors contributing positive organisational design, climate and culture*
- *Culture shocks and managing multicultural work force*
- *Emerging models of organisation behaviour in AD 2020*
- *Easternization/Indigenization of western management: a practical approach*

INTRODUCTION

An organisation is a social entity that has a collective goal and is linked to an external environment. The word is derived from the Greek word *organon*, itself derived from the better-known word *ergon* which means 'organ'—a compartment for a particular task. There are formal organisations and informal organisations exists in this world. There are a variety of legal types of organisations, including corporations, governments, non-governmental organisations, international organisations, armed forces, charities, non-for-profit corporations, partnerships, cooperatives, and universities. A hybrid organisation is a body that operates in both the public sector and the private sector simultaneously, fulfilling public duties and developing commercial market activities. A voluntary association is an organisation consisting of volunteers. Such organisations may be able to operate without legal formalities, depending on jurisdiction, including informal clubs. Organisations may also operate in secret and/or illegally in the case of secret societies, criminal organisations and resistance movements. In this final chapter, we are going to focus on their structure, design, climate and most importantly the organisation behaviour models in detail. We begin our discussion with structure first. There are two types of organisation in general; such as formal and informal organisations.

10.1 FORMAL AND INFORMAL ORGANISATIONS

The informal organisation is the interlocking social structure that governs how people work together in practice. It is the aggregate of, norms, personal and professional connections through which work gets done and relationships are built among people who share a common organisational affiliation or cluster of affiliations. It consists of a dynamic set of personal relationships, social networks, communities of common interest and emotional sources of motivation. The informal organisation evolves, and the complex social dynamics of its members.

Tended effectively, the informal organisation complements the more explicit structures, plans, and processes of the formal organisation: It can accelerate and enhance responses to unanticipated events, foster innovation, enable people to solve problems that require collaboration across boundaries, and create footpaths showing where the formal organisation may someday need to pave a way. The nature of the informal organisation becomes more distinct when its key characteristics are juxtaposed with those of the formal organisation.

(a) Key characteristics of the informal organisation: It is evolving constantly, have strong grass roots, always dynamic and responsive, excellent at motivation. It requires insider knowledge to be seen and treats people as individuals like flat and fluid; it is cohered by trust and reciprocity and difficult to pin down. It is collective decision making and essential for situations that change quickly or are not yet fully understood.

(b) Key characteristics of the formal organisation: It is enduring, unless deliberately altered, follows top-down approach and missionary style and static in nature. It has excellent at alignment, plain to see quick result, equates "person" with "role". It is hierarchical, bound together by codified rules and order and is easily understood and explained. It is critical for dealing with situations that are known and consistent.

Historically, some have regarded the informal organisation as the byproduct of insufficient formal organisation—arguing, for example, that "it can hardly be questioned that the ideal situation in the business organisation would be one where no informal organisation existed." However, the contemporary approach—one suggested as early as 1925 by Mary Parker Follett, the pioneer of community centers and author of influential works on management philosophy—is to integrate the informal organisation and the formal organisation, recognizing the strengths and limitations of each. Integration, as Follett defined it, means breaking down apparent sources of conflict into their basic elements and then building new solutions that neither allow domination nor require compromise. In other words, integrating the informal organisation with the formal organisation replaces competition with coherence.

At a societal level, the importance of the relationship between formal and informal structures can be seen in the relationship between civil society and state authority. The power of integrating the formal organisation and the informal organisation can also be seen in many successful businesses.

A leader in a formal, hierarchical organisation, who is appointed to a managerial position, has the right to command and enforce obedience by virtue of the authority of his position. However, he must possess adequate personal attributes to match his authority, because authority is only potentially available to him. In the absence of sufficient personal competence, a manager may be confronted by an emergent leader who can challenge his role in the organisation and reduce it to that of a figurehead. However, only authority of position has the backing of formal sanctions. It follows that whoever wields personal influence and power can legitimize this only by gaining a formal position in the hierarchy, with commensurate authority.

In contrast to the appointed head or chief of an administrative unit, a leader emerges within the context of the informal organisation that underlies the formal structure. The informal organisation expresses the personal objectives and goals of the individual membership. Their objectives and goals may or may not coincide with those of the formal organisation. The informal organisation represents an extension of the social structures that generally characterize human life—the spontaneous emergence of groups and organisations as ends in themselves.

Leaders emerge from within the structure of the informal organisation. Their personal qualities, the demands of the situation, or a combination of these and other factors attract followers who accept their leadership within one or several overlay structures. Instead of the authority of position held by an appointed head or chief, the emergent leader wields influence or power. Influence is the ability of a person to gain cooperation from others by means of persuasion or control over rewards. Power is a stronger form of influence because it reflects a person's ability to enforce action through the control of a means of punishment.

10.2 DEFINITION AND DETERMINANTS OF ORGANISATIONAL DESIGN

(a) Definition

Organisational design is the overall configuration of structural components that defines jobs, groupings of jobs, the hierarchy, patterns of authority and approaches to coordination and line-staff differentiation into a single and unified organisational system. Consider, for example, the differences in organisational design that might exist between a computer manufacturer and university. Since the computer manufacturer has to respond to frequent technological breakthroughs and changes in its competitive environment, it is likely to have a relatively flat affected by technology. Therefore, it has a more centralized structure with numerous rules and regulations.

(b) Determinants of Organisational Design

The key situational determinants of organisational design are technology, organisational environment and organisation size and life cycle.

1. *Technology:* Technology is the set of processes that an organisation uses to transform various resources such as materials and labour into products or services. Joan Woodward was the first person to see the link between technology and organisational design. In particular, Woodward defined three basic types of technology. In unit or small-batch technology, products are manufactured according to customer specifications in small quantities. Examples are printing press and studios.

In large batch or mass-production technology, products are manufactured in assembly-line fashion by combining component pans to create finished goods. Examples are home-appliance, automobile and computer manufacturers. In continuous-process technology, products are transformed from raw materials into finished goods through a series of machine transformations that change the composition of the materials themselves. Examples are petroleum refiners, food processors and chemical manufacturers.

Woodward viewed unit or small-batch technology as the least complex while the continuous process technology as the most complex. She found that organisations within each set had similar designs but the designs varied somewhat from set to set. Bums and Stalker argued that managers should examine the rate of change in technology to determine the best organisational structure. They recommended a bureaucratic or mechanistic structure for organisations with slowly changing technology and an organic or flexible structure for organisations with rapidly changing technology.

Charles Perrow concluded that the key question concerning an organisation's technology is whether it is routine or non-routine. In his view, a highly formalized centralized structure is appropriate for an organisation that uses the same routine technology while a more flexible structure is necessary for an organisation that often uses new technology. An organisation that uses continuous process, non-routine or intensive technology needs to ensure that its structure can adapt to changes in the technologies. Technology can affect all aspects of an organisation, not just production and the same technological change can have very different effects on different organisations.

2. *Environment:* The environment also influences the type of design an organisation is likely to adopt. The environment of an organisation consists of all the factors and conditions outside the organisation that might affect it which include customers, shareholders competitors, legislatures and regulatory agencies, economic factors, which include interest rates, unemployment rate, finance, objects, which include buildings, machines and events, which include as elections, war, floods etc.

If the managers are good at analyzing and predicting changes in the environment, then, they can help the organisation to take advantage of any change. Since the environment affects organisation both directly and indirectly, therefore, the managers must keep an eye on it and be ready to modify organisation's design to respond to environmental changes.

3. *Organisational Size and Life Cycle:* Organisation size refers to how large the organisation is, usually, in terms of the number of its full-time employees. Life cycle refers to organisation's maturity relative to that of other organisations. Size can affect organisation design in many different ways. A group of researchers in England found that large organisations tend to have more job specialization, more standard operating procedures, more rules and regulations, and more decentralization than small organisations. Thus, as organisations grow in size, they should be prepared to adapt their design accordingly.

Many people equate organisation design with an organisation's structure: The words "lean" and "flat" are used to describe organisation design as well as its structure. In fact, organisational design encompasses much more than simply the structure: Organisation design is the process of aligning an organisation's structure with its mission. This means looking at the complex relationship between tasks, workflow, responsibility and authority, and making sure these all support the objectives of the business.

Good organisational design helps communications, productivity, and innovation. It creates an environment where people can work effectively. Many productivity and performance issues can be traced back to poor organisation design. A company can have a great mission, great people, great leadership, etc. and still not perform well because of poor organisational design.

Take the example of a company whose sales department and production department both work well as separate units. Yet they need to communicate about customer needs and have not been organized to do so: Company performance suffers as a result. Then take the example of a company that wants to grow by acquiring new customers. Yet its sales team is rewarded for customer retention instead. Again, company performance is compromised as a result.

How work is done, business processes, information sharing and how people are incentivized; all of these directly affects how well the organisation performs. All of these factors are facets of the organisation's design and each facet is important to organisation's success. Given the importance of organisational design, why is it so often to blame for inefficiency and ineffectiveness? The reason is because organisations often evolve rather than get designed. With little or no planning and intervention, the organisation design that emerges is likely to be flawed with misaligned incentives, processing gaps and barriers to good communications.

Without due planning, an organisation's design often takes on a hierarchical structure. This structure is common because business executives and managers are often reluctant to relinquish control. However, such structures can lack flexibility, soak up resources and underuse key people and skills. When it comes to good organisation design, it's a question of getting the right balance, getting the right controls, the right flexibility, the right incentives; and getting the most from people and other key resources.

The organisational structure defines the organisation's hierarchy of people and departments as well as how information flows within the organisation. The organisational structure determines how and when information is distributed as well as whom makes what decisions based on the information available. How job tasks are formally divided, grouped and coordinated. The organisational structure is important because it ensures that there is an efficient operation of a business and it clearly defines its workers and their functions. The organisational structure also helps define the hierarchy and the chain of command. Structure helps influence behaviour and relationships of jobs and functions. Structure defines recurring activities and processes and structure provides a purposeful and goal-oriented behaviour.

Organisational design activities such as task allocation, coordination and supervision, which are directed towards the achievement of organisational aims. It can also be considered as the viewing glass or perspective through which individuals see their organisation and its environment. Organisations are a variant of clustered entities. An organisation can be designed in many different ways, depending on their objectives. The design of an organisation will determine the modes in which it operates and performs. Organisational design allows the expressed allocation of responsibilities for different functions and processes to different entities such as the branch, department, workgroup and individual.

Organisational design affects organisational action in two big ways. First, it provides the foundation on which standard operating procedures and routines rest. Second, it determines which individuals get to participate in which decision-making processes, and thus to what extent their views shape the organisation's actions. The set organisational design may not coincide with facts, evolving in operational action. Such divergence decreases performance, when growing. For example, a wrong organisational design may hamper cooperation and thus hinder the completion of orders in due time and within limits of resources and budgets. Organisational design shall be adaptive to process requirements, aiming to optimize the ratio of effort and input to output. Organisational design developed from the ancient times of hunters and collectors in tribal organisations through highly royal and clerical power structures to industrial structures and today's post-industrial structures.

As pointed out by L. B. Mohr, the early theorists of organisational design and structure, Taylor, Fayol, and Weber "saw the importance of design and structure for effectiveness and efficiency and assumed without the slightest question that whatever structure was needed, people could fashion accordingly. Organisational structure was considered a matter of choice. When in the 1930s, the rebellion began that came to be known as human relations theory, there was still not a denial of the idea of structure as an artifact, but rather an advocacy of the creation of a different sort of structure, one in which the needs, knowledge, and opinions of employees might be given greater recognition". However, a different view arose in the 1960s, suggesting that the organisational design and structure is "an externally caused phenomenon, an outcome rather than an artifact". In the 21st century, organisational theorists such as Lim, Griffiths, and Sambrook (2010) are once again proposing that organisational design and structure development is very much dependent on the expression of the strategies and behaviour of the management and the workers as constrained by the power distribution between them, and influenced by their environment and the outcome.

An organisation's life cycle is related to its size. Organisations tend to follow a predictable pattern of growth. After they are created, they grow for some period of time and then eventually stabilize as a mature organisation. To summarize, an organisation design needed by a small but rapidly growing business is different from an organisation design needed by an established and entrenched industry giant growing at a stable and predictable rate. An organisation's life cycle and growth rates are directly linked to the strategy that the organisation is pursuing.

10.3 TYPES OF ORGANISATIONAL DESIGN

According to management science, most human organisations fall roughly into four types such as committees or juries, ecologies, matrix organisations and pyramids or hierarchies.

(a) Committees or juries: These consist of a group of peers who decide as a group, perhaps by voting. The difference between a jury and a committee is that the members of the committee are usually assigned to perform or lead further actions after the group comes to a decision, whereas members of a jury come to a decision. In common law countries, legal juries render decisions of guilt, liability and quantify damages; juries are also used in athletic contests, book awards and similar activities. Sometimes a selection committee functions like a jury. In the middle ages, juries in continental Europe were used to determine the law according to consensus amongst local notables. Committees are often the most reliable way to make decisions. Condorcet's jury theorem proved that if the average member votes better than a roll of dice, then adding more members increases the number of majorities that can come to a correct vote (however correctness is defined). The problem is that if the average member is subsequently worse than a roll of dice, the committee's decisions grow worse, not better; therefore, staffing is crucial.

(b) Ecologies: This organisation design has intense competition. Bad parts of the organisation starve. Good ones get more work. Everybody is paid for what they actually do, and runs a tiny business that has to show a profit, or they are fired. Companies who utilize this organisation type reflect a rather one-sided view of what goes on in ecology. It is also the case that a natural ecosystem has a natural border—ecoregions do not in general compete with one another in any way, but are very autonomous. The pharmaceutical company GlaxoSmithKline adopted this philosophy.

(c) Matrix organisation: This organisational design assigns each worker two bosses in two different hierarchies. One hierarchy is "functional" and assures that each type of expert in the organisation is well-trained and measured by a boss who is super-expert in the same field. The other direction is "executive" and tries to get projects completed using the experts. Projects might be organized by products, regions, customer types, or some other schema. As an example, a company might have an individual with overall responsibility for products X and Y, and another individual with overall responsibility for engineering, quality control etc. Therefore, subordinates responsible for quality control of product X will have two reporting lines.

(d) Pyramids or hierarchical organisation: A hierarchical organisation is an organisational design where every entity in the organisation, except one, is subordinates to a single other entity. This arrangement is a form of a hierarchy. In an organisation, the hierarchy usually consists of a singular/group of power at the top with subsequent levels of power beneath them. This is the dominant mode of organisation among large organisations; most corporations, governments, and organized religions are hierarchical organisations with different levels of management, power or authority. For example, the broad, top-level overview of the general organisation of the Catholic Church consists of the Pope, then the Cardinals, then the Archbishops, and so on. Members of hierarchical organisational structures chiefly communicate with their immediate superior and with their immediate subordinates. Structuring organisations in this way is useful partly because it can reduce the communication overhead by limiting information flow; this is also its major limitation.

A hierarchy exemplifies an arrangement with a leader who leads other individual members of the organisation. This arrangement is often associated with bureaucracy. These structures are formed on the basis that there are enough people under the leader to give him support. Just as one would imagine a real pyramid, if there are not enough stone blocks to hold up the higher ones, gravity would irrevocably bring down the monumental structure. So one can imagine that if the leader does not have the support of his subordinates, the entire structure will collapse. Hierarchies were satirized in The Peter Principle (1969), saying that "in a hierarchy every employee tends to rise to his level of incompetence".

A hierarchy is typically visualized as a pyramid, where the height of the ranking or person depicts their power status and the width of that level represents how many people or business divisions are at that level relative to the whole—the highest-ranking people are at the apex, and there are very few of them; the base may include thousands of people who have no subordinates. These hierarchies are typically depicted with a tree or triangle diagram, creating an organisational chart or organigram. Those nearest the top have more power than those nearest the bottom, and there being fewer people at the top than at the bottom. As a result, superiors in a hierarchy generally have higher status and command greater rewards than their subordinates. All governments and most companies have similar structures. Traditionally, the monarch was the pinnacle of the state. In many countries, feudalism and manorialism provided a formal social structure that established hierarchical links at every level of society, with the monarch at the top.

In modern post-feudal states the nominal top of the hierarchy still remains the head of state, which may be a president or a constitutional monarch, although in many modern states the powers of the head of state are delegated among different bodies. Below the head, there is commonly a senate, parliament or congress, which in turn often delegate the day-to-day running of the country to a prime minister. In many democracies, the people are considered to be the notional top of the hierarchy, over the head of state; in reality, the people's power is restricted to voting in elections.

In business, the business owner traditionally occupied the pinnacle of the organisation. In most modern large companies, there is now no longer a single dominant shareholder, and the collective power of the business owners is for most purposes delegated to a board of directors, which in turn delegates the day-to-day running of the company to a managing director or CEO. Again, although the shareholders of the company are the nominal top of the hierarchy, in reality many companies are run at least in part as personal fiefdoms by their management; corporate governance rules are an attempt to mitigate this tendency.

Hierarchies and hierarchical thinking has been criticized by many people, including Susan McClary who is vehemently opposed to hierarchical organisation: Anarchism is generally opposed to hierarchical organisation in any form of human relations. Heterarchy is the most commonly proposed alternative to hierarchy and this has been combined with responsible autonomy by Gerard Fairtlough in his work on Triarchy theory.

Amidst constant innovation in information and communication technologies, hierarchical authority structures are giving way to greater decision-making latitude for individuals and more flexible definitions of job activities and this new style of work presents a challenge to existing organisational forms, with some research studies contrasting traditional organisational forms against groups that operate as online communities that are characterized by personal motivation and the satisfaction of making one's own decisions.

Let us again focus on the organisational design in detail by focusing on organisational philosophies and guiding principles.

1. ***Pre-bureaucratic structure designs:*** Pre-bureaucratic (entrepreneurial) Structure Designs lack standardization of tasks. This structure is most common in smaller organisations and is best used to solve simple tasks. The structure is totally centralized. The strategic leader makes all key decisions and most communication is done by one on one conversations. It is particularly useful for new (entrepreneurial) business as it enables the founder to control growth and development. They are usually based on traditional domination or charismatic domination in the sense of Max Weber's tripartite classification of authority.

2. ***Bureaucratic structure designs:*** Weber (1948) gives the analogy that "the fully developed bureaucratic mechanism compares with other organisations exactly as does the machine compare with the non-mechanical modes of production. Precision, speed, unambiguity, strict subordination, reduction of friction and of material and personal costs, these are raised to the optimum point in the strictly bureaucratic administration." Bureaucratic structures have a certain degree of standardization. They are better suited for more complex or larger scale organisations, usually adopting a tall structure. The tension between bureaucratic structures and non-bureaucratic is echoed in Burns and Stalker's distinction between mechanistic and organic structures. The Weberian characteristics of bureaucracy are:

- Clear defined roles and responsibilities
- A hierarchical structure design
- Respect for merit.

Bureaucratic structures design has many levels of management ranging from senior executives to regional managers, all the way to department store managers. Since there are many levels, decision-making authority has to pass through more layers than flatter organisations. Bureaucratic organisation have rigid and tight procedure, policies and constraints. This kind of structure design is reluctant to adapt or change what they have been doing since the company started. Organisational charts exist for every department, and everyone understands who is in charge and what his responsibilities are for every situation. Decisions are made through an organized process, and a strict command and control structure is present at all times. In bureaucratic structure designs, the authority is at the top and information is then flowed from top to bottom. This causes for more rules and standards for the company which operational process is watched with close supervision. Some advantages for bureaucratic structure designs for top-level managers are they have a tremendous control over organisational structure decisions. This works best for managers who have a command and control style of managing. Strategic decision making is also faster because there are less people it has to go through to approve. Some disadvantages in bureaucratic structures are it can discourage creativity and innovation in the organisation. This can make it hard for a company to adapt to changing conditions in the marketplace.

3. *Post-bureaucratic:* The term Post-Bureaucratic is used in two senses in the organisational literature: One generic and one much more specific. In the generic sense the term post bureaucratic is often used to describe a range of ideas developed since the 1980s that specifically contrast themselves with Weber's ideal type bureaucracy. This may include total quality management, culture management and matrix management, amongst others. None of these however has left behind the core tenets of bureaucracy. Hierarchies still exist, authority is still Weber's rational, legal type, and the organisation is still rule bound. Heckscher, arguing along these lines, describes them as cleaned up bureaucracies, rather than a fundamental shift away from bureaucracy. Gideon Kunda, in his classic study of culture management at 'Tech' argued that "the essence of bureaucratic control—the formalization, codification and enforcement of rules and regulations—does not change in principle; it shifts focus from organisational structure to the organisation's culture".

Another smaller group of theorists have developed the theory of the post-bureaucratic Organisation and provides a detailed discussion which attempts to describe an organisation that is fundamentally non bureaucratic. Charles Heckscher has developed an ideal type, the post-bureaucratic organisation, in which decisions are based on dialogue and consensus rather than authority and command, the organisation is a network rather than a hierarchy, open at the boundaries (in direct contrast to culture management); there is an emphasis on meta-decision making rules rather than decision making rules. This sort of horizontal decision making by consensus model is often used in housing cooperatives, other cooperatives and when running a non-profit or community organisation. It is used in order to encourage participation and help to empower people who normally experience oppression in groups.

Still other theorists are developing a resurgence of interest in complexity theory and organisations, and have focused on how simple structures can be used to engender organisational adaptations. For instance, Miner et al. (2000) studied how simple structures could be used to generate improvisational outcomes in product development. Their study makes links to simple structures and improviser learning.

Contemporary Forms of Organisational Design

Every organisation has its own unique design depending on its technology, limits and potentials of its environment and the life cycle stage it follows. Following are the various forms of an organisation based on their design:

(i) The U-Form Organisation: In the U-Form Organisation, U stands for Unity. It is also called as "functional design" as it relies exclusively on the functional approach to departmentalization. Members of the organisation who perform the same functions are grouped together into departments. Such organisation requires perfect coordination to operate smoothly aiming the various departments, since each department is highly dependent on another.

The U-Form design has several advantages. It allows an organisation to staff each department with experts; it also facilitates wide spans of management and helps the Managing Director to maintain centralized authority. However, the U-form design shows decision-making and employees within each department may concentrate on their own function forgetting overall organisational goals. It tends to make it hard for organisation to monitor the performance of individual managers within each functional area. When the organisations grow, they often find that the disadvantages of the U-form tend to become more significant and adopt different designs as they evolve through their life cycles.

(ii) The H-Form Organisation: In the H-Form Organisation, H stands for Hybrid and is also known as Conglomerate. The design relics on product departmentalization with the various products constituting different businesses. This design usually results from the corporate strategy of unrelated diversification of the products. This design has two advantages. First, such an organisation can protect itself from cyclical fluctuations in a single industry. The loss in one product is compensated by profit in another. Secondly, an organisation can buy and sell its individual businesses with little or no disruption to the others. The main disadvantage of this form of organisation is that it is complex and diverse thereby creating difficulty for top managers in having knowledge about all products.

(iii) The M-Form Organisation: In the M-Form Organisation, M stands for Multi-Divisional and it is called the Divisional Design. It is similar to the H-form design but has one notable distinction. Most of its businesses are in the same or related industries. For example, an organisation with an M-form design might own one business that manufactures automobile batteries, other that manufactures tyre and still another that manufactures car polish. Although each is distinct from the other but still related, in terms of manufacturing products that is used by automobile owners. Thus, the M-form design is used to implement a corporate strategy of related diversification.

A primary advantage of the M-form organisation is that it can achieve a great deal of synergy in its operations. For example, a consumer familiar with an organisation's batteries will be inclined to buy its tyres and car polish. Moreover, because the various units are in the same or related businesses, it is easy for top managers to understand, coordinate and control them. However, if the businesses are too closely related, the organisation cannot escape from the effect of cyclical fluctuations.

(iv) Functional Organisational Design: A Functional Organisational Design is a design that consists of activities such as coordination, supervision and task allocation. The organisational design determines how the organisation performs or operates. The term organisational design refers to how the people in an organisation are grouped and to whom they report. One traditional way of organizing people is by function. Some common functions within an organisation include production, marketing, human resources, and accounting. Example of such organisational design is shown in Fig. 10.1.

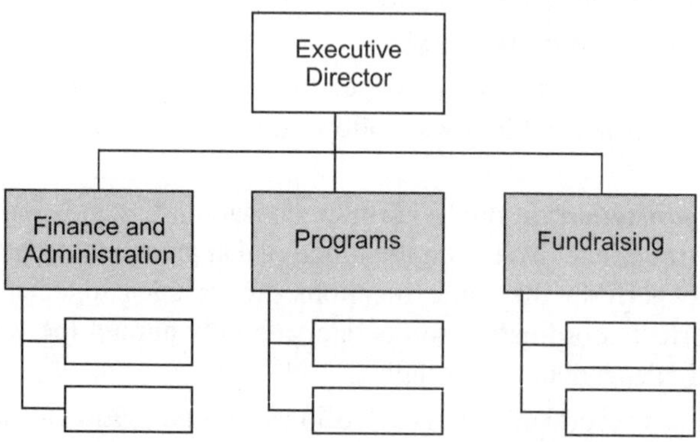

Fig. 10.1: Showing functional organisational design

This kind of organisational structure classifies people according to the function they perform in the organisation. The organisation chart for a functional based organisation consists of: Vice President, sales department, customer service department, engineering or production department, accounting department and administrative department.

This organizing of specialization leads to operational efficiencies where employees become specialists within their own realm of expertise. The most typical problem with a functional organisational structure is however that communication within the company can be rather rigid, making the organisation slow and inflexible. Therefore, lateral communication between functions becomes very important, so that information is disseminated, not only vertically, but also horizontally within the organisation.

Employees within the functional divisions of an organisation tend to perform a specialized set of tasks, for instance the engineering department would be staffed only with software engineers. This leads to operational efficiencies within that group. However it could also lead to a lack of communication between the functional groups within an organisation, making the organisation slow and inflexible.

As a whole, a functional organisation is best suited as a producer of standardized goods and services at large volume and low cost. Coordination and specialization of tasks are centralized in a functional structure, which makes producing a limited amount of products or services efficient and predictable. Moreover, efficiencies can further be realized as functional organisations integrate their activities vertically so that products are sold and distributed quickly and at low cost. For instance, a small business could make components used in production of its products instead of buying them.

Communication in organisations with functional organisational design can be rigid because of the standardized ways of operation and the high degree of formalization. This can further make the decision-making process slow and inflexible.

Even though functional units design often perform with a high level of efficiency, their level of cooperation with each other is sometimes compromised. Such groups may have difficulty working well with each other as they may be territorial and unwilling to cooperate. The occurrence of infighting among units may cause delays, reduced commitment due to competing interests, and wasted time, making projects fall behind schedule. This ultimately can bring down production levels overall, and the company-wide employee commitment toward meeting organisational goals.

(v) Divisional Structure Design: The Divisional Structure Design or product structure design is a configuration of an organisation, which breaks down the company into divisions that are self-contained. A division is self-contained and consists of collections of functions which work to produce a product. It also utilizes a plan to compete and operate as a separate business or profit center. According to Zainbooks.com, divisional structure in America is seen as the second most common structure for organisation today.

Employees, who are responsible for certain market services of types of products, are placed in divisional structure in order to increase their flexibility. The process can be further broken down into geographic (for example a US Division and an EU division), and product services for different consumers; companies or households). Another example of divisional structure design would be an automobile company which utilizes a divisional structure. The company would have one division for trucks, another for SUV'S, and another for cars. The divisions may also have their own departments such as marketing, sales, and engineering.

The advantage of divisional structure design is that it uses delegated authority so the performance can be directly measured with each group. This results in managers performing better and high employee morale. Another advantage of using divisional structure design is that it is more efficient in coordinating work between different divisions, and there is more flexibility to respond when there is a change in the market. Also, a company will have a simpler process if they need to change the size of the business by either adding or removing divisions. When divisional structure design is utilized more specialization can occur within the groups. When divisional structure is organized by product, the customer has their own advantages especially when only a few services or products are offered which differs greatly. When using divisional structures design that are organized by either markets or geographic areas they generally have similar function and are located in different regions or markets. This allows business decisions and activities coordinated locally.

The disadvantages of the divisional structure design are that it can support unhealthy rivalries among divisions. This type of structure design may increase costs by requiring more qualified managers for each division. Also, there is usually an over-emphasis on divisional more than organisational goals which results in duplication of resources and efforts like staff services, facilities, and personnel.

(vi) Product Structure: A Product Structure is based on organizing employees and work on the basis of the different types of products. If the company produces three different types of products, they will have three different divisions for these products. Following is the product based organisational design. Example of such organisational design is shown Fig. 10.2:

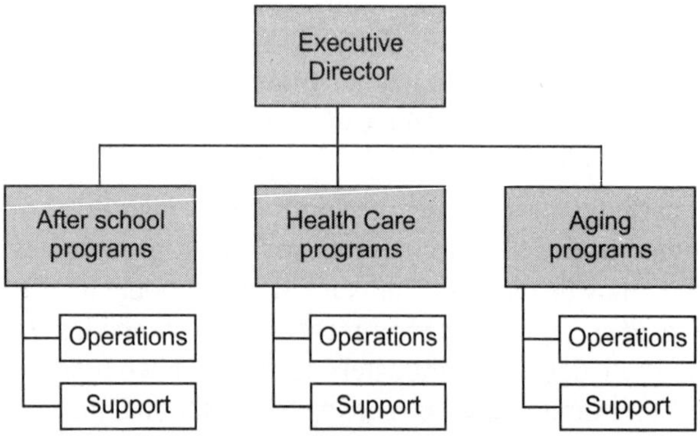

Fig. 10.2: Showing product structure based organisational design

(vii) Line Structure: This has a very specific line of command. The approvals and orders in this kind of structure come from top to bottom in a line. Hence the name is line structure. This kind of structure is suitable for smaller organisations. This is the sort of structure allows for easy decision making, and is very informal in nature. They have fewer departments, which makes the entire organisation a much decentralized one.

(viii) Line and Staff Structure: Line and Staff Structure combines the line structure where information and approvals come from top to bottom, with staff departments for support and specialization. Line and staff organisational structures are more centralized. Managers of line and staff have authority over their subordinates, but staff managers have no authority over line managers and their subordinates. The decision making process becomes slower in this type of organisational structure because of the layers and guidelines that are typical to it, and the formality involved. Example of such organisational design is shown in Fig. 10.3:

(ix) Market Structure: Market Structure is used to group employees on the basis of specific market. The company sells in a company could have three different markets they use and according to this structure, each would be a separate division in the structure.

(x) Matrix Structure Design: The Matrix Structure Design groups' employees by both function and product. This organisational design can combine the best of both separate structures. A matrix

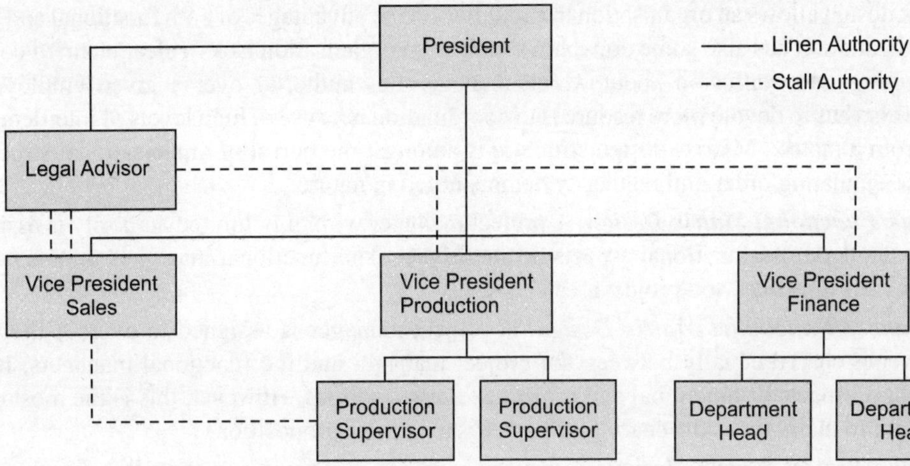

Fig. 10.3: Showing line and staff based organisational design

organisation frequently uses teams of employees to accomplish work, in order to take advantage of the strengths, as well as make up for the weaknesses, of functional and decentralized forms. An example would be a company that produces two products, "product A" and "product B". Using the matrix structure, this company would organize functions within the company as follows: "product A" sales department, "product A" customer service department, "product A" accounting, "product B" sales department, "product B" customer service department, "product B" accounting department. Matrix is a structure, which has a combination of function and product structures. This combines both the best of both worlds to make an efficient organisational structure. This structure is the most complex organisational structure, Example of such organisational design is shown in Fig. 10.4.

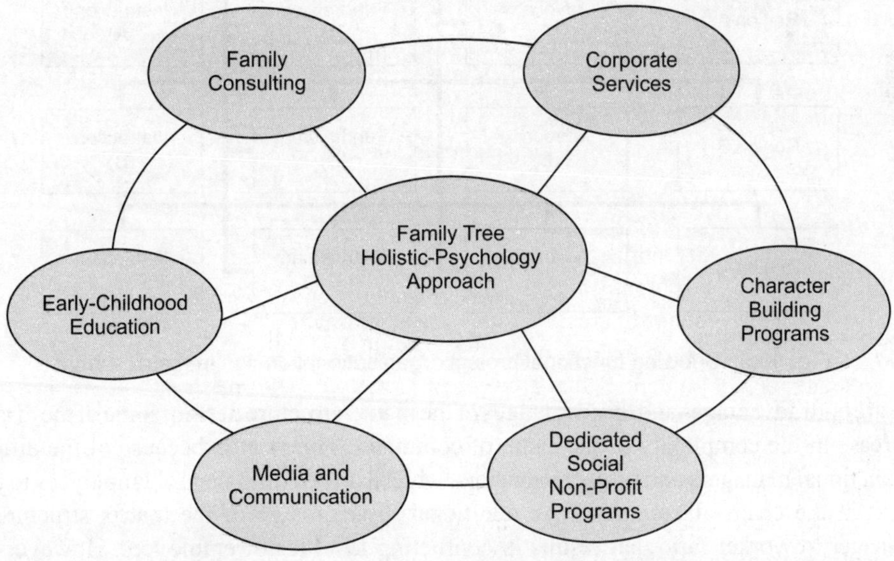

Fig. 10.4: Showing matrix organisational design

A matrix design allows an organisation to capitalize on the advantages of both functional and product departmentalization. It has also some drawbacks such as an organisation lacks a clear chain of command thereby resulting into confusion about which manager lies authority over a given employee. The organisation also has to devote more resources to coordination because of high levels of interdependence that result from a matrix. Matrix design structure is amongst the purest of organisational structures, a simple lattice emulating order and regularity demonstrated in nature.

(*a*) ***Weak/Functional Matrix Design:*** A project manager with only limited authority is assigned to oversee the cross-functional aspects of the project. The functional managers maintain control over their resources and project areas.

(*b*) ***Balanced/Functional Matrix Design:*** A project manager is assigned to oversee the project. Power is shared equally between the project manager and the functional managers. It brings the best aspects of functional and projectized organisations. However, this is the most difficult system to maintain as the sharing of power is a delicate proposition.

(*c*) ***Strong/Project Matrix Design:*** A project manager is primarily responsible for the project. Functional managers provide technical expertise and assign resources as needed.

Matrix structure design is only one of three major structures such as Functional and Project structure. Matrix management is more dynamic then functional management, in that it is a combination of all the other structures and allows team members to share information more readily across task boundaries. It also allows for specialization that can increase depth of knowledge in a specific sector or segment. Example of such organisational design is shown in Fig. 10.5.

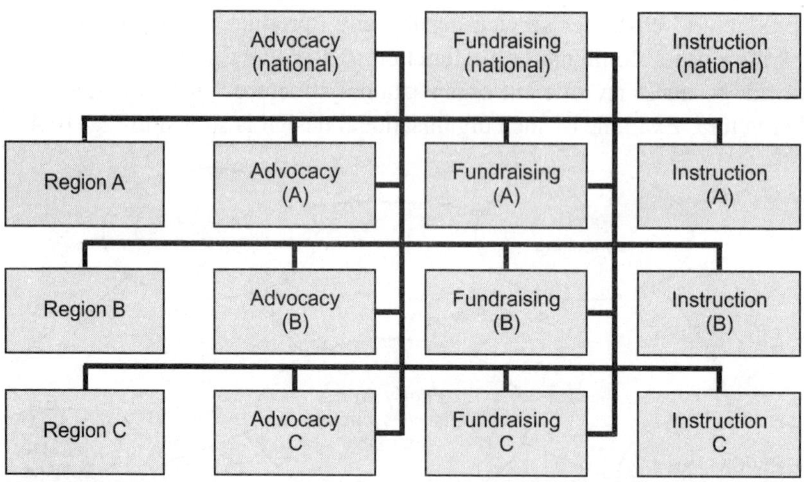

Fig. 10.5: Showing functional/project organisational design in matrix format

There are both advantages and disadvantages of the matrix structure design; some of the disadvantages are an increase in the complexity of the chain of command. This occurs because of the differentiation between functional managers and project managers, which can be confusing for employees to understand who is next in the chain of command. An additional disadvantage of the matrix structure design is higher manager to worker ratio that results in conflicting loyalties of employees. However the matrix structure also has significant advantages that make it valuable for companies to use. The matrix structure design improves upon the "silo" critique of functional management, in that it diminishes the vertical structure of functional management and creates a more horizontal structure which allows the spread of information across task boundaries to happen much quicker. Moreover, matrix structure design allows for specialization that can increase depth of knowledge & allows individuals to be chosen according to project needs. This correlation between individuals and project needs is what produces the concept of maximizing strengths and minimizing weaknesses. This leads to the emergence of hybrid organisation by combining various models but giving more emphasis in one model. Example of such organisational design is shown in Fig. 10.5.

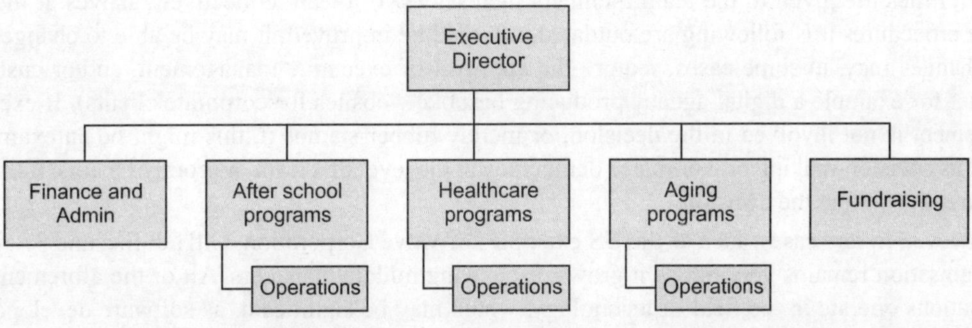

Fig. 10.6: Showing horizontal organisational design in matrix format

(xi) Flat or Horizontal Organisational Design: A flat organisation (also known as horizontal organisation or delayering) is an organisation that has an organisational structure with few or no levels of middle management between staff and executives. The idea is that well-trained workers will be more productive when they are more directly involved in the decision making process, rather than closely supervised by many layers of management.

This structure is generally possible only in smaller organisations or individual units within larger organisations. When they reach a critical size, organisations can retain a streamlined structure but cannot keep a completely flat manager-to-staff relationship without impacting productivity. Certain financial responsibilities may also require a more conventional structure. Some theorize that flat organisation designs become more traditionally hierarchical when they begin to be geared towards productivity.

The flat organisation design model promotes employee involvement through a decentralized decision-making process. By elevating the level of responsibility of baseline employees and eliminating layers of middle management, comments and feedback reach all personnel involved in decisions more quickly. Expected response to customer feedback becomes more rapid.

The flat design is common in small companies (entrepreneurial start-ups, university spin offs). As companies grow they tend to become more complex and hierarchical, which leads to an expanded structure, with more levels and departments.

The "strong form" of a flat organisation design is an organisation with no middle managers at all. Very small businesses may lack middle managers because there are too few staff to justify hiring middle managers; in this type of organisation, the business owner or the CEO may perform some of the functions performed by middle managers in larger organisations. However, some organisations do not take on middle managers even as they become larger, and remain extremely flat.

An organisation which has self-managing teams, that organize their own work without the need for a middle manager or supervisor above the team, may meet or closely approximate this model. This can cause conflicts with people whose career path expectations include a promotion, which may not be available within the organisation due to its flat structure. However, alternative "horizontal" career paths may be available, such as developing greater expertise in a role or mastery of a craft, and/or receiving pay rises for loyalty.

An absence of middle managers does not preclude the adoption and retention of mandatory work procedures, including quality assurance procedures. However, due to the fact that significant responsibilities are given to the team members themselves, if a team collectively arrives at the view that the procedures it is following are outdated, or could be improved, it may be able to change them. Such changes may, in some cases, require the approval of executive management, and/or customers (consider for example a digital agency producing bespoke websites for corporate clients). If executive management is not involved in the decision, or merely rubber-stamps it, this might be an example of consensus decision-making or workplace democracy at the level of a team or group of teams, if multiple teams are involved in the decision.

However, in rare cases, such as the US examples of Valve Corporation, GitHub Inc. and 37 signals, the organisation remains very flat as it grows, eschewing middle managers. All of the aforementioned organisations operate in the field of technology, which may be significant, as software developers are highly skilled professionals, much like lawyers. Senior lawyers also enjoy a relatively high degree of autonomy within a typical law firm, which is typically structured as a partnership rather than a hierarchical bureaucracy. Some other types of professional organisations are also commonly structured as partnerships, such as accountancy companies like KPMG or Ferguson.

(xii) Team Organisational Design: One of the newest organisational designs developed in the 20th century is team. In small businesses, the team design can define the entire organisation. Teams can be both horizontal and vertical. While an organisation is constituted as a set of people who synergize individual competencies to achieve newer dimensions, the quality of organisational design revolves around the competencies of teams in totality. For example, everyone of the Whole Foods Market stores, the largest natural-foods grocer in the US developing a focused strategy, is an autonomous profit centre composed of an average of 10 self-managed teams, while team leaders in each store and each region are also a team. Larger bureaucratic organisations can benefit from the flexibility of teams as well. Xerox, Motorola, and Dailmer Chrysler are all among the companies that actively use teams to perform tasks.

(xiii) Network Organisational Design: Another modern design structure is network. While business giants risk becoming too clumsy to pro-act (such as), act and react efficiently, the new network organisations contract out any business function that can be done better or more cheaply. In essence, managers in network structures spend most of their time coordinating and controlling external relations, usually by electronic means. H&M is outsourcing its clothing to a network of 700 suppliers, more than two-thirds of which are based in low-cost Asian countries. Not owning any factories, H&M can be more flexible than many other retailers in lowering its costs, which aligns with its low-cost strategy. The potential management opportunities offered by recent advances in complex networks theory have been demonstrated including applications to product design and development, and innovation problem in markets and industries.

(xiv) Virtual Organisational Design: Virtual Organisational Design is defined as being closely coupled upstream with its suppliers and downstream with its customers such that where one begins and the other ends means little to those who manage the business processes within the entire organisation. A special form of boundaryless organisation is virtual. Hedberg, Dahlgren, Hansson, and Olve (1999) consider the virtual organisation as not physically existing as such, but enabled by software to exist. The virtual organisation design exists within a network of alliances, using the Internet. This means while the core of the organisation can be small but still the company can operate globally be a market leader in its niche. According to Anderson, because of the unlimited shelf space of the Web, the cost of reaching niche goods is falling dramatically. Although none sell in huge numbers, there are so many niche products that collectively they make a significant profit, and that is what made highly innovative Amazon.com so successful.

(xv) Hierarchy-Community Phenotype Model of Organisational Design: In the 21st century, even though most, if not all, organisations are not of a pure hierarchical design structure, many managers are still blind-sided to the existence of the flat community structure within their organisations.

The business firm is no longer just a place where people come to work. For most of the employees, the firm confers on them that sense of belonging and identity, the firm has become their "village", their community. The business firm of the 21st century is not just a hierarchy which ensures maximum efficiency and profit; it is also the community where people belong to and grow together, where their affective and innovative needs are met.

Lim, Griffiths, and Sambrook (2010) developed the Hierarchy-Community Phenotype Model of Organisational Structure borrowing from the concept of Phenotype from genetics. A phenotype refers to the observable characteristics of an organism. It results from the expression of an organism's genes and the influence of the environment. The expression of an organism's genes is usually determined by pairs of alleles. Alleles are different forms of a gene. In their model, each employee's formal, hierarchical participation and informal community participation within the organisation, as influenced by his or her environment, contributes to the overall observable characteristics (phenotype) of the organisation. In other words, just as all the pair of alleles within the genetic material of an organism determines the physical characteristics of the organism, the combined expressions of all the employees' formal hierarchical and informal community participation within an organisation give rise to the organisational structure. Due to the vast potentially different combination of the employees' formal hierarchical and informal community participation, each organisation is therefore a unique phenotype along a spectrum between a pure hierarchy and a pure community (flat) organisational structure. Example of such organisational design is shown in Fig. 10.7.

Virtual organisational design popularly known as 'E' Organisation will have the following characteristics:

1. ***There are no generally accepted rules:*** There are no established and proven e-org models or strategic plans. What worked in March may be scrapped in May. E-orgs in their infancy and players are being forced to experiment.
2. ***Victory goes to the quick:*** Fast to no longer fast enough. It used to be that the big would eat the small. In an e-word, the fast eat the slow. Competition is forcing e-organisations to make decisions quickly, develop new products and service in record time, move into market fast, and be able to respond to competitive actions immediately. The old saying "Ready, Aim, Fire" has been replaced by "Fire, Ready, Aim".

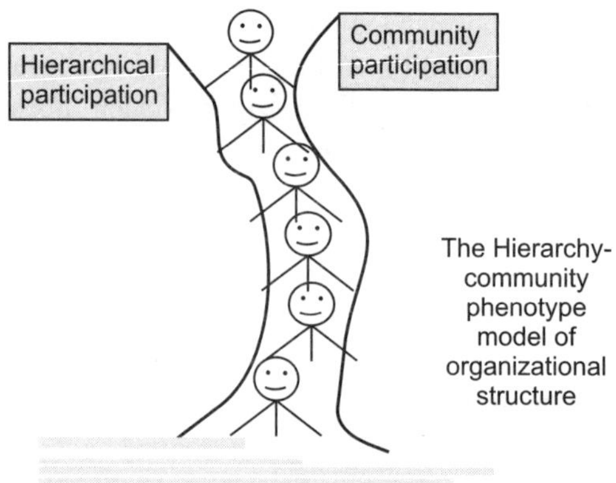

Fig. 10.7: Showing Hierarchy-Community phenotype model of organisational design

3. ***Location doesn't matter:*** In the past, the people you hired, the suppliers you used and the customers you serviced were largely defined by your geographic location. For instance, you hired from the labour pool from Bangalore to New Delhi or tried to entire prospective employees to move from where they lived to where your organisation was located. Now, through network linkages, employers in remote locations can have access to the best and brightest. And talented people no longer have to move their residence to pursue job opportunities in faraway places.
4. ***Integrated information is everything:*** Intranets, Extranets and the Internet have changed the way that information can move inside organisations. Open and integrated information systems allow bypassing of traditional organisational hierarchies; making it easy for employees and managers alike to track projects, democratising internal decision making; and closely linking organisations to their suppliers, partners and customers.

(xvi) Global Organisation: An organisation, which has assets in more than one country other than its home country is called as Global Organisation. Such companies have offices and/or factories in different countries and usually have a centralized head office where they coordinate the global management. These organisations have centralized head office in their home country that controls their various offices in other parts of the world. A global organisation must modify and adapt its design to allow it to function effectively, e.g. Nestle is a big global organisation and highly decentralized. US organisational design is like an umbrella. Nestle's various organisations scattered around the world are operated by its own general managers, who are empowered with a great deal of autonomy and authority to make decisions. As a result, Nestle is almost a confederation of independent operating organisations. Its design is similar to the M-form but because the operating units are so far apart that there is little synergy.

It is to be remembered that there is no one best form of design that all organisations should adopt. Each organisation has to carefully assess its own strategy, its strengths and weaknesses, its history, its technology, environment, life cycle and size. It must then choose a design that fit these elements most effectively.

10.4 ORGANISATION STRUCTURES AND THEIR EFFECT ON HUMAN BEHAVIOUR

The structure of any organisation will affect the following:

(*a*) Behaviour of how people act and work

(*b*) Motivation of workers

(*c*) Performance

(*d*) Teamwork and cooperation

(*e*) Intergroup and interdepartmental relationships.

Management decisions and actions that result in a specific organisation structure and work specification including (1) Work Specification; specify to what degree the tasks are subdivided into separate jobs, (2) Departmentalization 'the basis in which jobs will be grouped together, (3) Chain of Command, to whom do individuals and groups report to, (4) Span of Control, the number of people that a can manage efficiently and effectively direct, (5) Centralization and Decentralization where is the decision making authority? (6) Formalization to what degree be rules and regulations to direct employees and managers? (7) Division of Labour/specialization is a process of identifying the specific jobs that need to be done and designing the people who will perform them. Job specialization can occur in 3 different ways (*a*) Personal Specialties like occupational and professional specialties e.g., accountants, engineers, scientists, (*b*) Horizontal Specialties means work is divided by the natural sequence order e.g., manufacturing plants divide work into fabricating and assembly and (*c*) Vertical Specialties means work is divided along the vertical plane of an organisation from the lowest level manager to the highest level manager.

Delegation of Authority means process of distributing authority downwards in an organisation. Whether an organisation chooses to centralize or decentralize will be guided by:

1. How routine and straightforward are the job's required decisions?
2. Are individuals competent to make decisions?
3. Are individuals motivated to make the decisions?

Reasons to decentralize authority are as follows: It encourages the development of professional managers. Managers are able to exercise more autonomy but it can lead to a competitive climate. Reasons to centralize authority are as follows: When the managers are not skilled enough and would need further training which can be expensive. When there are new administrative costs because new divisions need to be formed. Decentralization can mean duplication of functions.

The process of grouping jobs into logical units. The process in which an organisation is structurally divided by combining jobs in departments according to some shared characteristics. Functional Departmentalization, Geographical and Product Span of Control is the number of individuals who report to a specific manager. Three factors are important in determining optimum span of control such as Required Contact, Degree of Specialization and Ability to Communicate.

Often, growth would result in bureaucracy, the most prevalent structure in the past. It is still, however, relevant in former Soviet Republics, China and most governmental organisations all over the world. Shell Group used to represent the typical bureaucracy: Top-heavy and hierarchical. It featured multiple levels of command and duplicate service companies existing in different regions. All this made Shell apprehensive to market changes, leading to its incapacity to grow and develop further. The talents in the structure will neither be recognized nor be appreciated and the promotion is based on seniority. Employees are frustrated and productivity and output remain either negative or very low. The failure of this structure became the main reason for the company restructuring into a matrix.

Starbucks is one of the numerous large organisations that successfully developed the matrix structure supporting their focused strategy. Its design combines functional and product based divisions, with employees reporting to two heads. Creating a team spirit, the company empowers employees to make their own decisions and train them to develop both hard and soft skills. Some OB experts also mention the multinational design, common in global companies, such as Procter & Gamble, Toyota and Hindustan Unilever. This structure can be seen as a complex form of the matrix, as it maintains coordination among products, functions and geographic areas. The talents in the structure will always be recognized and appreciated. Moreover the promotion is based on merit and achievements. Employees are motivated and productivity and output remain very high.

In general, over the last decade, it has become increasingly clear that through the forces of globalization, competition and more demanding customers, the structure of many companies has become flatter, less hierarchical, more fluid and even virtual. However, e-orgs create social isolation and uncertainty. These conditions foster a need by employees for strong emotional bonds. Managers in e-orgs should consider, therefore, encouraging employees to more openly express their emotions than should managers in more traditional organisations. As the line separating employee's home life and work life increasingly blurs, employees need guidance as to which online behaviours are and are not acceptable.

Managers need to inform employees if, when, and how their work will be monitored; and managers need to create clear policy guidelines to reduce ethical ambiguities. Motivating employees in an e-org creates unique challenges for managers. For example, managers need to make jobs interesting to minimize the distraction of "going online". And to hire and keep professional and technical employees, who are in short supply, management should design creative compensation and benefit program that will appeal to these employee's varied needs. Communication in e-orgs is able to cut across vertical and horizontal levels. Employees can communicate instantly anytime, with anyone, anywhere. But this openness also increases the likelihood that employees will experience communication overload. To help employees, managers should encourage people to screen communications carefully, prioritized demands on their time, and engage in other time-management techniques.

Managers who have worked in both traditional and e-organisations say that leadership is different in e-orgs because of the increased importance of speed, flexibility, and the need to provide direction through vision. Additionally, the change and instability typical in an e-org places a higher premium on managers creating a trusting climate with their employees. Politics in e-organisations is not limited to face-to-face interactions. Traditional political activities, such as water cooler conversation, are expanded in e-orgs to include cyber-schmoozing via the electronic grapevine.

Effective managers in e-orgs will recognise this added dimension to political channels and attempt message. Monitoring electronic communications is made further necessary to ensure that the Internet and e-mail are not used to harass or discriminate against others. Electronic communication networks are reshaping the workplace and redesigning jobs. But they are also putting employees in front of CRT monitors for hours at a time and increasing the risk of fatigue, eyestrain, and repetitive-motion injuries. Management, in cooperation with architects and industrial engineers need to design workplaces that are ergonomically effective. The success or failure of an organisation depends, to a large degree, on the quality of the people it hires. Managers in e-orgs need to pay particular attention in hiring to finding job candidates who are not only competent in their area of expertise, but who can handle high levels of uncertainty and change, who work well on teams, can endure long hours, and handle intense work pressures.

(a) Making Organisation Design Decisions

Given the many choices of structure, how do you go about making organisation design decision for business in hand? Different organisation structures have different benefits in different situations. What matters is the overall organisation design is aligned with the business strategy and the market environment in which the business operates. It must then have the right business controls, the right flexibility, the right incentives, the right people and the right resources.

Develop a clear mission statement for the organisation. Focus the organisation structure around the mission statement. The mission statement should include the inter-relationship between workers at every level as well as inspiring innovation and ensuring efficiency. Decide whether the organisation structure will be centralized and formal or decentralized and informal. For centralized and formal organisations, the organisation structure takes more of a top-down approach with strictly defined work roles. For decentralized and informal organisations, there is more of a cooperative approach with workers often performing a wide range of functions. The organisation structure can be department based or based on a particular project or process. Department-based organisation structure is often divided into line functions (such as manufacturing) and staff functions (such as human resources).

Design the overall chain of command for the organisation. If there is a single overall director or leader, determine the title for that role. If there are dual or multiple leaders, divide the overall company function between the various roles in a way that there is a clear unity of command. Add subordinate roles to the chain of command. Determine the process of reporting from subordinate to supervisor and make allowances for special circumstances (such as an emergency). Indicate if and how interactions across departments or projects will take place. Determine the authority and responsibility to be assigned to each position in the organisation structure. Attempt to achieve a minimum of overlapping functions. Also, attempt to minimize any possible confusion by subordinates concerning which supervisors to consult with on specific issues.

Following are the essential factors that you can consider when thinking about the structure of organisation in question:

1. ***Strategy:*** The organisation design must support the business strategy. If organisation intends to be innovative then a hierarchical structure will not work. If however, business strategy is based on low cost, high volume delivery then a rigid structure with tight controls may be the best design.
2. ***Size:*** The design must take into account the size of organisation. A small organisation could be paralyzed by too much specialization. In larger organisations, on the other hand, there may be economies of scale that can be gained by maintaining functionally specialist departments and teams. A large organisation has more complex decision making needs and some decision making responsibilities are likely to be devolved or decentralized.
3. ***Environment:*** If the environment in which the business functions in customers, suppliers, regulators, etc., is highly unpredictable or volatile, then the organisation needs to be flexible enough to react to this.
4. ***Controls:*** What level of control is right in business in question? Some activities need special controls (such as patient services in hospitals, money handling in banks and maintenance in air transport) whilst others are more efficient when there is a high degree of flexibility.

5. ***Incentives:*** Incentives and rewards must be aligned with the business's strategy and purpose. When these are misaligned, there is a danger that units within the organisation become self-serving.

There is much more to organisation design than deciding on its structure. The above lists show just some of the facets organisation design that can be taken into accounting thinking about this. With each stage of growth or each change, the organisation design needs to be reassessed and realigned as necessary. Now just think of designing a global organisation in AD 2020 after completing your education and hopefully after serving few years in the industry. Before that, look at the symptoms of ineffective organisation design and likely root causes.

Symptoms of an ineffective organization	Likely root causes: Leadership	Decision-making & structure	People	Work processes & systems	Culture
Lack of coordination: work unfinished, teams isolated, out-of step	X	X		X	
Excessive conflict: Needless friction among internal groups	X	X	X		
Unclear roles: Functions overlap and/or fall through the cracks		X			
Gap in skills or misused resources: missing or underutilized skills or resources	X		X	X	
Poor work flow: Disruptions, cumbersome processes				X	
Reduced responsiveness: Slow reactions to environmental shifts	X	X			X
Conflicting communications: external stakeholders confused, complaining				X	
Low staff morale: lack of confidence or drive; poor teaming	X				X

Note: "People" causes of excessive conflict are typically related to poor performance measures or incentives, not lack of talent or skill per se.

Source: Strategic Organization Design: An Integrated Approach, Mercer Delta Consulting (2000); Interview with Peter Thies, Equinox Organizational Consulting; Bridgespan analysis.

Fig. 10.8: Showing symptoms of ineffective organisation design and likely root causes

Source: http://www.bridgespan.org/getmedia/b1139597

(b) Designing a Global Organisation in AD 2020—Some Thoughts

Imagine that you make electronic components for the auto industry. You receive a large order from a global auto manufacturer for rapidly designing and delivering a new type of electronic sensors in three different sizes. Completing the order requires frequent consultation among design experts, material suppliers, software developers and strategic allies who are stationed in three different time zones, and speak five different languages. Or, you are a manufacturer and exporter of industrial chemicals. You find that you must frequently communicate with vendors, customers, chemical experts, freight forwarders, foreign banks, regulatory agencies, and custom officials from all across the globe to effectively run your business.

More and more business now finds themselves operating amidst such global scenarios. Increasingly, they find the need for consultative interaction among diverse experts, separated by functional lines, geographic boundaries and language barriers. Dramatic changes in science, information technology, consumer lifestyle and government legislation has globalised markets and complicated business decision-making, thereby intensifying the need for frequent managerial consultation and information exchange. To effectively facilitate this exchange, firms must restructure their organisation. The emphasis in this new organisation will not be on managing men and material flow but on managing human intellect and information flow. To be congruent with this shift in focus, managerial philosophy, structural forms and management practices must also correspondingly change.

1. ***Traditional Vs Today's Organisation:*** The Traditional Organisation aimed at operational efficiency that yesterday's markets and competitive environment demanded. Markets of the past were homogenous, staid and most importantly, regional. Customer tastes were stable and local, technological change was predictable and foreign competitive entry in the form of superior products was non-existent. The single factor contributing to competitive success in this steady environment was efficiency in current operations. Companies achieved this by standardising tasks and sequentially organising work. Any behaviour-related deviation to this arrangement was controlled through rules and standard operating procedures. Market related deviations were controlled by vertical integration strategies. What emerged was a rigid organisation that guaranteed efficiency by performing the current task repeatedly and preventing change. That was a machine bureaucracy.

Today's environment demands an organisation that is flexible, besides being efficient and global. Customer tastes have become differentiated and a firm should customize design, packaging, and delivery to effectively serve multiple segments. Technologies are rapidly changing and it is imperative for a firm to frequently innovate and offer higher quality products at standard prices to remain competitive. Markets have become global and a firm must employ global procurement, processing and distribution strategies to be effective. It must design products in one place, make the components in another, assemble them in a third place and market/deliver them globally.

To be successful in this environment, a firm must have the ability to efficiently manage and move information across the globe rapidly. Moving materials, from one stage of processing to the next, will be uneconomical and unwise in the emerging scenario. The focus in today's organisation is thus on the management and transfer of knowledge and information globally as opposed to the management and transfer of tangible materials.

2. ***Create a Learning Environment:*** If information sharing is a vital attribute for a global firm, its personnel must be capable of sending and receiving critical information. To effectively achieve this, organisational members must be well informed all the time. A learning environment is thus sine quinine for a global firm. Managerial decisions and organisational systems in this firm must emphasis continuous company-wide learning as a dominant value. For a learning environment to emerge, top management commitment towards pursuit and acquisition of new information, distribution mechanisms to share learned information and an adaptive mentality must be present.

To realize these, managers must act more as coaches, information providers and facilitators of knowledge acquisition, rather than as allocators and controllers of organisational resources. They must aggressively empower employees and additionally foster a risk-driven organisational culture, wherein employees experiment and encounter failures but learn from their mistakes. 3-M, Sony, and Motorola are some examples of successful global firms that adopt an experimentation approach in organising, to encourage risk-taking and consequent learning. Seeking management's permission to try a new method is considered as loathsome in these firms. What is viewed as an appropriate behaviour is, asking forgiveness rather than requesting permission.

Some successful global firms use benchmark techniques as a learning tool. Ford Motor Company learned how to create an "invoice-less system" in its supplier relations by benchmarking Mazda's accounts payable operations. Xerox learned to be efficient in order fulfillment by benchmarking L.L. Bean's order filling techniques. Japanese firms generally use job rotation techniques for learning and some use temporary assignment of personnel to the customer, supplier or strategic alliance partner sites for this purpose. Some, such as 3-M, create a university type of environment within the firm by organizing educational seminars through which R&D personnel share their research results. Others regularly invite academicians for this purpose or send their personnel to seminars/workshops conducted by outsiders.

Yet others provide company-paid foreign travel to employees as a means to learn. Organisational learning is not just about acquiring new knowledge or updating current insights. It is also about unlearning what was previously learned. To be successful, learning strategies should include unlearning outmoded assumptions (for example), it is extremely difficult for Indian products to enter and successfully compete in the US market and old methods that are now obsolete. By encouraging employees to accept change and rewarding them for it, a firm can bring about the unlearning of previously learned information that is no longer relevant.

3. ***Adopt a Network Structure:*** A global organisation is one that transcends its home base by competing in international markets. To be successful as a global firm, it must be capable of responding to customer needs from diverse and distant markets, rapidly and effectively. Not only in virtual information flow from these markets to the firm's headquarters critical, but the headquarters should be capable of processing the received information effectively. A network structure is an appropriate arrangement for this purpose.

It has a well-informed headquarters staff; arranged according to functional lines, but with minimal hierarchy and maximal horizontal interaction that is achieved through cross-functional teams and committees. The field staff, spread across the globe, consists of specialist firms with whom the headquarters has a temporary relationship. Thus, one firm in the field may design the product, the second may make the components, and the third may assemble the end product, and so on, whereas the headquarters is responsible for coordinating activities among the field units.

The network is thus a flexible organisation with several loosely hanging satellites as members of the network. Members are held together by partnership or alliance contracts that emphasis the pursuit of common goals. Membership in the network often changes, depending on the needs of the headquarters firm or when a member is no longer needed because goals have been met.

Nike is a good example of a network organisation with field subcontractors operating in China, South Korea, Taiwan and Thailand. The subcontractors act as independent units, making and selling sneakers globally while Nike engages in R & D activities, providing design information to the subcontractors. Nike is able to respond faster to changes in the fashion environment by rearranging the network.

4. *Cultivate a Global Manager Mindset:* A global firm requires a band of managers with a global knowledge-frame and mindset. These managers must have the knowledge, attitude and requisite competence to effectively deal with foreign government agencies and non-business stakeholder. This means proficiency in communication and in cross-country politics, cultures and economics. Managers of global firms should especially be: familiar with the functioning of the supranational entities such as the WTO and the European Union and various regional trading blocks such as ASEAN and NAFTA, skilled in representing his/her company at international business gatherings, trade shows and conferences; able to effectively handle foreign TV media and press conferences; aware of the norms and values of predominant foreign cultures; and well-informed about diplomatic protocol, etiquette and practice. By encouraging managers to take university courses that cover the gamut of international politics, diplomacy and trade issues, a firm can satisfy its needs in this area. Alternatively, these criteria may be included in managerial selection and in house training.

To summarize, designing a global organisation is complex and requires several competing elements to be judiciously balanced. No model recipe exists and one can proceed in this area only through incremental adjustments. By fine-tuning organisational elements in a methodical and systematic manner, a firm must be able to arrive at a structure that is ideal for its purpose.

10.5 ORGANISATIONAL CLIMATE

Perhaps one of the most important and significant characteristics of a great workplace is its organisational climate. Organisation climate is the properties of the business environment in a workplace observed by staff that strongly influence their actions and job performance. For example, a perceptive business manager might take the trouble to survey employees about the organisational climate to identify and promote those aspects that are most conducive to achieving corporate objectives, also called corporate climate. Organisational climate, while defined differently by many researchers and scholars, generally it refers to the degree to which an organisation focuses on and emphasizes:

- Innovation,
- Flexibility,
- Appreciation and recognition,
- Concern for employee well-being,
- Learning and development,
- Citizenship and ethics,
- Quality performance,
- Involvement and empowerment, and
- Leadership.

Organisational climate (sometimes known as Corporate Climate) is the process of quantifying the "culture" of an organisation; it precedes the notion of organisational culture. It is a set of properties of the work environment, perceived directly or indirectly by the employees, that is assumed to be a major force in influencing employee behaviour. Climate and culture are both important aspects of the overall context, environment or situation.

Even though organisational culture and organisational climate are sometimes used interchangeably, there are certain differences between the two. According to Bowditch and Buono, "Organisational culture is concerned with the nature of beliefs and expectations about organisational life, while climate is an indicator of whether those beliefs and expectations are being fulfilled". Organisational climate is a relatively enduring quality of the internal environment that is experienced by its members, influences their behaviour, and can be described in terms of the values of a particular set of characteristics. In short organisational climate is a set of characteristics and factors of the organisation that are perceived by the employees and which serve as a major force in influencing their behaviour. These factors may include job descriptions, performance arid evaluation standards, leadership style, challenges and innovations.

(a) Factors Affecting Organisational Climate: In every organisation, there exist certain factors that exert deep influence on the climate. Schneider and Barlett describe six factors that have an influence over organisational climate such as managerial support, inter-agency conflict, agent dependence and general satisfaction. Lawrence James and Allan Jones have identified five factors influencing climate, which include management philosophy, organisational structure and process, which include communication, motivation and leadership, physical environment and values.

Similarly, Kahn has identified factors such as rules orientation, the nurture of subordinates, strict supervision and promotional achievement orientation. Thus, it is very difficult to generalize exactly the factors affecting the climate. Organisational climate has a major influence on human performance through its impact on the motivation, job satisfaction and attitudes of people.

The organisation climate is something that is senses rather than something that is recognized cognitively. Climate is a set of attributes which can be perceived about a particular organisation and/or its sub systems, and that may be induced from the way the organisation and/or its sub systems deal with their members and environments. It is the combined perceptions of individuals that are useful in differentiating organisations according to their procedures and practices. In short it is the combined and collective view of people within the organisation as to the nature of the environment in which they work.

Further, organisational culture tends to be shared by all or most members of some social group; is something that older members usually try to pass on to younger members; shapes behaviour and structures perceptions of the world. Cultures are often studied and understood at a national level, such as the American or French culture. Culture includes deeply held values, beliefs and assumptions, symbols, heroes and rituals. Culture can be examined at an organisational level as well. The main distinction between organisational and national culture is that people can choose to join a place of work, but are usually born into a national culture.

Organisational climate, on the other hand, is often defined as the recurring patterns of behaviour, attitudes and feelings that characterize life in the organisation while an organisation culture tends to be deep and stable. Although culture and climate are related, climate often proves easier to assess and change. At an individual level of analysis the concept is called individual psychological climate. These individual perceptions are often aggregated or collected for analysis and understanding at the team or group level, or the divisional, functional, or overall organisational level.

Organisational climate, manifested in a variety of human resource practices, is an important predictor of organisational success. Numerous research studies have found positive relationships between positive organisational climates and various measures of organisational success, most notably for metrics such as sales, staff retention, productivity, customer satisfaction and profitability:

- Denison (1990) found that an organisational climate that encourages employee involvement and empowerment in decision-making predicts the financial success of the organisation.
- Schneider (1996) found that service and performance climates predict customer satisfaction.
- Patterson, Warr and West (2004) found that manufacturing organisations that emphasized a positive organisational climate, specifically concern for employee well-being, flexibility, learning and performance, showed more productivity than those that emphasized these to a lesser degree.
- Potosky and Ramakrishna (2001) found that an emphasis on learning and skill development was significantly related to organisational performance.
- Ekvall (1996) found a positive relationship between climates emphasizing creativity and innovation and their profits.
- Hansen and Wernerfelt (1989) found that organisational climate factors explain about twice as much variance in profit rates as economic factors.
- Thompson (1996) found that companies utilizing progressive human resource practices impacting climate such as customer commitment, communication, empowerment, innovation, rewards and recognition, community involvement/environmental responsibility and teamwork outperformed organisations with less progressive practices.

Organisational climate clearly influences the success of an organisation. Many organisations, however, struggle to cultivate the climate they need to succeed and retain their most highly effective employees.

Hellriegel and Slocum (2006) explain that organisations can take steps to build a more positive and employee-centered climate through:

- ***Communication:*** How often and the types of means by which information is communicated in the organisation.
- ***Values:*** The guiding principles of the organisation and whether or not they are modeled by all employees, including leaders.
- ***Expectations:*** Types of expectations regarding how managers behave and make decisions.
- ***Norms:*** The normal, routine ways of behaving and treating one another in the organisation.
- ***Policies and rules:*** These convey the degree of flexibility and restriction in the organisation.
- ***Programs:*** Programming and formal initiatives help support and emphasize a workplace climate.
- ***Leadership:*** Leaders that consistently support the climate desired.

(b) Creating Positive Organisational Climate: Making a climate change in an organisation is one of the core fundamental steps to begin, to create a great place to work. There are two difficulties in defining organisation climate: How to define climate, and how to measure it effectively on different levels of analysis. Furthermore, there are several approaches to the concept of climate. Two in particular have received substantial patronage: The cognitive schema approach and the shared perception approach.

Organisational climate has also been defined as "the shared perception of the way things are around here". There is great deal of overlap in the two approaches.

1. *Cognitive Schema Approach:* Cognitive representations of social objects are referred to as schemas. These schemas are a mental structure that represents some aspect of the world. They are organized in memory in an associative network. In these associative networks, similar schemas are clustered together. When a particular schema is activated, related schemas may be activated as well. Schema activation may also increase the accessibility of related schemas in the associative network. When a schema is more accessible this means it can more quickly be activated and used in a particular situation. When related schemas are activated, inferences beyond the information given in a particular social situation may influence thinking and social behaviour, regardless of whether those inferences are accurate or not. Lastly, when a schema is activated a person may or may not be aware of it.

Two processes that increase the accessibility of schemas are salience and priming. Salience is the degree to which a particular social object stands out relative to other social objects in a situation. The higher the salience of an object the more likely that schema for that object will be made accessible. For example, if there is one female in a group of seven males, female gender schemas may be more accessible and influence the group's thinking and behaviour toward the female group member. Priming refers to any experiences immediately prior to a situation that caused a schema to be more accessible.

2. *Shared Perception Approach:* Some researchers have pursued the shared perception model of organisational climate. Their model identifies the variables which moderate an organisation's ability to mobilize its workforce in order to achieve business goals and maximize performance. One of the major users of this model is departments of the Queensland State Government, Australia. These departments use this model of climate to survey staff in order to identify and measure those aspects of a workplace which impact on: Stress, morale, quality of work life, well-being, employee engagement, absenteeism/presenteeism, turnover and performance.

While an organisation and its leaders cannot remove every stressor in the daily life of its employees, organisational climate studies have identified a number of behaviours of leaders which have a significant impact on stress and morale. For instance, one Queensland State Government Employer, Queensland Transport, has found that increasing managers' awareness of these behaviours has improved quality of work life of employees and the ability of QT's to deliver its organisational goals.

In short, the cognitive schema approach regards the concept of climate as an individual perception and cognitive representation of the work environment. From this perspective, climate assessments should be conducted at an individual level. The shared perception approach emphasizes the importance of shared perceptions as underpinning the notion of climate.

3. *Climate Surveys:* Theories of Cognitive and Neuropsychology and Emotional Intelligence provide additional scientific rationale for why leaders should improve stress and morale in the workplace to achieve maximum performance. Climate surveys can provide concrete evidence of how this works in action. Organisational climate surveying enables the impact of Human Resource (HR) strategies to be evaluated to create HR Return on Investment (HRROI) calculations. This data has been found to be highly effective in changing the perspective of people-based initiatives as being an "investment" rather than a "cost" and transforming HR into a "mission-critical strategic partner" from its perception of "personnel administration".

A number of studies by Dr. Dennis Rose and colleagues between 2001–2004 have found a very strong link between organisational climate and employee reactions such as stress levels, absenteeism and commitment and participation. A study has found that Hart, Griffin et al. (1996) organisational climate model accounts for at least 16% single-day sick leave and 10% separation rates in one organisation. Other studies support the links between organisational climate and many other factors such as employee retention, job satisfaction, well-being and readiness for creativity, innovation and change. Hunter, Bedell and Mumford have reviewed numerous approaches to climate assessment for creativity. They found that those climate studies that were based on well-developed, standardized instruments produced far higher effect sizes than did studies that were based on locally developed measures.

In order to make the organisational climate work, there must be a clear common understanding and congruent applications by senior managers and their staff regarding simply stated organisational goals, objectives, priorities and command philosophies. Understanding of nature of organisational climate, its principal components and its interactive dynamics as well.

Finally taking actions to make organisational climate directly supports the organisation's goals, objectives, priorities and command philosophies. Embedding within the climate the principle of rationality i.e., do what seems right and sensible and questioned the policies, procedures and requirements that seem otherwise. Starting from the top management/boss. Demonstrate downwards the willingness to take calculated risks, with the calculations based on the principle of rationality. As the expected mode of leaderships permeates downwards, encourages, reward and tell stories about incidents of independent but disciplined actions in the absence of positive control.

10.6 ORGANISATIONAL CULTURE

Organisational Culture is the set of values that states what an organisation stands for, how it operates and what it considers important. According to Deal and Kennedy, a strong culture is, "A system of informal rules that spells out how people have to behave most of the time". Schein defines organisational culture as the pattern of basic assumptions that a given group has invented, discovered and developed while learning to cope with its problems of external adaptation and internal integration.

All the above definitions stress acceptable and unacceptable behaviour of its members. For instance, one organisation might value solidarity and loyalty to organisation more than any other value whereas another organisation might stress on good relations with customers. Such values are part of organisational culture in spite of not being formally written like rules and regulations of the organisation. They do not usually appear in the organisational training program and in fact, many organisations have difficulty in expressing their cultural values. However, an organisation's values automatically enter every employee's personal values and actions over a period of time. Organisational culture has a profound influence on individual employees because it is generally an accepted set of values rather than a written set of rules with which employees might not argue.

Organisation culture helps integrate an organisation's subsystems and processes. The integration lets the organisation coordinate its various actions effectively. Common language develops within a culture, helping communication. Conceptual categories develop that filter unimportant detail and focus attention on important matters. Perceptual filtration reduces the likelihood that an individual will become overloaded by stimuli defined as unimportant by the culture. Organisational cultures define rules for power, rules for social stratification, and the ways in which social status is determined. Some accord social status and power to people of high achievement. Others base status and power on seniority.

Further an organisational effectiveness may be anlaysed in terms of an open systems framework and also can be examined in terms of interrelated sub-systems, for example tasks to be undertaken by technology employed, formal structure, behaviour of people and the process of management. The state of the sub-systems will reflect upon the effectiveness of the organisation as a whole. This chapter discusses organisational culture, criteria and technique of evaluating the effectiveness of an organisation in detail. See the contrasting dimensions of culture with climate in an organisation in Table 10.1.

Table 10.1: Contrasting dimensions or organisational culture and climate

Sl. No	Organisational climate	Organisational culture
1	Met organisational expectations	Nature of expectations
2	Create temperature	Create work pressure
3	Transactual	Transformational
4	Tactical	Strategic
5	Norms–Behaviour	Values–Beliefs

The chemistry of successful turnarounds of organisations that became pro-active only when after crossing certain stages such as in the chaotic state, there is total lack of direction. People just do what they are supposed to do, as a matter of routine. In the absence of proper leadership, all efforts of different departments aren't properly coordinated and there is a total lack of synergy between action and goals, as the goals and the means lack clarity, at every stage of the process. A visionary leader comes along, wakes up the organisation from its deep slumber, gets goals, targets and clarifies roles of each individual.

Efforts are made to communicate what the organisation needs to do, when, where and how. Since each individual is clear what he/she is working for, the corrective action taken by the leader becomes result oriented and the organisation becomes more confident of working in a fairly systematic manner. This may be called the "*State of Equilibrium*". The leader then concentrates on systems in the organisation and takes far-reaching, progressive and professional action that results in the elimination of useless systems and introduction of systems that really mean business. At this stage, the organisation becomes proactive.

For instance, the "*Internal Customer Concept*" introduced in dozens of Indian organisations like Kirloskar, Cummins, Widia India Ltd., and Crompton Greaves, Eicher Tractors and go on, a system that makes the organisation customer-oriented and in plain common sense translated into action for building up real team spirit in the organisation. The spread of the ISO-9000 and TQM messages to the nook and corner of the country is a refreshing change. And the leading international guru of quality, Dr.Joseph Juran has himself acknowledged that many Indians have already achieved top quality. Organisations or such companies, for example, ICICI Bank has taken efforts to statistically analyze consumer feed-back, eliminate non-value adding activities from every process, use technology to speed up communications and cut cycle time, delegate specified decision-maiming, power down the line and calculate profitability by putting a cost on every activity.

The Madras-based Alacrity group's success in building flats for thousands has provided a pro-active rule in customer relations. They have guaranteed their customer that absolutely white money is involved, no cost escalation once the agreement is signed with the buyer, interest at commercial rates for delays, and such other actions in a market unknown for values is what has made the difference. Alacrity has provided the right answer to the question "What should happen?" and achieved a massive 45% market-share in the business. The time to act in such a pro-active organisation cultures are not a matter of choice it is just that only these organisations will survive, grow and develop at all times.

Organisational culture is a complex and deep aspect of organisations that can strongly affect organisation members. Organisational culture includes the values, norms, rites, rituals, ceremonies, heroes and scoundrels in the history of the organisation. It defines the content of what a new employee needs to learn to be accepted as a member of the organisation. Key aspects of organisational culture include a sharing of a value and a structuring of experiences in an organisation. Different sets of values can coexist among different group of people throughout an organisation. Although values differ from group to group, members of each group can share a set of values.

Also, not all people in an organisation will fully agree about the dominant values and norms. An organisation that has adapted successfully to its external environment can develop a culture with a consensus among members about the organisation's mission. Specific goals derived from the mission and the means to reach those goals will be part of the culture. A consensus about a mission among veteran members lets the organisation move forward smoothly towards those goals. Members agree about what needs to be done and how it will be done. In short, an organisation's culture help its members develop a sense of identity with the organisation and a clear vision of the organisation's direction. An organisational culture that gives its members a clear vision of the organisation's mission also percents consistent image to its markets, customers, and clients. Overtime, that image can give an organisation a competition advantage by building commitment to its products or services.

(a) Importance of Culture

Culture plays a very significant role in any organisation by communicating information about the overall acceptable and unacceptable behaviour. Culture communicates whether the organisation expects its managers to be aggressive or conservative in decisions-making, generous or moderate in supporting social causes and ruthless or kind in competitive dealings.

Some organisations have clear, strong and well-defined culture whereas others have ambiguous, weak and poorly defined cultures. Most managers agree that a strong and clear culture is preferable to weak and vague culture because it helps to provide a common frame of reference for managerial decision-making and a wide variety of other organisational activities.

An organisational culture generally takes shape overtime and is often deeply influenced by the values of the organisational founders. As organisational culture evolves, various symbols, stories, heroes, slogans and ceremonies also come into being. These, then, serve to maintain and perpetuate the culture through subsequent generations of employees.

Creating organisational culture is a deliberate effort to build a specific type of organisational culture. It happens when an entrepreneur forms an organisation to pursue a vision or when managers of an existing organisation form a new operating unit. The new culture needs an ideology that is understandable, convincing, and widely discussed. The ideology is a key tool for getting commitment from members of the organisation of the vision. Culture maintenance requires managers to be aware of what organisational culture is and how it manifests itself in their managers to be aware of what organisation. It requires knowing the existing organisational culture's artefacts, values, and ideologies. A key way managers can become familiar with their culture is by doing a culture diagnosis, as described in an earlier section. By maintaining their culture, managers want to maintain commitment of organisation members to key parts of that culture. The best way managers can be familiar with their culture is by doing a culture diagnosis.

An organisation's culture can be seen as its members' collective mental models which is why nobody can change an organisation without investing its cultural assumptions. In Edgar Schein's model, cultural assumptions are deeply influenced by beliefs founders and leaders, carrying on for years after the founders themselves have ceased to run the company. Unlike Chris Argyris, Schein see most organisations as essentially healthy and willing and patient with employees. They lack certain skills and may be handicapped by dysfunctional values, but these gaps can be remedied through careful organisational change and recruitments.

Culture maintenance also requires managers to carefully examine any new practices for consistency with their culture's ideology. Introducing drug testing for employment screening in an organisation with a culture built around trust might be a contradiction. Such testing might not appear contradictory in an organisation that strongly values safety when working in hazardous areas. Changing organisational culture requires breaking of some features of the old culture and creating new features. The size and depth of the change will vary depending on the degree of difference between the desired new culture and the old. For example, changing the culture of an organisation that has a homogeneous workforce to one that values diversity will require an extended effort.

(b) Changing Organisational Culture

Change is most often needed when the organisation has lost its effectiveness and is struggling to either carry out or change its strategic goals. The manager trying to change an organisational culture faces lots of difficulties. Because organisational culture embody the organisational values, which are embedded in organisation's soul that stays stable irrespective of the changes in leadership and environment.

It is, however, possible to change organisational culture, to improve the organisation performance. For this managers must change employee's ideas about what is and what is not appropriate behaviour. They must create new role model and new stories to help employees understand the meaning of what is happening around them. One way to brine about such changes is to manage the symbols that are important to the organisation. An organisation's suggestion box is a symbol of an organisation's openness to the ideas of the employees. Some organisations try to emphasize the importance of employees' ideas by rewarding them for their suggestions. However, if the suggestion box remains just a symbol and organisation never translates the suggestions into actions, the box will have little effect on organisation morale.

The change will reach deep into the cultural fabric of the organisation over a period of many years. Successfully managing the change process requires managers to attend to several issues. One is choosing the proper time for change. They are advised to act when the times seen right for culture change or when the situation clearly demands it. An opportune time for culture change or when the organisation wishes to pursue favourable new markets. IBM, for example, changed its culture when it shifted its emphasis away from its historical roots in mainframe computers to small personal computers and workstations. Change also might be required when the organisation is performing poorly and faces clear threats to its viability. Once successfully made changes in the organisational culture will be as stable as the old culture was. However, any organisation willing to change its culture must realize that such a change is never easy and cannot be brought about simply by ordering employees.

Multinational organisations typically have employees from many countries working side by side. Those employees do not shed their national culture when they come to work. The heterogeneity of values in such organisations is extremely high, as is the change of subcultures forming along national lines. Some research evidence suggests that instead of masking local differences with organisational culture, multinational cultures may increase ties with people to have their native cultures. This "culture synergy" view urges managers to view multinational cultural diversity as a resource. That diversity could lead to better product ideas for culturally diverse markets and better communication with culturally diverse customers.

(c) A Framework for Assessing Cultures

Edgar Schein in his classic work organisational culture and leadership describing how cultural artefacts such as dress codes, ways of talking to the boss and other visible evidence. He collected data from the newest in the organisation to the senior most on shared values and its correlation with visible cultural artefacts. Finally in order to understand shared underlying assumptions, he conducted focus group discussions of inconsistencies between artefacts and espoused values that are readily offered reasons for the visible artefacts. Finally the researcher pulled together all data and made conclusions from the groups and pinpoint what hinders or aids progress on the stated organisations goal.

One of the most widely referenced approaches for analysing variations among cultures has been done by Geert Hofstede. He surveyed more than 116,000 IBM employees in 40 countries about their work-related values. He found that managers and employees vary on five value dimensions of national culture. They are listed and defined as follows:

1. ***Power distances:*** The degree to which people in a country accept that power in institutions and organisations is distributed unequally. Ranges from relatively equal (low power distance) to extremely unequal (high power distance).
2. ***Individualism versus collectivism:*** Individualism is the degree to which people in a country prefer to act as individuals rather than as members of groups. Collectivism is the equivalent of low individualism.
3. ***Quantity of life versus quality of life:*** Quantity of life is the degree to which values like assertiveness, the acquisition of money and material goods, and competition prevail. Quality of life is the degree to which people value relationships and show sensitivity and concern for the welfare of others.
4. ***Uncertainty avoidance:*** The degree to which people in a country prefer structured over unstructured situations. In countries that score high on uncertainty avoidance, people have an increased level of anxiety, which manifests itself in greater nervousness, stress and aggressiveness.
5. ***Long-term versus short-term orientation:*** People in cultures with long-term orientations look to the future and value thrift and persistence. A short-term orientation values the past and present, and emphasizes respect for tradition and fulfilling social obligations.

Table 10.2: Showing the findings of the study of hofstede

Country	Power distance	Individualism*	Quantity of life**	Uncertainty avoidance	Long-term orientation***
China	High	Low	Moderate	Moderate	High
France	High	High	Moderate	High	Low
Germany	Low	High	High	Moderate	Moderate
Hong Kong	High	Low	High	Low	High
Indonesia	High	Low	Moderate	Low	Low
Japan	Moderate	Moderate	High	Moderate	Moderate
Netherlands	Low	High	Low	Moderate	Moderate

Russia	High	Moderate	Low	High	Low
United States	Low	High	High	Low	Low
West Africa	High	Low	Moderate	Moderate	Low

**A low score is synonymous with collectivism.*

***A low score is synonymous with high quality of life.*

****A low score is synonymous with a short-term orientation.*

Source: Adapted from G.Hofstede, "Cultural Constraints in Management Theories", Academy of Management Executive, February 1993, p. 91.

A company succeeds as a result of what the company does, its strategy, and how it does it, its culture. The culture is linked to the strategic values, whether one is starting up a new company or trying to change the culture of an existing company. The process of creating an organisation culture is really a process of linking its strategic values with its cultural values, much as the structure of the organisation is linked to its strategy. Strategic values are the basic beliefs about an organisation's environment that shape its strategy.

Cultural values are the values that employees need to have and act on for the organisation to act on the strategic values. Cultural values are the values employees need to act on for the organisation to carry out its strategic values. They should be grounded in the organisation's beliefs about how and why the organisation can succeed. Organisations that attempt to develop cultural values that are not linked to their strategic values may end up with an empty set of values that have little relationship to its business. In other words, employees need to value work behaviours that are consistent with and support the organisation's strategic values: Low-cost production, customer service, or technological innovation.

Indian culture can be characterised as fatalistic context sensitive, tolerant of ambiguity, convergent, future-oriented, collectivist, other-directed, embedded, role bound, androgynous and power-distance tolerant. The profile is not as clean, however, the nature and the development of self is the key element in the formation of the culture. The Type Z firm is committed to retaining employees, evaluate worker's performance based on both qualitative and quantitative information, emphasizes broad career paths, exercises control through informal, implicit mechanisms, requires that decision making occur in groups and be based on full information sharing and consensus, expects individuals to take responsibility for decisions, and emphasizes concern for people. Ouchi suggested that typical USA firms do not have the same cultural commitment to employees as Japanese firms and US type Z firms.

In reality, US workers and managers often spend their entire careers in a relatively small number of companies. Still, there is a cultural expectations that if there is a serious downturn in a firm's fortunes, change of ownership or a merger, workers and managers will be let go. For example, when Wells Fargo Bank bought first Inter-State Bank in Arizona, they expected to lay off about 400 employees in Arizona and 5,000 in the corporation as a whole. However, eight months after the purchase it had eliminated over 1,000 in Arizona and a total of 10,800. Wells Fargo has a reputation as a vicious cutter following a takeover and seems to be living up to that reputation.

Table 10.3: Showing cultural difference among Japanese and US firms

Cultural Value	Expression in Japanese Companies	Expression in Type Z, US Companies	Expression in Typical US Companies
Commitment to Employees	Lifetime employment	Long-term employment	Short-term employment
Evaluation	Slow and qualitative	Slow and qualitative	Fast and quantitative
Careers	Very broad	Moderately broad	Narrow
Control	Implicit and informal	Implicitly and informal	Explicit and formal
Decision Making	Group and consensus	Group and consensus	Individual
Responsibility	Group	Individual	Individual
Concern for people	Holistic	Holistic	Narrow

(d) The Peters and Waterman Approach

Tom Peters and Robert Waterman, in their bestseller in search of excellence, focused even more explicitly than Ouchi on the relationship between organisational culture and performance. Peters and Waterman chose a sample of highly successful US firms and sought to describe the management practices that led to their success. Their analysis rapidly turned to the cultural values that led to successful management practices.

10.7 MANAGING AN INTERNATIONAL WORKFORCE

Whenever an organisation expands its operations to other countries, it tends to become multicultural and will then face the challenge of blending various cultures together. The managerial personnel entering another nation need to adjust their leadership styles, communication patterns and other practices to fit their host country. Their role is to provide fusion of cultures in which employees from both countries adjust to the new situation seeking a greater productivity for the benefit of both the organisation and the people of the country in which it operates.

(a) Barriers to Cultural Adaptation

- Managers and other employees who come into a host country tend to exhibit different behaviours and somewhat see situation around them from their own perspectives. They may fail to recognize the key differences between their own and other cultures. These people are called, 'parochial'.
- Another category of managers called 'individualistic' place greatest emphasis on their personal needs and welfare. They are more concerned about themselves than the host country.
- Another potential barrier to easy adaptation of another culture occurs; when people are predisposed to believe that their homeland conditions are the best. This predisposition is known as the 'self-reference criterion' or 'ethnocentrism'. This feeling interferes with understanding human behaviour in other cultures and obtaining productivity from local employees.

(*i*) ***Cultural Distance:*** To decide the amount of adaptation that may be required when personnel moves to another country, it is helpful to understand the cultural distance between the two countries. Cultural distance is the amount of distance between any two social systems. Whatever may be the amount of cultural distance, it does affect the responses of all individuals to business. The manager's job is to make the employees adapt to the other culture and integrate the interests of the various cultures involved.

(*ii*) ***Cultural Shock:*** When employees enter another nation they tend to suffer cultural shock, which is the insecurity and disorientation caused by encountering a different culture. They may not know how to act. May fear losing face and self-confidence or may become emotionally upset. Cultural shock is virtually universal. Some of the more frequent reasons for cultural shock are as follows:

- Different management philosophies
- New language
- Alternative food, dress, availability of goods
- Attitude towards work and productivity
- Separation from family, friends and colleagues
- Unique currency system.

Many expatriates report difficulty in adjusting to different human resource management philosophies, the language, the different currency and work attitudes in another culture.

(*iii*) ***Overcoming Barriers to Cultural Adaptation***

- Careful selection of employees, who can withstand/adjust cultural shocks for international assignments is important.
- Pre-departure training in geography, customs, culture and political environment in which the employee will be living will help for cultural adaptation.
- Incentives and guarantees for better position will motivate employees for cultural adaptation in the new country.
- Employees who return to their home country after working in another nation for sometime tend to suffer cultural shock in their own homeland. After adjusting to the culture of another nation and enjoying its uniqueness, it is difficult for expatriates to readjust to the surroundings of their home country. Hence, organisations need repatriation policies and programs to help returning employees obtain suitable assignments and adjust to the 'new' environments.

(b) Cultural Contingencies

Productive business practices from one country cannot be transferred directly to another country. This reflects the idea of cultural contingency that the most productive practices for a particular nation will depend heavily on the culture, social system, economic development and employee's values in the host country. Hence, the expatriate managers must learn to operate effectively in a new environment with certain amount of flexibility. Labour policy, personnel practices and production methods need to be adapted to a different labour force. Organisation structures and communication patterns need to be suitable for local operations.

(c) Multicultural Organisation as Competitive Advantage

Developing the multicultural organisation requires commitment from top management and a clear vision of the benefits of multiculturalism for the future of the organisation. The multicultural organisation has six characteristics: Pluralism, full structural integration, full integration of informal networks, an absence of prejudice and discrimination, equal identification among employees with organisational goals for majority and minority groups and low levels of intergroup conflict.

Table 10.4: Showing competitive advantage of firms

Advantage	Contribution
Cost	Trim the cost of integrating diverse workers.
Resource acquisition	Companies that have the best reputation for managing diverse employees will have the best chance of hiring the best available diverse personnel.
Marketing	Increased insight and cultural sensitivity will improve the development and marketing of products and services for diverse segments of the population.
Creativity	Diversity of perspectives will improve levels of creativity throughout the organisation.
Problem solving	Problem solving and decision making will improve through groups with more diverse perspectives.
System flexibility	Tolerance and valuing of diverse perspectives throughout the organisation will make the organisation more fluid, more flexible and more responsive to environmental changes.

Movement towards better management of a diverse workforce usually begins for one or more of three reasons. Some companies, such as Xerox, were obliged to develop better management of a workforce made more diverse by affirmative action. Other companies, such as Digital Equipment and Hewlett-Packard, grew very quickly to remain competitive and then realised that they had to work with multicultural constituencies. A third group of companies, which includes Avon products, needed to have a diverse workforce to match the diversity in the marketplace. Companies of all three types need to better manage their multicultural workforce to gain a competitive advantage in the market place. Business leaders' consultants and academic scholars contended that having a multicultural organisation can create competitive advantage in the six ways shown in Table 10.5.

Table 10.5: Showing various cultural advantages of firms

Advantage	Contribution
Pluralism	Training and orientation programs, ensuring minority group input, putting diversity into mission statements.
Full structural integration	Education, training, affirmative action, performance appraisals and reward systems, benefits, work schedules.
Integration of informal networks	Mentoring, social events, support groups.
Absence of prejudice	OD seminars, focus groups, bias-reduction training programs, task forces.
Equal identification with Goals	Input of minority group into mission, goals, and strategies.
Minimal intergroup conflict	Survey feedback, conflict reduction training.

(d) Integrating the Individual in the Culture

Interest in culture has been aroused by the examples of Japanese successes. Some organisations in India have adopted Japanese practices, notable amongst these being Maruti Udyog and Sundaram Clayton. Maruti adopted some practices because of the positive pressure of Suzuki: 7 hours 45 minutes shift, zero-defect production, cost cutting, and discipline. A new organisational culture developed. Organisational culture can be defined as cumulative ways of thinking and behaving shaped by the values, attitudes, rituals, and sanctions in an organisation. Operationally, development of culture would involve developing a strong corporate identify, development of important values, building healthy traditions and developing consistent management practices.

1. ***Cultural Change:*** People learn to depend on their culture. It gives them stability and security, because they can understand what is happening in their community and know how to respond. However, two types of cultural change may confront employees. One, involves a move to a new location and its culture, the other, a gradual change in their existing environment. Employees need to learn to adapt to both situation in order to avoid possible negative consequences.

2. ***New Culture:*** Companies frequently transfer employees between different cities for new job assignments. The employees who move to new job locations often experience various degrees of cultural shock, which is a feeling of confusion, insecurity and anxiety caused by a strange new environment. They are concerned about not knowing how to act and about losing their self-confidence when the wrong responses are made. A cultural change does not have to be dramatic to cause some degree of shock. For example, when an employee moves from a small town to Mumbai both the employee and family are likely to suffer cultural shock. A similar shock may occur when a Mumbai employee is transferred to a small town in an isolated rural area. The whole family may not know what to do with their time or how to act and dress. Cultural shock is even greater when there is a move from one nation to another, especially if the languages are different. For unprepared employees, the environment can appear to be chaos. They become disoriented, retreat into isolation, and want to return home on the next aeroplane. But a different culture is not behavioural chaos. It is a systematic structure of behavioural patterns, probably as systematic as the culture in the employee's home country. It can be understood if employees have receptive attitudes and receive advance preparation.

(e) Emerging Issues

Emerging issues in the area of organisational culture include innovation, employee empowerment and procedural justice. Innovation is the process of creating and doing new things that are introduced into the marketplace as products, processes, or services. The organisational culture can either help or hinder innovation. Employee empowerment, in addition to being similar to employee participation as a motivation technique, is now viewed by some as a type of organisational culture. Empowerment occurs when employees make decisions, set their own work goals and solve problems in their own area of responsibility. Procedural justice is the extent to which the dynamics of an organisation's decision-making processes are judged to be fair by those most affected by them.

Organisational culture requires attention to three factors. First, managers can take advantage of cultural values that already exist and use their knowledge to help subordinates understand them. Second, employees need to be properly socialised, or trained, in the cultural values of the organisation, either through formal training or by experiencing and observing the actions of higher-level managers. Third, managers can change the culture of the organisation through managing the symbols, addressing the extreme difficulties of such a change, and relying on the durability of the new organisation culture once the change has been implemented.

10.8 MODELS OF ORGANISATIONAL BEHAVIOUR

The bottom line for the developing organisation is not the company's net profit, but the growth of the individuals and societies with whom it is involved. The individuals and organisations within the organisations worldwide will be continually renewing themselves, thereby actualizing their interdependent potential. The philosophical grounds upon which their cooperation is based reach across the globe, from ancient Buddhism to modern existentialism, from anthroposophy to humanistic psychology. The author believes that through self-management frameworks and potential performance programming will redefine the concept of management development/self-management in the New Millennium. This final section focuses the latest concepts in Indigenization of Western management in depth.

As we learn more human behaviour at work, we apply improved models of organisational behaviour. Modern organisations are increasing their use of supportive, collegial and Theory Y models. In order to provide review and perspective, Table 10.1 presents the four models of organisational behaviour from earlier in the book and then relates them to other ideas on the subject. By reading the figure, one can determine the McGregor's Theory Y is related to the supportive and collegial models. Similarly, Herzberg's maintenance factors apply mostly to the autocratic and custodial models.

Table 10.6: Showing various modes of organisational behaviour

	Autocratic	**Custodial**	**Supportive**	**Collegial**
Basis of model	Power	Economic resources	Leadership	Partnership
Managerial orientation	Authority	Money	Support	Team work
Employee orientation	Obedience	Security and benefits	Job performance	Responsibility
Employee psychological result	Dependence on boss	Dependence on organisation	Participation	Commitment; self-discipline
Employee needs met	Subsistence	Security	Status and recognition	Self-actualisation
Performance result	Minimum	Passive cooperation	Awakened drives	Enthusiasm
Relations to Other Ideas				
Maslow's hierarchy of needs	Physiological	Security	Middle-order	Higher-order
Alderfer's need levels	Existence	Existence	Relatedness	Growth
Herzberg's factors	Maintenance	Maintenance	Motivational	Motivational
Motivational environmental	Extrinsic	Extrinsic	Intrinsic	Intrinsic
McGregor's theories	Theory X	Theory X	Theory Y	Theory Y

Leadership style	Negative	Mostly neutral on job	Positive	Positive
Blake and Mouton's managerial grid	9, 1	5, 5	6, 6	9, 9

Source/credit: Prof. Subash Sharma, IIMA.

As shown in Table 10.6 the trend of each subsequent model of organisational behaviour is towards more open human organisations. Generally there is also movement towards a wider distribution of power, more intrinsic motivation, a more positive attitude towards people, and a better balance of concern for both employee and organisational needs. Discipline has become more a matter of self-discipline instead of being imposed from the outside. The managerial role has advanced from one of strict authority to leadership and team support.

(a) Emphasis on Higher-Order Needs

One reason for emphasis on improved models of organisational behaviour is the evolution of employee need structures. Postindustrial nations have reached a condition wherein higher-order (growth) needs are the prime motivators for many employees. Consequently, managers, of these workers must seek to design organisational behaviour systems that provide a greater probability of satisfying those needs that was possible in the past. In addition, the emergence of a knowledge society requires more use of intellectual abilities across a wide range of employees, and advanced organisational behaviour systems tend to be more effective with knowledge workers. A manager cannot make employees think; they must be internally motivated to do so.

Table 10.7: Paradigm shift in organisation development

From	To
Closed systems	Open systems
Materialistic orientation	Human orientation
Centralized power	Distributed power
Extrinsic motivation	Intrinsic motivation
Negative attitudes about people	Positive attitudes about people
Focus on organisation needs	Balanced focus on employee and organisation needs
Imposed discipline	Self-discipline
Authoritative managerial role	Managerial role of leadership and team support

(b) A Social Approach

A social approach recognized that what happens outside the firm will influence organisational behaviour practices within the firm. Also, what happens inside the firm will influence society? Management must be constantly aware of and responsive to this external environment, because it is an important influence on internal operations.

Table 10.8: Organisation environment

Organisational Characteristics	Environment	
	Stable	**Changing**
Structure	More rigid hierarchy	More flexible (some project and matrix)
Production system	More specialization	More job enrichment
Leadership style	More structure	More consideration
Communication	More vertical	More multidirectional
Model of organisational behaviour	More autocratic	More supportive
Performance measure	More management by rules	More management by objectives

Source/credit: Prof. Subash Sharma IIMA.

10.9 INDIGENIZATION OF WESTERN MANAGEMENT

(a) Combining the Best of the East & the West in Management Education*

Management education deals with the art and science of directing and controlling or handling any organisation, specially under resource constraint situation, be it business, industry, public system or government. Such education not only covers a thorough understanding of Behavioural Sciences, Human Resource Development, Financing, Marketing, Operations and Information Systems, but also calls for adequate grasp of the National and Global Economics, Politics, Sociology, Legal Framework, Technological Trends and Natural Environment in which the organisation has to function and prosper through the formulation of effective strategies. All organisations need to have a Vision and a Mission with Milestones to achieve a common goal.

(b) Foundation of the Western Model

The Western Model of Management Education is based on the following hypotheses:

1. Human behaviour and motivation is guided by the fulfillment of human need as propounded by Freud, Maslow, McGregor, Mintzberg and others. The primary human need is defined as materials need with the non-materials dimension playing a relatively minor role. Human Resource Management organisations are based on this fundamental hypothesis.
2. Organisations must survive and flourish under the competition resulting in only a few dominant organisations in each segment of industry. However, the regulatory authorities ensure avoidance of monopolies. This approach leads to concentration on core competence using latest technologies and massive economy of scale requiring minimal human intervention (in the manufacturing sector). The stress is on quality, efficiency and productivity, the keystones of material prosperity and higher standard of living. Such material prosperity invariably leads to high level of consumption of energy generated from organic fuels leading to global warming through the generation of unabsorbed green house gases.

*Resource Person: Dr. Subir Chowdhury, Professor, IIM-Calcutta.

3. The focus of business and industry is to serve the customers to their fullest satisfaction at the lowest possible price leading to a higher share of market and a high rate of return on the shareholder's capital. Market led economy and consumerism are the main forces guiding the economy.
4. Organisations are free to hire and fire employees based on the behaviour of the market and technological change. However a strong social security net provided by the State looks after the interests of the unemployed workmen.

10.10 WISDOM OF THE EAST

(a) 'Giving' Vs 'Needing' Model

Each human being has a soul. Narrow self-centred material need based activities denote a lower order animal existence for human beings or corporates. We need to rise above our selfish interests and supplement it with enlightened self-interest. This is the message of the spirit of human existence. If we do not follow this basic message of humanity as propagated by our great spiritual leaders like Swmai Vivekananda, Rabindranath Tagore and Rishi Aurobindo, we may heading for the doomsdays in distant future. Intrinsic and enduring motivational strategic need to be based on the 'Giving' model rather that on the 'Needing' model.

(b) Blending Spiritualism with Materialism

In the East, spiritualism is a way of life, differentiating human values from animal existence. While we do have our material needs for the self and family, our ultimate goal is spiritual enlightenment. We therefore need to blend our material and spiritual needs for a holistic view of happy living. We do not believe that the search of material prosperity alone can lead to a balanced and satisfying life. Our belief is that a process of meditation in search of a quality mind helps us to understand ourselves and leads to a better synchronization between the body and the mind towards a richer life. We also believe that having met the basic material requirement of life, spiritual pursuit is the main motivator helping human beings to achieve great heights. Instead of acting on external stimuli in search of excellence, we should be guided by internal inspirations.

(c) Developing Both Left & Right Side of the Brain

Management education model of the West fully develops the left side of the brain which controls the logical, sequential and analytical aspects of decision making. There is hardly any emphasis on developing the right side of the brain controlling the holistic, intuitive and random access features, that are so vitally important for a complex decision making process. Meditation or a quality mind—process is a proven mechanism for the development of the right side of the brain.

10.11 BLENDING THE BEST OF THE EAST AND THE WEST

(a) A Holistic Approach

The West has taught us how to organise efficiently using technological innovations like information technology and biotechnology in a market economy. The east however advocates a holistic approach with respect to human happiness through a balanced view of environmental protection and distribution of purchasing power to avoid the disaster implied in the Western model. We should certainly work towards higher standards of living with a drastic reduction of people living below the poverty line. But at the same time we may not strive to catch up worth the standard of living in Europe or America since that is unlikely to be sustainable due to environmental degradation.

(b) The Future of Organisational Behaviour

Interest in the four goals of describing, predicting, explaining and controlling human behaviour at work has increased throughout be twentieth century. This evolving interest in organisational behaviour stems from both a philosophical desire by many people to create more humanistic workplaces and a practical need to design more productive work environment. As a result of these force, organisational behaviour is now a key part of business school, engineering and medical school curriculums. Furthermore, its role in both academic programs and corporate management development seminars is expected to increase further as a response to endorsements such as the one described below.

The field of organisational behaviour has grown in depth and breadth, and it will continue to mature. The keys to its past and future success revolve around the related processes of theory development, research and managerial practice. Theories offer explanations of how and why people think, feel, and act as they do. Research is the process of gathering and interpreting relevant evidence that will either support a behavioural theory or help change it. Neither research nor theory can stand alone and be useful, however. Managers apply the theoretical models to structure their thinking; they use research results to provide relevant guides to their own situations. In these ways, there is a natural and healthy flow from theory and research to practice, which is the conscious application of conceptual models and research results with the goals of improving individual and organisational performance. Fortunately, one of the major trends today is the increasing acceptance of theory and research by practising managers. Please refer appendix for more details. By building a better climate for people, organisational behaviour way organisational behaviour may contribute to social improvements that stretch far beyond the confines of any one organisation.

A system of 'Feed back - Feed forward' (*i.e.*, a system of integrating past experience with future learning and vice versa) is envisaged for evolving a universal developmental model under diverse environment in the new millennium. This approach called for indigenization of western management through a process of restructuring the orientation and objectives of our management development programmes, procedures and system. This approach, it is hoped that, will nourish human capabilities required for sustained high performance and resilience of the organisations.

SUMMARY

- Workforce diversity is a function of the similarities and differences among employees in such characteristics as age, gender, ethnic heritage, physical ability or disability, race, and sexual orientation. Managers of diverse work groups need to understand how their members' social conditioning affects their beliefs about work and must have the communication skills to develop confidence and self-esteem in their employees.
- A multicultural organisation is one in which employees of different backgrounds, experiences, and cultures can contribute and achieve their fullest potential for the benefit of both themselves and the organisation. Developing a multicultural organisation is a significant step in managing a

diverse workforce and may be crucial to sustaining a competitive advantage in the marketplace. A multicultural organisation has six characteristics: Pluralism, full structural integration, full integration of informal networks, an absence of prejudice and discrimination, equal identification with organisational goals among employees from both majority and minority groups and low levels of intergroup conflict.

- The ultimate purpose of increasing an organisation's ability to adapt to a changing environment is to make it more effective. Barnard makes the distinction between organisation effectiveness, which is the accomplishment or organisational objectives, and efficiency, which involves the satisfaction of member's needs. Etziend has suggested that effectiveness is the degree of goal achievement or as the further elaborates, the amount of resources and organisation needs to use in order to produce units of output. In general, OD programs are aimed at three basic organisational dimensions, which affect performance. Effectiveness refers to the accomplishment of specific organisational goals and objectives. Please see chapter 12 for more reference.
- Same motivational tools may not suit the employees of all the nations. Hence, appropriate motivational techniques need to be implemented depending on the requirement of employees of that particular nation.
- Similarly, communication problems may also arise between the expatriate manager and the employees of the host country. Hence, managers need to make adjustments in their communication suited to local cultures. If local culture is ignored, the resulting imbalance in the social system interferes with the productivity.
- Eventually, a cadre of employees with cross-cultural adaptability can be developed in organisations with large international operations. These employees are 'trans-cultural' employees because they operate effectively in several cultures. They are low in ethnocentrism and adapt readily to different cultures without major cultural shock. They usually can communicate fluently in more than one language.

REVIEW QUESTIONS

1. Discuss the similarities and differences between the organisational culture approaches of Ouchi, Peters and Waterman.
2. Discuss the role of organisational climate in developing, maintaining and changing the organisational culture.
3. Why does multiculturalism contribute to competitive advantage for an organisation?
4. How do you assess the OB models? What criteria you apply when you measure success of new generation companies like Infosys and ICICI Ltd?
5. Explain cultural shocks. How do you manage multicultural workforce?

DISCUSSION QUESTIONS

1. Summarize in your own words what the statistics tell us about the organisational culture of new generation service sector companies from emerging markets?
2. Identify ways in which the internationalization of business affects the businesses we do in India.

3. If all things considered, do you think people from diverse cultures are more alike or more different? Give the reasons for your answer.
4. What is the role of leadership in developing, maintaining and changing positive organisational culture and climate?
5. Describe how the culture of an organisation can induce product and business innovation.

STUDENT EXERCISE

Globalization provides the opportunity for Indian managers to work in different cultures. People in low-context cultures, such as Germany, the US and Canada, derive key information from precise and brief written and spoken messages. In high-context cultures, such as China, Japan and Mexico, people derive great meaning from situational cues above and beyond written and spoken words. These cultural differences have a significant effect on the effectiveness of management where the manager is from a different culture. With globalization comes the opportunity for living and working in foreign countries.

When an individual is assigned to a foreign country outside of their home country, they are referred to as an expatriate. Indian expatriate managers usually are characterized as culturally inept and prone to failure on international assignments. Research supports this view in early 1990s. There is a high cost for software companies to send employees and their families to foreign countries. For this reason and to insure effectiveness of expatriate employees, individuals need to understand and be sensitive to the cultural values, norms, and practices of the host country.

Assume that you will become an expatriate employee for a Germany based firm. What might you do to prepare yourself for a successful transition to your new assignment?

SKILL TEST

Are you Self-Reliant?

Each of the following questions relates to how you form relationships with people at work, home and other areas of your life. Please read each statement carefully and rate each on a scale from 0 (strongly disagree) to 5 (strongly agree) to describe your degree of agreement or disagreement with the statement. Please answer all 15 questions.

1. It is difficult for me to delegate work to others.
2. Developing close relationships.
3. I avoid depending on other people because I feel crowded by close relationships.
4. I am frequently suspicious of other people's motives and intentions.
5. Asking for help makes me feel needy and I do not like that.
6. It is difficult for me to leave home or work to go to the other.
7. People will always be there when I need them.
8. I regularly and easily spend time with other people during the workday.
9. I trust at least two other people to have my best interests at heart.
10. I have a healthy, happy home life.

11. I need to have colleagues or subordinates close in order to feel secure about my work.
12. I become very concerned when I have conflict with family members at home.
13. I get very upset and disturbed if I have conflicts in relationship(s) at work.
14. I prefer very frequent feedback from my boss to know I am performing well.
15. I always consult others when I make decisions.

Scoring

Follow the instructions to determine your score for each subscale of the Self-Reliance Inventory. Note: Question 6 is used twice in scoring:

Self-Reliance/Counter dependence

Step 1 : Total your responses to Question 1–6.

Step 2 : Total your responses to Question 7–10.

Step 3 : Subtract your Step 2 total from 20(20—Your Score).

Step 4 : Add your results in Steps 1 and 3.

Step 5 : Total your responses to Questions 6 and 11–15.

A score lower than 16 in Step 4 or Step 5 indicate self-reliance on that particular subscale.

A score higher than 20 in Step 4 suggest possible counter dependence and a score higher than 20 in Step 5 suggests possible overdependence.

Source: J.C. Quick, D.L. Nelson and J.D. Quick, The Self-Reliance Inventory: 1991.

If you wish to know more insight on your test score, then you are welcome to contact author via e-mail: shaangrila@gmail.com or social media drs.shajahan.7@facebook.com.

11

CHAPTER

CASE STUDIES AND INTERNET EXERCISE

11.1 CASE STUDY METHOD

A case is written description of an organisation (or any of its parts) covering all or some of its aspects for a certain period of time. It sets forth of events and organisational circumstances surrounding a particular managerial situation. Despite its known deficiencies, the case method is widely used by universities and professional institutes throughout the world, especially for imparting knowledge and developing skills in the area of services marketing. The goal of case analysis is not developing a set of "correct" facts but to learn to reason well with available data. Cases mirror the uncertainty of the real-world managerial environment. In that the information present is often imprecise and ambiguous. You may perhaps be frustrated that there is no one right answer or correct solution to any given case. Instead, there may be a number of feasible strategies management might adopt, each with somewhat different implications for the future of the organisation, and each involving different trade-offs.

The managers cannot afford to delay making decisions until they are satisfied with the quality and quantity of available information. Such a time perhaps may never arrive. Like a real world manager, a student of service marketing must make a decision, making best use of whatever information is available and making assumptions about whatever is unknown or is not available. If you're using this book in a course or seminar, you'll be exposed to a wide range of different management situations within a relatively short time. As a result, the cases presented in this book will collectively provide a much broader exposure to service marketing problems than most managers' experience in many years on the job. Recognizing that managerial problems are not unique to a particular institution (or even to a specific service industry) forms the basis for developing a professional approach to management.

(a) Objectives of Case Method Analysis

The objectives of the case method analysis are to:

- Help you to acquire the skills of putting text book knowledge about management into practice. Managers succeed not so much because of what they know but because of what they do.

- Get you out of the habit of being a receiver of facts, concepts and techniques and get into the habit of diagnosing problems, analyzing and evaluating alternatives and formulating workable plans of action.
- Train you to workout answers and solutions for yourselves, as opposed to relying upon the authoritative crutch of the teacher/counsellor or a text book.
- Provide your exposure to a range of organisations and managerial situations (which might take a life time to experience personally), thus offering you a basis for comparison in your working as a career manager.

(b) Advantages and Disadvantages

It's important to recognize that even though case writers try to build realism into their cases; these cases differ from real-world management situations in several important respects. First, the information is prepackaged in written form. By contrast, managers accumulate their information through memoranda, meetings, conversations, research studies, observations, news reports and other externally published materials and of course, by rumour. Second, case tends to be selective in their reporting because most of them are designed with specific teaching objectives in mind. Each must fit a relatively short class period and focus attention on a defined category of management problems within a given subject area.

To provide such a focus—and to keep the length and complexity of the case within reasonable bounds—the writers may need to omit information on problems, data, or personnel that are peripheral to the central issues in the case. In the real world, management problems are usually dynamic in nature. They call for some immediate action, with further analysis and major decisions being delayed until some later time. Managers are rarely able to wrap up their problems, put them away, and go on to the next "case". In contrast, discussing a case in class or writing an analysis of a case is more like examining a snapshot taken at a particular point in time although sometimes a sequel case provides a sense of continuity and poses the need for future decisions within the same organisations.

A third, and final contrast between case analysis and real-world management is that participants in case, discussions and authors of written case reports aren't responsible for implementing their decisions, nor do they have to live with the consequences. However, this doesn't mean that you can be frivolous when making recommendations. Instructors and classmates are likely to be critical of contributions that aren't based on careful analysis and interpretation of the facts. The pedagogical objective of case method is very much different from the usual teaching in the class room. Instead of the professor/ instructor/counsellor; it is the students who do most of the talking. The counsellor/instructor's role is to solicit students participation and guide the discussion.

Since a case assignment emphasizes students participation, it is obvious that the effectiveness of the class discussion depends upon each student having studied the case before hand. A case assignment therefore requires conscientious preparation before class. The case analysis and discussion help the students in developing analytical, communication and interpersonal skills which are vital for success in management. The method also provides some opportunity to the students to relate their viewpoints with those of the others. While defending his own viewpoint, a student has also to develop an appreciation for the viewpoints held by others.

(c) Preparing a Case

In case study method, issues are discussed and various alternatives and approaches are evaluated in detail. Usually, a good argument can be made for more than one course of action. The important thing for students to understand in case analysis is that it is the exercise of *identifying, diagnozing* and *recommending* that counts rather than discovering the "right answer". The essence of case analysis is to become skilled in the process of designing workable action plans through evaluation of the prevailing circumstances. Just as there is no one right solution to a case, there is also no single correct way of preparing a case. However, the broad guidelines outlined in "Preparing a Case" may help familiarize you with the job of case preparation. A case may be prepared for:

- Oral analysis for discussion (by individuals).
- Oral analysis for discussion (by groups).
- Written analysis (by individuals).
- Written analysis (by groups).
- Oral/written analysis and presentation (by individuals/groups).

What particular method would be followed in the counselling sessions would depend upon the thinking of the counsellor and other factors, including the nature of the company and the length of the case. However, with practice, you should be able to establish a working style with which you feel comfortable.

(d) Initial Analysis

A case is a technical paper. As such it deserves careful reading. A good approach is to read the case three times: Once rapidly, scanning quickly any exhibits; a second time thoroughly and slowly, putting careful attention to the exhibits and making some notes about apparent organisational objectives, strategies, symptoms of problems, root causes, unresolved issues and the role of key individuals; and a third time rapidly again to reinforce the main points. First, it's important to gain a feel for the overall situation by skimming quickly through the case. Ask yourself:

- What sort of organisation does the case concern?
- What is the nature of the industry (broadly defined).
- What is going on in the external environment?
- What problem does management appear to be facing?

While no standard procedure can be laid down, the following successive steps will be helpful for analyzing the case (whether for oral discussion or written presentation):

- Know the facts.
- Understand the environment of the organisation (external and internal).
- Gather relevant information from outside sources, if necessary.
- Appraise and evaluate the environment.
- Consider and keep in mind the mission of the organisation, while making recommendations.

As you precede the case further, try to make notes in response to such questions as:

- What decisions need to be made, and who will be responsible for making them?

- What are the objectives of the organisation itself and of each of the key players in the case? Are these objectives compatible? If not, can the problem be reconciled, or will it be necessary to redefine the objectives?
- What resources and constraints are present that may help or hinder attempts by the organisation to meet its objectives.

You should make a particular effort to establish the significance of any quantitative data presented in the text of the case or, more often, in the exhibits. See if new insights may be gained by combining and manipulating data presented in different parts of the case. But don't accept the data blindly. In the cases, as in real life, not all information is equally reliable or equally relevant. On the other hand, case writers won't deliberately misrepresent data or facts to try to trick you.

(e) Developing Recommendation

Once you have thoroughly diagnosed the company's situation and weighed the pros and cons of various alternative courses of action, you may decide on what the company should do to tackle the problems or improve its performance. Draw up your set of recommendations and prepare an "action agenda". This is the most crucial part of the analysis. Bear in mind that proposing realistic, workable solution is not the same as offering a hasty, or not a properly conceived possibility. Do not recommend anything you would not be prepared to do yourself if you were in the shoes of the decision maker. Your recommendations won't be complete unless you give some thought to how the proposed strategy should be implemented.

- What resources human, financial, or others will be required?
- Who should be responsible for implementation?
- What time frame should be established for the various actions proposed?
- How should subsequent performance be measured?

In other words, offer a definite agenda for action, stipulate a time-table and sequence for initiating actions, indicating priorities and suggesting who should be responsible for doing what.

(f) What an Evaluator Looks for in a Case Analysis

The important elements that a counsellor (or evaluator) would generally look for in case analyses are:

- Care with which facts and background knowledge have been used.
- Ability to state problems and issues clearly.
- Use of appropriate analytical techniques.
- Evidence of sound logic and arguments.
- Consistency between analysis and recommendations.
- Ability to formulate reasonable and feasible recommendations for action.

In short, both future managers as well as the present managers can make use of the case study method for developing a sense of responsibility, commitment and commonsense while taking decision in modern business environment. Efforts have been taken by the author for simulating most of the service marketing problems.

CASE STUDY NO. 1

Samsung Pays a Heavy Price for Communication

South Korea is making enormous strides in the international business community by supporting the development of new industries that export products around the world. One of its major stars has been the Samsung group. The country's largest conglomerate, it operates primarily in consumer electronics, and in 1991 had 187,000 employees and worldwide sales of more than $43 billion. It is so large and so dominates the South Korean economy that it has been referred to as "the republic of Samsung". The government allowed Samsung to enter a wide range of new industries over the past decade or so, including automobiles and aerospace. Its Chairman, Lee Kun Hee, was regularly seen conferencing with prominent Heads of State and breaking ground for new factories.

Working closely with the government is essential in South Korea because the government tightly controls the right to be in business. The government has everything to say about what companies are permitted to do: What to produce, where and when to build factories and what types of mergers and acquisitions are allowed. The President of South Korea, Kim Young Sam, is the country's first civilian leader in more than three decades and has officially declared that his administration is trying to untangle the close ties between government and business. There are indications to the contrary, however. In 1995 Samsung seemed to fall from favour with the Kim administration. Chairman Lee was openly critical of the South Korean Government, calling the Kim administration "second class" and local politics "fourth class" in remarks in Beijing and China. At the time, Samsung was submitting a funding proposal for a new auto plant and developing a bid to buy a $378 million stake in AST research in California.

Suddenly, government finance officials were less friendly to the funding proposal and foreign exchange regulators stopped the purchase bid. The purchase was finally approved many months after it should have been and in a form that will make AST much more expensive to operate. A project to build a $1 billion semiconductor plant in Texas is also being held up, as it's approval to participate in an international consortium with Northrop Grumman and Bristol Aerospace. It is clear that Samsung no longer has favoured status. Samsung is not alone in having to put up with this type of government interference. Five of South Korea's top six conglomerates have had difficulties with the administration. In February 1995, the Chairman of Sunkyong group, Chey Jong Hyon, described the administration as "anachronistic" and criticized tax rates as "unbearably" high. Within a month the government initiated antitrust investigations of four of its affiliate companies and began examinations of another for manipulating its accounts. Then, in March, when Ssangyong group Chairman Kim Suk Won ran for an important assembly seat, Sangyong affiliate shares plummeted on the stock market. After Hyundai group founder Chung Ju Yung ran against Kim for President several years ago, Chung was convicted of violating securities laws and the Hyundai group was cut off from government loans for new investments and was denied the opportunity to raise equity capital overseas. The administration claims it did not interfere in the stock market or in various approvals and that the investigations were routine. Growth has been hobbled by everything from slow approvals to investigations for various problems. In each situation, the troubles began when a top executive in the company criticized the Kim administration. Although the government is supposed to be supporting business and exporting, problems such as these are stifling growth and especially outside investment in South Korean companies.

Questions

1. What role does communication play in relations between business and government in South Korea?
2. Where is the communication process breaking down in this situation?
3. If you were advising a major US company that is planning investments in South Korea, how would you advise them to handle the Kim administration?

Courtesy: Steve Glain, "For South Korea Firms, Speaking Too Freely May Carry Steep Price", Wall Street Journal, 1995.

CASE STUDY NO. 2

Indya.com's Touch Decisions

Indya.com an online internet service was created in June 2000 and in September 2000 it made its global launch with great success, backed by three giant corporate partners Satyam, Economic Times and Shoppers Stop. It seemed that this was the perfect marriage, a giant from each of three key areas: Computers, media, and retailing. It was a "can't miss" combination. The partners had a clear vision of what they were creating. They expected that consumers would eventually pay bills, buy stock, arrange their travel and do a myriad of other things electronically. Within a month, it had more than 500,000 subscribers and 1 crore national advertising campaign featured celebrities, authors and futurists. ET dropped out early so it could concentrate on its other businesses and because it was tired of putting so much money into Indya. But the others stayed convinced of the soundness of the investment. Within one year it had over a million subscribers. But then a series of decisions started to cut into their lead over other services, America online (AOL) and rediff.com. First, when subscribers started using Indya for e-mail and sending lots of messages to each other, started charging for sending more than thirty e-mails per month. Customers were angry because they had become accustomed to the all you can use pricing that had made Indya.com popular.

After a change in leadership due to retirement, the new CEO, reaffirmed Indya's strategy to serve the mass electronic consumer. Although it had more than 1.2 million subscribers, more than five times as many as rediff.com, the really large mass market did not exist in 2000. Satyam and Shoppers Stop considered the venture a money pit and were very concerned. When rediff.com came out with its Windows version and indya.com did not, Indya lost customers and did not pick up as many as rediffmail.com. Almost a year later indya.com came out with a Windows version. It helped, but rediff.com was already ahead and chasing AOL for number one. Finally, in 2002 indya.com created a new pricing structure to match AOL and rediff.com a structure that took almost a year to design and approve. AOL undercut it the next day. After even more aggressive price cutting, following a year of red ink, indya.com showed a small profit for the first quarter of 2002. Less than month later Mr.Aravind took over as new CEO. Excited by the challenge, he asked for over $ 200 million to create new content and capabilities for the service to capitalise on the Internet. The partners turned him down. Finally, losing money at the rate of $10 to $ 12 million per month, wanted out. They tried to sell it for $ 500 million, a paltry amount compared to what they had put into it over the years. No takers in May 2002, they finally sold it to Reliance International for $ 200 million. Indya.com now aspires to become the biggest online service in the world under the new management.

Questions

1. Identify the many different decisions indya.com made that eventually led to its problems.
2. What type of decisions was each of these?
3. Which of the decision-making problems may have occurred at Indya.com?

CASE STUDY NO. 3

The Men Who Command

They were Para-dropped over the enemy territory. Their combined objective was to blow up a bridge, cut the lines of communication and destroy the fuel dump of the enemy. It was well protected by mine fields around it, barbed wires and machine guns and heavy caliber cannons in pill boxes. There were nearly 200 men guarding the fuel dump. The plan was to drop the Para Command at two different zones. The first group to be under the command of a Major. The Major and his men (175) had the task of silencing the heavy guns, destroying the pill boxes and capturing or blowing up the fuel depot. Reconnaissance had shown that the supply depot was surrounded by machine gun and a belt of barbed wires. Outside this was the minefield 30 yards wide. Intelligence report had shown that it was manned by at least 10 machine guns and a few duel purpose cannon. The major and his men were to be dropped very close to the enemy minefield but outside the field of fire. The 'Packets' were supposed to go little deeper and drop another group under the command of a Lieutenant. He would be taking a group of 20 men. Their job was to blow the bridge connecting the main enemy land, immediately, thereby cutting the supply line by road and then to cut off all the lines of communication of the enemy. After that they should go back and join the main body and clear a way through the minefields and barb wires so that they can together blow up the fuel depot. After this the Major (who is in overall command) must retreat and rendezvous with the infantry. The infantry and the artillery wanted to by pass this area next day without much opposition. So this task had to be done in the night. This area had another strategic importance. If it could be brought under control then it was easier for the army to surround a temporary enemy air field operating very close to the border playing havoc with the supply conveys' of our army.

The first group under Major Gupta was dropped. This air drop was a little scattered one. By the time they assembled only 162 of them could be found. The remaining ones were either dead or lost. Or may be they hit the mines since there were explosions to be heard. They advanced immediately the alert enemy opened up. Major Gupta and his men returned the fire. What followed was a massacre. 30 of Gupta's men were shot and killed and twenty of them were wounded. All this happened in twenty minutes. Major Gupta knew the enemy was very powerful. Aimed the heavy guns and plenty of machine guns they could keep off the attacking forces. He immediately contacted the Command HQ and asked for artillery support. He was not given it. He requested the Air force to make a go at it. That also was turned down. He was reminded that it was his job. He was advised to end volunteers to gun positions crawling and blow up with grenade or to open another front and to cover it with gun fire. He radioed back and said it was murder. He swore into the mouth piece desperately. He did not cell for volunteers. The senior N.C.O. came and said that the casuality was very high. Many of them needed medical help. He further said unless something is done the enemy may launch a counter attack on them. The Major sat quiet. Thought for sometime. Bullets were missing them by inches. He studied through his glasses. He rushed forward and threw grenades into a gun pit and opened up with his automatic machine gun. He was shot dead by accurate enemy fire.

Immediately the Captain Bindra who was second in Command ordered his men to withdraw to safe positions. He assumed Command of his men. He told them they should avenge their Major's death. But they should fight an intelligent war. He was young and had the look of a competent Officer. He had just finished a command course along the new principles of leadership. The Major was very well liked by his men. He discussed the plan. Captain Bindra ordered all the wounded to be evacuated. He called for medical orderlies to help them. Then he divided the group into four and gave independent Commands and targets to 3 different senior men and assumed command of the fourth himself. He explained to them their objective and plans clearly and wished them good luck.

In the mean time the other group was dropped exactly as they practiced it at the Para Training School. They blew the bridge, cut the lines of communication and were advancing forward to clear a way through the minefield to help blow the fuel depot. One by one the enemy guns fell. There were heavy losses on both sides. Captain Bindra urged them forward. They fought under him as a coordinated team. They were joined by the 2nd group. Together they blew up the fuel depot. They were later picked up by the choppers. Nearly 200 of them were dropped. Now only 90 of them were alive. On their way back the Captain asked the Subedar how long he had known the Major. He said 8 years. "was he Coward"? "No" replied the Subedar. Did he not faith in his men? "Yes". Then why did he not do as he was told? Why was he fighting his own personal war? The Subedar said that his men liked him very much. He too liked them very much. But he always suffered for others. He was like a father. A father cannot afford to see his sons getting killed. Captain Bindra noded but he was not sure. The major had sacrificed his life for his men. Captain Bindra was awarded Virchakra for his courage, leadership and ability shown in the battle against the enemy. He is major now. Analyse the case and state the leadership theories applied in this case.

CASE STUDY NO. 4

What Action Should be Taken Against Ram Nivas?

Mr. Ram Nivas is an Electrical Engineer working with the Kamath Engineering (Private) Limited. He has a diploma in Electrical Engineering and after joining the company he has been trained in the Inventory Control and Repair department. On 16th December, 2001, Mr. Shankar, Foreman of the Repairs department retired due to ill health. The management of the company promoted Ram Nivas and he was made the Foreman of the Repairs Department. The Repairs department has four Supervisors assigned to different types of repair work. The organisation chart of the Repairs department is shown in Figure below. The Supervisors working under Ram Nivas were senior people with an average experience of 15 years in the company. P. Mane was the youngest among them with 9 years experience in the company. S. Kapoor was the senior most Supervisor with 20 years experience. Mr. Kapoor had joined the company as a Watchman and after completing some training course has become the Supervisor. Even though, he did not possess formal education; he was the popular leader among the employees of the Repairs department.

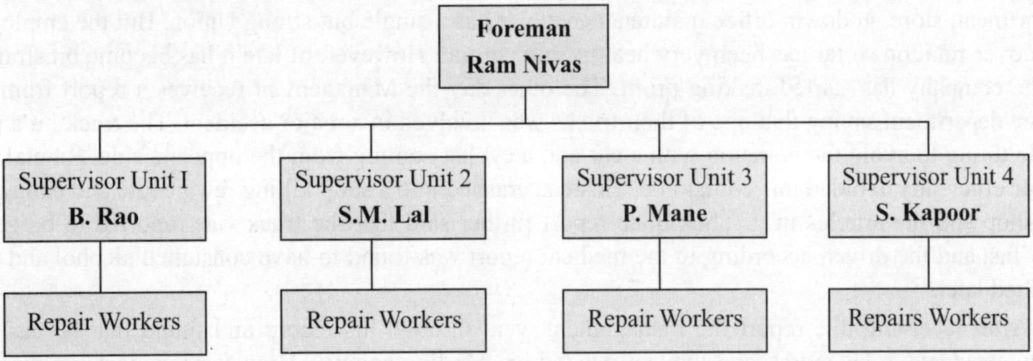

Since Ram Nivas a new comer to the department, he did not want to make any major changes in the established procedures and practices. Ram Nivas noticed that quite frequently, workers and other Supervisors referred the problems to S. Kapoor. Ram Nivas did not object since he was interested in developing good working relations with his subordinates. At the end of June 2002 the accounting department notified Mr. Ram Nivas that the monthly expenditure on equipment purchases for the repairs department has exceeded the budget. Mr. Ram Nivas was asked to give and explanation. On checking the accounts, it was found that spare part No.1004 costing Rs.15,000 was purchased even though Mr. Ram Nivas had only authorized @ loss expensive part costing Rs.9,000. On further enquiry it was revealed that Mr. S. Kapoor suggested the purchases of No.1004 spare part and the concerned billing clerk agreed with S. Kapoor. When this was brought to the notice of Ram Nivas, he remarked it is all old Kapoor's fault. During the early part of July 2002. Mr. Ram Nivas received a telephone call from an old friend Mr. Nitin Guha, Mr. Guha was a management consultant specialising in the area of human relations.

Mr. Guha visited Ram Nivas at the letter's residence on a Sunday afternoon. After a general discussion about social and family matters, Mr. Ram Nivas narrated the incident that took place in the Repairs department a few days ago. He suggested the following alternatives and he wanted to get the advice of Mr. Guha regarding the best possible course of action. Alternative suggested by Ram Nivas, were as follows:

1. Mr. Kapoor should be warned he should be told about the scope of his authority.
2. Mr. Ram Nivas should send a report recommending the dismissal of Mr. Kapoor.
3. The billing clerk should be punished for his mistake.
4. Mr. Ram Nivas should establish closer control over Mr. Kapoor and other subordinates.

Mr. Guha was more interested in analyzing the problem before prescribing possible course of action. Analyse case and suggests a suitable remedy.

CASE STUDY NO. 5

Black Panther Transporting Company

Black Panther Transporting Company is a flourishing company whose main activity is transporting goods from one place to the other by road. It has a large fleet of heavy duty-trucks and employs a few hundred drivers. It also employs other people for other duties in various other departments such as repair department, store, godown, office maintenance etc. It has a single but strong Union. But the employer-employee relation so far has been very healthy and cordial. However, of late it has become bit strained as the company has started making profit. The other day the Management receives a report from the police department saying that one of their trucks was involved in a major accident. The truck hit a post while trying to avoid the collision with a car and a cyclist coming from the opposite side. Ramlal, the driver efficiently avoided this collision but instead crashed into a shop killing few people and damaging the shop and the articles in it. The police report further said that the truck was reported to be going very fast and the driver, according to the medical report was found to have consumed alcohol and was arrested later.

After receiving this report the management went through his record and found that he has had many accidents to his credit, and they suspended his pending enquiry. However this decision was not appreciated by other drivers of the company. The union has already given the warning. From reliable sources the Management has come to know that the drivers are planning to go on a sudden strike so as to paralyse the company's activities. The Management, knowing fully well; that this is the season of the year when they have maximum work and the chance to make very high profit decides to tackle it tactfully and so they have decided to call for a meeting. This is the meeting in which the Management is facing the leaders from the union. Analyze the case by applying suitable conflict management and negotiation process.

11.2 INTERNET EXERCISES

E-business is using the Internet to facilitate every aspect of running a business. E-business has significant implications for managing people at work because it eventually will seep into every corner of life both on and off the job. Determine how wide-spread E-business is in India. Using the Business standard and Economic Times web sites examine the information regarding E-Business and the use of the Internet. What can you conclude about e-mailing? What implications for global management does this have?

Exercise No. 1. http://www.toshiba.com

Toshiba America Group specializes in advanced electronics. It is recognized as a leader in products that enhance home, industry, and health environments. It currently has over 10,000 workers and has annual sales exceeding $7.5 billion. Toshiba America, Inc. is a subsidiary of the Toshiba Corporation, which has 321 consolidated subsidiaries worldwide. It established American operations in 1965.

How does this organisation train its managers for its global operations? What problems do you foresee these managers may encounter? How important are expatriates to this company? Provide suggestions that Toshiba may utilize to improve their training and support of its expatriates.

Discuss your responses to the following questions with the class. Prepare a two-page report indicating your answers.

Exercise No. 2. http://www.dupont.com

Today's Dupont was founded over 200 years ago as an explosives company. At approximately 100 years of age, this organisation changed its focus to one looking at global chemicals, materials, and energy. As Dupont organisation currently enters its third century of successful operations, it now concerns itself with providing science-based solutions to bring real differences into the lives of its customers. As you examine this informative site, you should focus on collecting the necessary information to prepare a two-page report that responds to the following questions. Explain how you perceive cultural differences are addressed within Dupont. How does this organisation assist its managers to become global managers? Provide suggestions that may improve this process for Dupont. Discuss a few of the methods utilized by this organisation to address any cross-culture difficulties it has or will encounter.

Exercise No. 3

One of the major threats to group effectiveness is "groupthink". Modern managers can easily become victims of groupthink if they are not aware of the danger. Janis defines groupthink as: "A mode of thinking that people engage in when they are deeply involved in a cohesive in-group, when members' strivings for unanimity override their motivation to realistically appraise alternative courses of action". Members of groups that have the dysfunction of groupthink tend to be friendly and tightly knit. Determine whether there is a real possibility for groupthink in a global context. Specifically, go to Asia and then to Singapore. What cultural and historical forces would you need to be aware of as a manager assigned to your firm's Singapore operation, in order to avoid the possibility of groups of your employees victimized by groupthink? (*Hint*: go to "Doing Business Around the World" and use the "worldskip.com" option. You may have to click on www.worldskip.com if the page does not load properly. Be sure to "skip" to Singapore using the drop-down menus. Look for the links to "People and Culture"). Assess the degree to which changes in self and self-concept are occurring in Japan. Using the Business Around the World Map, identify traditional cultural factors that influence Japanese notions of self and self-concept. Are there changes occurring in Japanese society that have an impact on self and self-concept?

Exercise No. 4

External and Internal forces provide organisations key "cues" that signal the need for change. Effective organisations "know" when they need to change by monitoring these forces. Awareness of the forces of change can help managers determine when they could consider implementing an organisational change. External forces for change occur outside of the organisation. These forces may have global effects and they may cause the organisation to reassess the essence of what business it is in and the development and deployment of goods and services. Social and political pressures, technological advancements, demographic characteristics, and market changes are all "external" forces that may signal the need for an organisation to change. The global manager must be sensitive to various cultural factors that combine with these external forces for change. A change in one society may signal a need for change in the global organisation in that geographical area, but not necessarily in another that the firm is doing business in.

There are several different models of change management. Each model is based on a different set of assumptions and therefore offers managers a unique set of recommendations for how organisational change should be implemented. Company expansion and growth represents a form of organisational change. Using the Business Around the World Map of www.worldskip.com , go to the Middle East and access Egypt. Under "Doing Business in the Middle East", select the option for AME. You will find several articles of interest regarding organisational change and expansion. Typically, the organisations are demonstrating globalization (such as MasterCard International). You may select the article on MasterCard International. The company announced that it will continue its rapid expansion plan in the Middle East & North America region with the opening of new offices in the Kingdom of Saudi Arabia. What implications for the firm does this type of expansion have? Consider Lewin's change model. What factors do you see that correspond to the three stages: unfreezing, changing, and refreezing? Provide examples of the three components of change, which include the inputs, target elements of change, and outputs.

Exercise No. 5

Ericsson is a Swedish electronics giant that is truly a global company. It has many decentralized business units around the world. Decentralization is a form of organisation that requires the development and deployment of strategies to insure effective communication and "knowledge" sharing throughout the organisation on a global level. A cornerstone of Ericsson's knowledge-sharing strategy is to provide free internet access to its employees and their families. The focus is on specialized websites that provide information about Ericsson to all its employees. It allows for the solicitation of opinions and it provides for a "knowledge map" by listing competence inventories of experts in different fields. Assume that you are heading Ericsson's global expansion team. You are interested in insuring the successful implementation of the firm's "knowledge-sharing" organisation design strategy in two different regions of the world: Russia and Argentina. Examine the key characteristics of people, literacy, education, and communications for each of the two countries using www.worldskip.com. What factors are important to consider in insuring the successful design of the organisation in these two countries?

Exercise No. 6

Self-esteem is the overall evaluation of oneself, one's perceived self-worth. People with high self-esteem view themselves in positive terms; those with low self-esteem view themselves in negative terms. Self-esteem as an organisational behaviour topic has been viewed from a uniquely Western perspective. However, the concept has cross-cultural implications. The data show that individualistic cultures exhibit stronger positive correlations between self-esteem and life satisfaction. Global managers need to remember to de-emphasize self-esteem when doing business in some contexts and to emphasize the concept when managing with others. Individual differences abound in organisations.

The vast array of individual differences can make the manager's job endlessly challenging. Growing workforce diversity compels managers to view individual differences in increasingly different ways. Self-concept is an important variable in organisational behaviour. Ideas of self and self-concept vary from one historical era to another, from one socioeconomic group to another, and from culture to culture. Success in international dealings can be enhanced based on the ability of the manager to detect and adjust to different cultural notions of self. According to research, Japanese-Indian communication and understanding often are hindered by significantly different degrees of self-disclosure.

A key element in understanding and adapting to these differences involves culturally rooted conceptions of self and self-disclosure. Assess the degree to which changes in self and self-concept are occurring in Japan. Identify traditional cultural factors that influence Japanese notions of self and self-concept. Are there changes occurring in Japanese society that have an impact on self and self-concept? Are there indications of change in the society? If so, what implications are there for the global manager in attempting to support self-esteem of employees?

If you wish to know more insight on this exercise, then you are welcome to contact author via e-mail: shaangrila@gmail.com or social media: drs.shajahan.7@facebook.com.

BIBLIOGRAPHY

Argyris Chris, *Personality and Organization*, New York: Harper & Row, 1957.

Understanding Organizational Behaviour, Homewood, III: Irwin, Dorsey Press, 1960.

Organization and Innovation, Homewood, III. Irwin Dorsey Press, 1965.

Beyond Freedom and Dignity, Harvard Educational Review, Vol 41, 1971.

Reasoning, Learning and Action: Individual and Organization, San Francisco; Jossey-Bass, 1982.

Increasing Leadership Effectiveness, Malabar, Fla; Krieger, 1984.

Strategy, Change and Defensive Routines, Pitman Pub., 1985.

Argyris, Chris and Richard M. Cyert, *Leadership in the Eighties; Essays on Higher Education*, Cambridge, Mass: Inst. Ed. Management, 1980.

Atkinson John William, *Motivation and Achievement,* New York: Halsted Press 1974.

Ajzen I and Fishbein M, *Understanding Attitudes and Predicting Social Behavior,* Englewood-Cliffs, NJ: Prentice-Hall 1980.

Ajzen I, *The Theory of planned behavior*, Organization Behavior and Human Decision Process, Vol 50: PP 179–211, 1991.

Ajzen Ice K, *Nature and Operation of Attitudes,* Annual Review of Psychology, Vol 52, PP 27–58, 2001

Allport, Gordon, *Attitudes in Handbook of Social Psychology*, ed. C. Murchison. Worcester, MA: Clark University Press, PP 789–844,1935.

Alpert S, Tjosvold D and Law KS, *Conflict Management, Efficacy and Performance in Organizational Teams*, Personal Psychology, 2000.

Bacheldor M, *The Elusive Intangible Intelligence*: *Conflict Management and Emotional Intelligence in the Workplace,* The Western Scholar, Fall, 2000.

Blake R and Mouton JS, *The managerial Grid,* Houston TX, Gulf 1964.

Breckler S J & Wiggins EC, *On defining attitude and attitude theory: Once more with feeling,* In A. R. Pratkanis, S. J. Breckler, & A. C. Greenwald (Eds.), Attitude structure and function. Hillsdale, NJ: Erlbaum. pp 407–427, 1992.

Berle, Adolf A, *Power,* New York: Harcort, Brace & World,1969.

Bankart CP And Powers SP, *Individual Decisions and Group Consensus*, Journal of Social Psychology, 126, June 1986.

Barnard Chester I, *The Functions of the Executive,* Cambridge, Mass: Harvard University Press, 1938.

Beck Don Edward, *Beyond the Grid and Situationalism; A Living Systems View*, Training and Development Journal, 36, August 1982.

Bennis Warren and Bert Nanus, *Leaders: The Strategies for Taking Charge*, New York: Harper & Row, 1986.

Berne Eric, *Transactional Analysis in Psychotherapy,* New York. Grove Press, 1961.

Blake Robert R and Jane S Mouton, *The Versatile Manage—A Grid Profile,* Homewood, III: Irwin, 1982.

Blanchard Kenneth and Spenser Johnson, *The One Minute Manager,* New York. Morrow, 1982.

Bradford David L, *Managing for Excellence*, New York: Wiley, 1984.

Bradford Leland P, *National Training Laboratories: Its History 1947–1970,* Bethel, Maine: National Training Laboratories, 1974.

Brink TL, *Psychology: A Student Friendly Approach Unit 13: Social Psychology,* PP 295, 2008.

Carlson Formost, *Psychology: the Science of Behaviour,* New Jersey, USA: Pearson Education PP 488, ISBN 978-0-205-64524-4, 2010.

Chandler AD, Jr., *Surgery and Structure,* Cambridge, Mass; MIT Press, 1962.

Cofer CN and Appley MH, *Motivation: Theory and Research*, New York: Wiley 1964.

Cuming Pamela, *The Power Handbook*, New York: Van Nostrand Reinhold, 1984.

Culbert Samuel A & McDonough John J, *Radical management: Power politics and the pursuit of trust,* New York: The Free Press, 1985.

Cyert Richard M and James G March, *A Behavioural Theory of the Firm,* Englewood Cliffs. N.J. Prentice-Hall, 1963.

Drucker Peter F., *The Practice of Management*, New York: Harper & Row, 1977.

The Discipline of Innovation, Harvard Business Review, 64, May-June 1985.

Effective Executive, New York: Harper & Row, 1985.

Managing in Turbulent Times, New York: Harper & Row, 1985.

Dolores Albarraci, Blair T Johnson and Mark P Zanna, *The Handbook of Attitudes Routledge*, ISBN 0805844937, 2005.

Dubrin Andrew J, *Leadership* (3rd Ed), New York: Houghton Mifflin, 2001.

Eagly A & Chaiken S, *Attitude strength, attitude structure and resistance to change,* in R. Pety and J. Kosnik (Eds.), Attitude Strength PP 413–432, 1995.

Eagly Alice H and Chaiken Shelly, *The Psychology of Attitudes*, Harcourt Brace Jovanovich College 1993.

Eagly Alice H and Shelly Chaiken 1998, *Attitude Structure and Function* in Handbook of Social Psychology, ed. DT Gilbert, Susan T Fisk and G.Lindsey, PP269–322. New York: McGraw-Hill 1998.

Ezigbo CA, *Advanced Management Theory: Theory and Application*, Enugu, Immaculate Publications Ltd. 2011.

Fazio R H, *How do attitudes guide behaviour* in R. M. Sorrentino & E. T. Higgins (Eds.), The Handbook of Motivation and Cognition: Foundations of Social Behaviour PP 204–243. New York: Guilford Press 1986.

Fazio R & Williams, C, *Attitude accessibility as a moderator of attitude-perception and attitude-behaviour relation: An investigation of the 1984 presidential election,* Journal of Personality and Social Psychology, 51, PP 505–514, 1986.

Fazio Russell H and Tamara Towles Schwen, *The MODE Model of Attitude-Behavior Processes* in Chaiken, Shelly, and Trope, Yaacov, Dual Process Theories in Social Psychology, New York: Guilford Press,1999.

Frank M Andrews, *Measures of Personality and Social Psychological Attitudes,* Gulf Professional Publishing ISBN 0125902441, 1991.

Fedler Fred E, *Engineer the Job to fit the Manager*, Harvard Business Review, Vol 51 pp 115–122, 1965.

Filley, Alan C, *Interpersonal Conflict Resolution* Glenview, III: Scott. Foreman, 1975.

Freud Sigmund, *New Introductory Lectures on Psychoanalysis* New York: Norton, 1933.

Fincham R & Rhodes, *Principles of Organizational Behaviour*, Oxford University Press, 4th Edn.

Gellerman Saul W, *Management by Motivation,* New York: American Management Association, 1968.

Gerd Bohner, *Attitudes and Attitude Change*, Social Psychology, Psychology Press. ISBN 0863777791, 2002.

Greg Maio and Geoffrey Haddock, *The Psychology of Attitudes and Attitude Change,* Sage Social Psychology Program, SAGE ISBN 141292975X, 2010.

Gibb Jack R, *A New View of Personal and Organizational Development*, LaJolla, Calif: Omicron Press, 1978.

Goddard Robert W, *The Rise of the New Organization*, Management World, January 1985.

Griffin Ricky, *Management*, Boston: Houghton, Miffin, 1984.

Gregory Moorehead and R.S. Griffin, *Organizational Behaviours: Managing People and Organizations*, Jaico, 1994.

Guest Robert H Paul Hersey, and Kenneth H Blanchard, *Organizational Change through Effective Leadership*, 2nd ed, Englewood Cliffs, N.J. Prentice Hall, 1986.

Haddock G, *Contemporary Perspectives on the Psychology of Attitudes,* Taylor & Francis, ISBN 184169326X, 2004.

Harris Philip R, *Management in Transition*, San Francisco: Jossey-Bass, 1985.

Harrist, *I'm OK - You're OK: A Practical Guide to Transactional Analysis*, New York: Harper & Row, 1969.

Hersey P Blanchard KH and Johnson DE, *Management of Organizational Behavior Leading Human Resources*, Prentice Hall India, 10th Edn.

Holt David H, *Management: Principles and Practice,* Englewood Cliffs. N.J: Prentice Hall, 1987.

Homans GC, *The Human Group*, New York: Harcourt, Brace & World, 1950.

House Robert J A, *Path-Goal Theory of Leader Effectiveness*, Administrative Science Quarterly, 16, 1971.

Icek Ajzen Attitudes, *Personality and Behaviour,* McGraw-Hill International, ISBN 0335224008, 2005.

Johnson David W, *Joining Together*, Englewood Cliffs, N.J.: Prentice-Hall, 1987.

Johnson RA, *Management, Systems, and Society: An Introduction*, Pacific Palisades, Calif: Goodyear Publishing Co. 1976.

Jones JE and Pfeiffer JW, *The 1973 Annual Handbook for Group Facilitators*, San Diego, Calif: University Associates, 1973.

John P Robinson and Phillip R Shaver, *Measures of Social Psychological Attitudes Survey Research Center*, Institute for Social Research, ISBN 0879441305, 1980.

Joseph P Forgas, Joel Cooper and William D Crano, *The Psychology of Attitudes and Attitude Change*, Routledge, ISBN 1848729081, 2010.

Judith R. Gordon, *A Diagnostic Approach to Organizational Behaviour*, Allyn & Bacon, 1993.

Katzell R and Thompson D, "Work Motivation: Theory and Practice", *The American Psychologist*, February 1990.

Katz R, *The Influence of Group Conflict on Leadership Effectiveness*, Organizational Behaviour and Human Performance, 20, 1977.

Kemp Geoffrey, *Projection of Power: Perceptives, Perceptions, and Problems*, Hamden Conn: Archon Books, 1982.

Keith Davis, *Human Behaviour at Work*, McGraw Hill Publishers, 1991.

Kepner CH and Tregoe BB, *The Rational Manager*, New York, McGraw-Hill, 1965.

Knapp Mark, *Nonverbal Communications in Human Interacting*, 2nd Ed. New York: Holt, Rinchart & Winston, 1978.

Koontz Harold and Cyril O'Donnell, *Essentials of Management*, 4th Ed. New York: McGraw-Hill, 1986.

Kotter JP, *Organizational Dynamics: Diagnosis and Intervention, Reading*, Mass: Addison-Wiley, 1978.

Lapinski, Maria Knight and Franklin J Boster (2001), *Modeling the Ego-Defensive Function of Attitudes,* Communication Monographs Vol 68(3): PP 314–324, 2001.

Lang M, *Conflict Management: A gap in Business Education Curricula*, Journal of Education for Business 84(4) 2009.

Lawrence PR and Lorsch JW, *Developing Organization: Diagnosis and Action*, Reading, Mass. Addison-Wiley, 1969.

Lewin K, *Frontiers in Group Dynamics*, Human Relations, 1, 1947.

Likert Rensis, *New Patterns of Management,* New York. McGraw-Hill, 1961.

Lippett Gordon, *Organizational Renewal,* New York: Appleton-Century-Crofts, 1969.

Livingston J Sterling, *Pygmalion in Management,* Harvard Business Review, 48, July–August 1969.

Luthans Fred, *Introduction to Management: A Contingency Approach,* New York: McGraw-Hill, 1976.

Mackenzie KD, *Virtual Position and Power*, Managerial Science, Vol 32 May 1985.

MacMillan Ian C. and Randall S Schuler, *Gaining a Competitive Edge through Human Resources*, Personnel, Vol 62 , 1985.

March JG and Simon HA, *Organizations* New York: Wiley, 1958.

Marrow Alfred J, *Behind the Executive Mask,* New York: American Management Association, 1965.

Maslow Abraham H, *Toward a Psychology of Being*, Princeton, N.J , Van Nostrand, 1962.

Mayo Elton, *The Human Problems of an Industrial Civilization,* Ayer Company, 1977.

McClelland David C, *The Achieving Society Princeton*, N.J.: Van Nostrand, 1961.

McGregor Douglas, *The Human Side of Enterprise,* New York: McGraw-Hill, 1960.

Mintzberg H, *The Nature of Managerial Work*, New York: Harper & Row, 1973.

Mills TM, *The Sociology of Small Groups*, Eaglewood Cliffs, New Jersey Prentice-Hall 1967.

Morgan Gareth, *Images of organization* (2nd ed), Newbury Park: Sage,1996.

Murnighan J Keith, *Group Decision Making: What Strategies should you use*? Management Review, 70, No.2, February 1981.

Naisbit T John, *Mega Trends* New York: Warner Books, 1982.

Olson James M and Zanna Mark P, *Attitudes and Attitude Change*, Annual Review of Psychology, Vol 44, PP 117-154, 1993.

Perrow Charles, *Organizational Analysis: A Sociological View,* Belmont, Calif: Wadsworth Publishing, 1970.

Pettigrew Andrew, *Strategy as process, power and change* in Stephen Cummings & David Wilson, Images of Strategy, Malden, MA: Blackwell, 2003.

Pfeffer Jeffrey, *Managing with power: Politics and influence in organizations,* Boston: Harvard Business School Press, 1992.

Petty RE & Cacioppo JT, *The effects of involvement on responses to argument quantity and quality: Central and peripheral routes to persuasion,* Journal of Personality and Social Psychology, PP 46, 69-81, 1984.

Peters Thomas J and Robert H Waterman Jr., *In Search of Excellence: Lessons from America's Best-Run Companies*, New York: Warner Books, 1982.

Portnoy Robert A, *Leadership*, Englewood Cliffs, N.J.: Prentice-Hall, 1986.

Rahim MA, *Toward a Theory of Managing Organizational Conflict,* The International Journal of Conflict management, Vol 13, 2002.

Robbins Stephen P, *The Essentials of Organization Behaviour,* Englewood Cliffs, N.J.: Prentice-Hall, 1983

Roethlisberger FJ and Dickson WJ *Management and the Worker* Cambridge, Mass: Harvard University, Press, 1939.

Rosenberg M J and Hovland CI, *Cognitive, Affective and Behavioral Components of Attitudes* in M J.Rosenberg and CI Hovland (eds.), Attitude Organization and Change: An Analysis of Consistency Among Attitude Components New Haven: Yale University Press 1960.

Schein Edgar H, *Organizational Culture and Leadership,* San Francisco: Jossey-Bass, 1985.

Shukla, Madhukar, *Understanding Organizations – Organizational Theory & Practice in India*, Prentice Hall India.

Shapiro Irving, S, *Management Communication-The View from Inside*, California Management Review, 27, Fall 1984.

Skinner BF, *Science and Human Behaviour*, New York: Macmillan, 1953.

Smith Jonathan E Kenneth, Carson P and Ralph A. Alexander, *Leadership: It can make a Difference*, Academy of Management Journal, 27, December 1984.

Stodgily RM, *Personal Factors Associated with Leadership: A Survey of the Literature*, Journal of Psychology, 25, 1948.

Tannenbaum Robert and Warren H Schmidt, *How to choose a Leadership Pattern*, Harvard Business Review, Vol 37, PP 95–102 , March-April 1958.

Tesser A and Shaffer David R, *Attitudes and Attitude Change,* Annual Review of Psychology Vol 41: PP 479–523, 1990.

Tesser A, *On the importance of Heritability in Psychological research: The case of attitudes,* Psychological Review, 100, PP 129–142,1993.

Theobald, Robert, *The Rapids of Change Indianapolis*, Ind.: Knowledge Systems, 1987.

Trist EL et al., *Organizational Choice*, London. Tavistock Publications, 1963.

Urwick Lyndall F, *The Theory of Organization*, New York: American Management Association, 1952.

Visser Penny S, Bizer, George Y and Krosnick Jon A, *Exploring the Latent Structure of Strength-Related Attitude Attributes*, Advances in Experimental Social Psychology, Vol 38: PP 1-67, 2006.

Weber Max, *The Theory of Social and Economic Organization*, trans. by A.H.Henderson and ed. by Talcott Parsons. New York: Oxford University Press, 1946.

Whitley B E, *The Psychology of Prejudice & Discrimination,* United States: Wadsworth Engage Learning 2010.

Wood W, *Attitude Change: Persuasion and Social Influence,* Annual Review of Psychology Vol 51, PP 539–570, 2000.

Wright N, *Leadership Styles which are Best when*, Business Quarterly, Winter 1984.

Yelsey Alan A, *Strategies and Actions for Improving Organizational Performance*, Academy of Management Review, 9, June 1984.

Yukl Gary A, *Leadership in Organizations*, Englewood Cliffs. N.J., Prentice-Hall, 1981.

Zajonc RB "Mr." Journal of Personality and Social Psychology Monograph Supplement 9: PP 1–27, 1968

e-Resources

Brandt M J and Wetherell GA, *What attitudes are moral attitudes? The case of attitude heritability Social Psychological and Personality Science*, 3(2), 172–179. Retrieved from http://journals2.scholarsportal.info.myaccess.library.utoronto.ca/tmp/10766316054165146494.pdf 2012.

Ferguson T J, *Perceiving Groups: Prejudice, Stereotyping, & Discrimination*, Retrieved from: www.usu.edu/psy3510/prejudice, 2004.

Fazio R H & Olson MA, *Implicit Measures in Social Cognition Research: Their Meaning and Use.* Retrieved from: http://commonsenseatheism.com/wp-content/uploads/2011/04/Fazio-Olson-Implicit-measures-in-social-cognition-research-Their-meaning-and-uses.pdf 2003.

Katz, Daniel 1960, *The Functional Approach to the Study of Attitudes,* Public Opinion Quarterly 24(2) http://poq.oxfordjournals.org/content/24/2/163.abstract1960.

Wikipedia open sources such as

http://en Wikipedia.org/conflict_ management

http://en Wikipedia.org/negotiation

http://en Wikipedia.org/bargaining

http://en Wikipedia.org/motivation

http://en Wikipedia.org/perception

http://en Wikipedia.org/personality

http://en Wikipedia.org/attitudes

http://en Wikipedia.org/groups

http://mahendrayoung.org